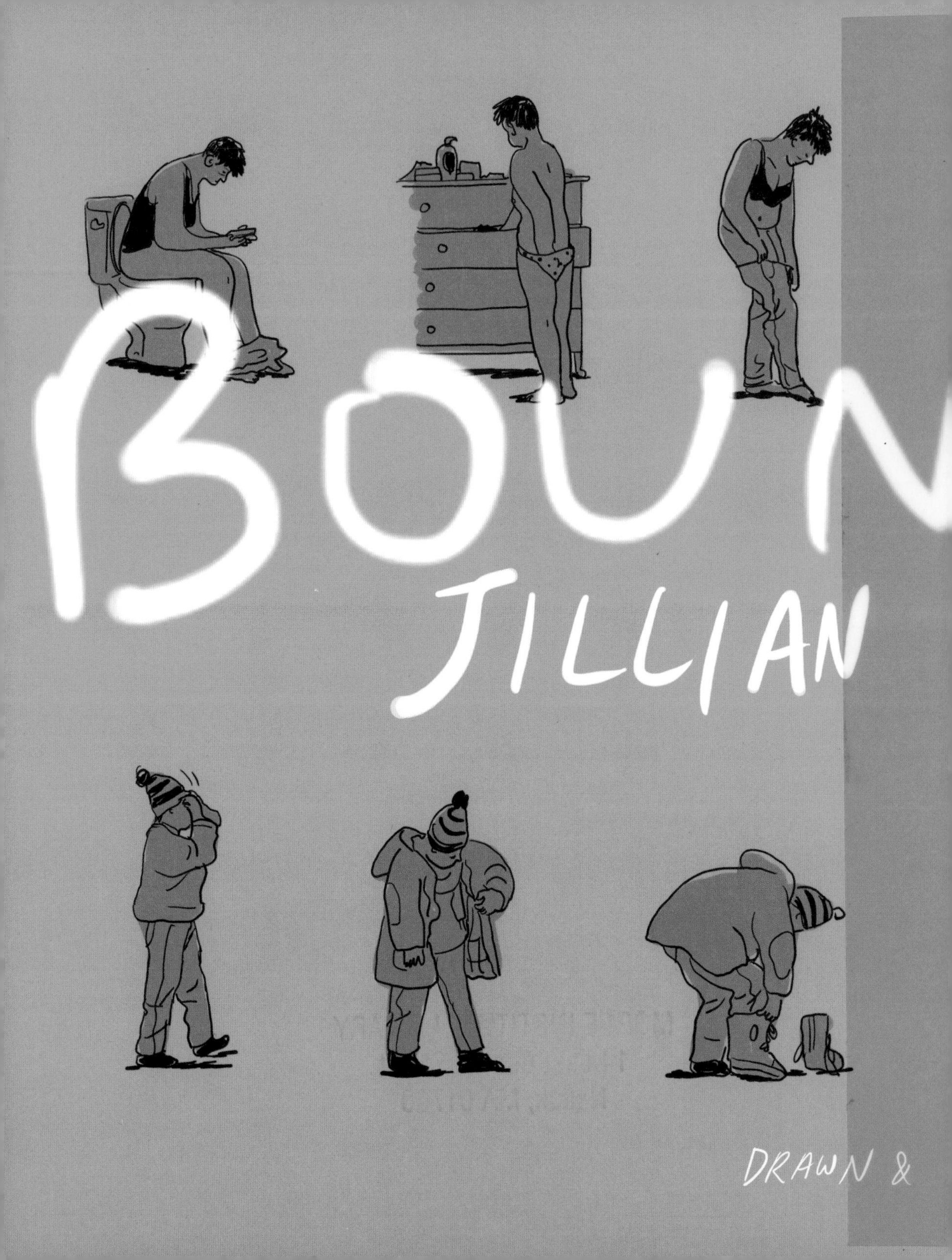
BOUN
JILLIAN
DRAWN &

DLESS

TAMAKI

QUARTERLY

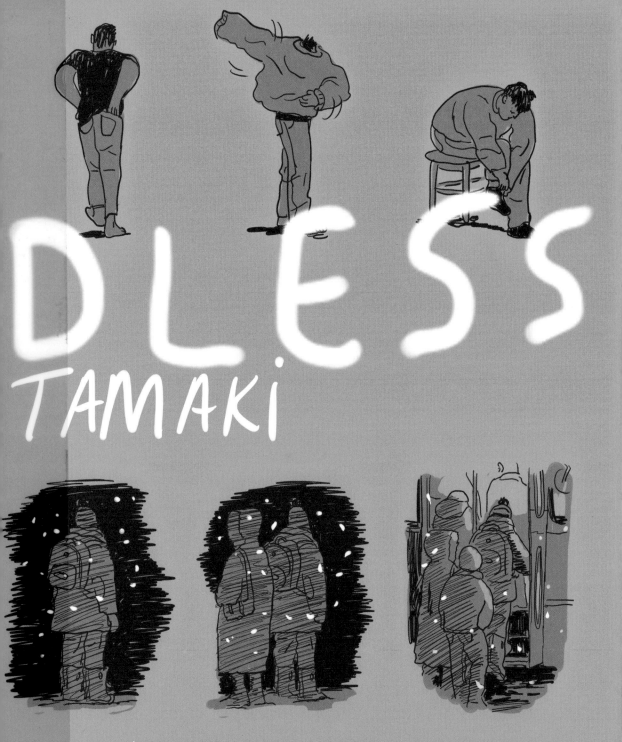

WORLD-
CLASS
CITY

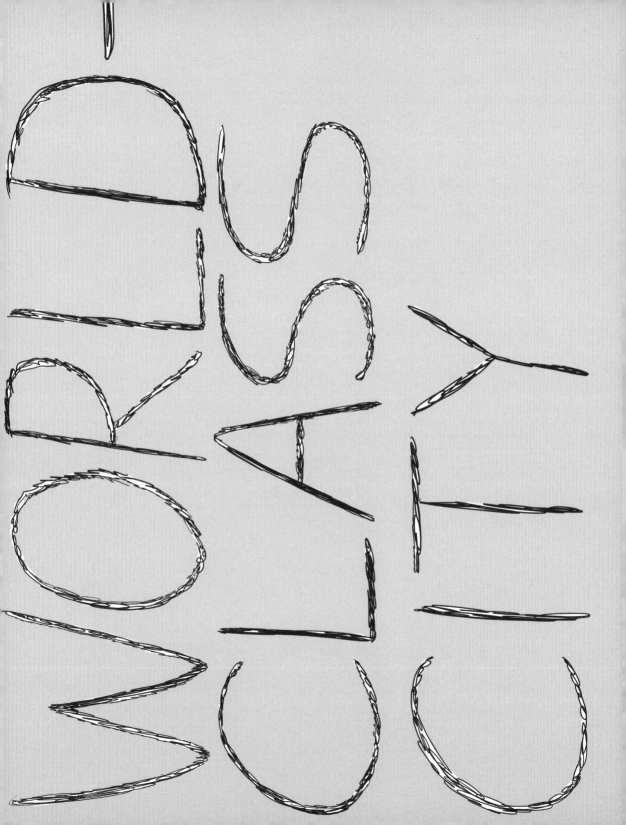

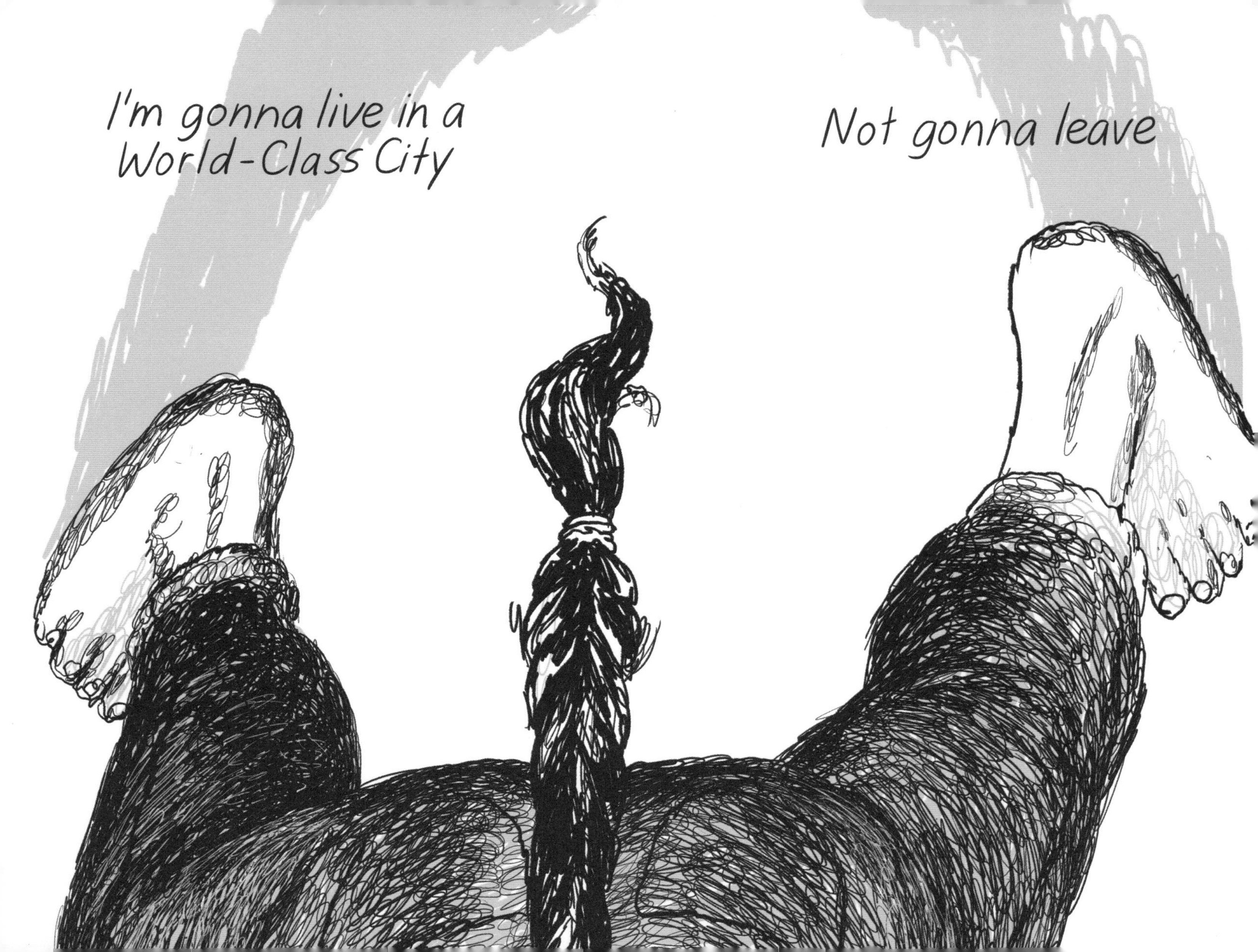
I'm gonna live in a World-Class City
Not gonna leave

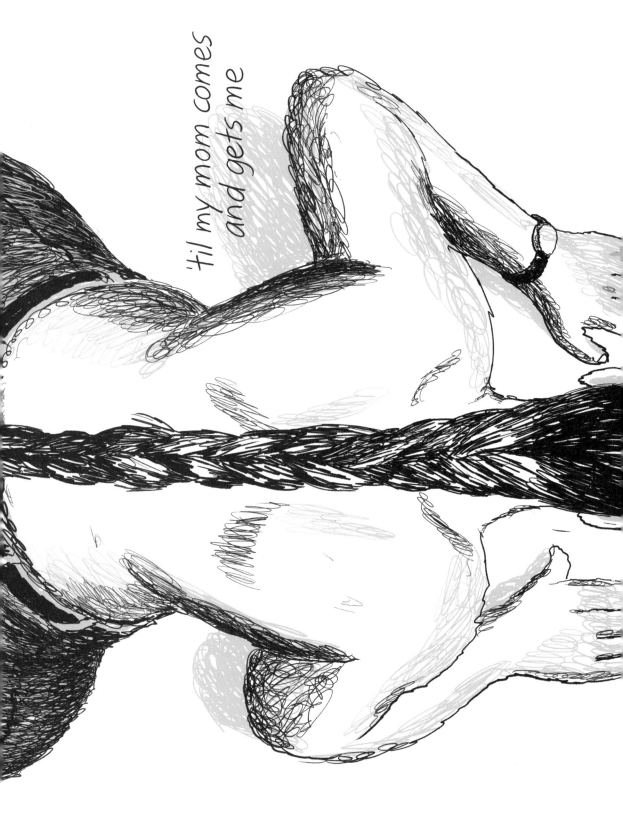

'til my mom comes and gets me

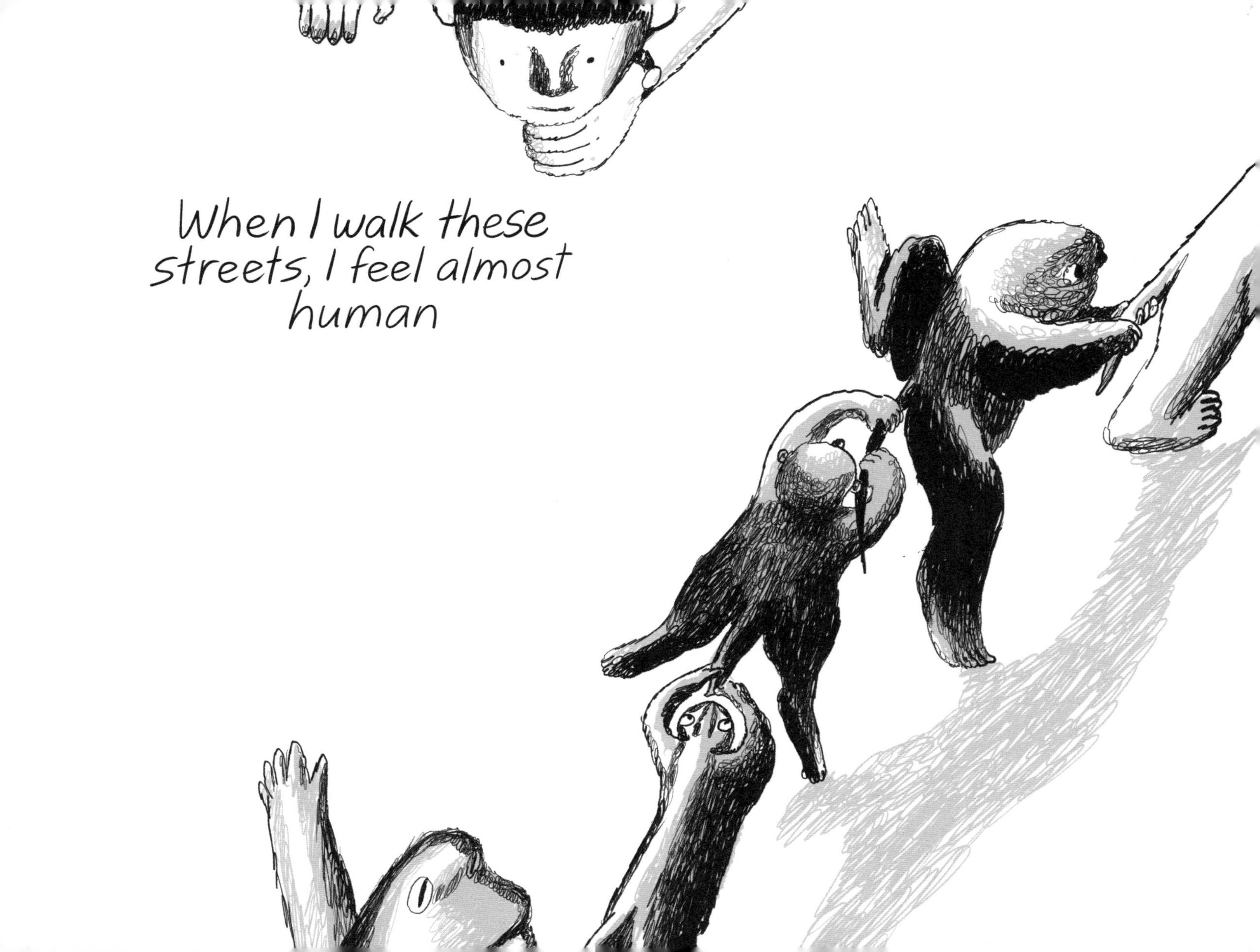
When I walk these streets, I feel almost human

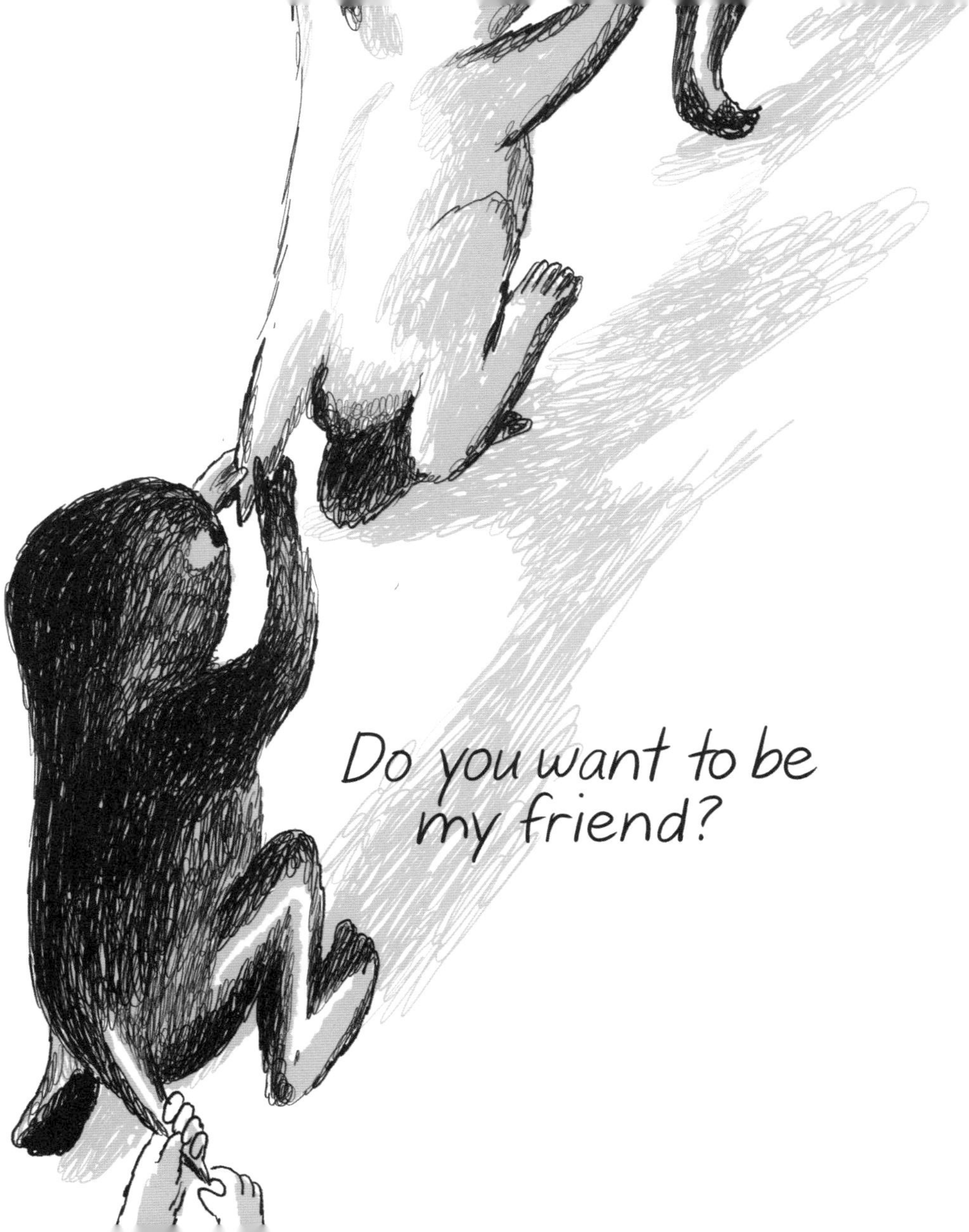
New face in the crowd
Do you want to be my friend?

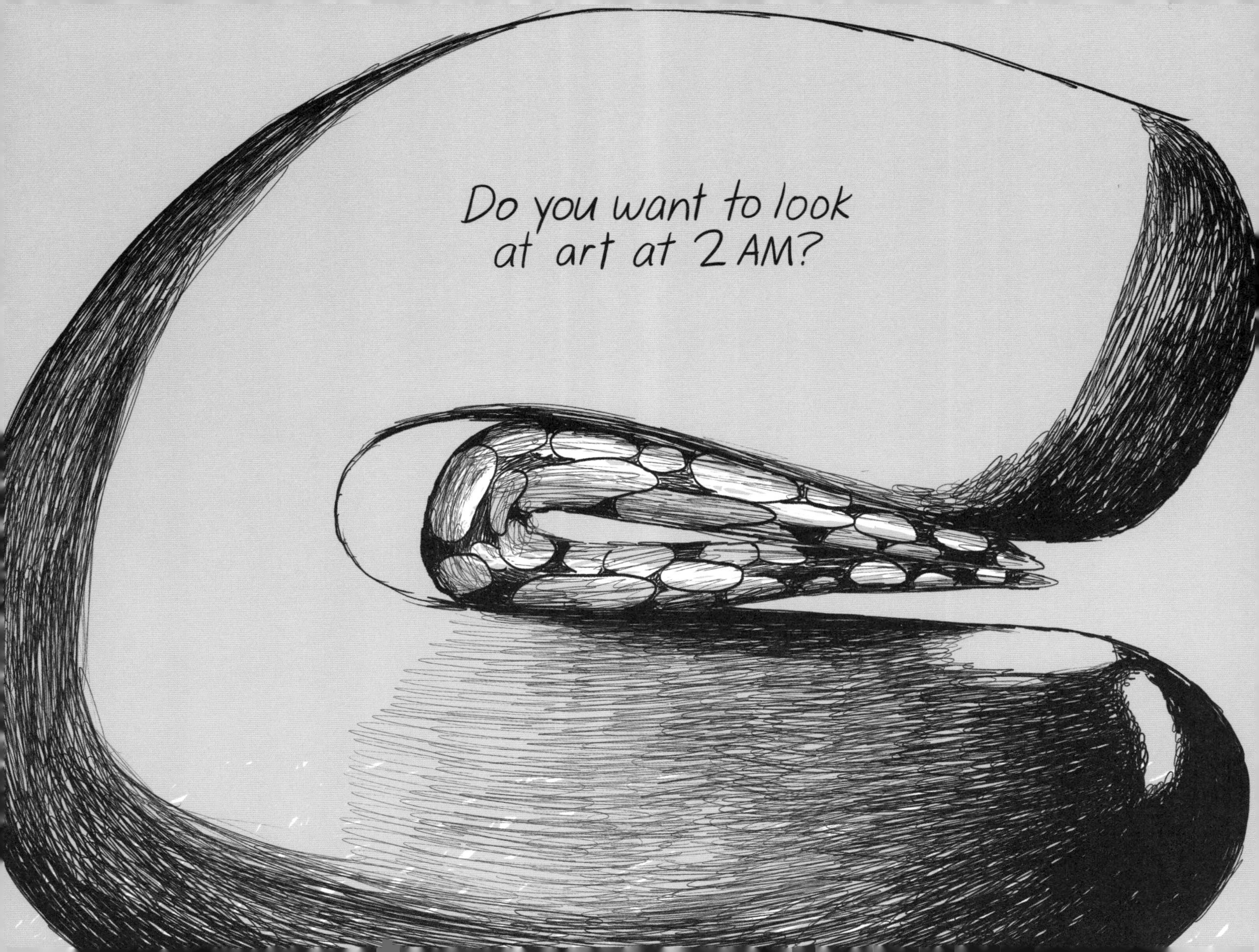
Do you want to look
at art at 2 AM?

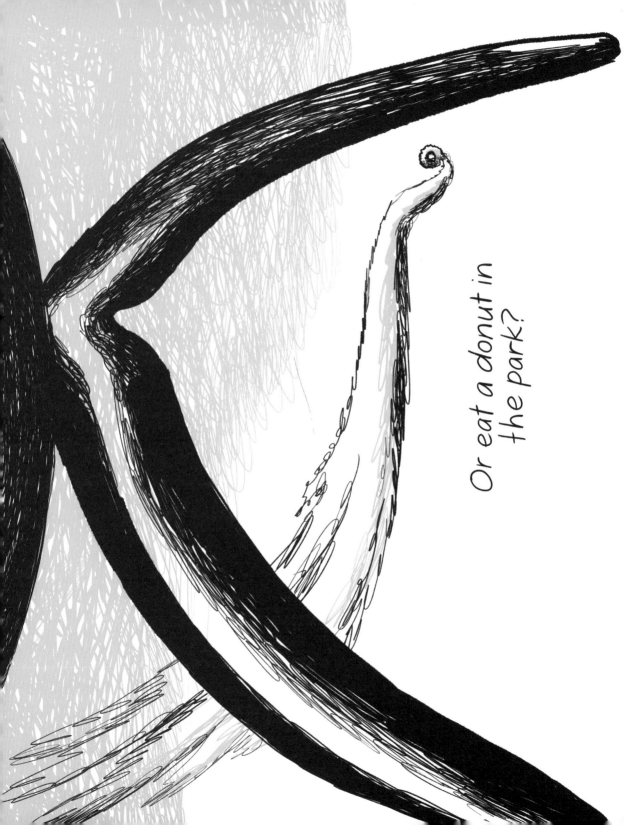

Or eat a donut in the park?

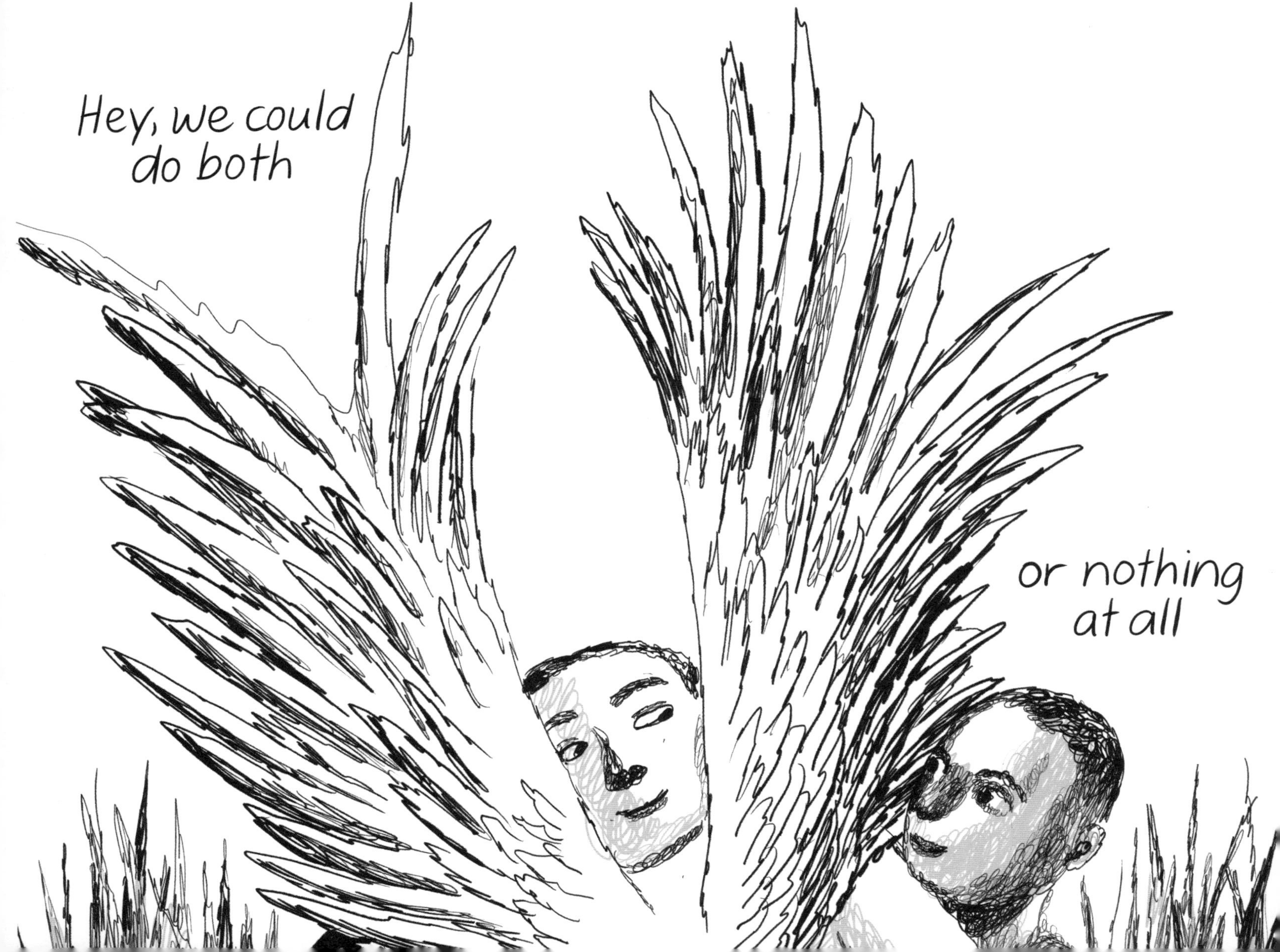
Hey, we could do both
or nothing at all

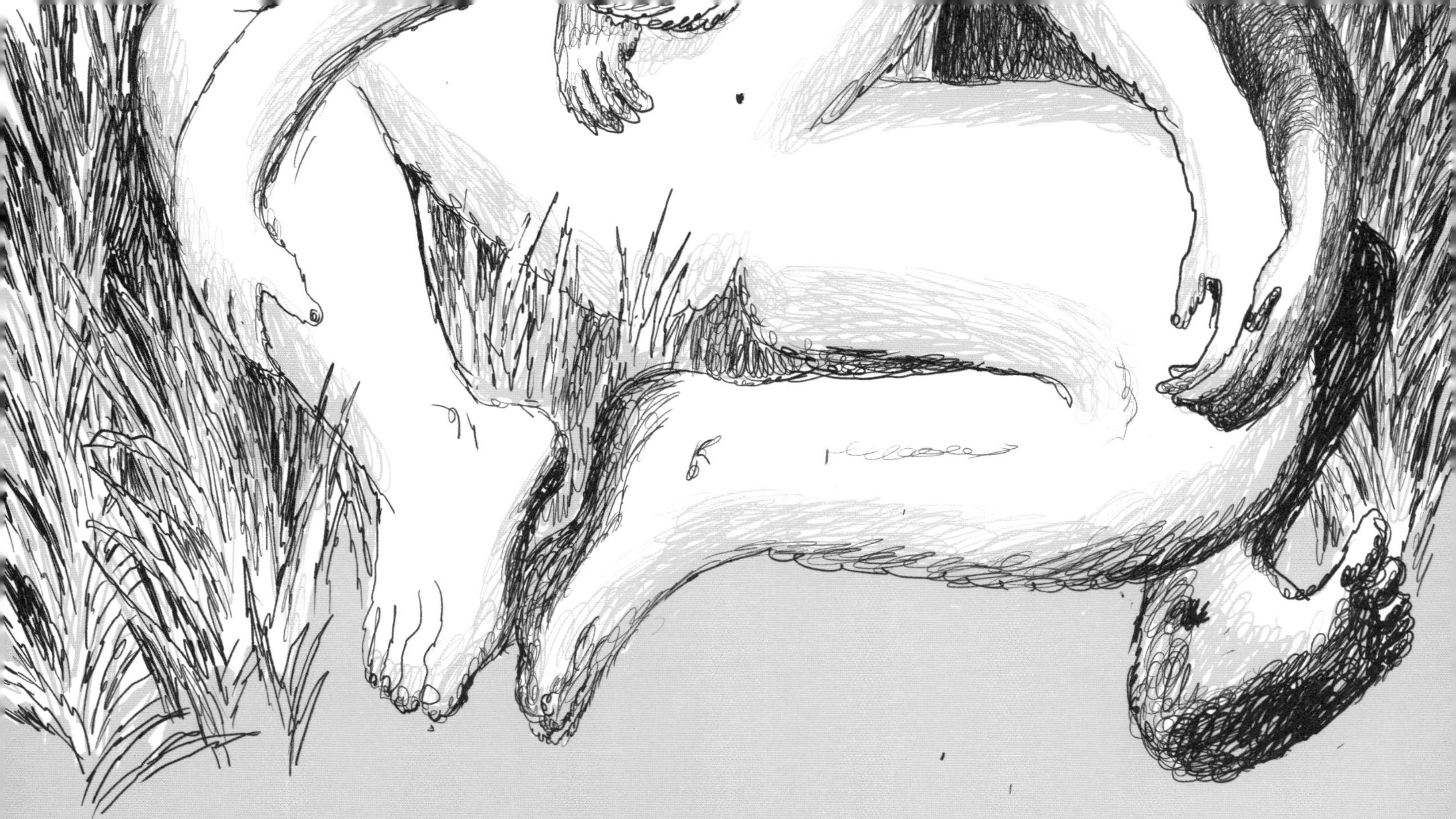

The dogs are so cute in
the World-Class City

The girls are so fine in
this World-Class City

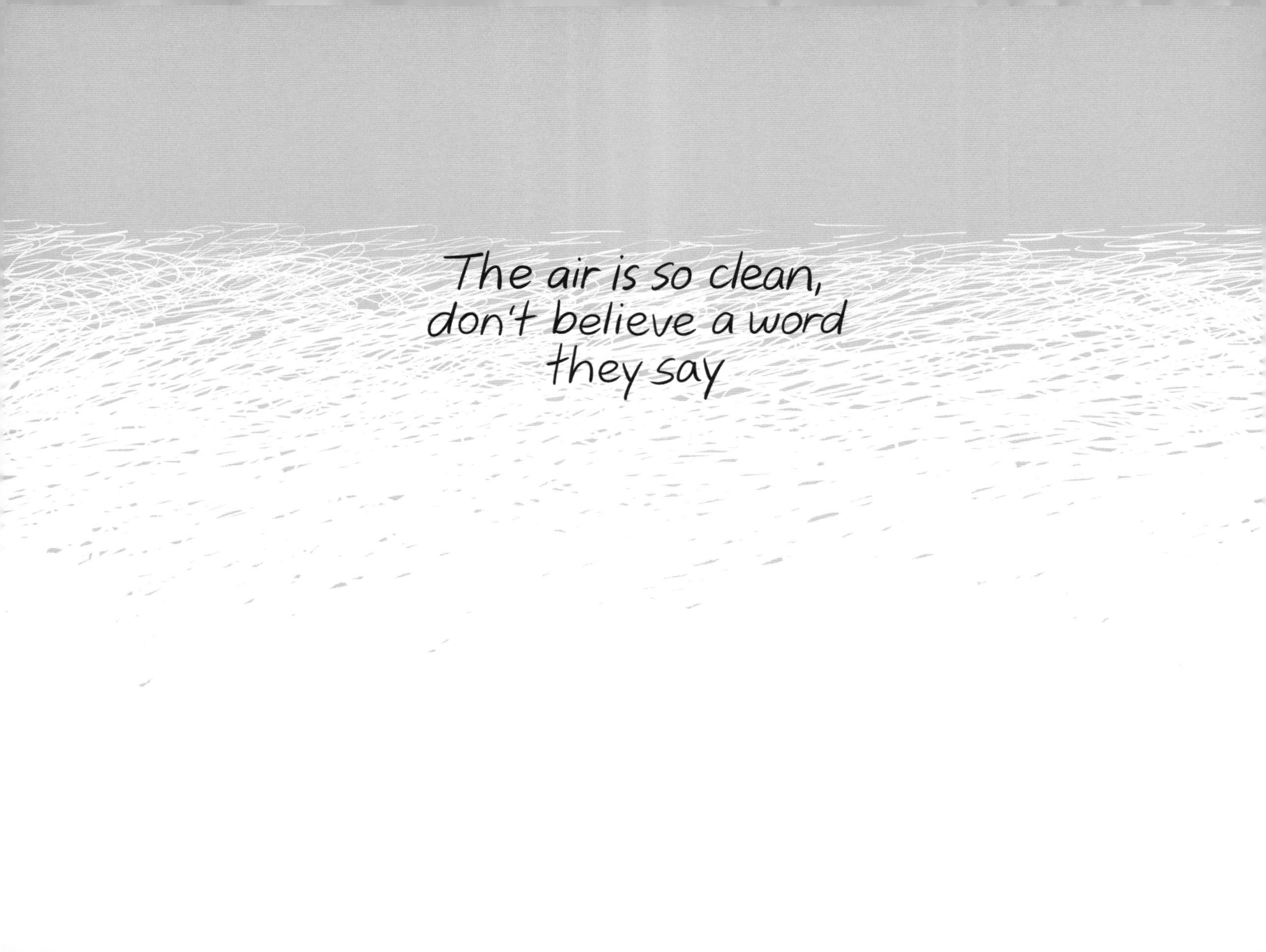
The air is so clean,
don't believe a word
they say

I get stronger with
every passing day

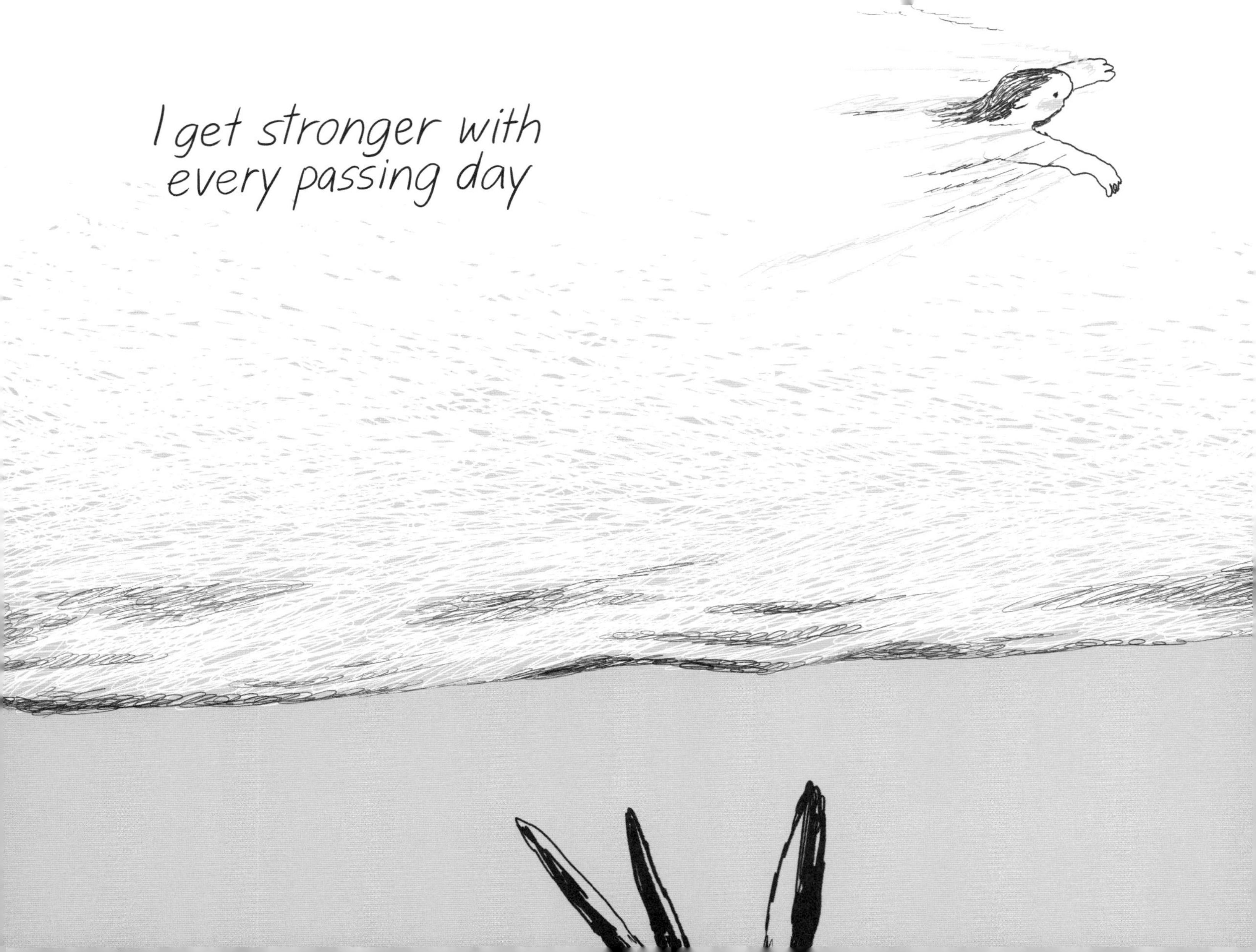

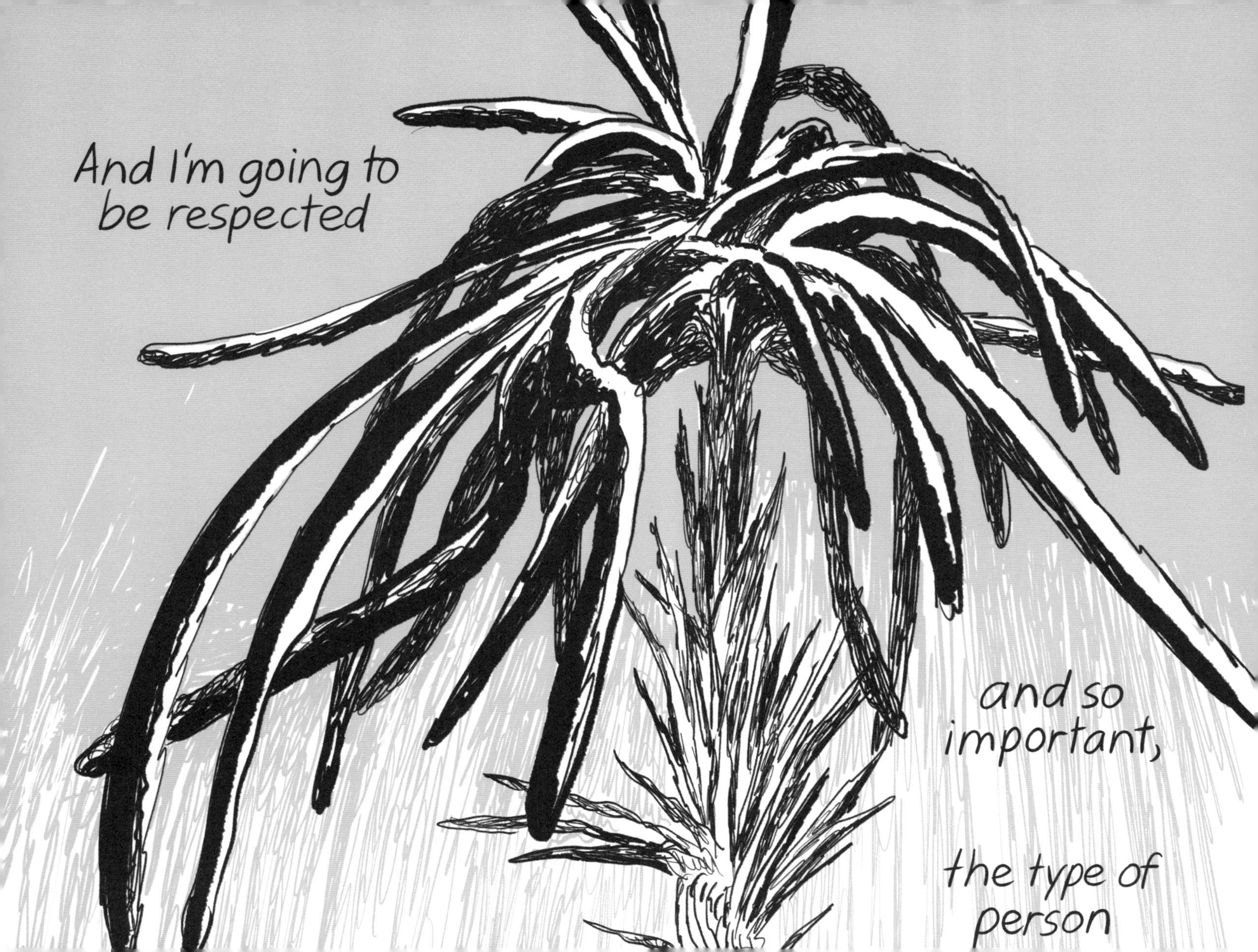
And I'm going to
be respected
and so
important,
the type of
person

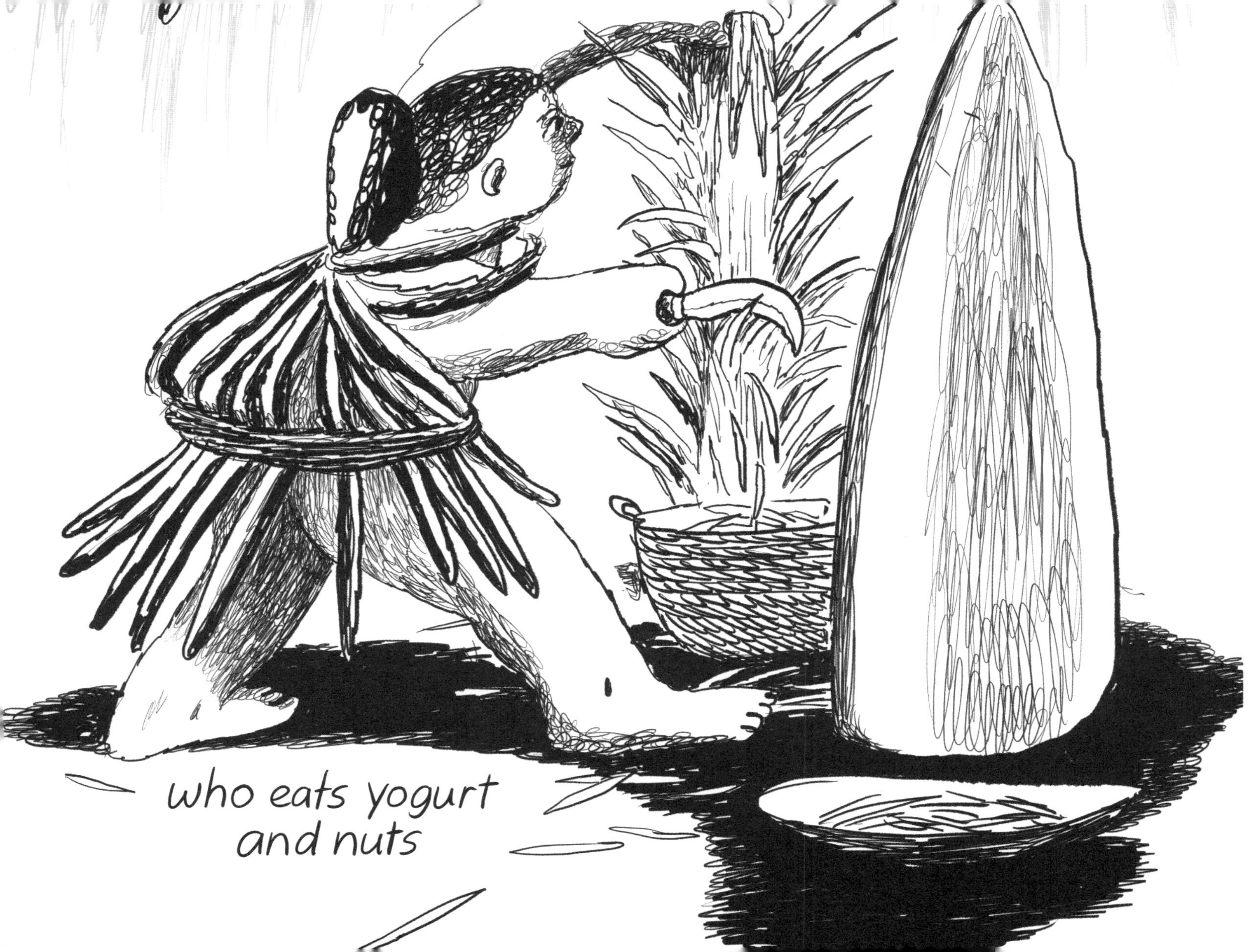

who eats yogurt
and nuts

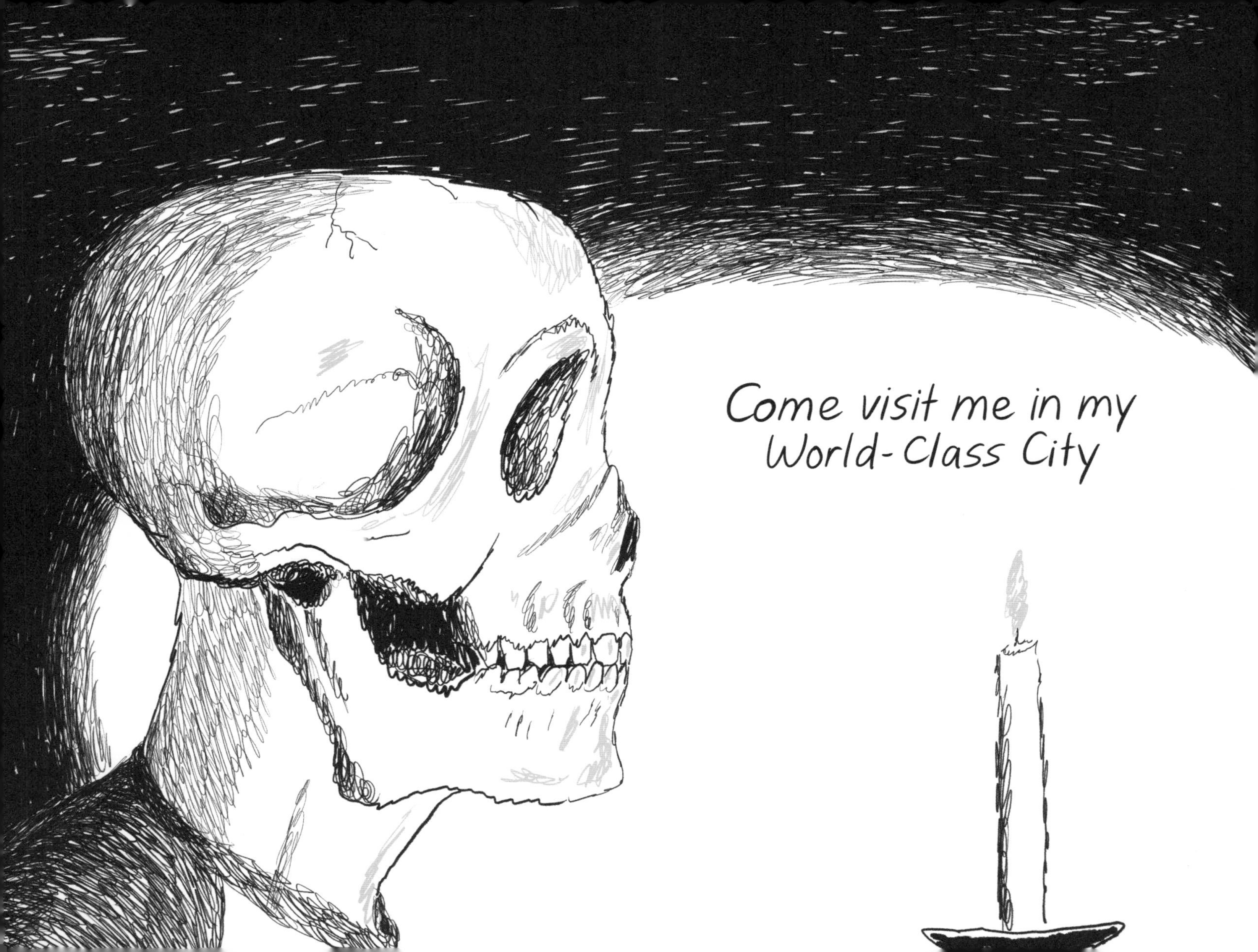
Come visit me in my
World-Class City

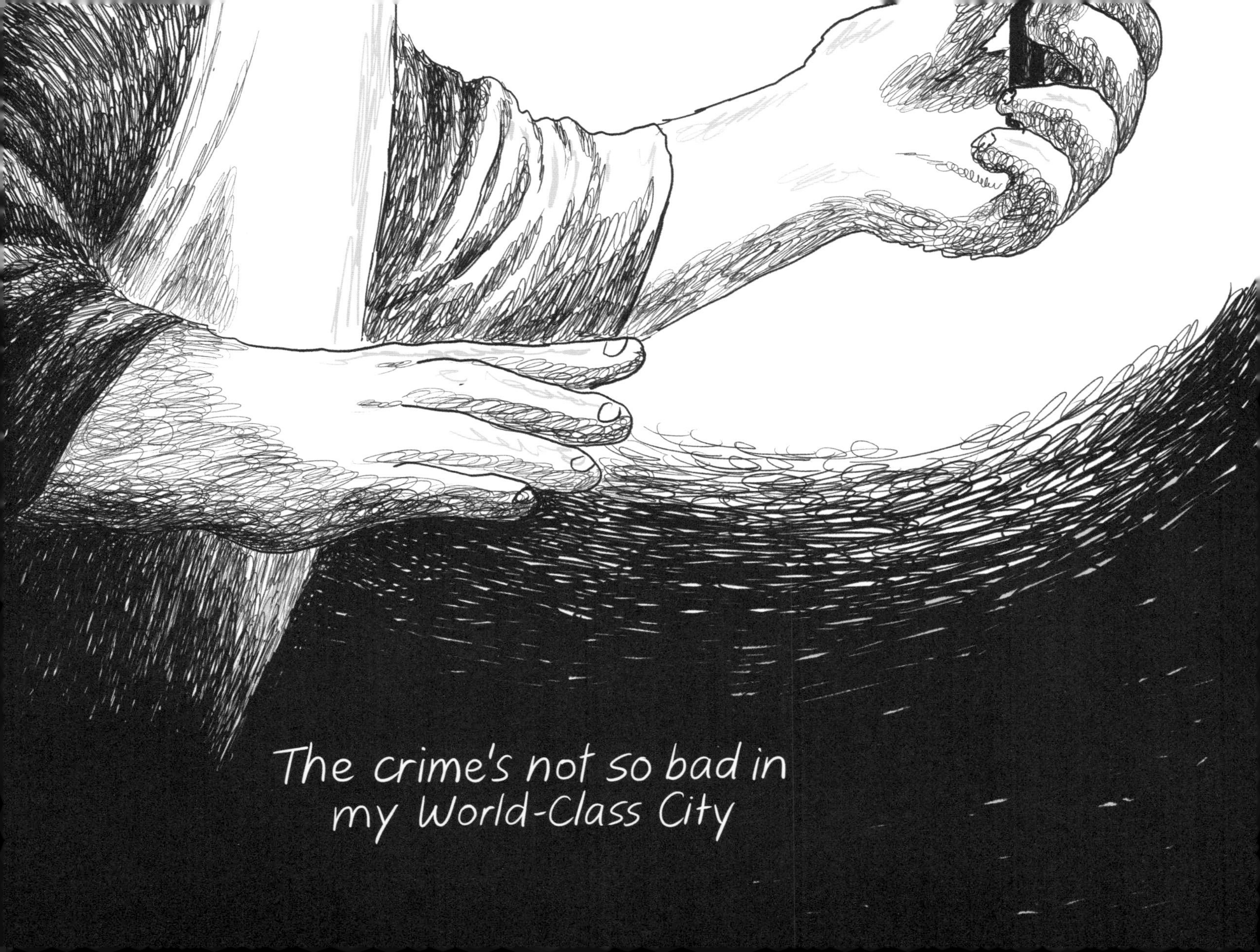
The crime's not so bad in
my World-Class City

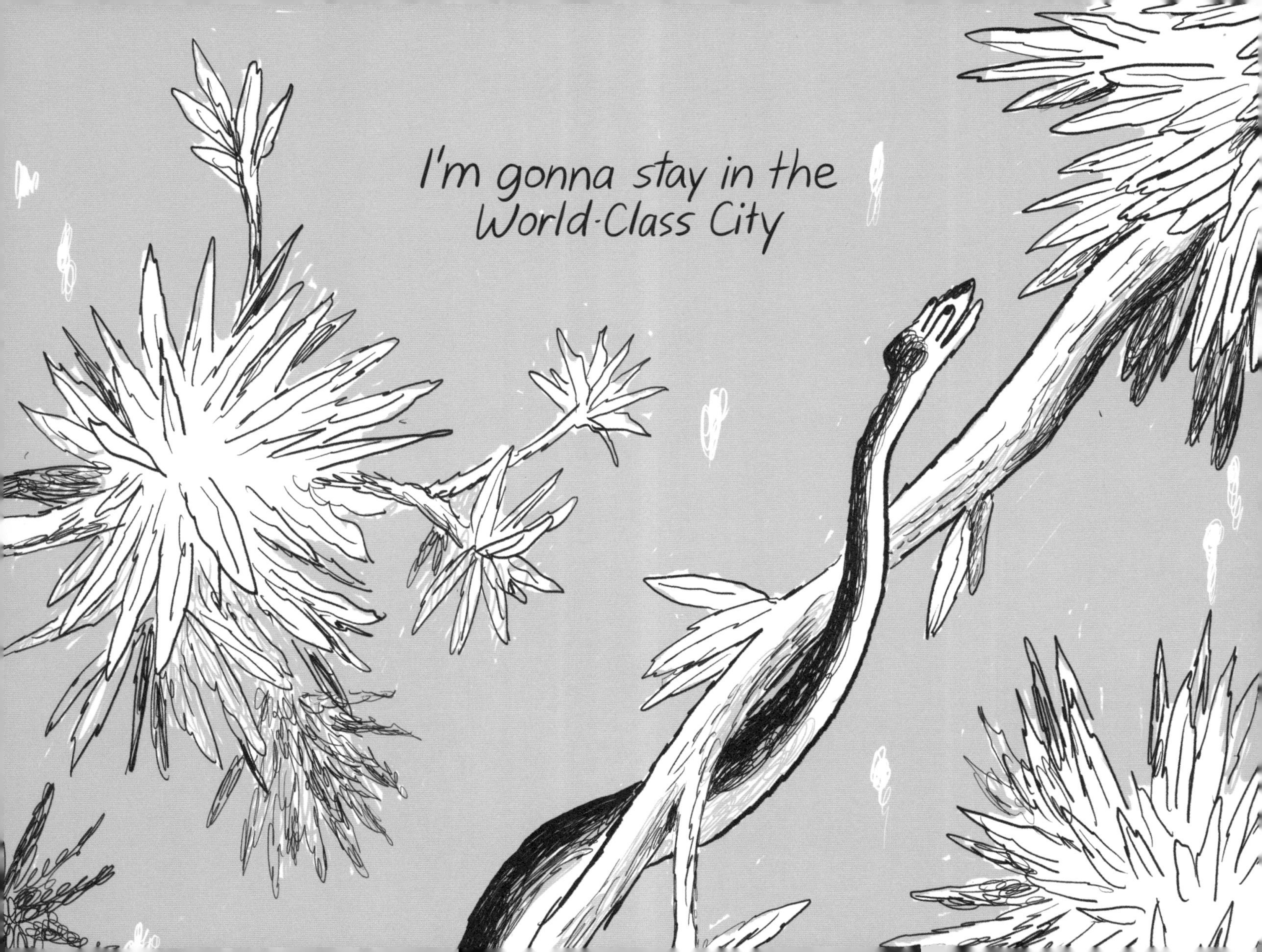
I'm gonna stay in the
World-Class City

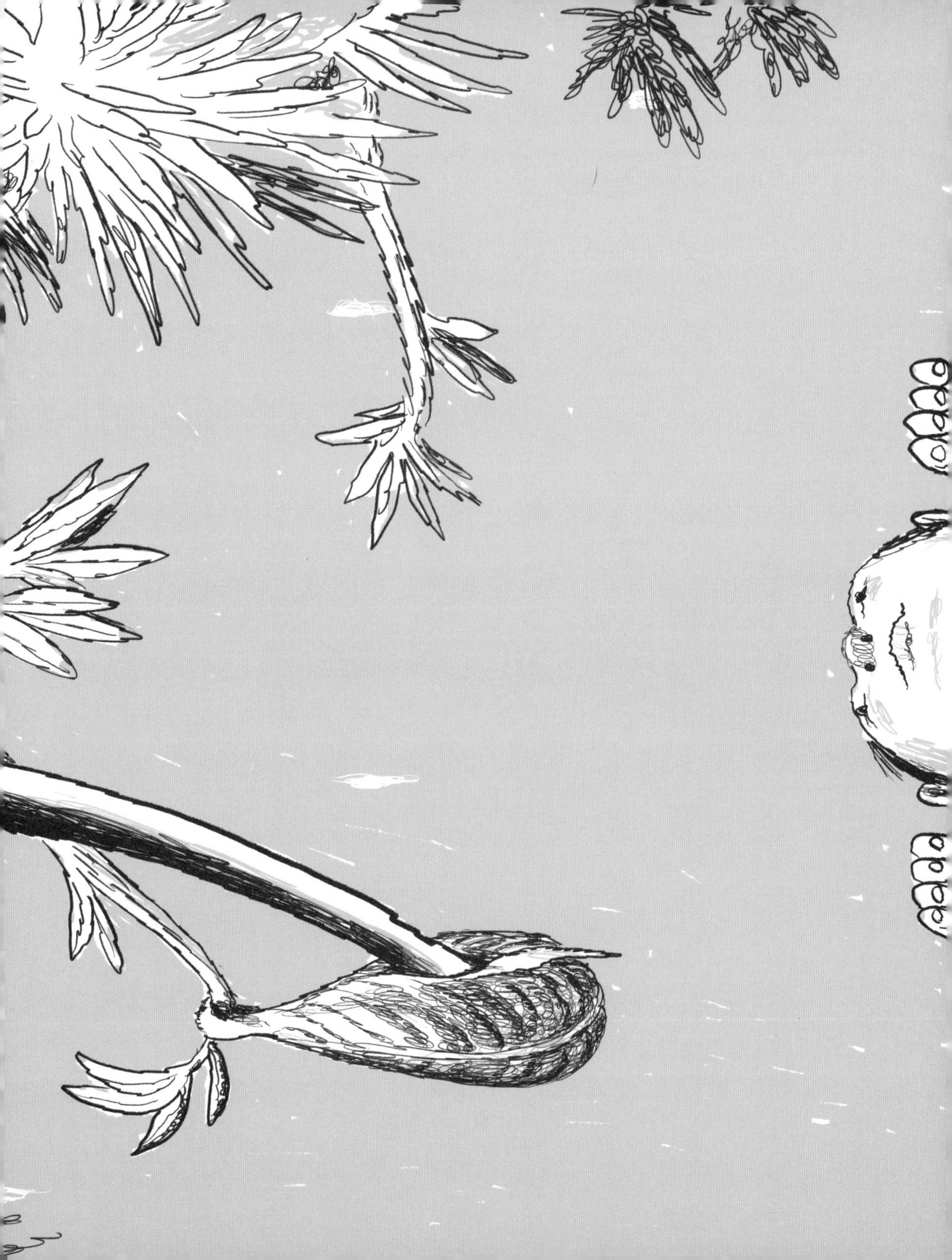

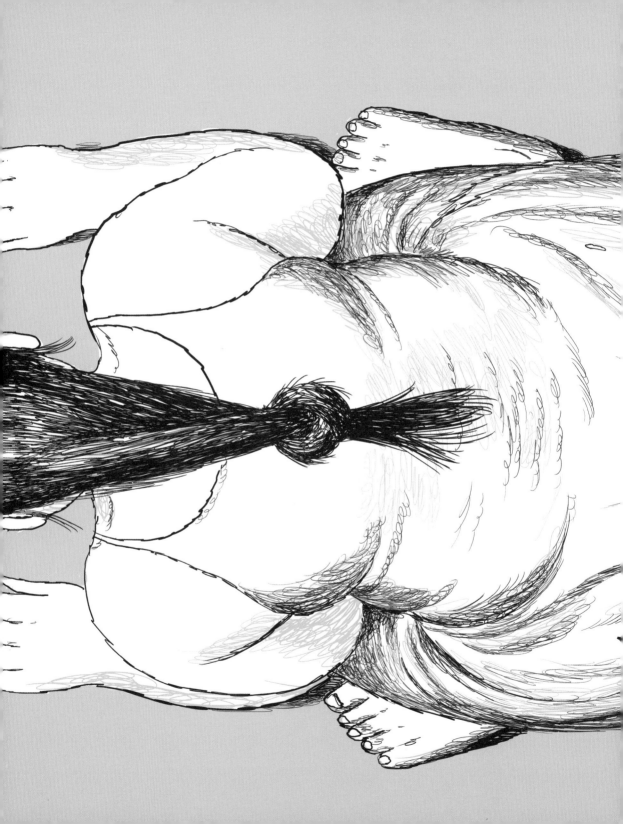

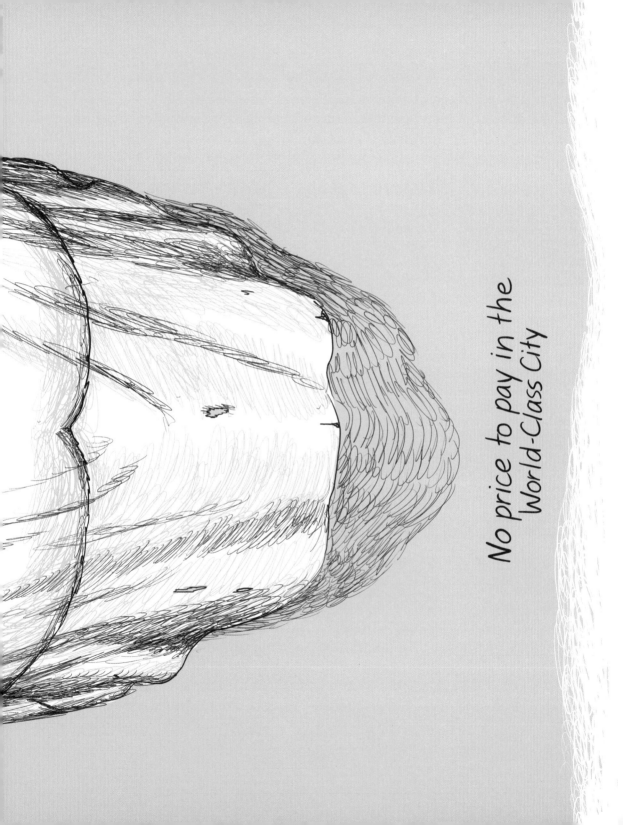

No price to pay in the
World-Class City

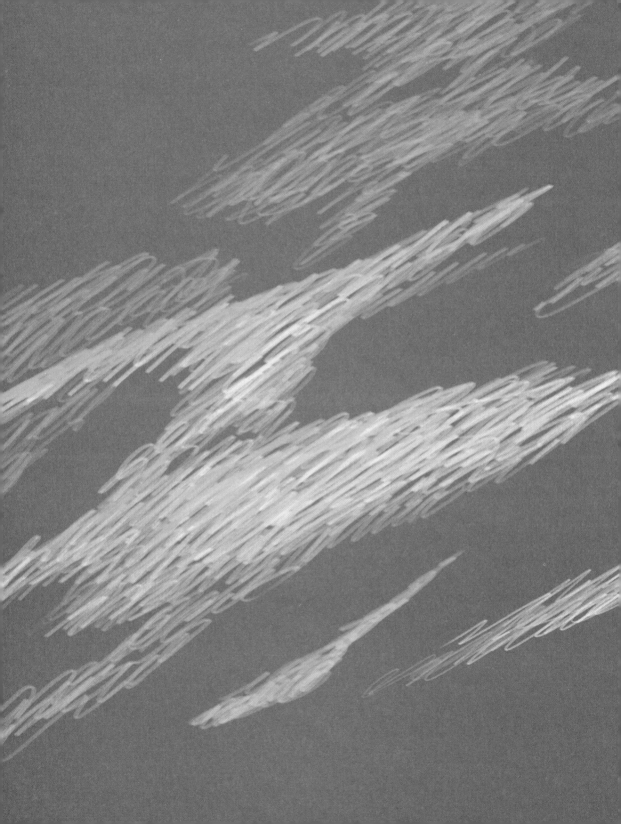

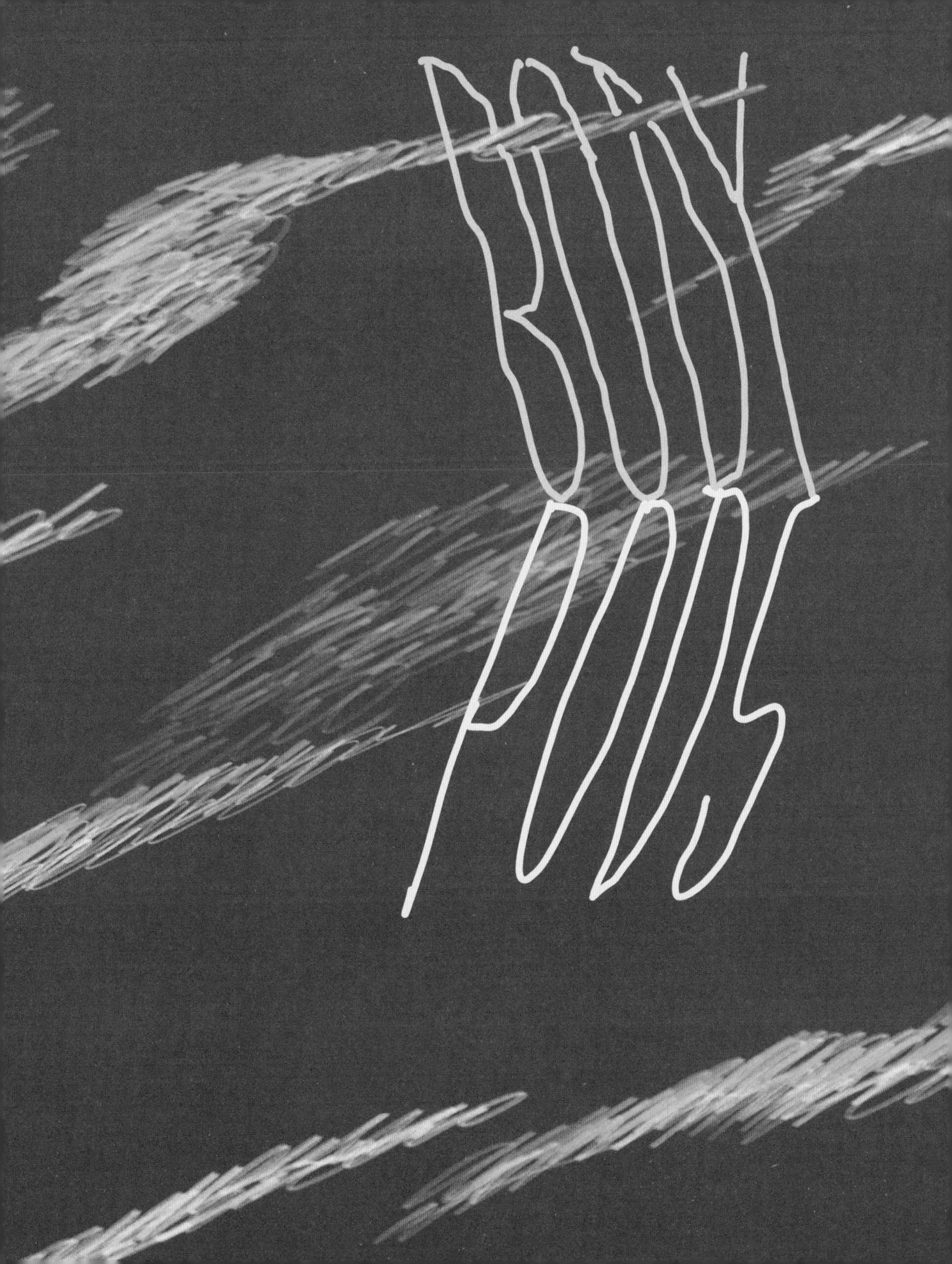
BODY
PODS

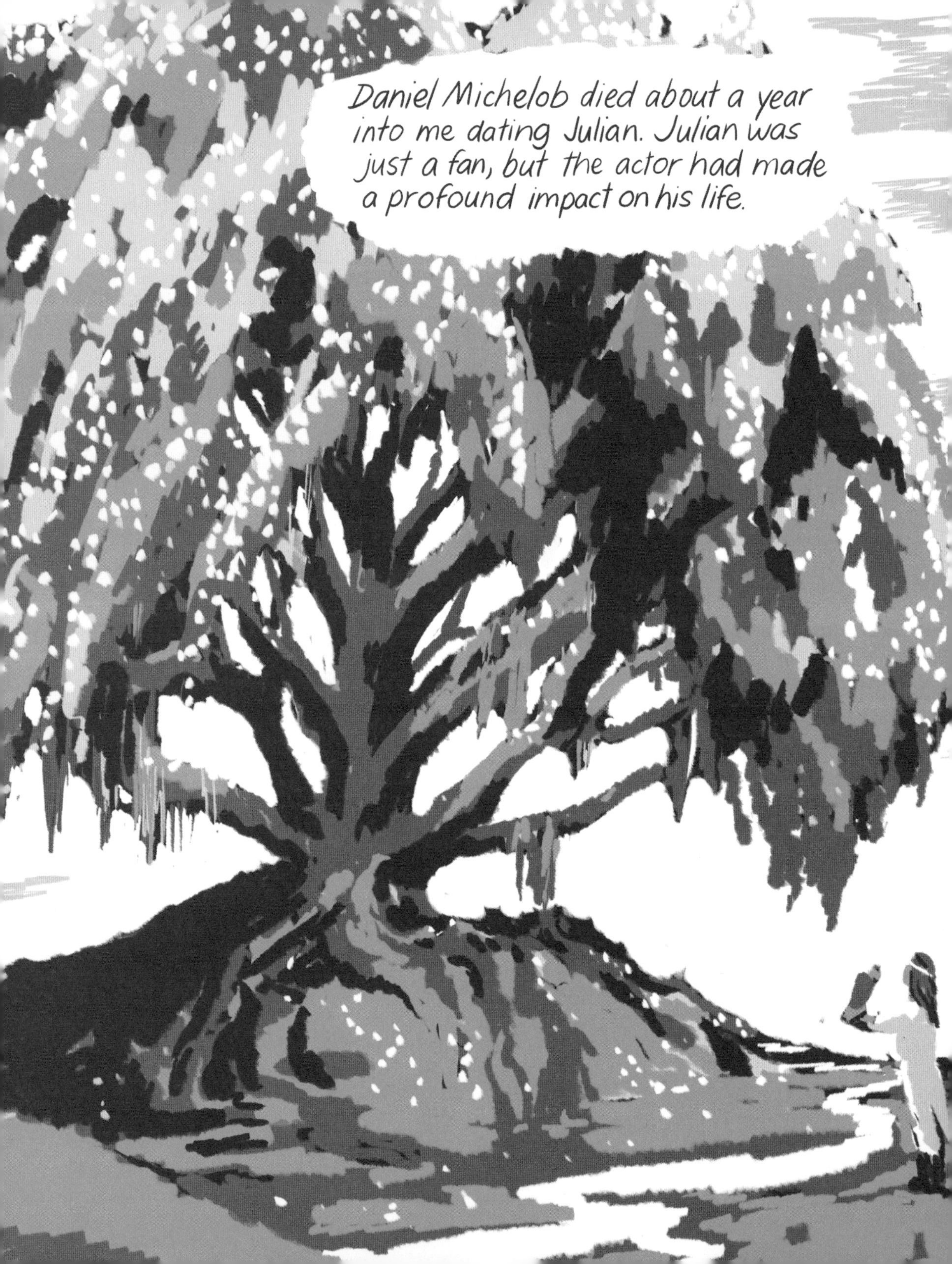
Daniel Michelob died about a year into me dating Julian. Julian was just a fan, but the actor had made a profound impact on his life.

Daniel Michelob
(as Derek O'Shaughnessy)

Body Pods had been a cultural touchstone for decades, but it seemed to hold a particular significance for males between the ages of 11 and 22. I'm not sure why. It's a pretty depressing movie, despite the action-adventure elements.

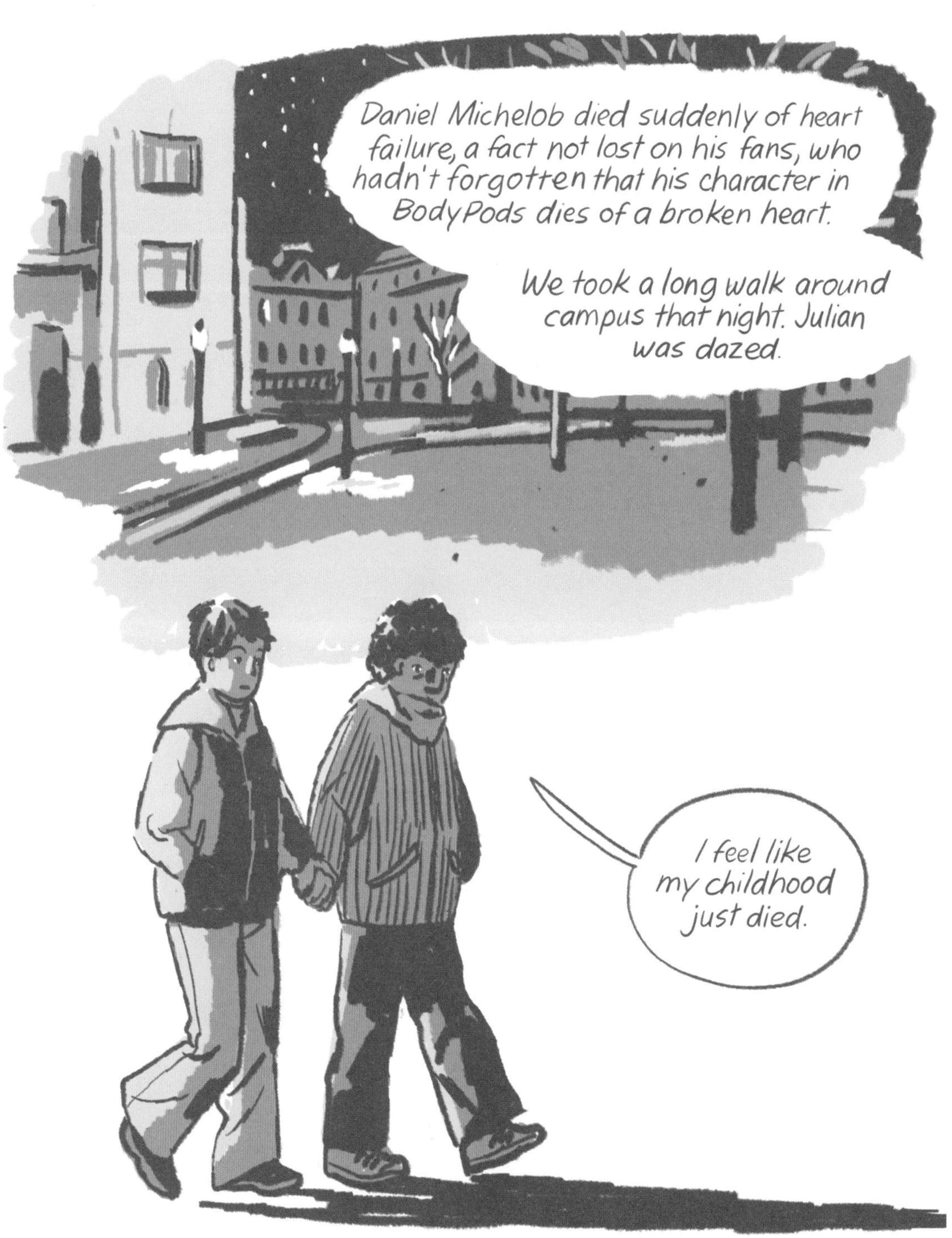
Daniel Michelob died suddenly of heart failure, a fact not lost on his fans, who hadn't forgotten that his character in BodyPods dies of a broken heart.
We took a long walk around campus that night. Julian was dazed.
I feel like my childhood just died.

We washed up at the engineers' pub.
The TVs were blasting the news.

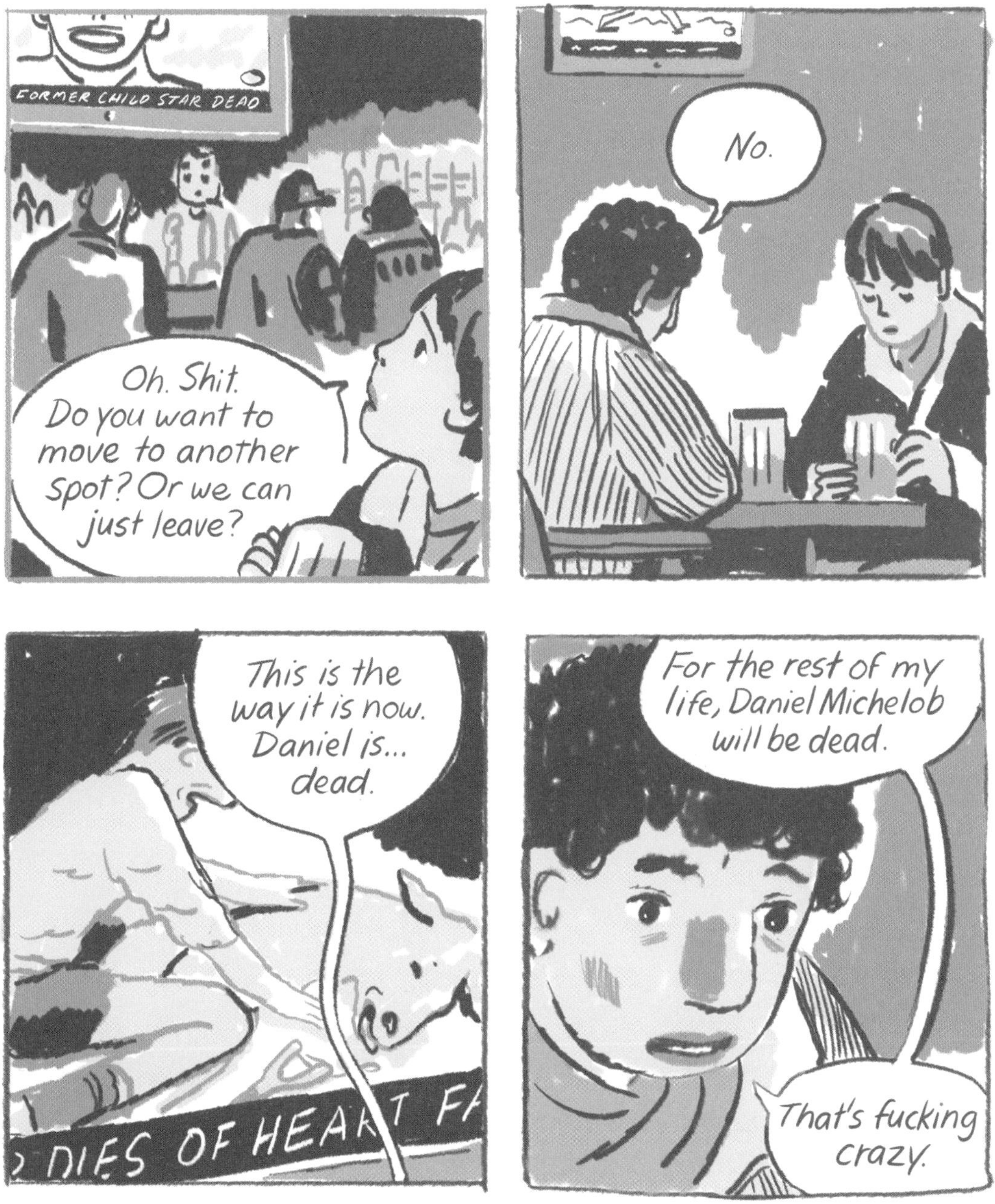
FORMER CHILD STAR DEAD
Oh. Shit. Do you want to move to another spot? Or we can just leave?
No.
This is the way it is now. Daniel is... dead.
DIES OF HEART FA
For the rest of my life, Daniel Michelob will be dead.
That's fucking crazy.

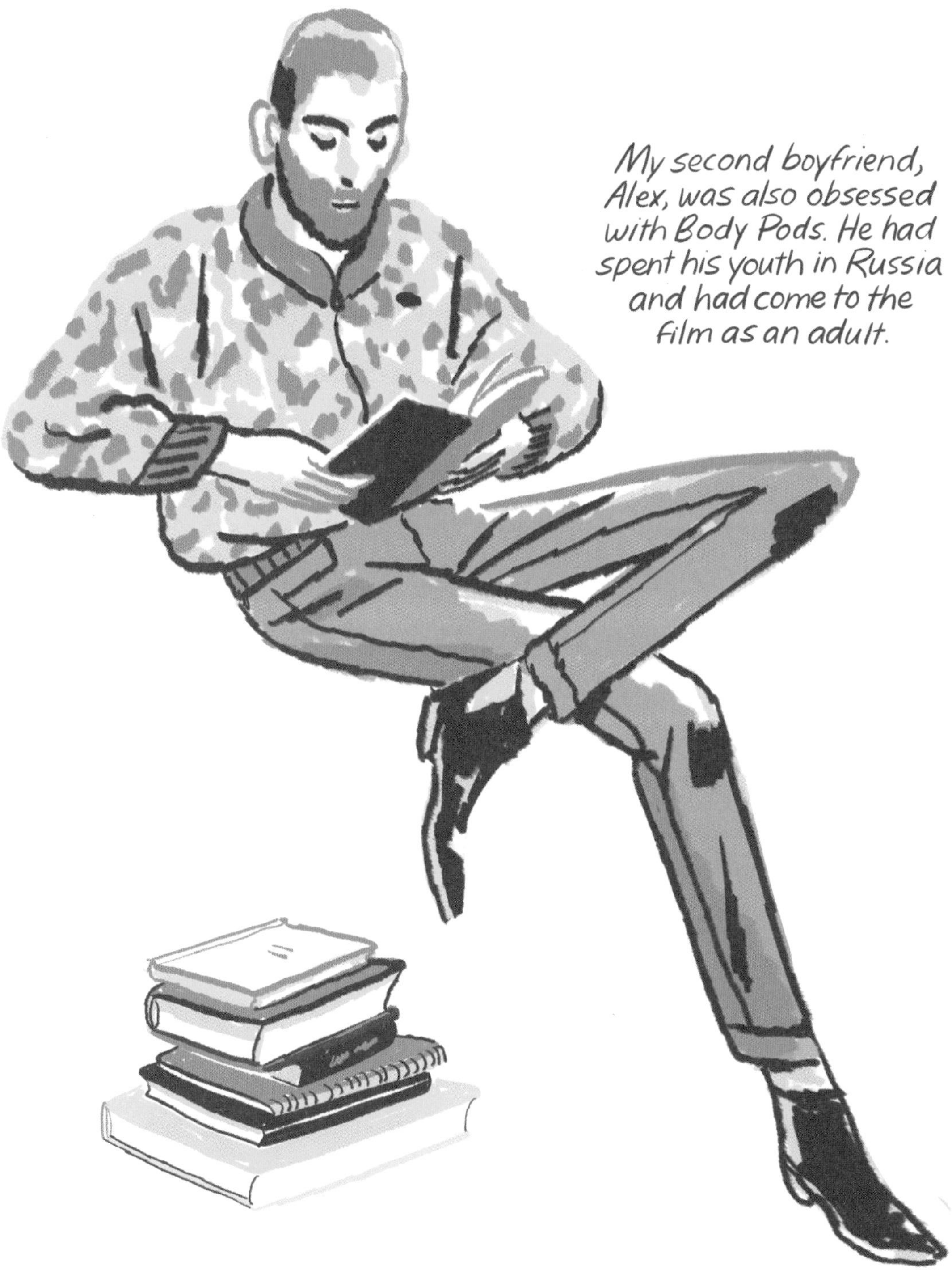
My second boyfriend, Alex, was also obsessed with Body Pods. He had spent his youth in Russia and had come to the film as an adult.

Alex was a grad student in film studies and his appreciation for Body Pods was largely aesthetic.

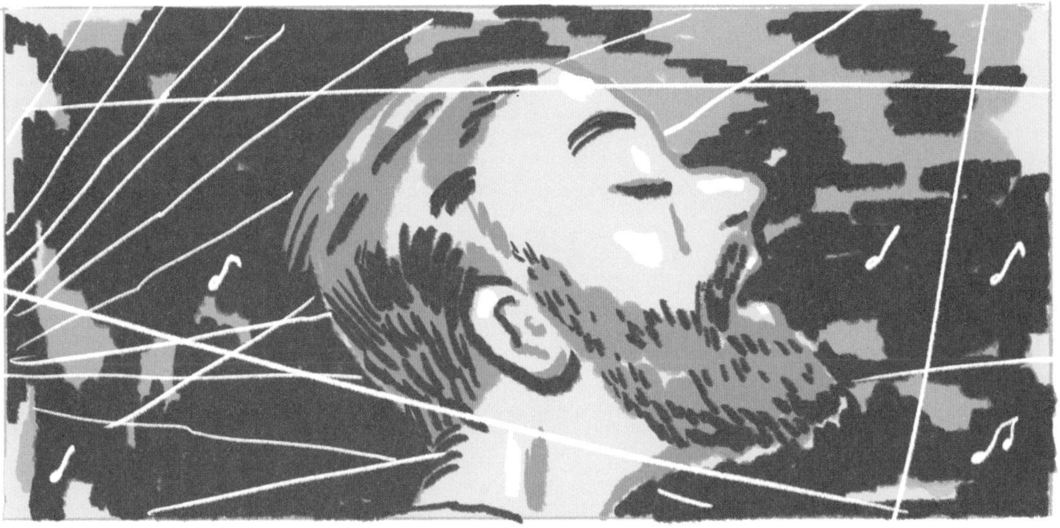

He said it was the apex of American filmmaking, before computer graphics had, in his words, "industrialized the craft."

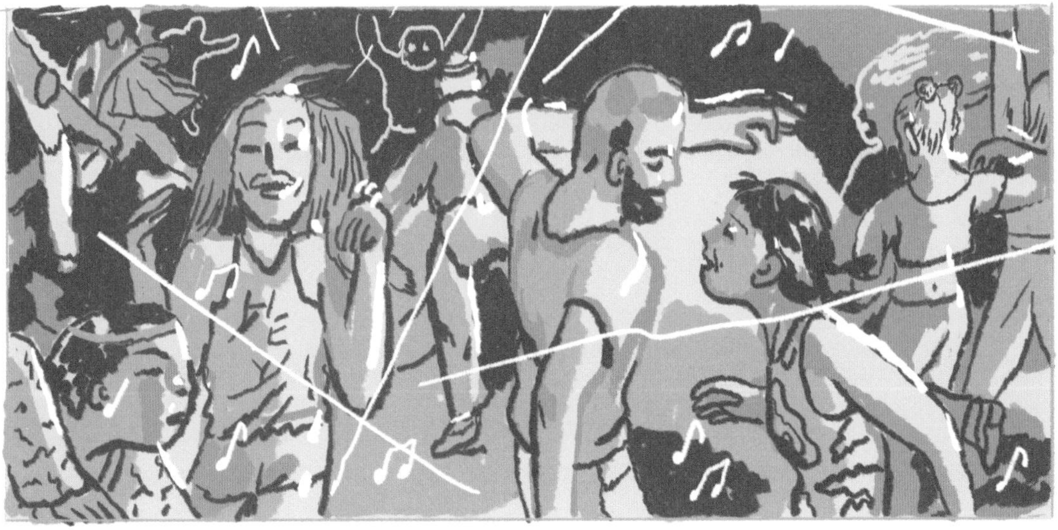

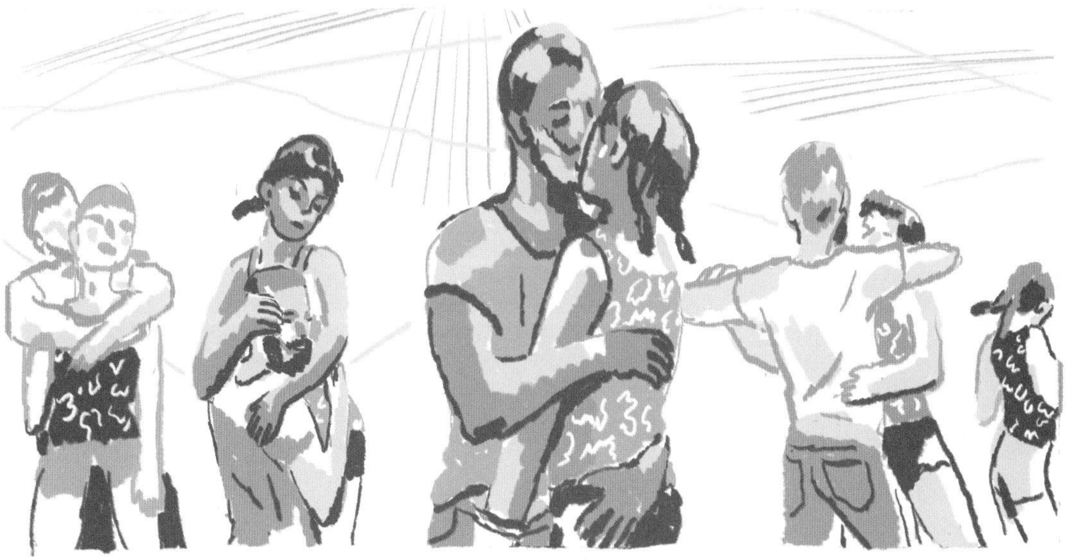

The paper-thin production values held more than charm for Alex. For him, the visible boom mics and shoddily painted background sets created an "intensely human" effect.

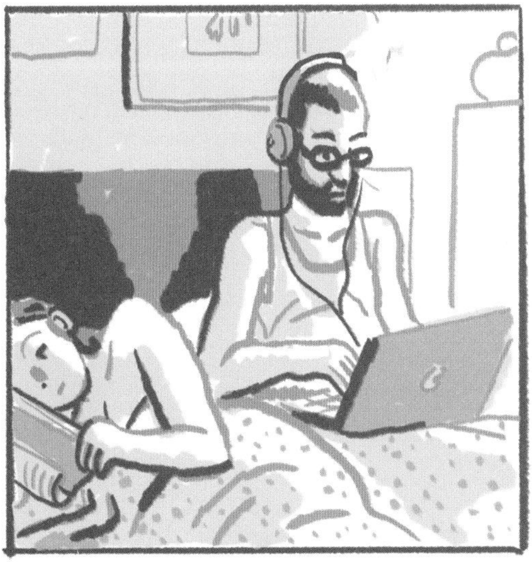

Of course, we'd still laugh at the flaws.

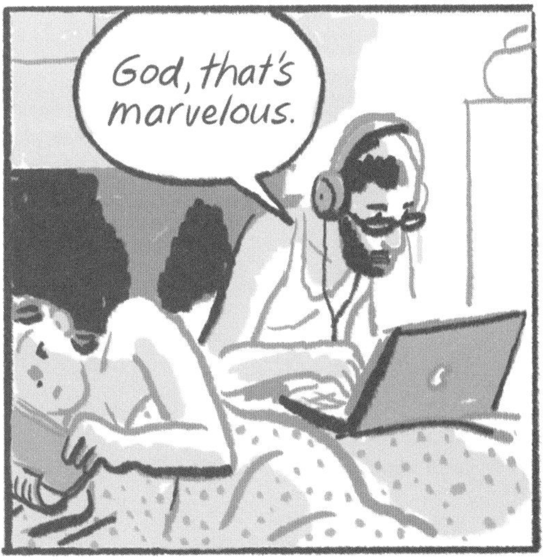
God, that's marvelous.

But after the outburst, Alex would lean in towards the screen with wonder.

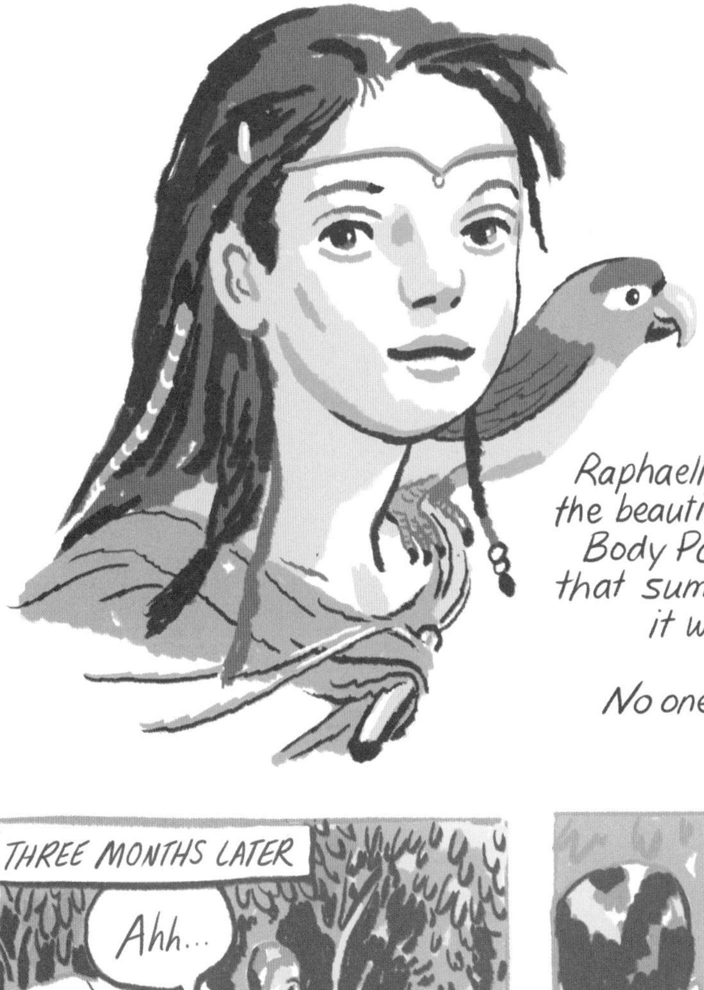

Raphaella Doig, who played the beautiful young heroine of Body Pods, died tragically that summer. I had to admit, it was pretty sad.

No one should die at 46.

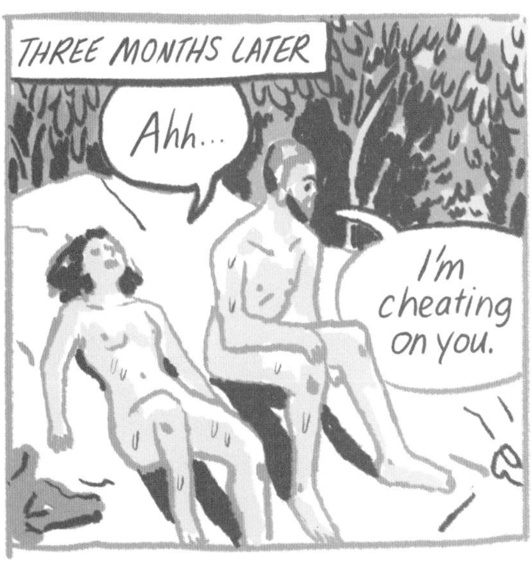
THREE MONTHS LATER
Ahh...
I'm cheating on you.

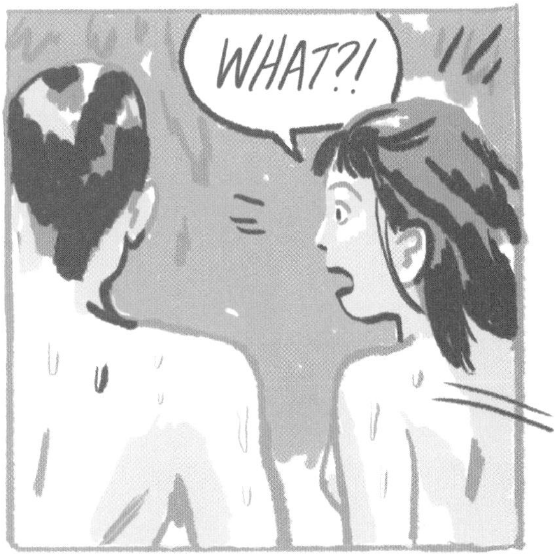
WHAT?!

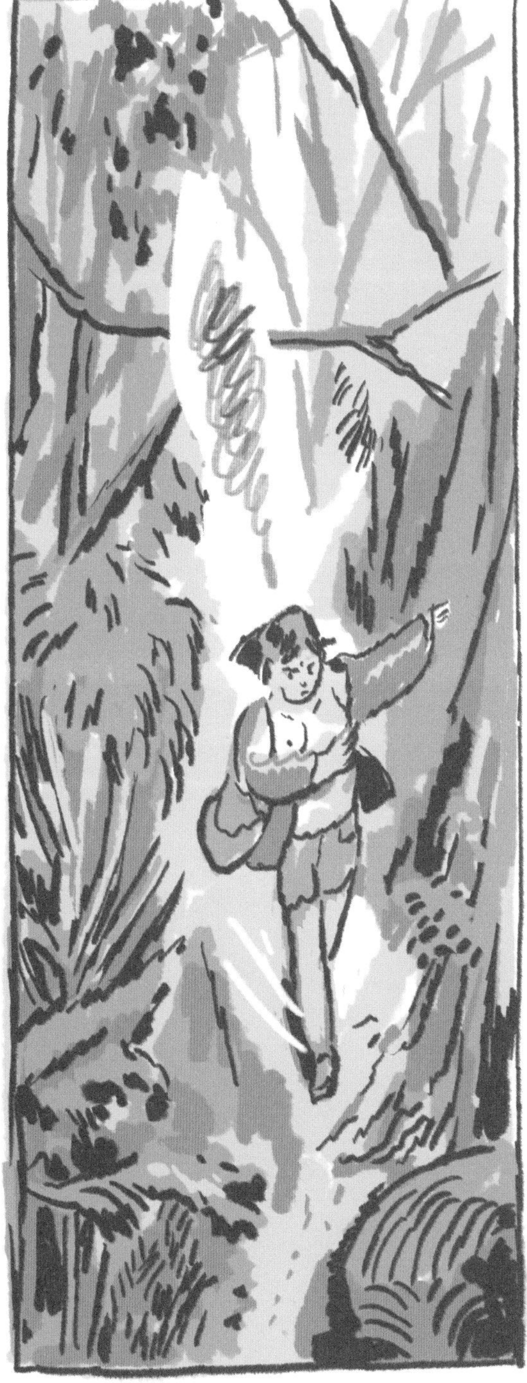

His reasons were elusive. He didn't cry or fight back or try to make me stay, which was extremely irritating.

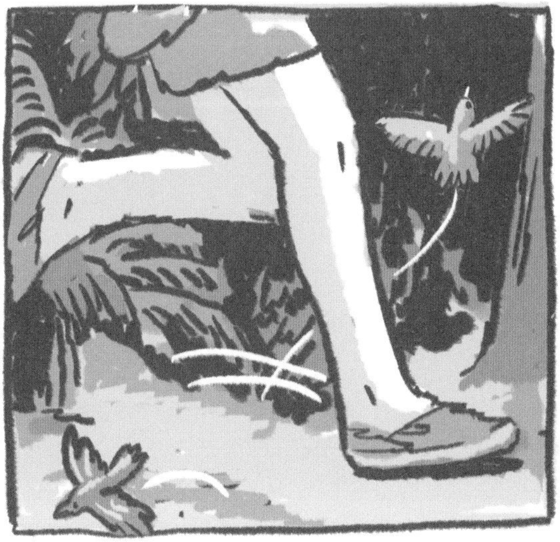

He just stared straight ahead, eyes distant, and murmured, "We're all going to die one day."

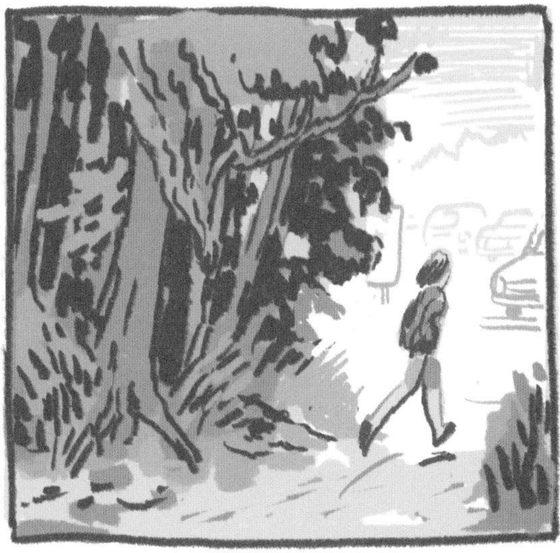

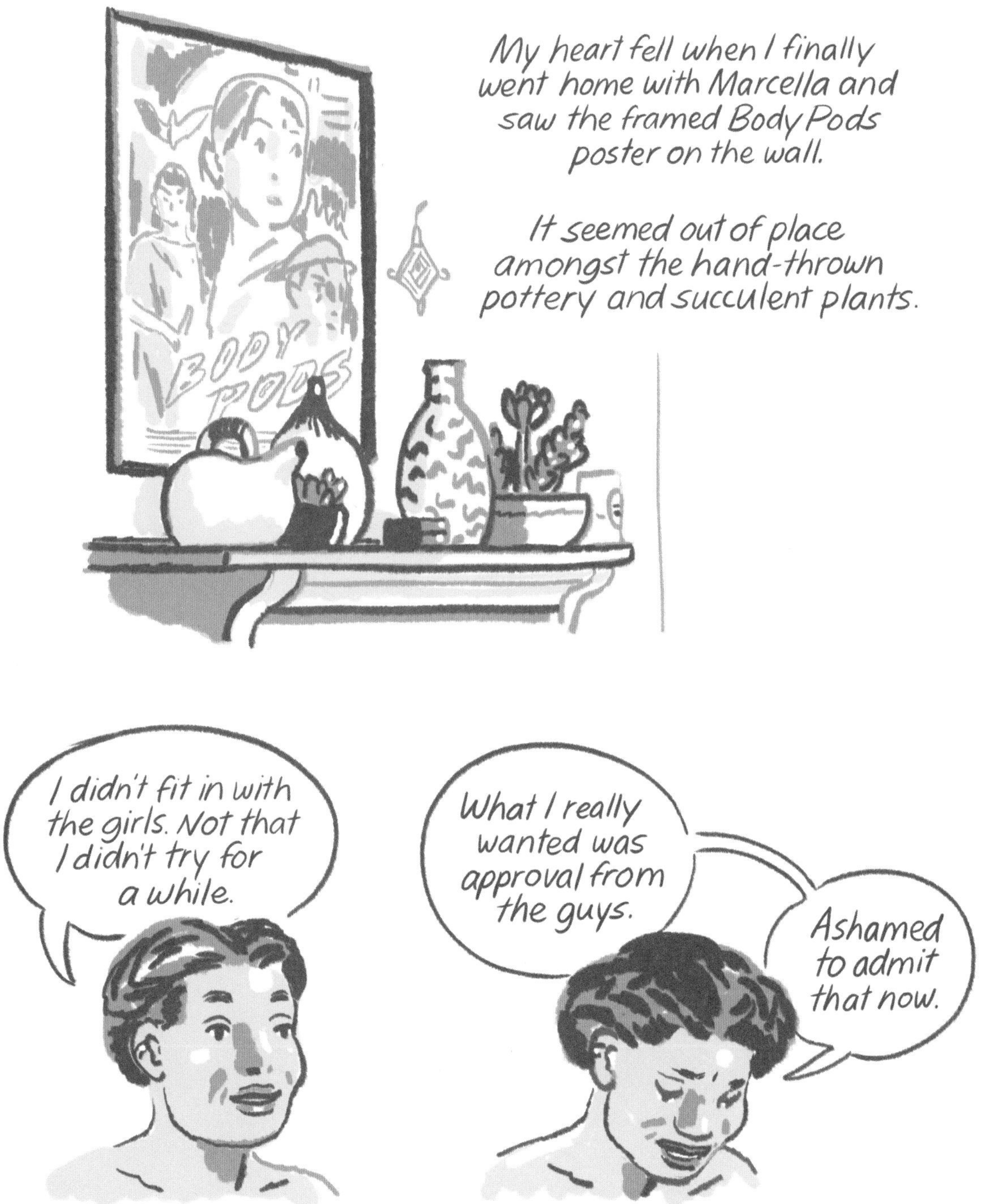
My heart fell when I finally went home with Marcella and saw the framed Body Pods poster on the wall.
It seemed out of place amongst the hand-thrown pottery and succulent plants.
BODY PODS
I didn't fit in with the girls. Not that I didn't try for a while.
What I really wanted was approval from the guys.
Ashamed to admit that now.

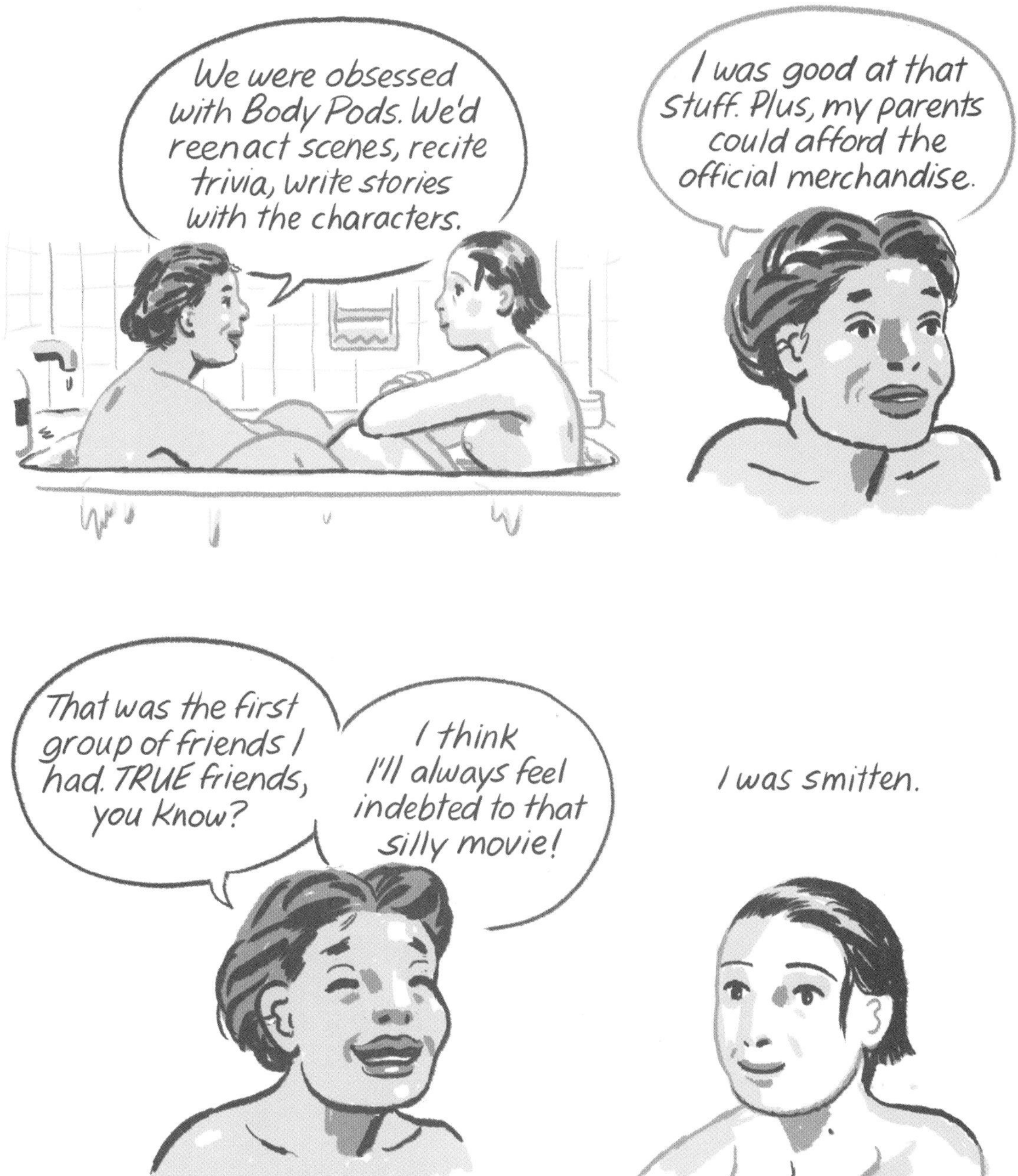
We were obsessed with Body Pods. We'd reenact scenes, recite trivia, write stories with the characters.
I was good at that stuff. Plus, my parents could afford the official merchandise.
That was the first group of friends I had. TRUE friends, you know?
I think I'll always feel indebted to that silly movie!
I was smitten.

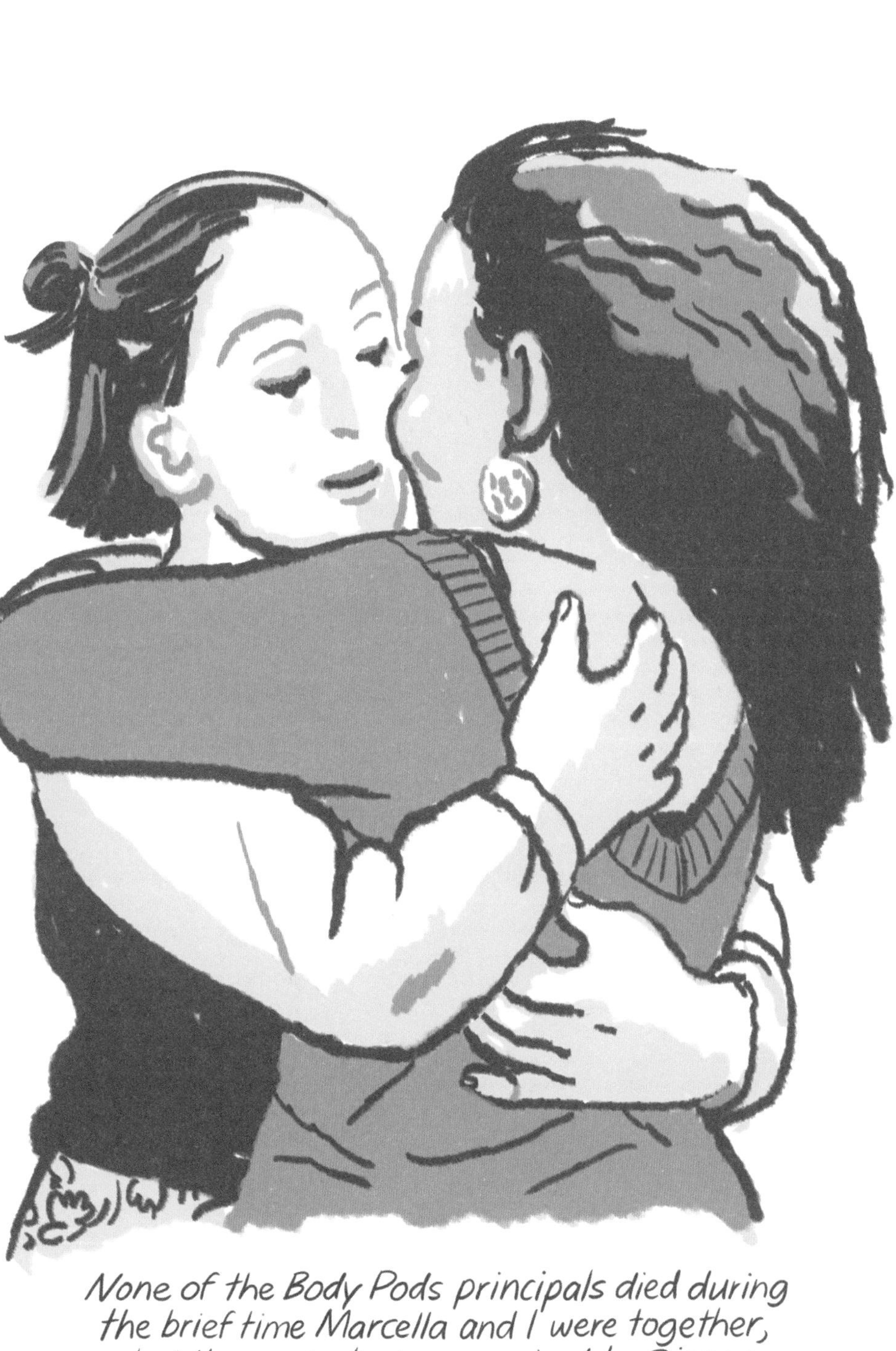

None of the Body Pods principals died during the brief time Marcella and I were together, but the property was acquired by Disney. I think it was something like 10 billion dollars.

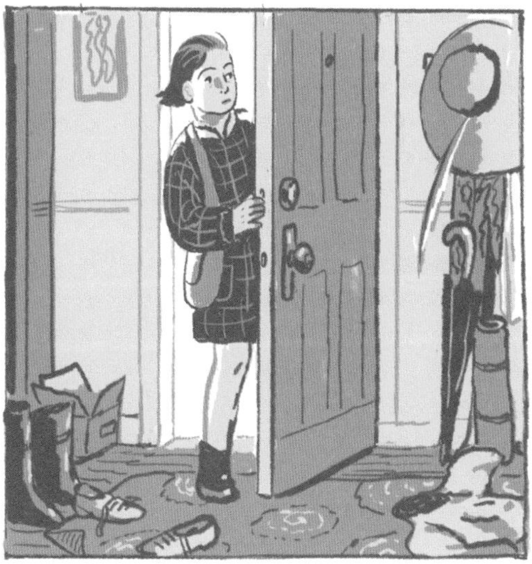

Marcella was disgusted. She fell deeper into depression with every announcement Disney made regarding their plans.

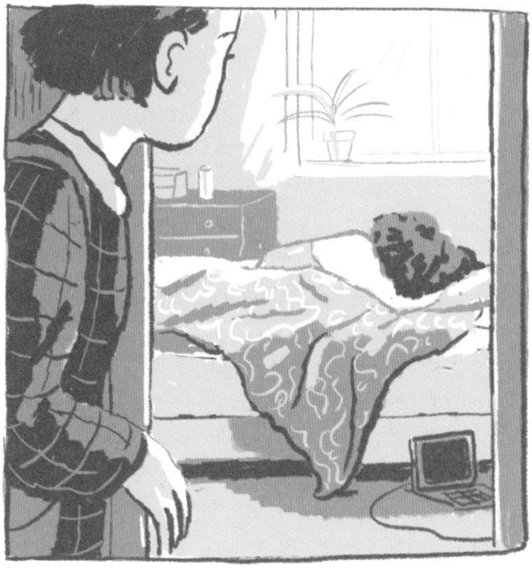

(It was a series of rolling announcements, dispatched from a week-long convention in Orlando.)

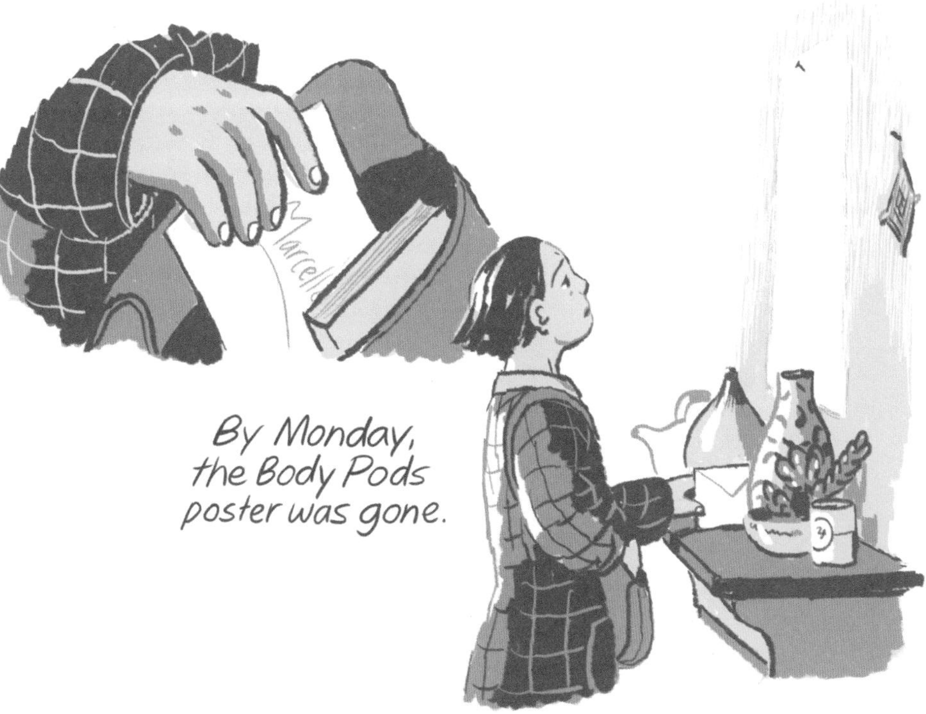

By Monday, the Body Pods poster was gone.

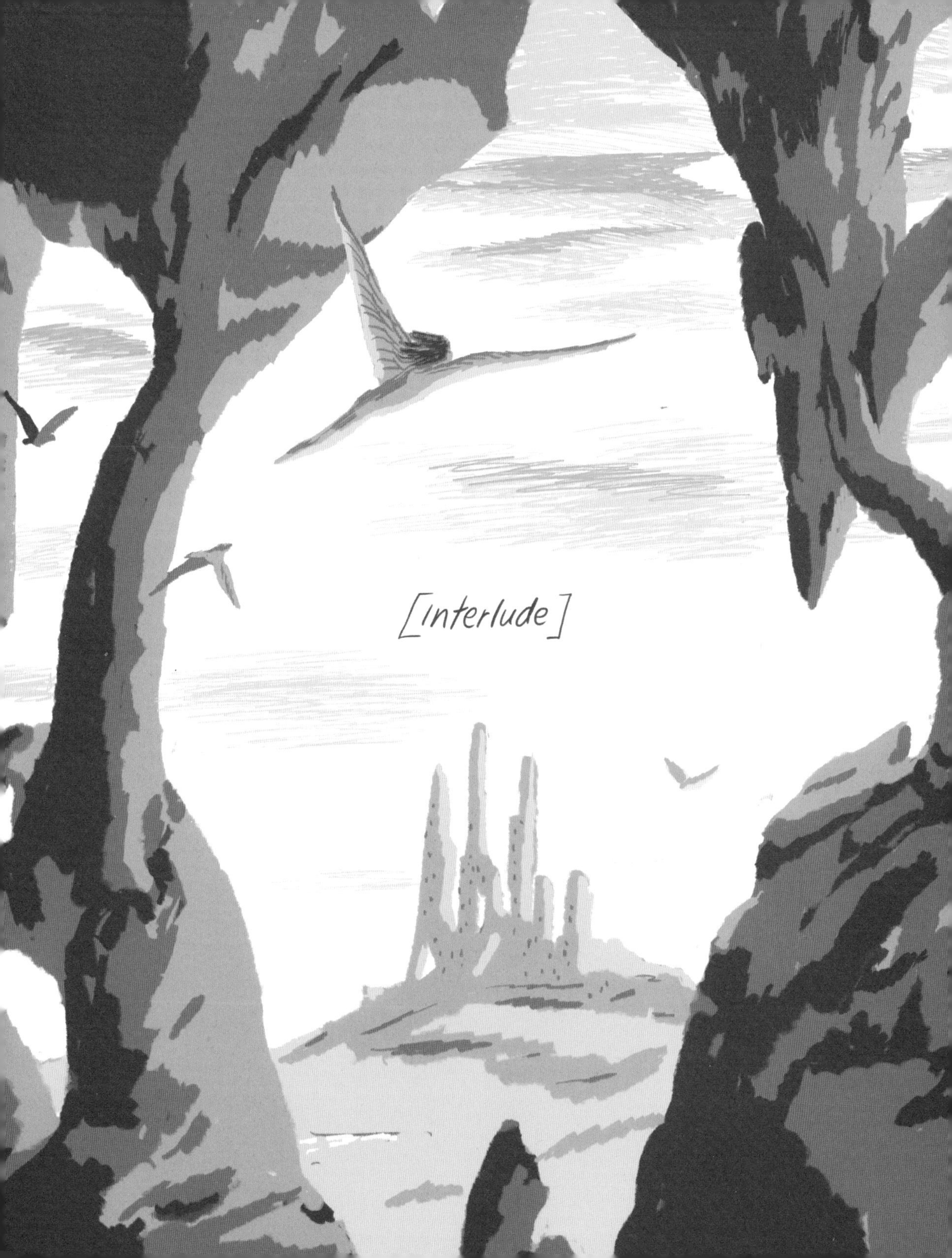
[interlude]

Mickey Rodriguez was a 39-year-old actor and waiter when he was cast in the role of Fivel Donovan, a friendless ex-military sniper gone rogue.

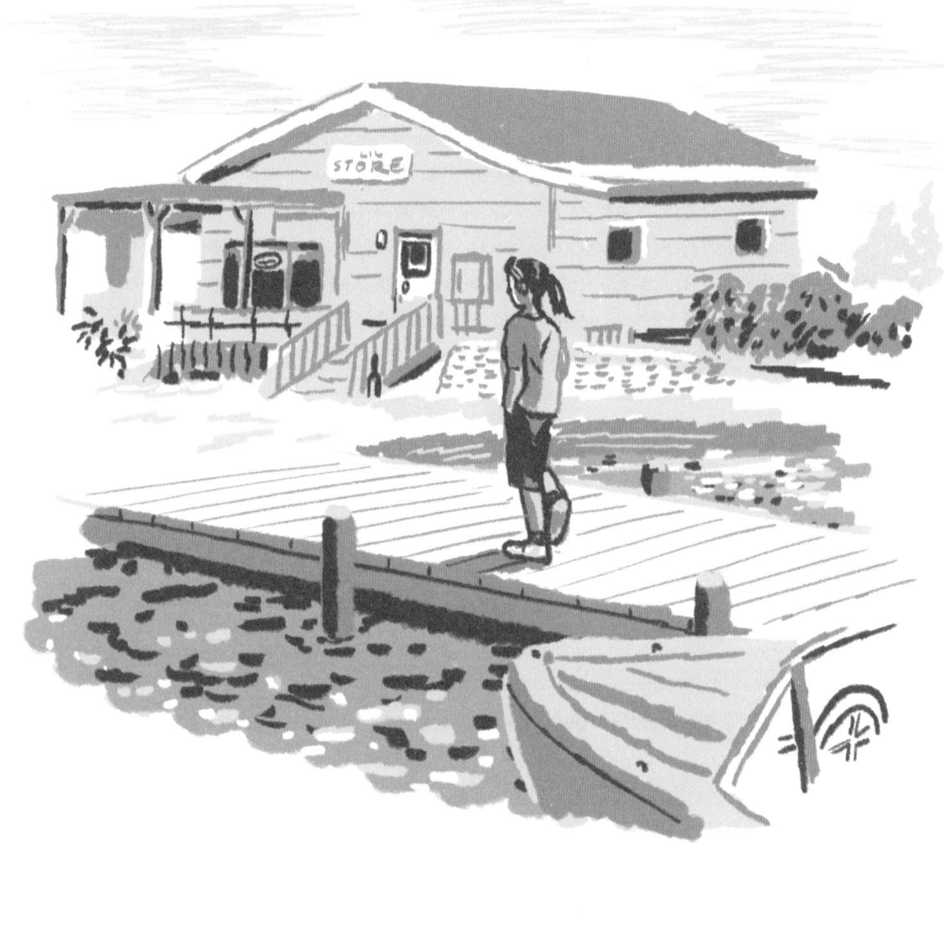
STORE

The character of Fivel could hardly resemble the actor who played him any less—in his thirty years in the public eye, Mickey seemed to have avoided scandal, embarrassment, and other pitfalls of fame. In fact, he was generally regarded as a very sweet man.

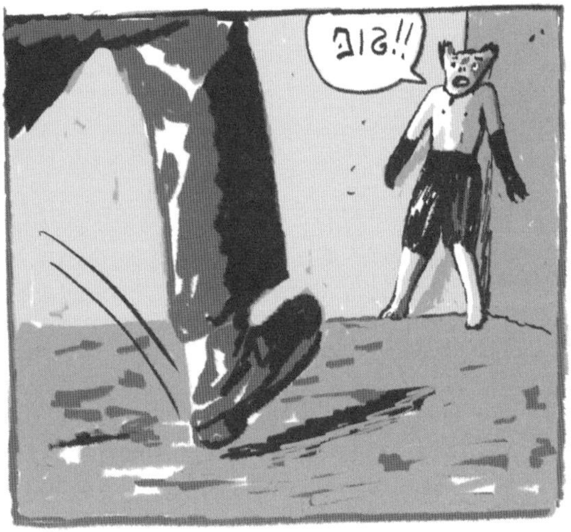

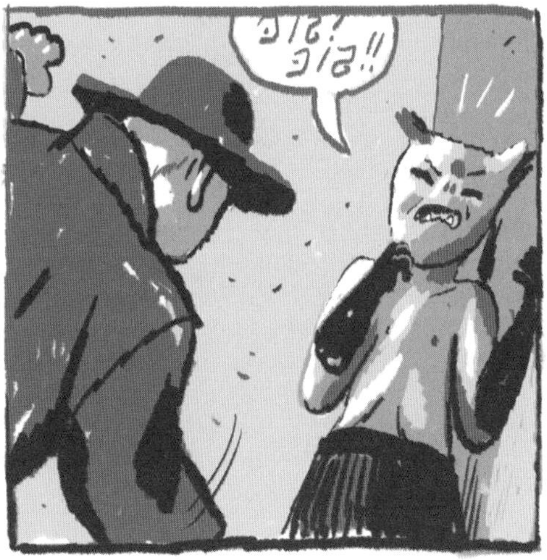

"Body Pods literally saved my life. I had been hustling in LA for fifteen years by that point and was ready to throw in the towel for good.

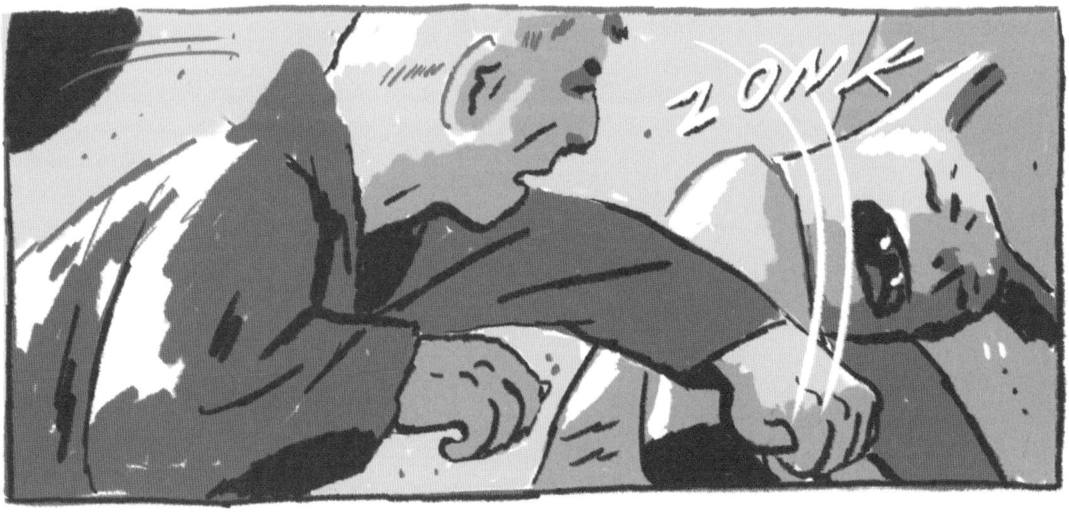
ZONK

"That's a hard way of living. Auditioning, the constant rejection, living hand-to-mouth. I was screwing up really bad. At one point, my wife kicked me out and I was sleeping in my car."

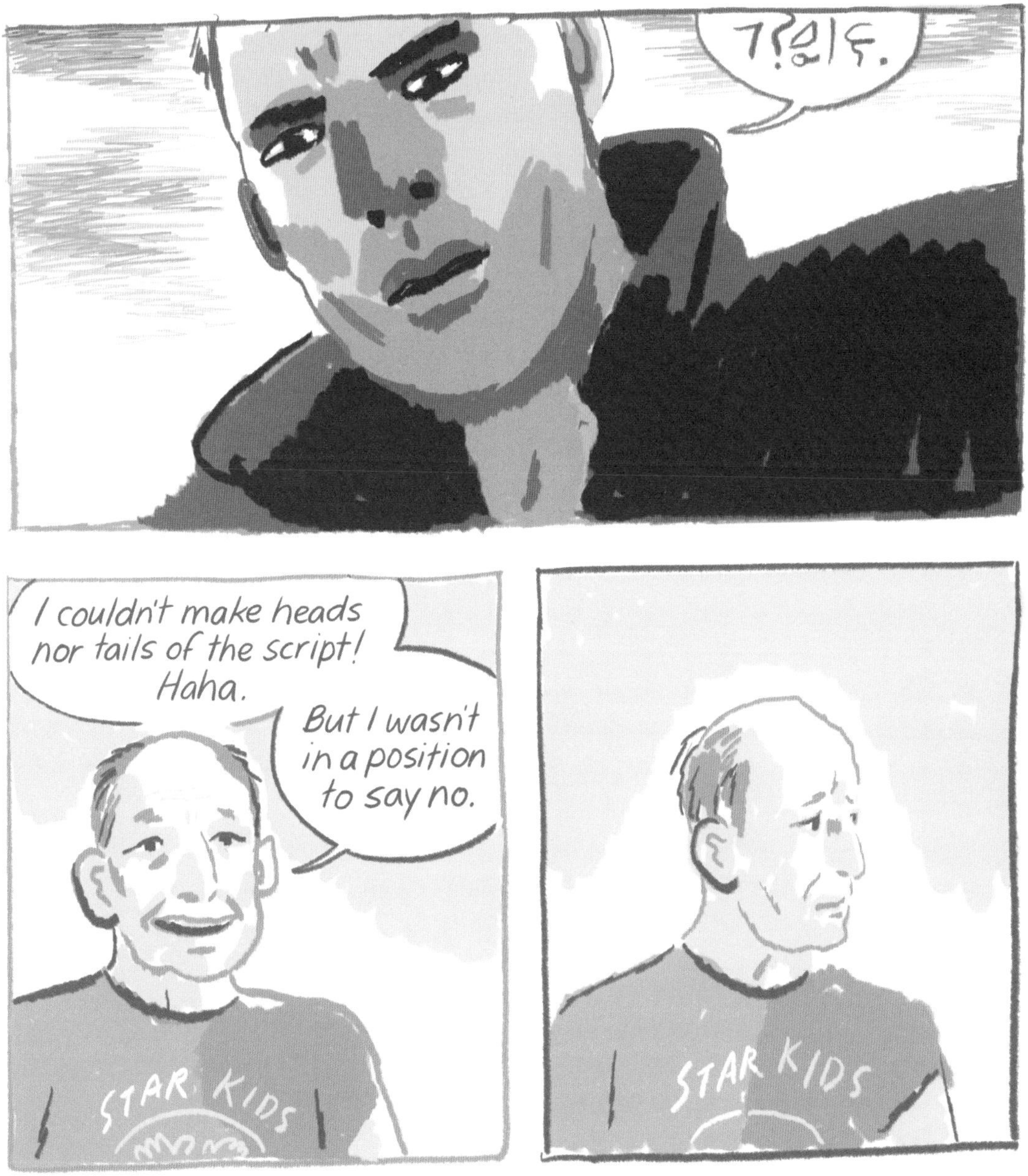
I couldn't make heads nor tails of the script! Haha.
But I wasn't in a position to say no.
STAR KIDS
STAR KIDS

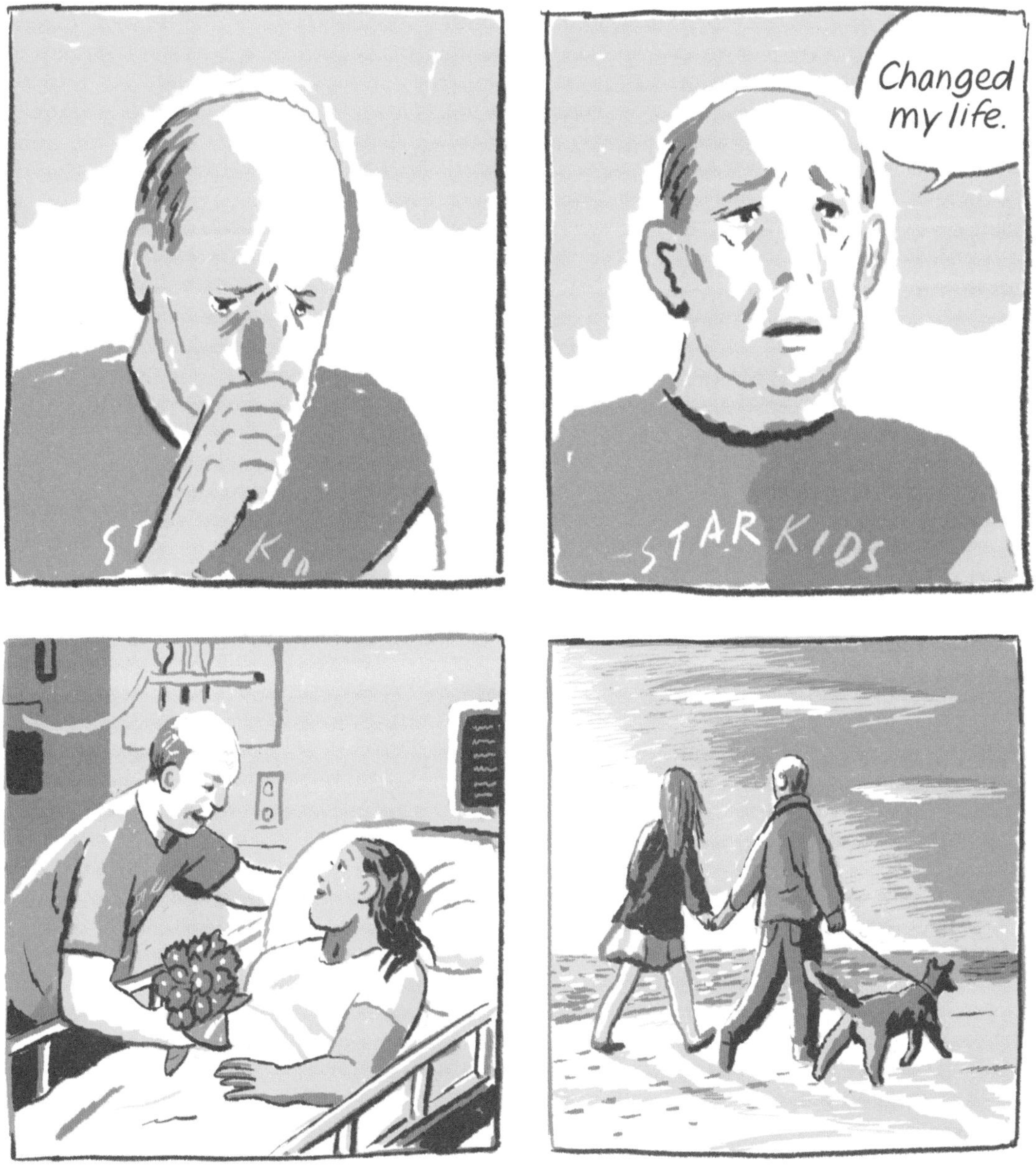
Changed my life.
STAR KIDS

"I owe it all to the fans. No matter the ups and downs, they've been there.

"I never forget that. Not for one day. I'm a grateful man."

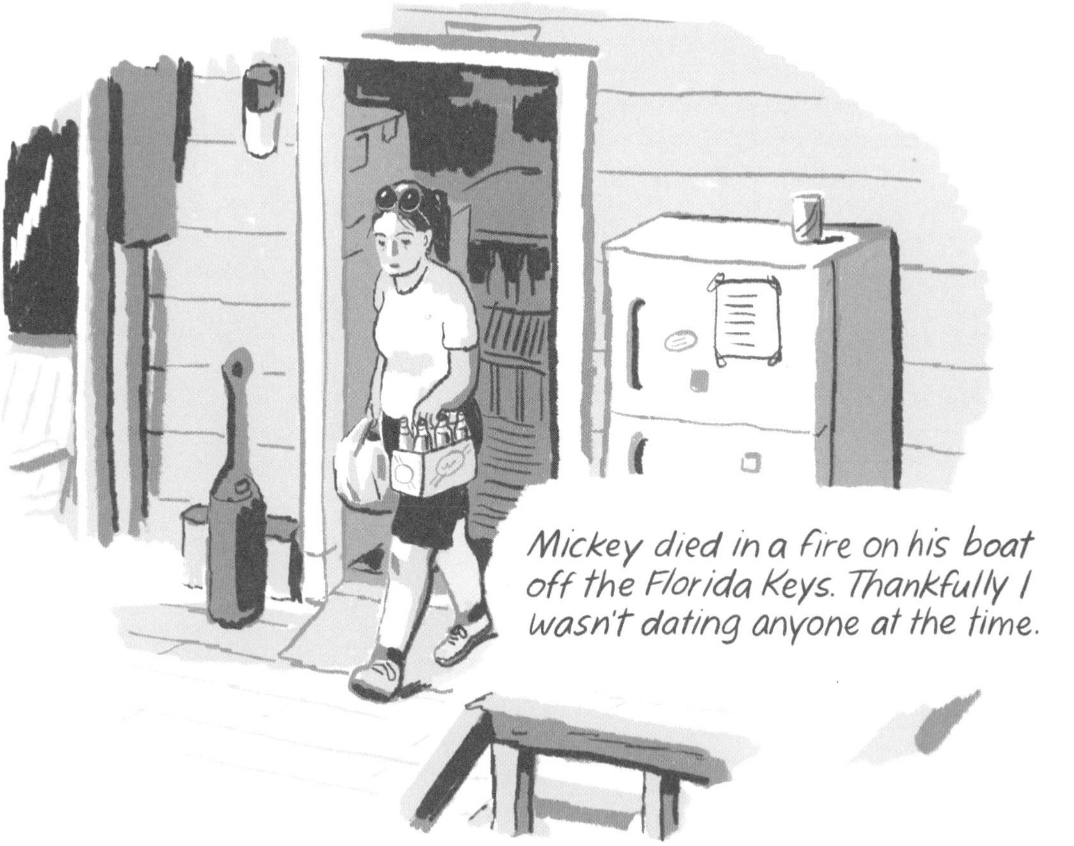
Mickey died in a fire on his boat off the Florida Keys. Thankfully I wasn't dating anyone at the time.

The incident eerily mirrored Fivel Donovan's death, which involved him starting a fire on an enemy spaceship, then getting double-crossed and trapped on the vessel.

The Internet went crazy. Talk of a curse and whatnot. The whole thing felt gross. I tried to stay offline for a few weeks.

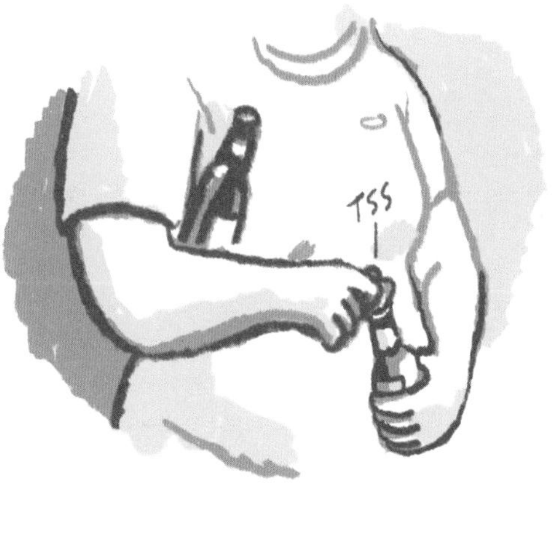
TSS

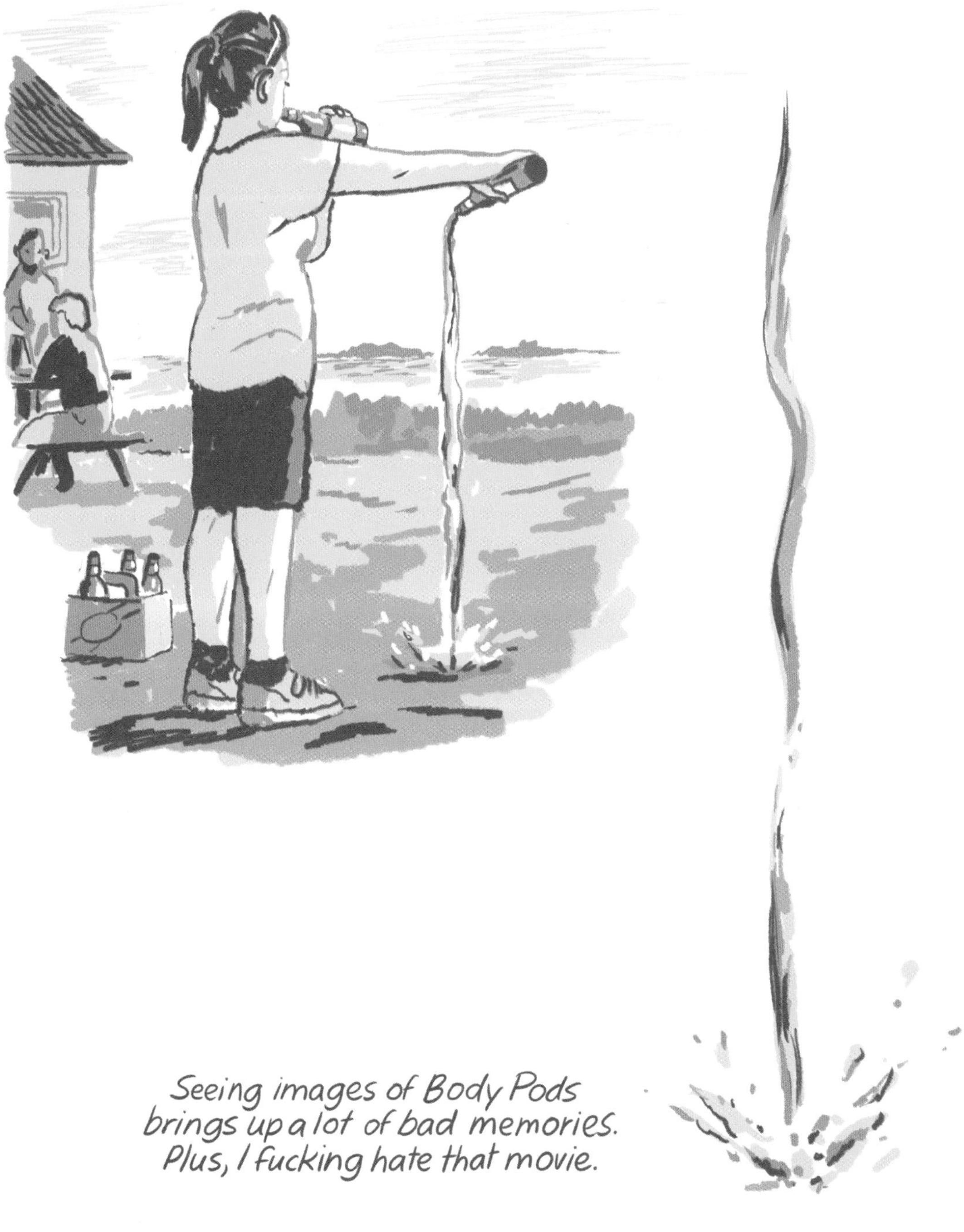
Seeing images of Body Pods
brings up a lot of bad memories.
Plus, I fucking hate that movie.

The ClairFree System

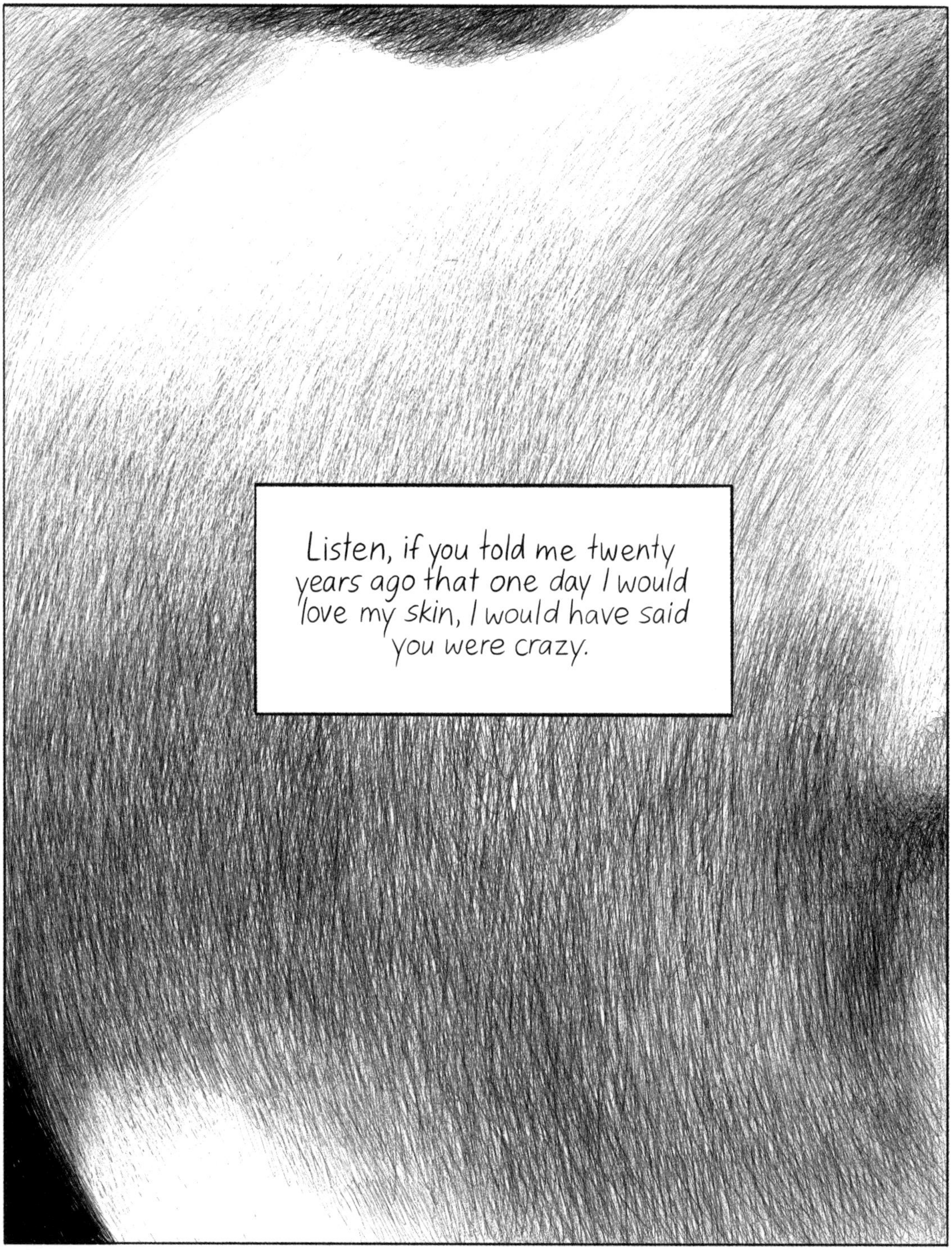
Listen, if you told me twenty years ago that one day I would love my skin, I would have said you were crazy.

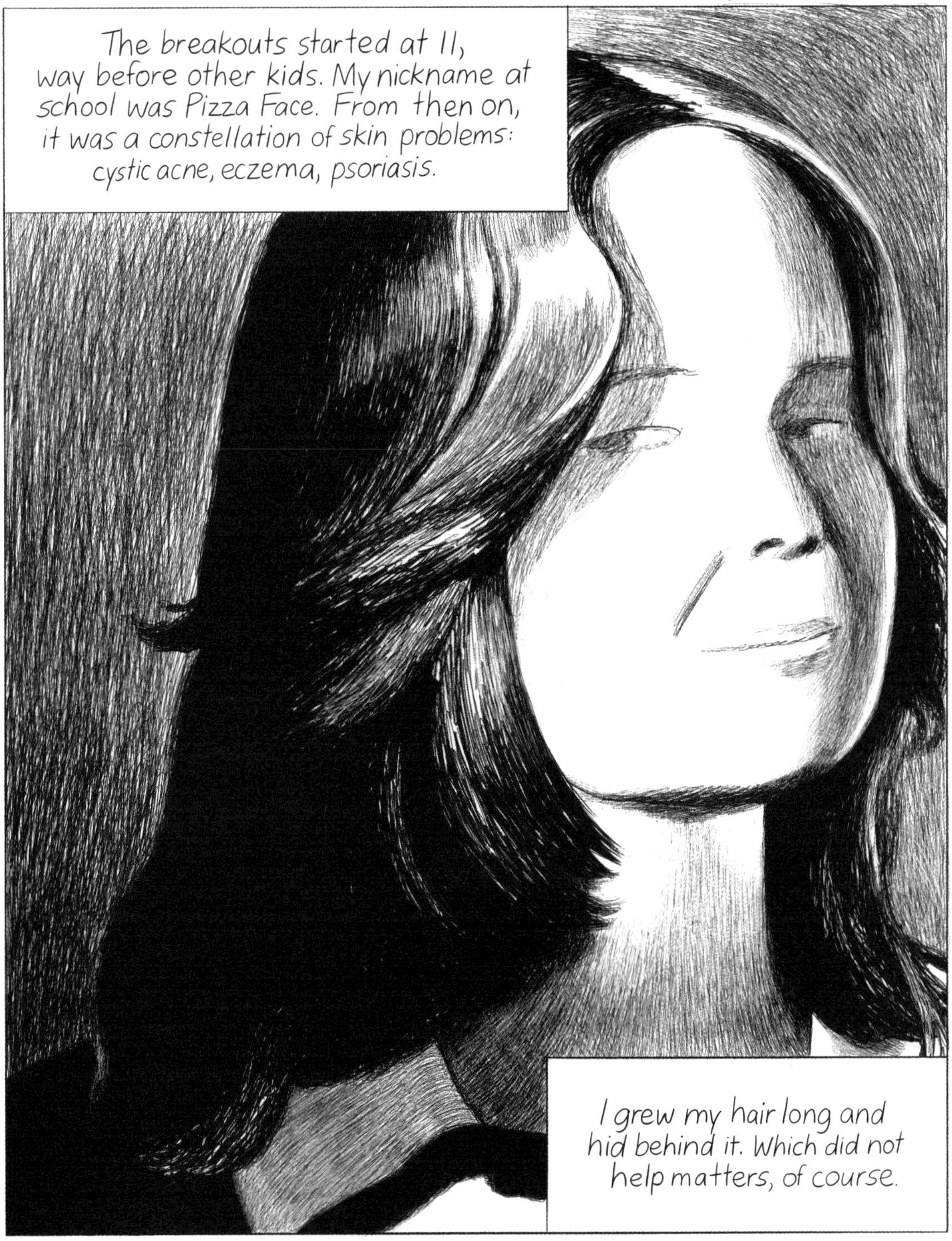
The breakouts started at 11, way before other kids. My nickname at school was Pizza Face. From then on, it was a constellation of skin problems: cystic acne, eczema, psoriasis.
I grew my hair long and hid behind it. Which did not help matters, of course.

I must have tried every product on the market. I shudder to think about the money I have spent on skin care over the years.

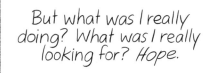

But what was I really doing? What was I really looking for? *Hope.*

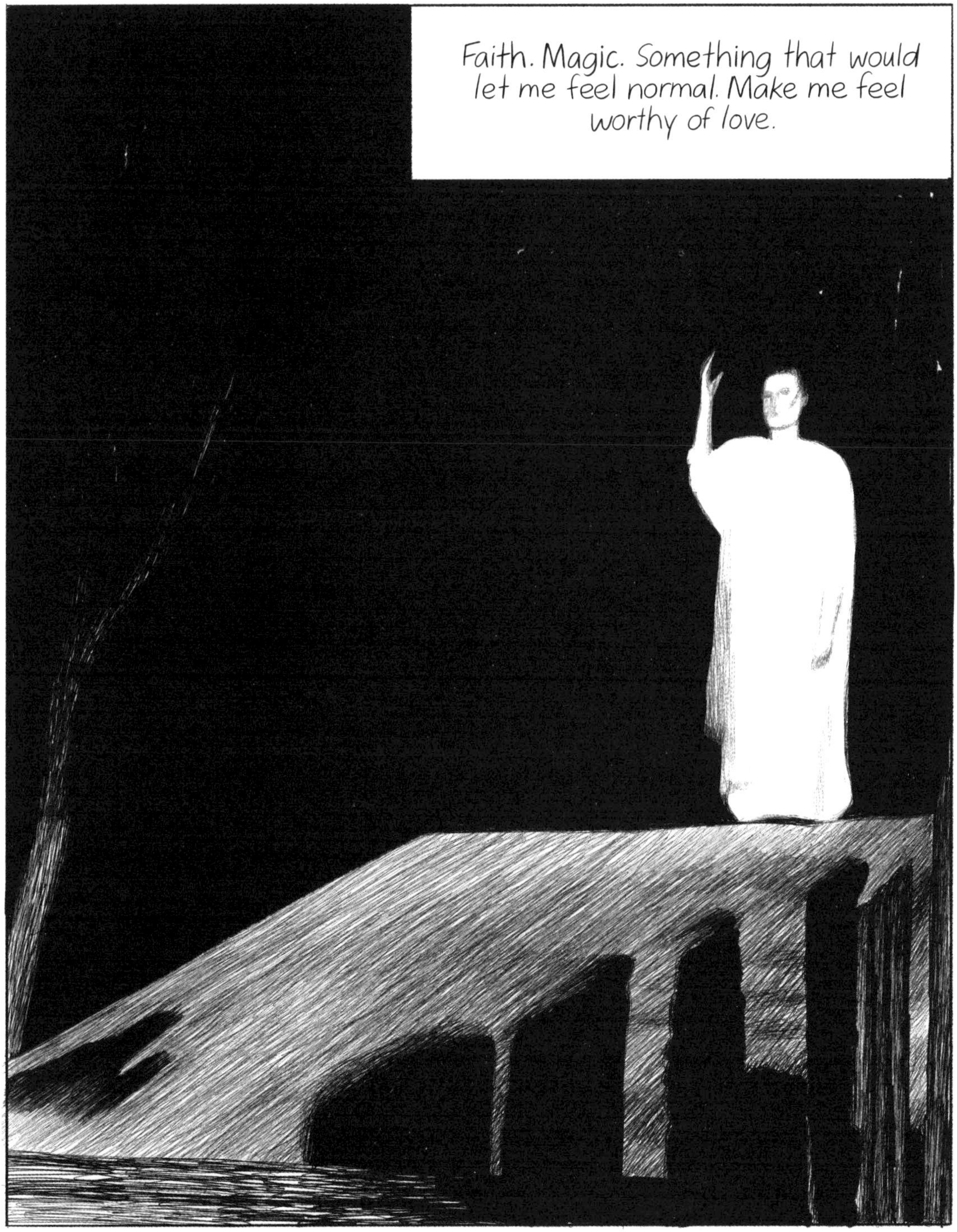
Faith. Magic. Something that would let me feel normal. Make me feel worthy of love.

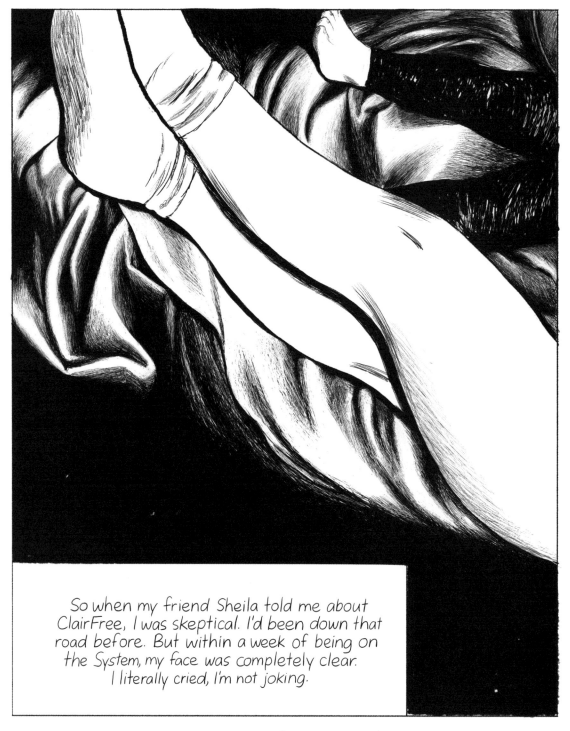

So when my friend Sheila told me about ClairFree, I was skeptical. I'd been down that road before. But within a week of being on the System, my face was completely clear. I literally cried, I'm not joking.

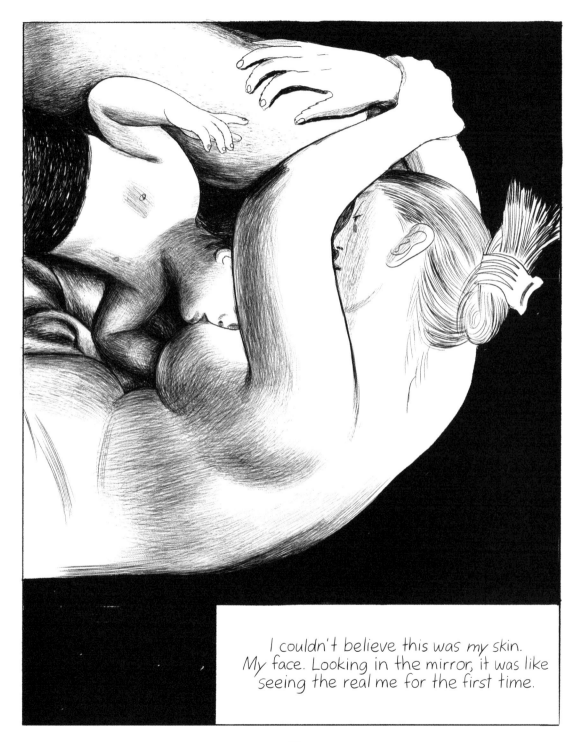

I couldn't believe this was *my* skin.
My face. Looking in the mirror, it was like
seeing the real me for the first time.

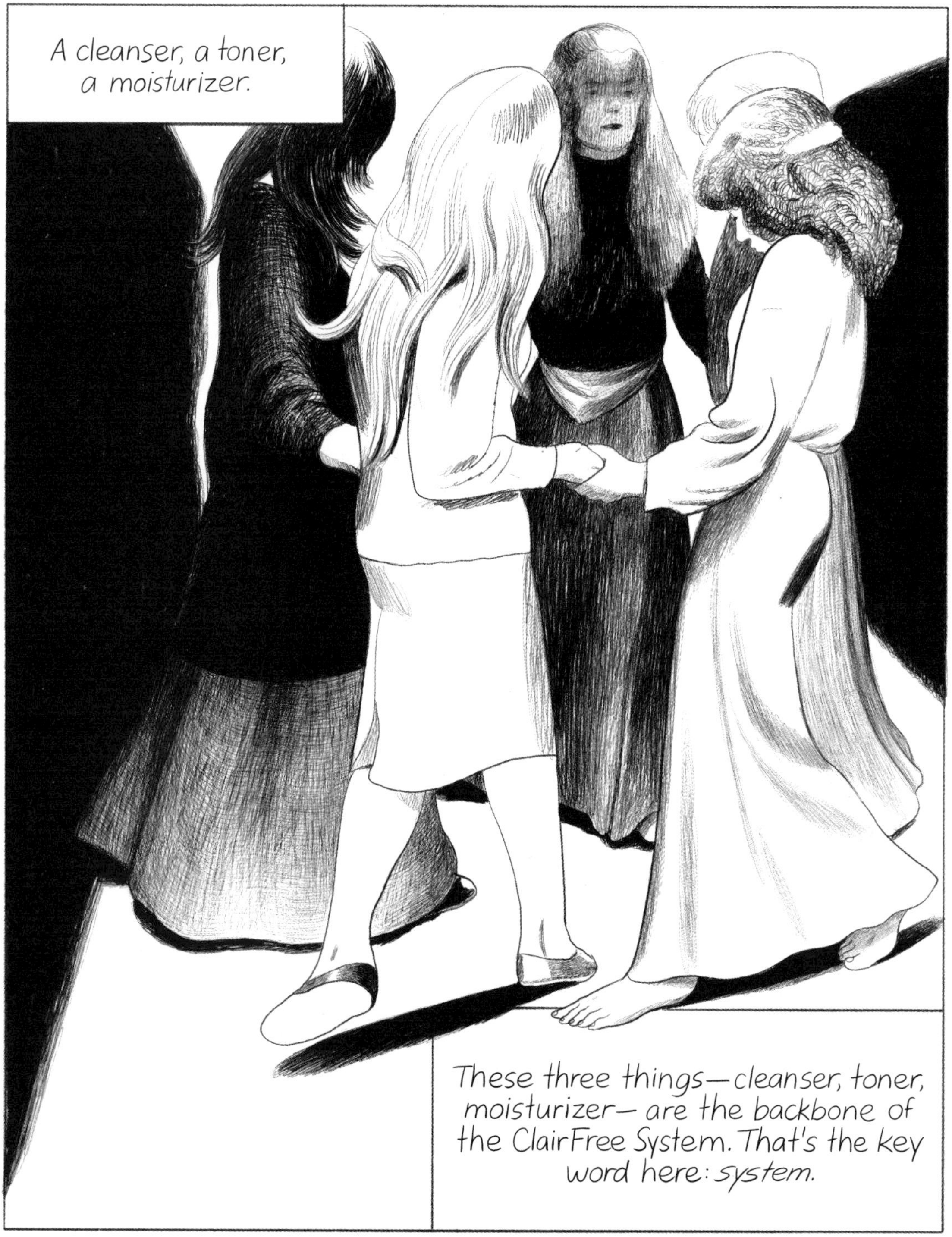
A cleanser, a toner, a moisturizer.
These three things—cleanser, toner, moisturizer— are the backbone of the ClairFree System. That's the key word here: *system*.

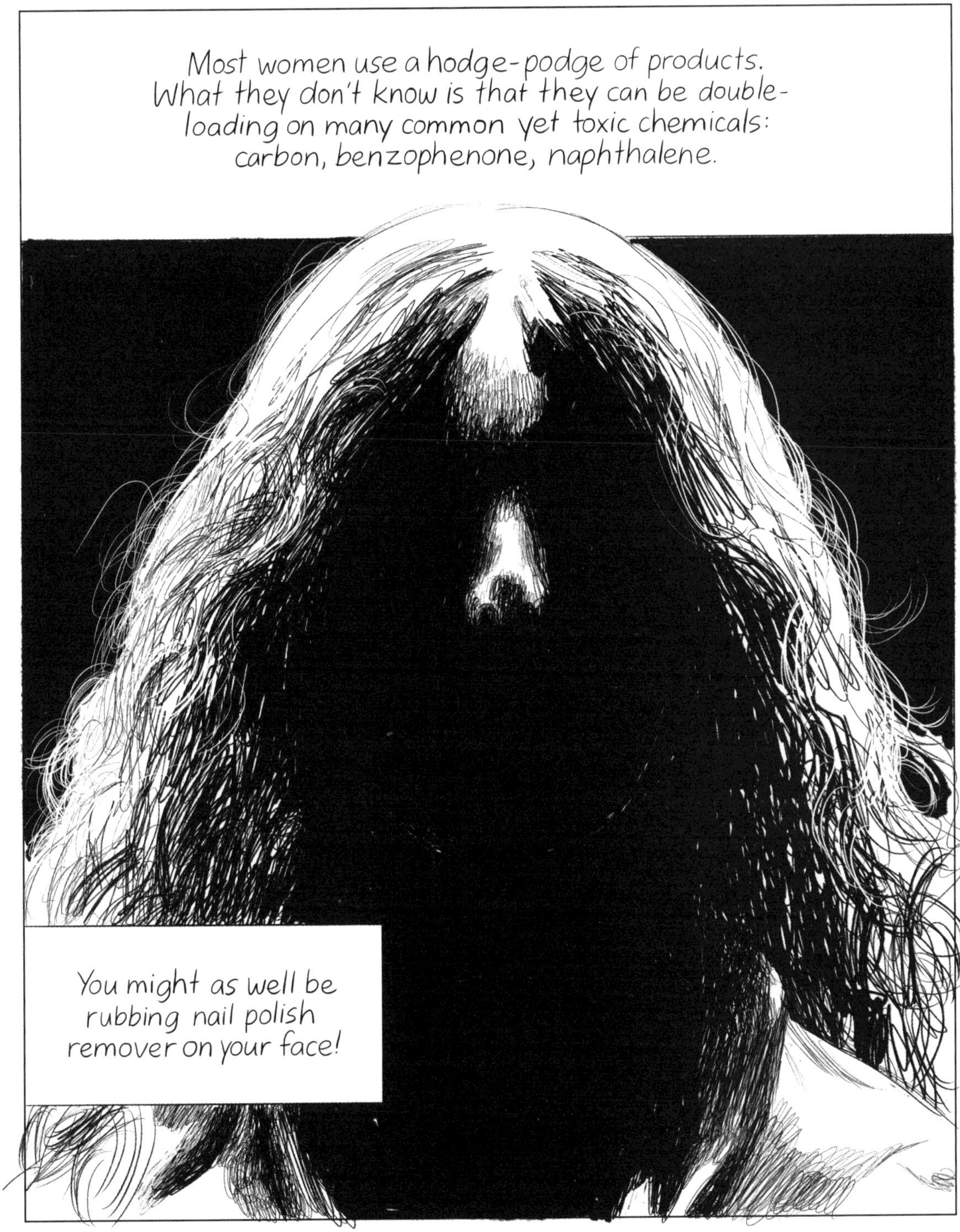
Most women use a hodge-podge of products. What they don't know is that they can be double-loading on many common yet toxic chemicals: carbon, benzophenone, naphthalene.
You might as well be rubbing nail polish remover on your face!

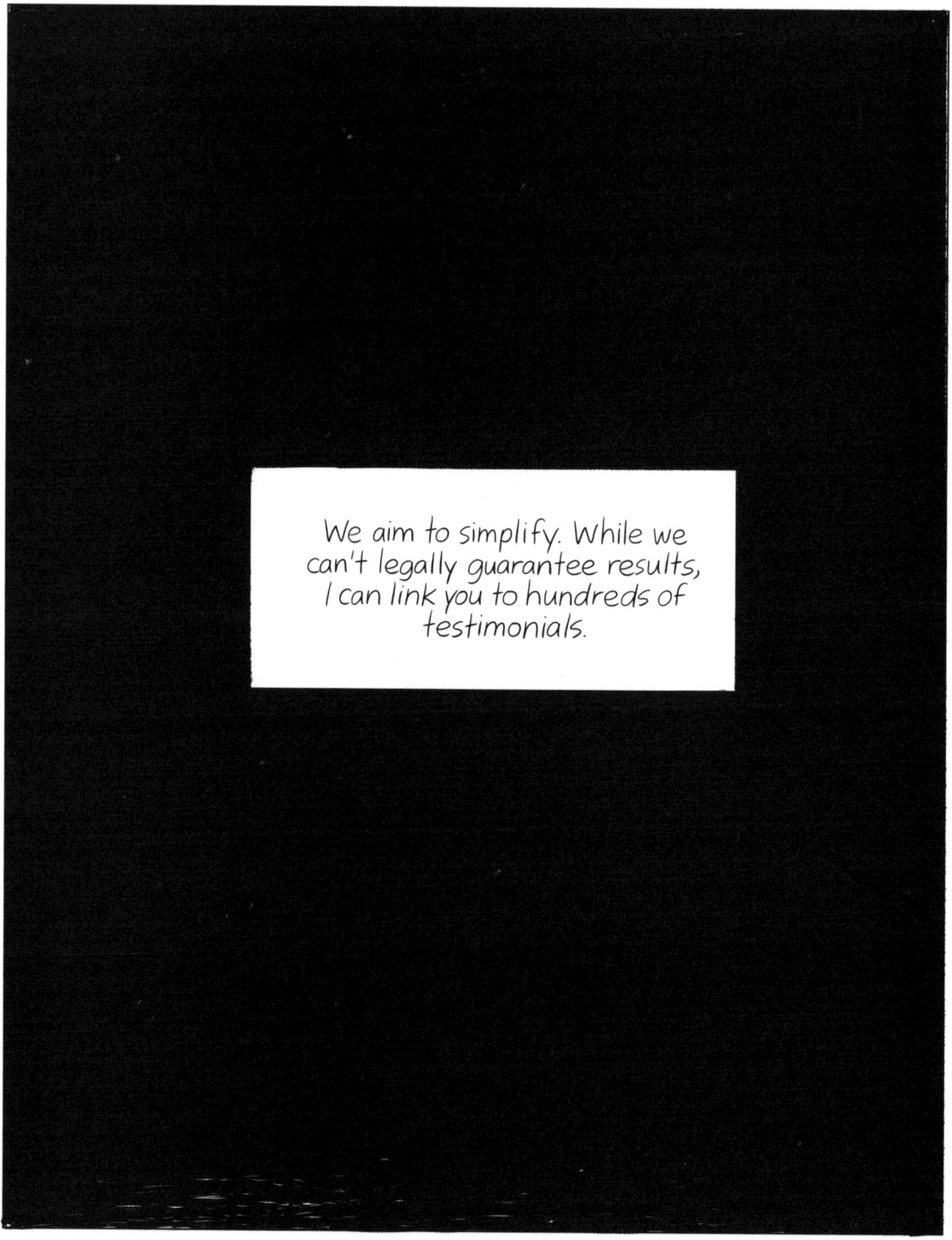
We aim to simplify. While we can't legally guarantee results, I can link you to hundreds of testimonials.

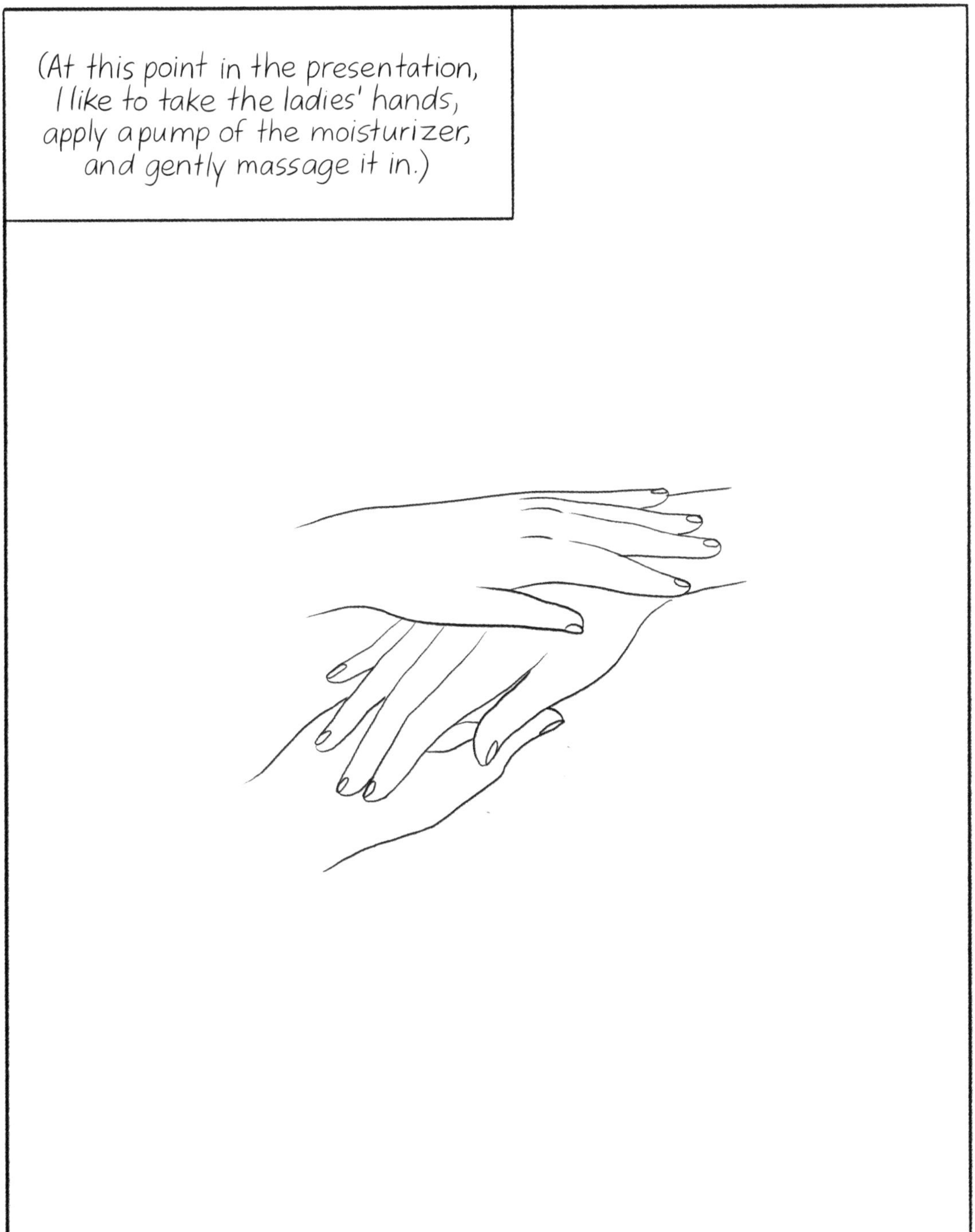
(At this point in the presentation, I like to take the ladies' hands, apply a pump of the moisturizer, and gently massage it in.)

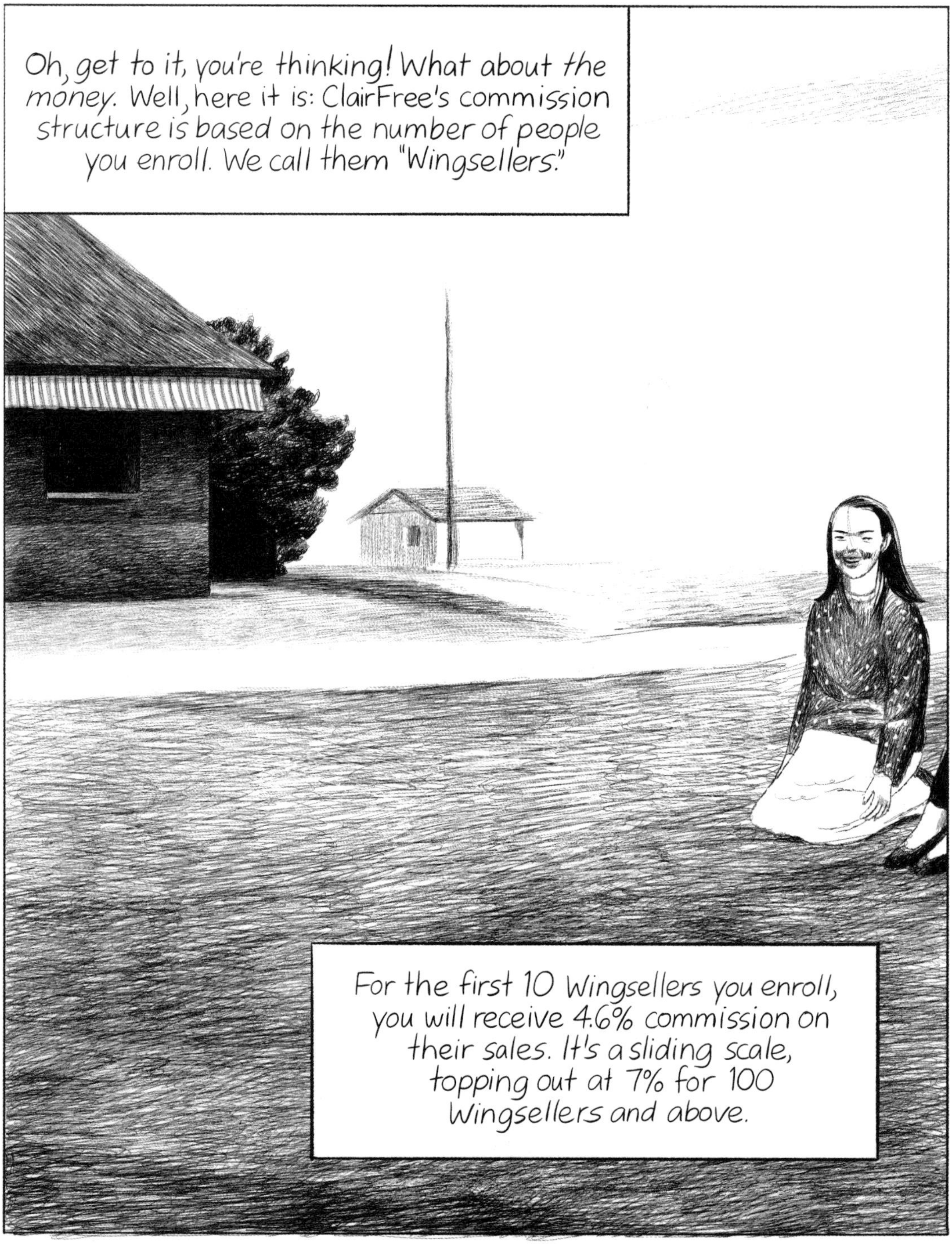
Oh, get to it, you're thinking! What about the money. Well, here it is: ClairFree's commission structure is based on the number of people you enroll. We call them "Wingsellers."
For the first 10 Wingsellers you enroll, you will receive 4.6% commission on their sales. It's a sliding scale, topping out at 7% for 100 Wingsellers and above.

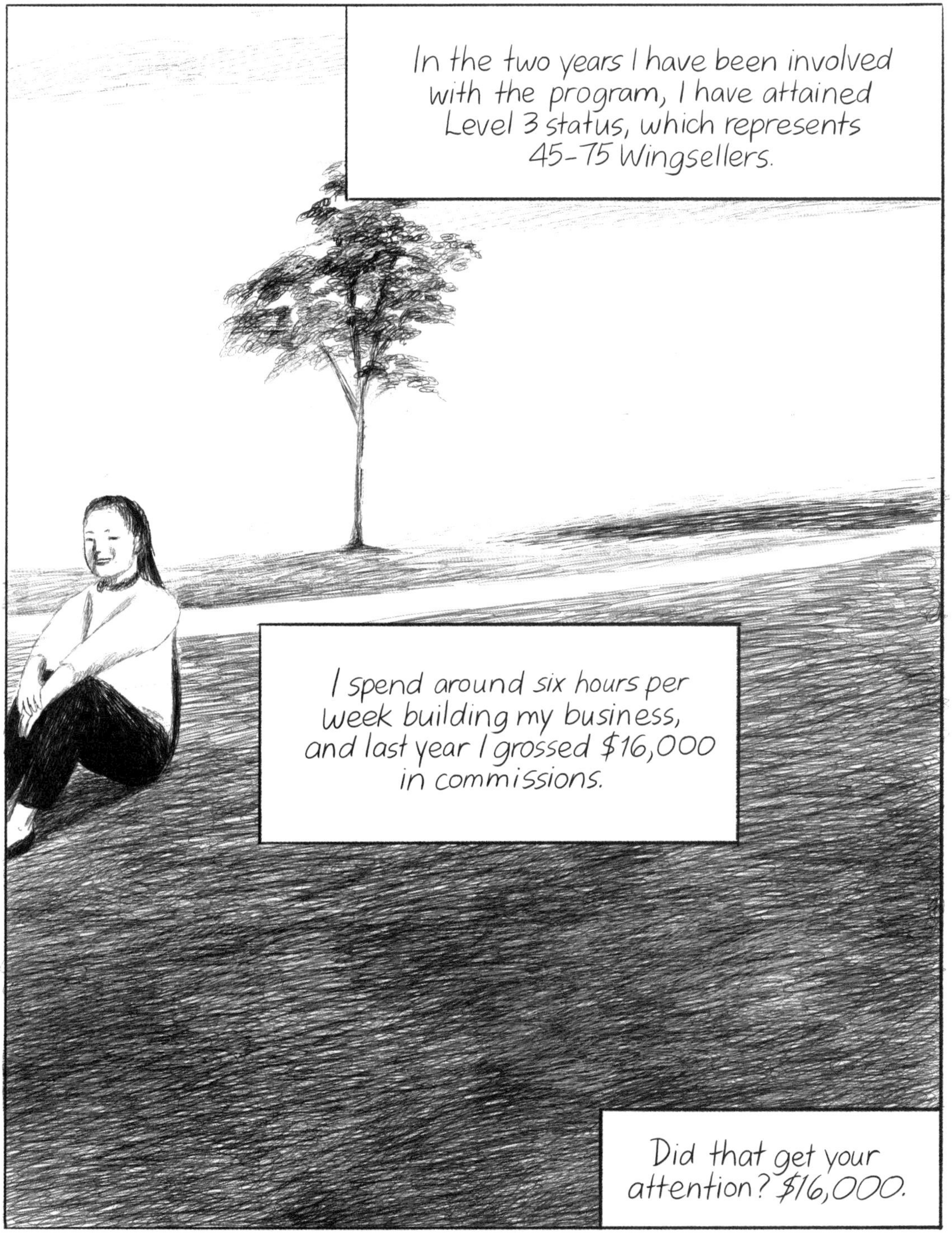
In the two years I have been involved with the program, I have attained Level 3 status, which represents 45-75 Wingsellers.
I spend around six hours per week building my business, and last year I grossed $16,000 in commissions.
Did that get your attention? $16,000.

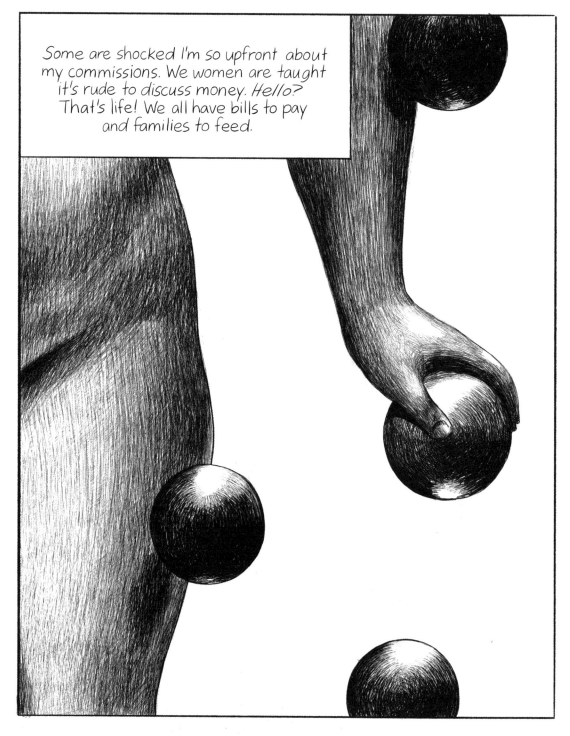

Some are shocked I'm so upfront about my commissions. We women are taught it's rude to discuss money. *Hello?* That's life! We all have bills to pay and families to feed.

The income from this program has been a godsend for me and my daughter. I don't have to pick up those extra shifts. I can say yes to the ballet classes, the jeans, the concert tickets.

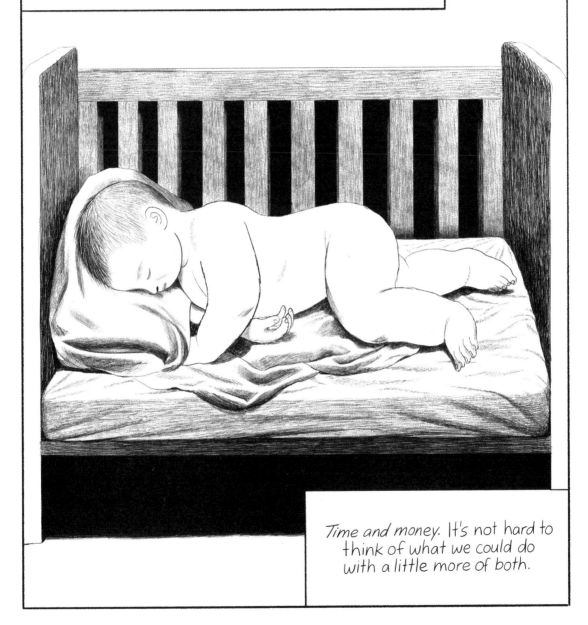

Time and money. It's not hard to think of what we could do with a little more of both.

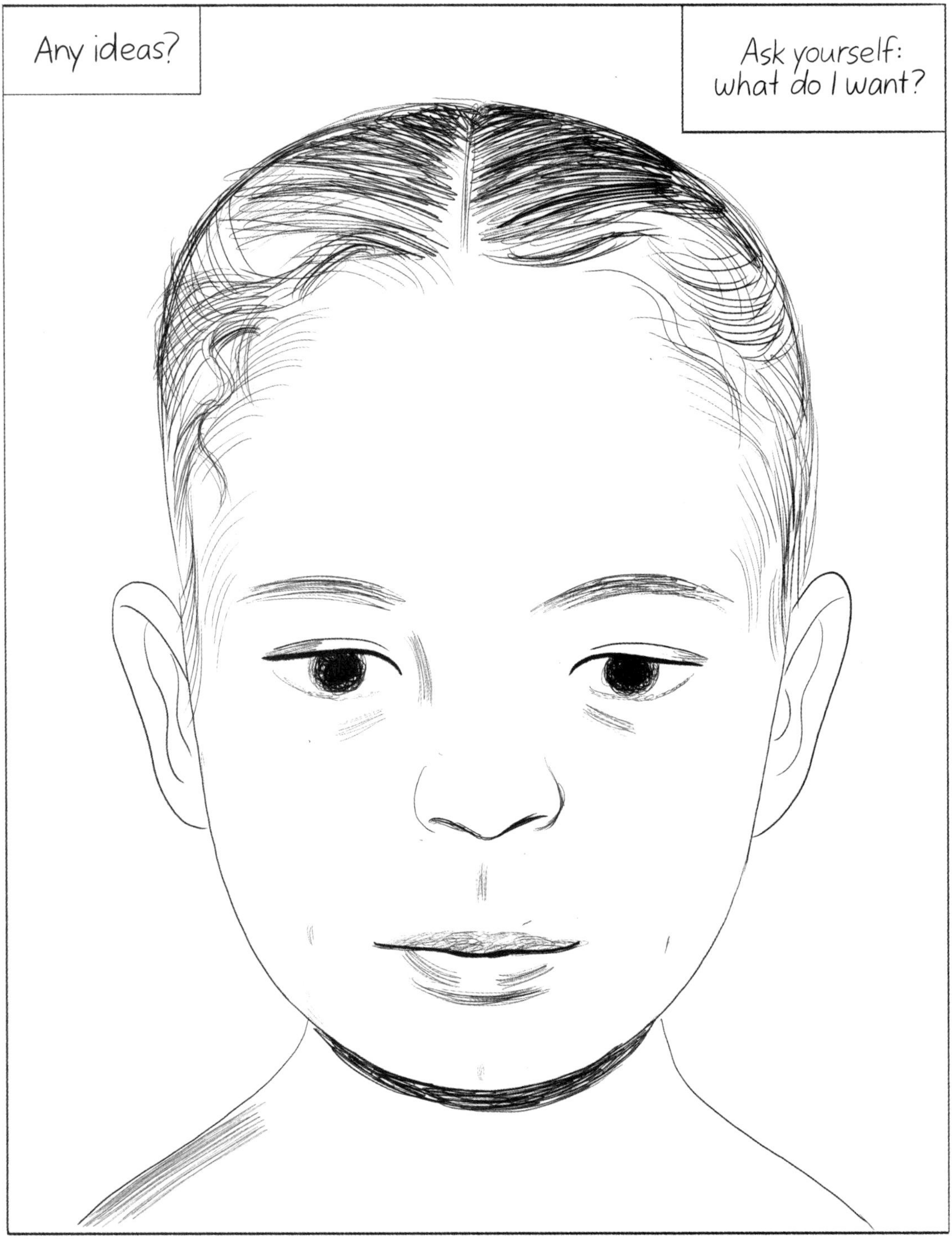
Any ideas?
Ask yourself: what do I want?

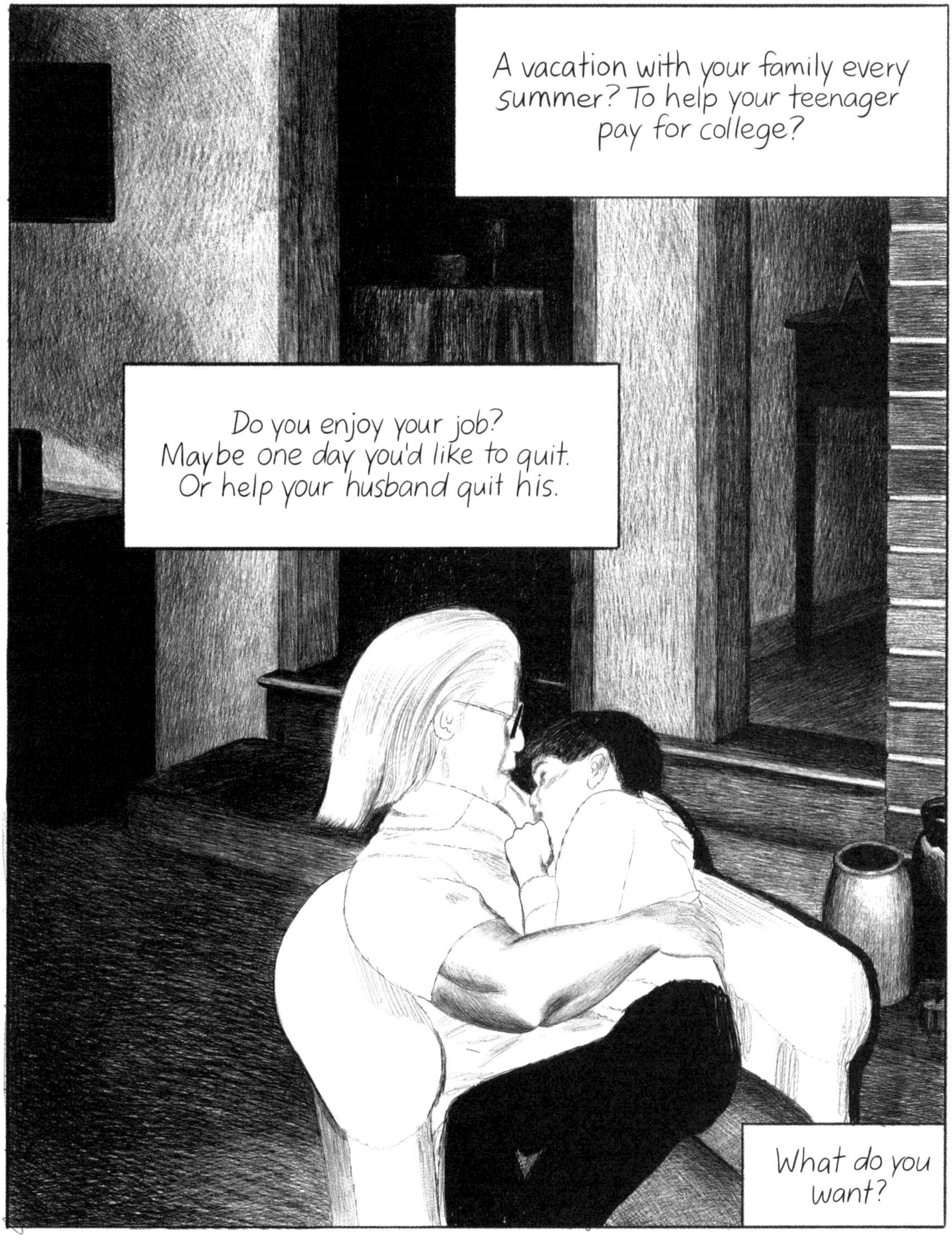
A vacation with your family every summer? To help your teenager pay for college?
Do you enjoy your job? Maybe one day you'd like to quit. Or help your husband quit his.
What do you want?

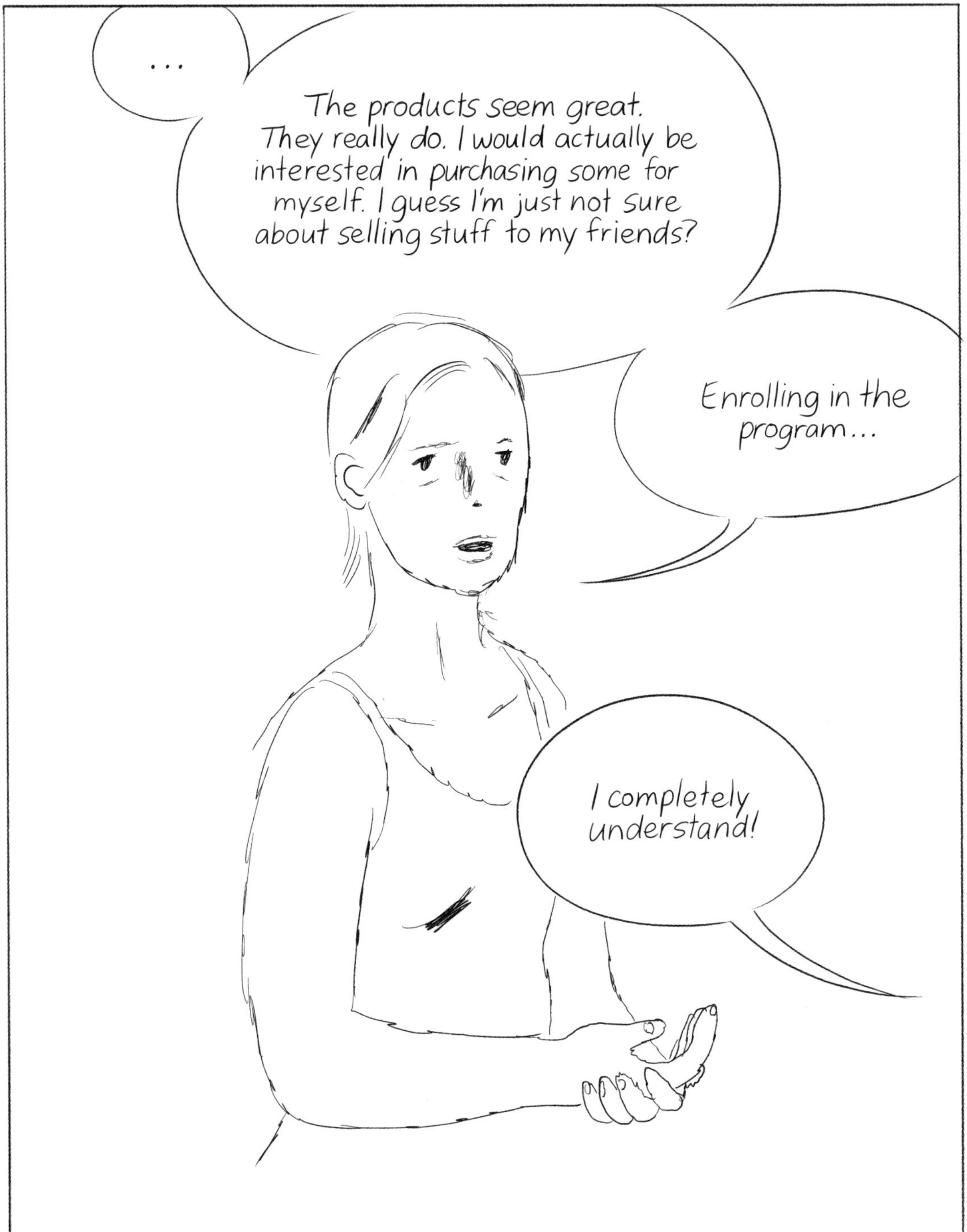
...
The products seem great. They really do. I would actually be interested in purchasing some for myself. I guess I'm just not sure about selling stuff to my friends?
Enrolling in the program...
I completely understand!

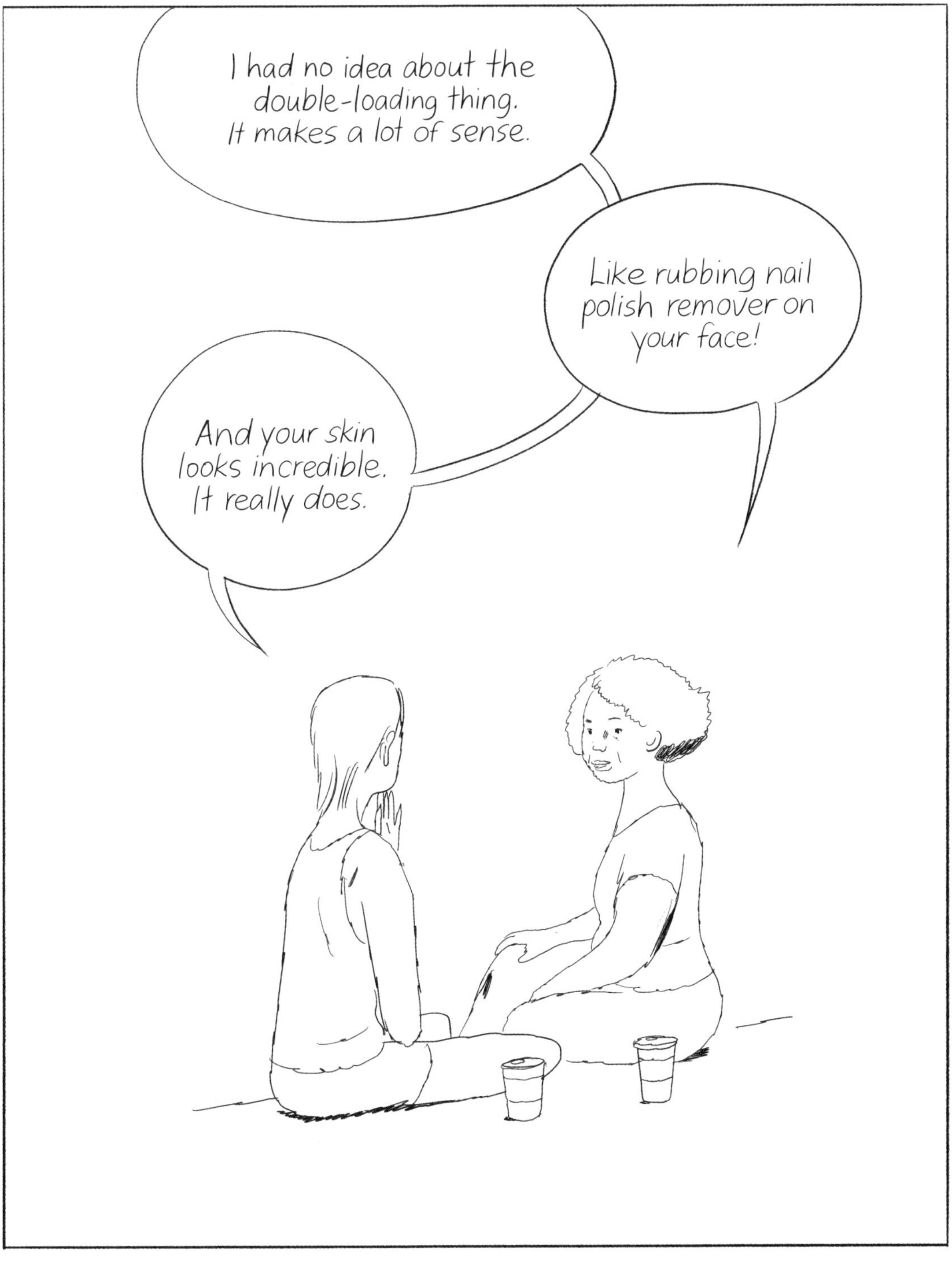
I had no idea about the double-loading thing. It makes a lot of sense.
Like rubbing nail polish remover on your face!
And your skin looks incredible. It really does.

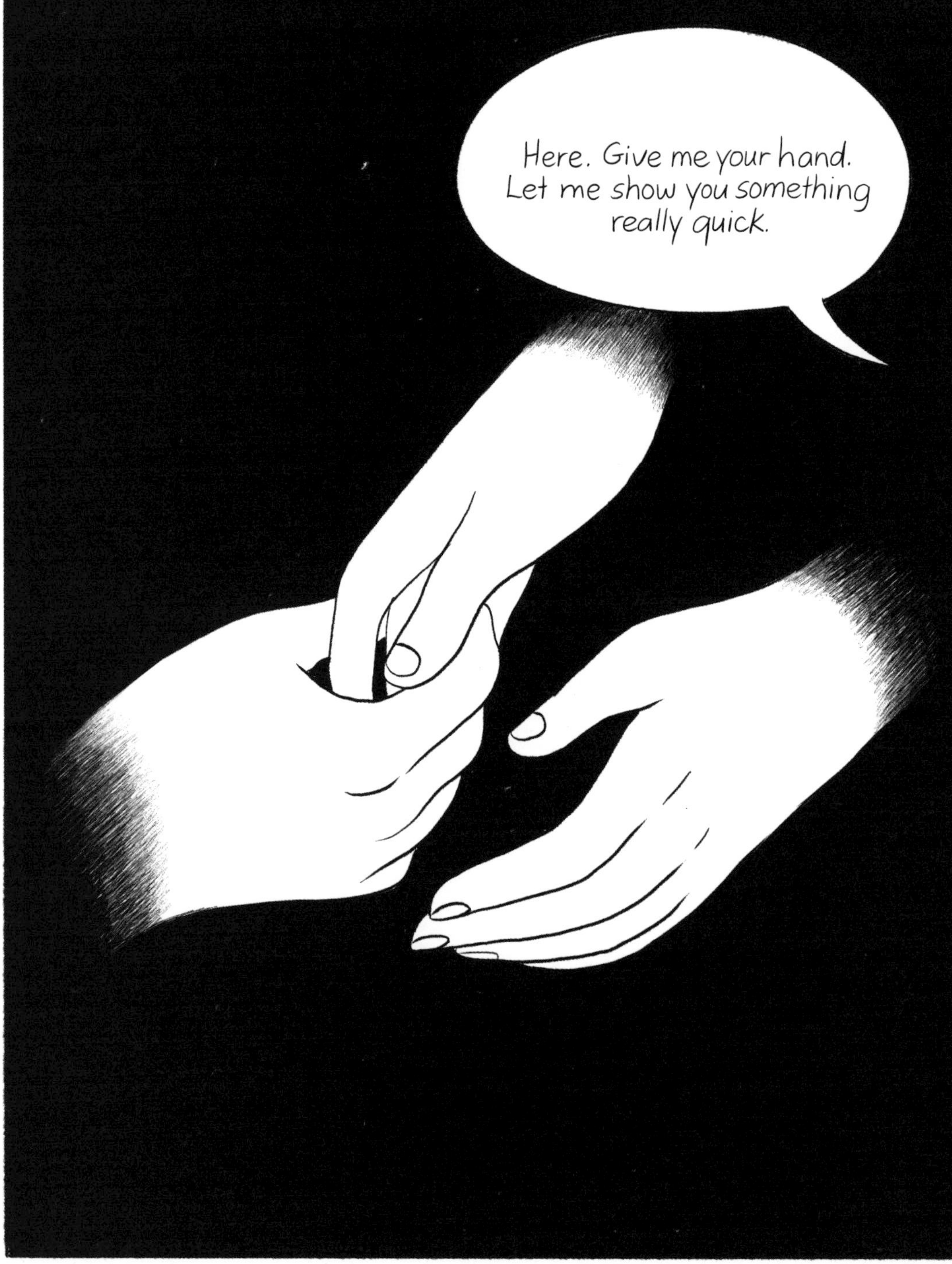
Here. Give me your hand. Let me show you something really quick.

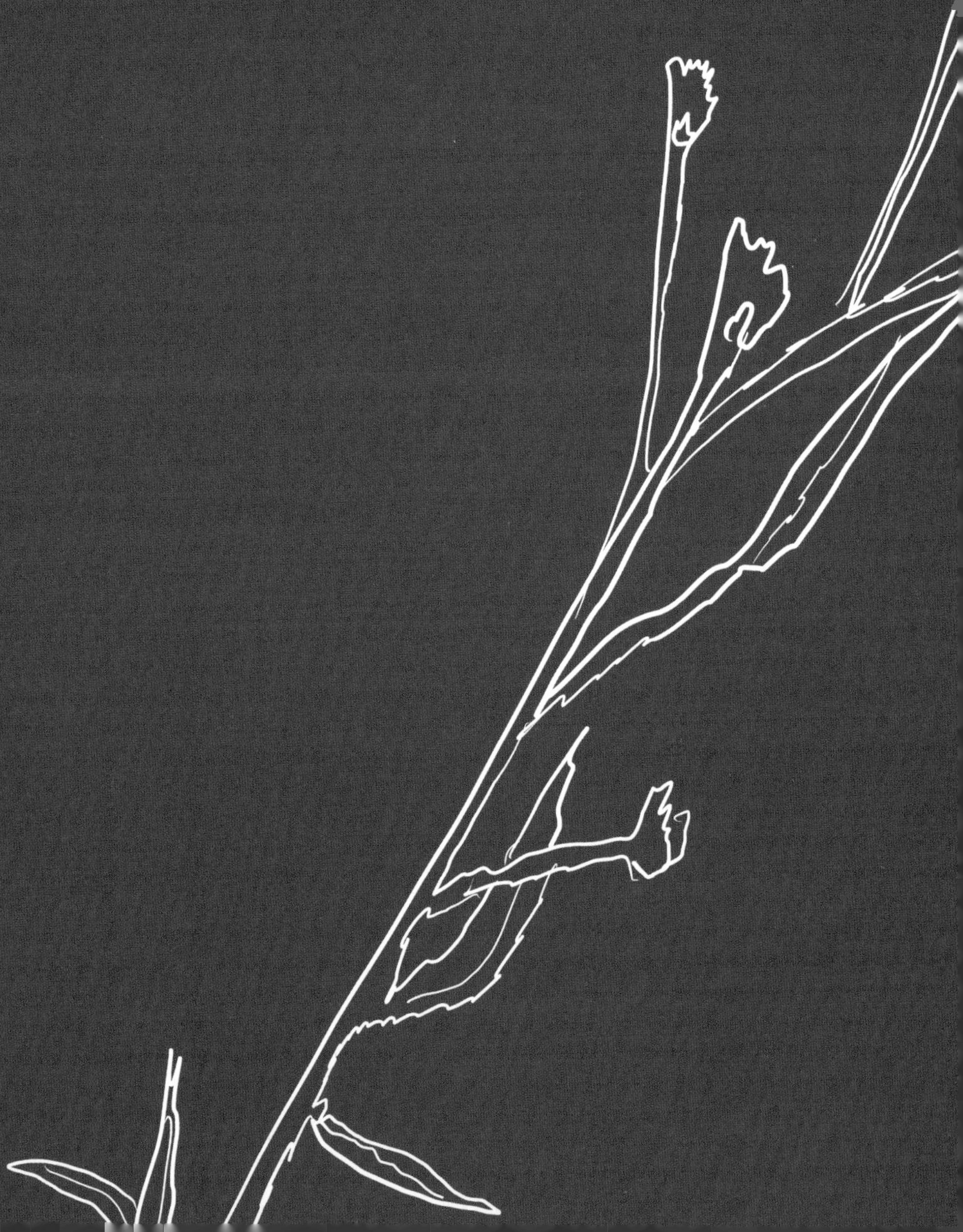

1.Jenny

The mirror Facebook was all anyone could talk about for two weeks.

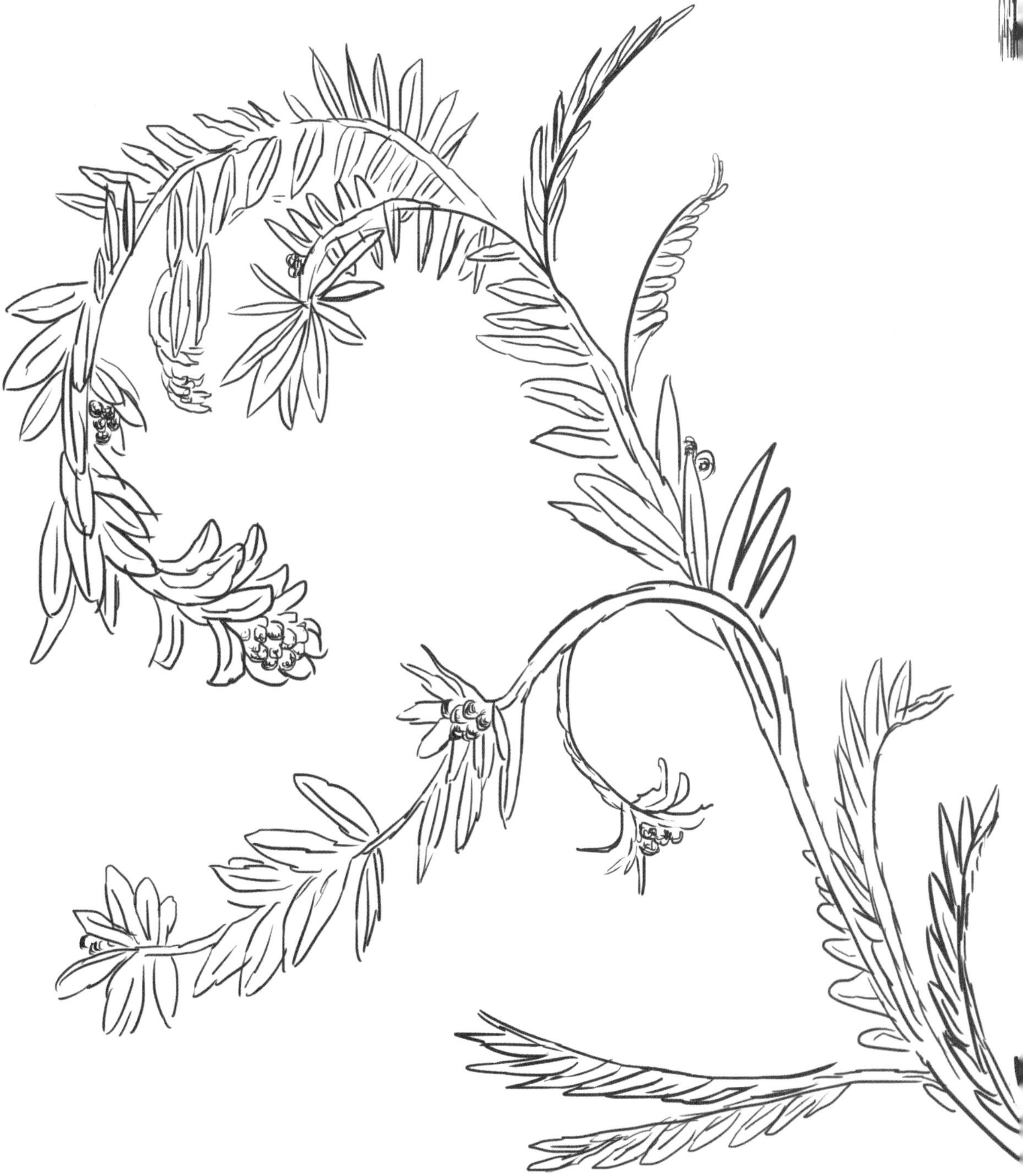

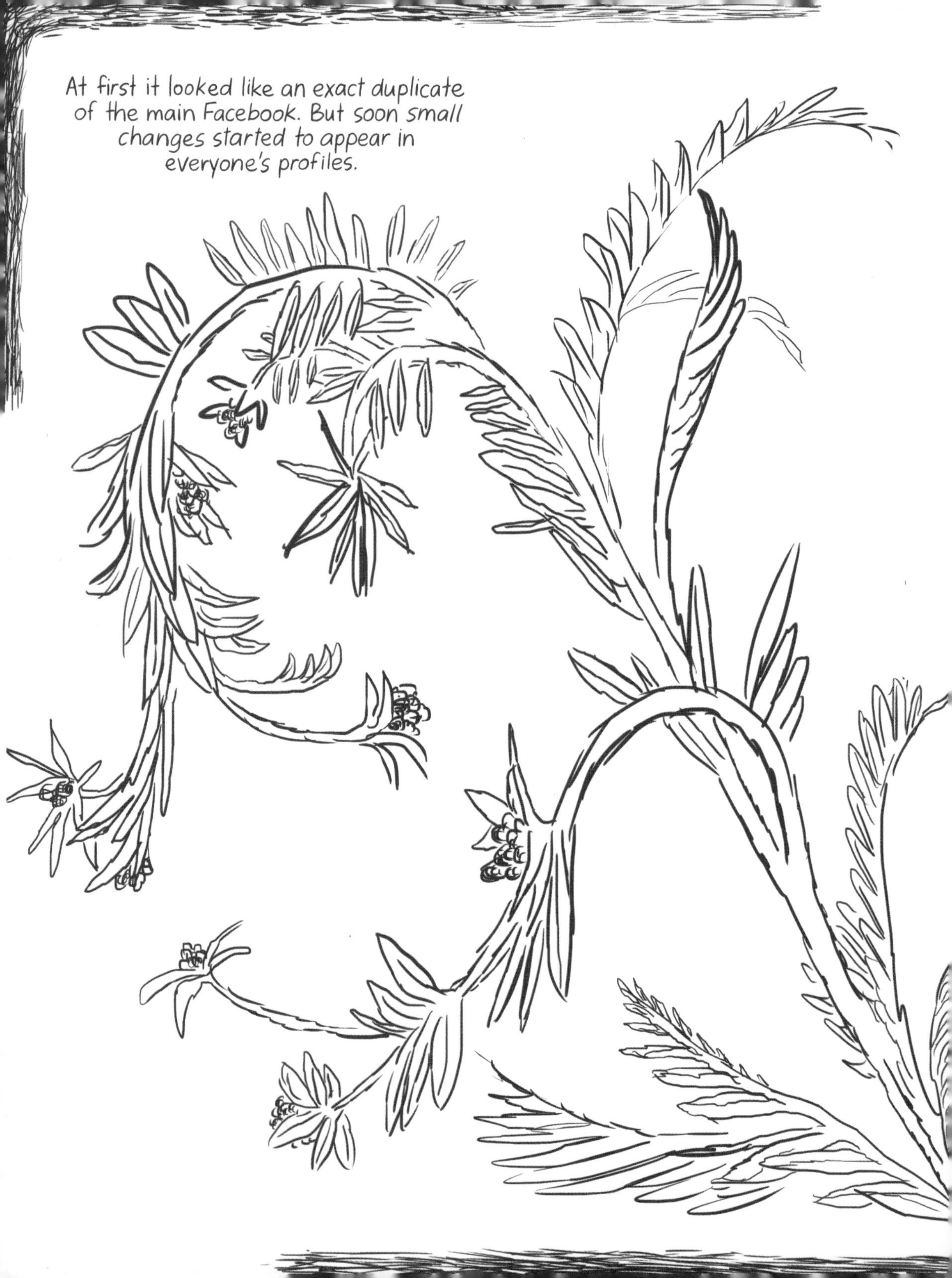
At first it looked like an exact duplicate of the main Facebook. But soon small changes started to appear in everyone's profiles.

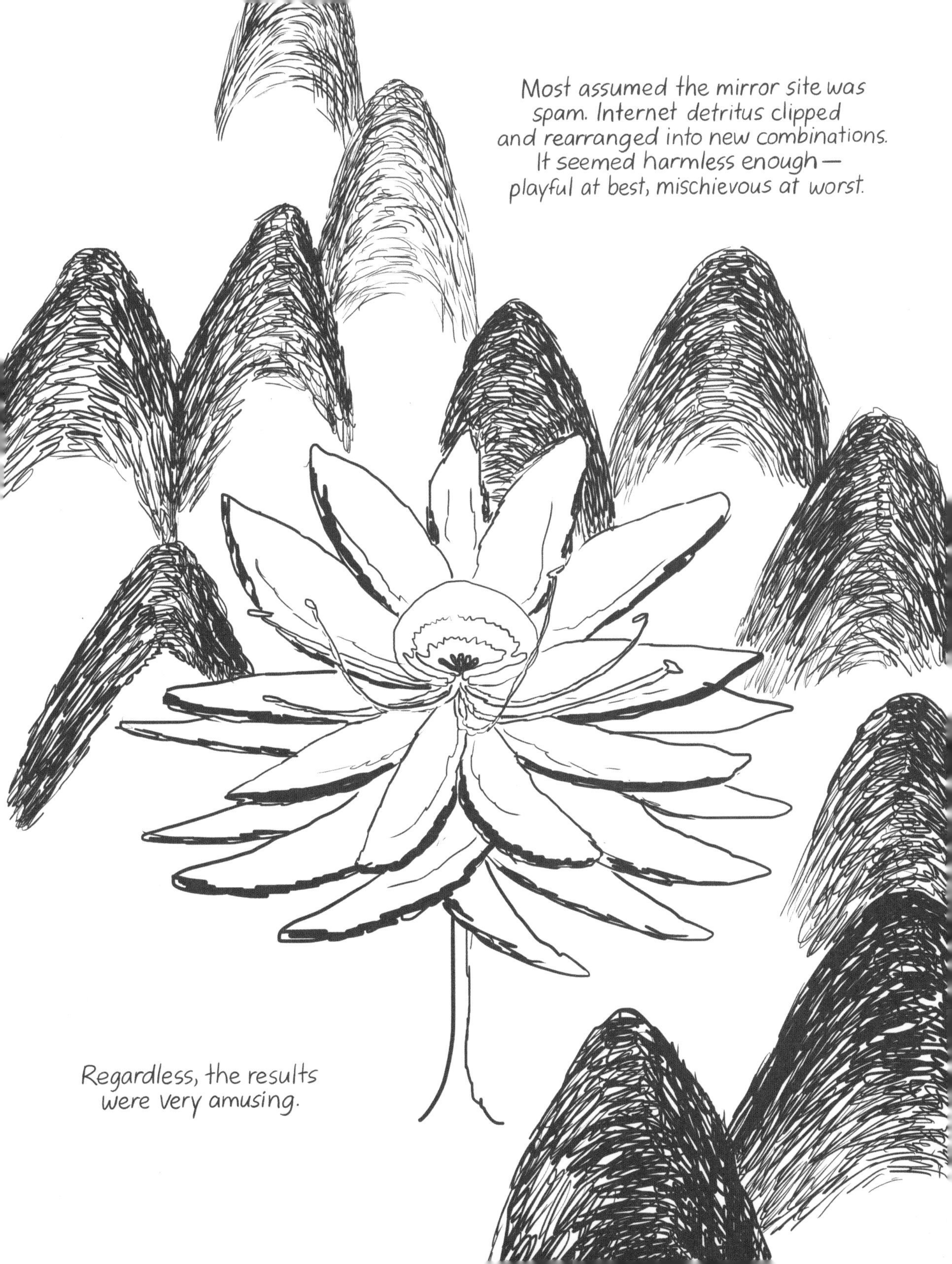
Most assumed the mirror site was spam. Internet detritus clipped and rearranged into new combinations. It seemed harmless enough— playful at best, mischievous at worst.
Regardless, the results were very amusing.

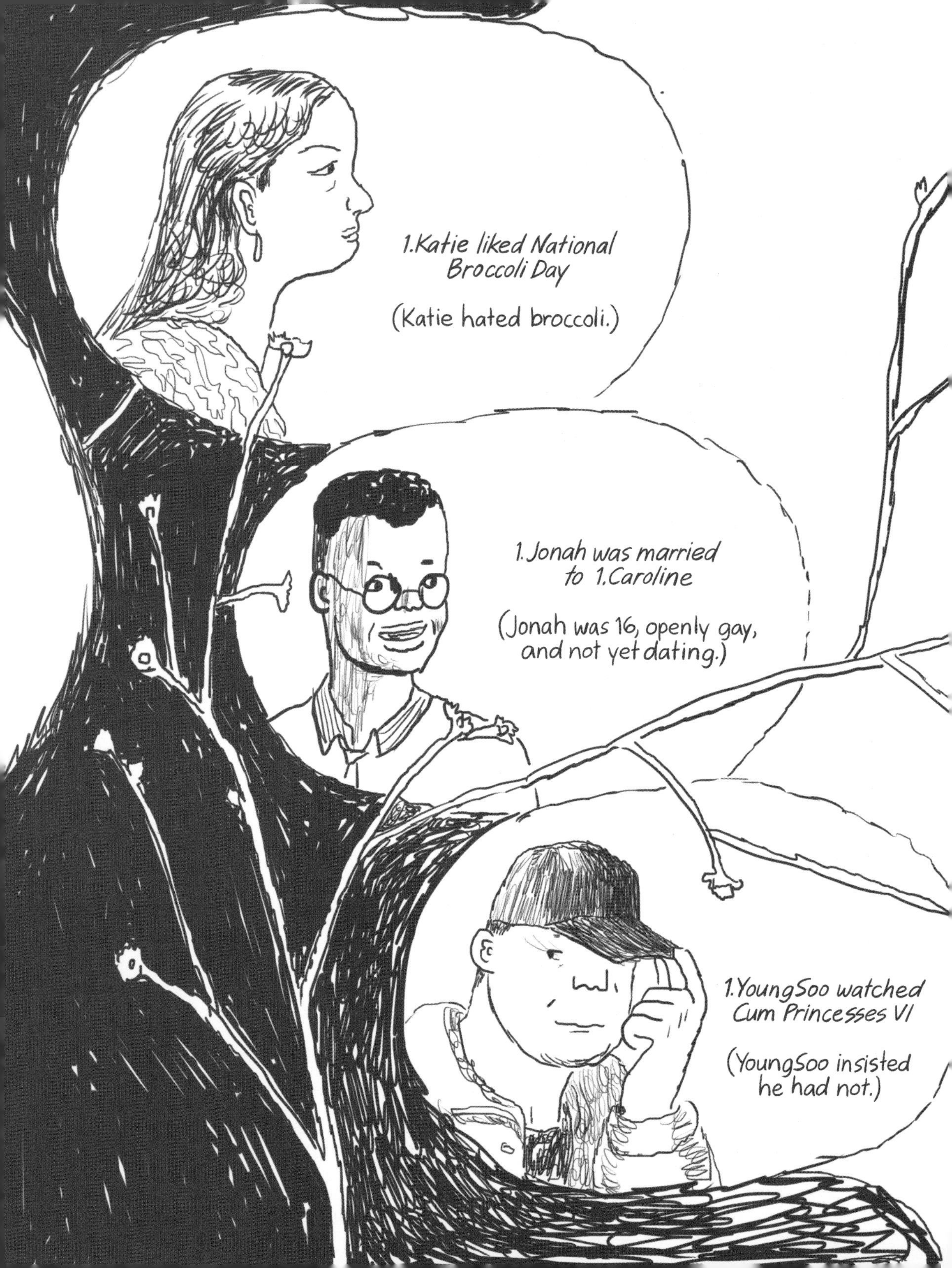
1.Katie liked National Broccoli Day
(Katie hated broccoli.)
1.Jonah was married to 1.Caroline
(Jonah was 16, openly gay, and not yet dating.)
1.YoungSoo watched Cum Princesses VI
(YoungSoo insisted he had not.)

Jenny could recognize she had gotten a little wrapped up with checking her mirror. At first she had been merely curious, but now it felt more like muscle memory.

Or a nervous tic.

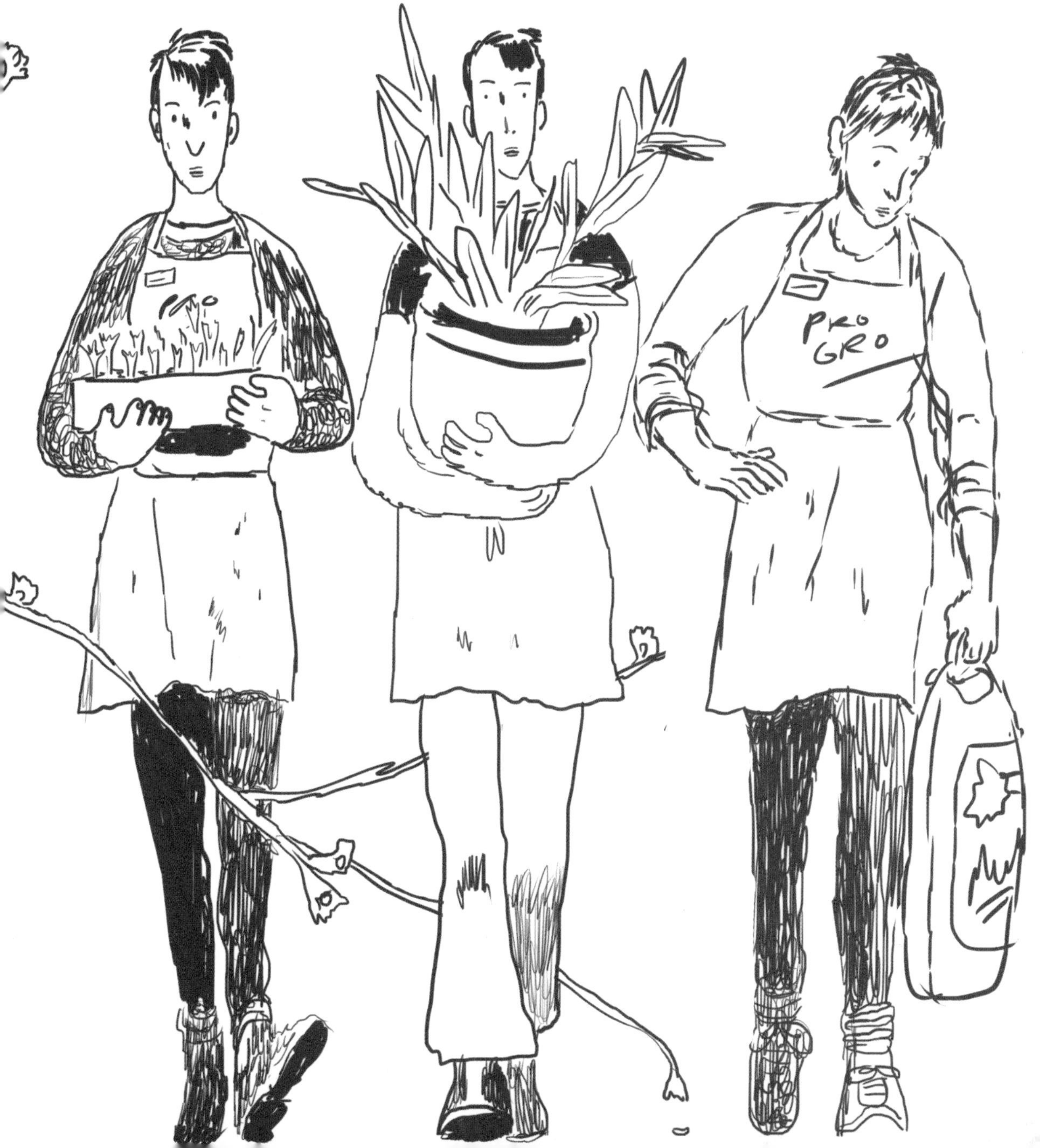
PRO GRO

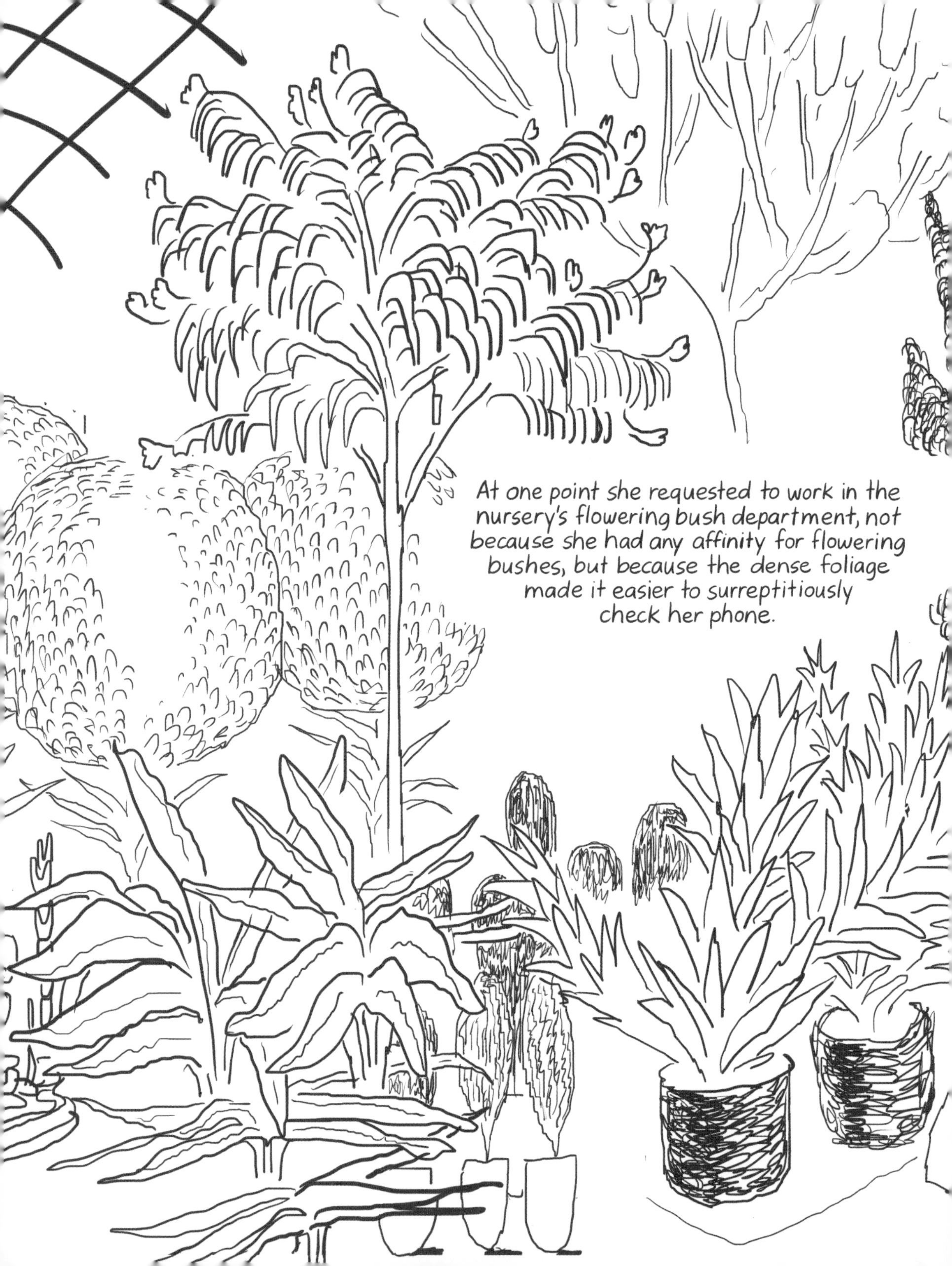
At one point she requested to work in the nursery's flowering bush department, not because she had any affinity for flowering bushes, but because the dense foliage made it easier to surreptitiously check her phone.

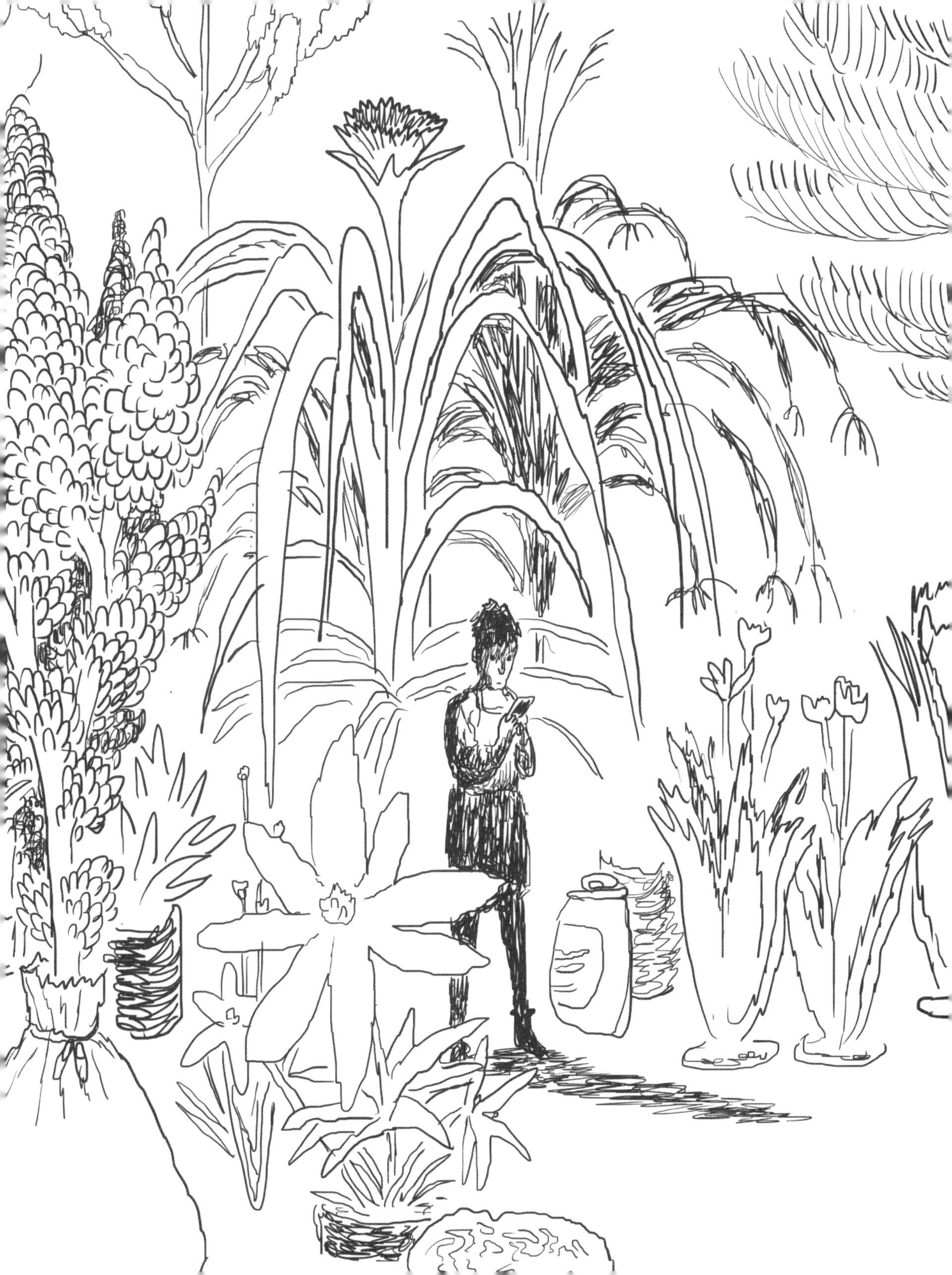

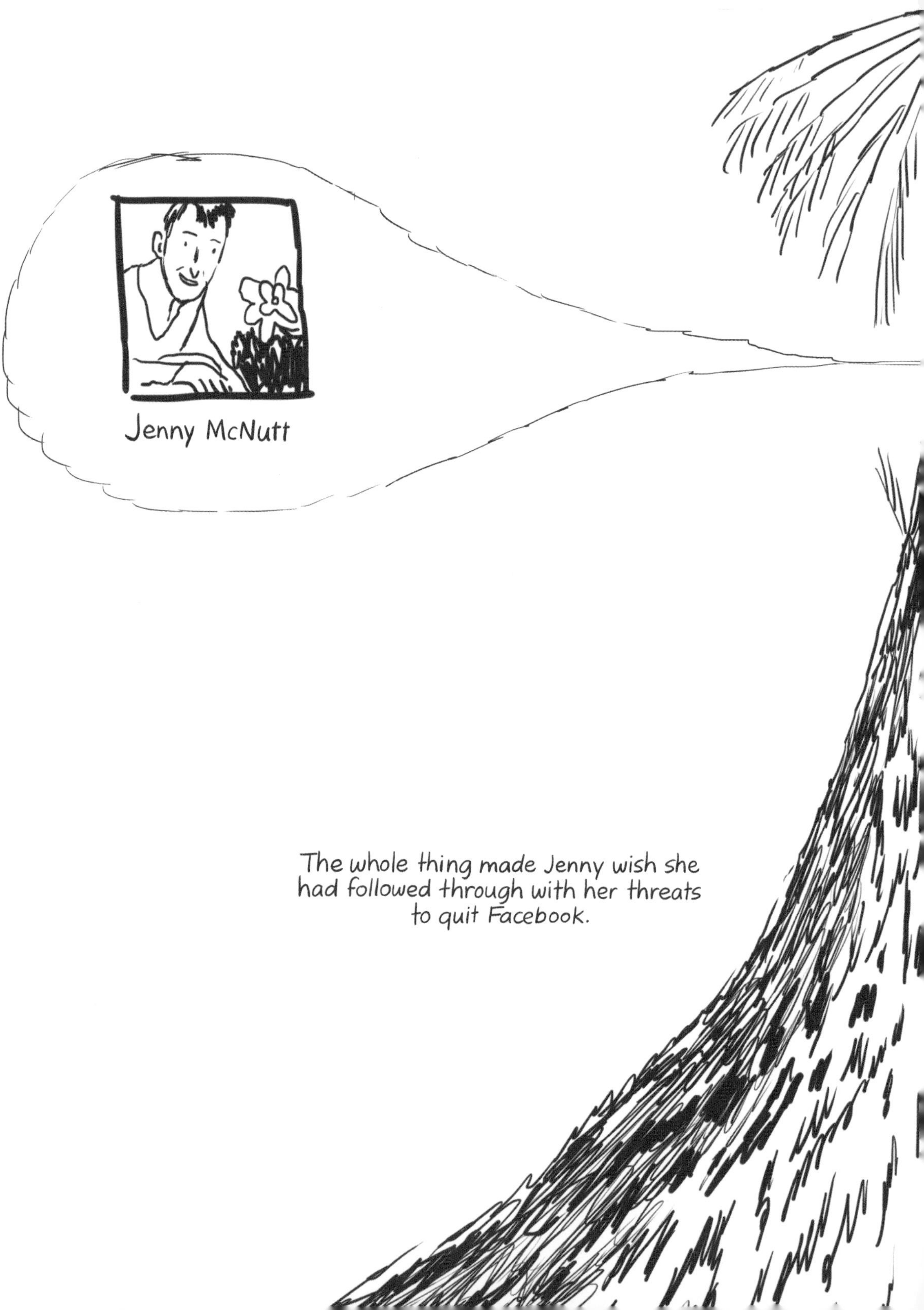
Jenny McNutt
The whole thing made Jenny wish she had followed through with her threats to quit Facebook.

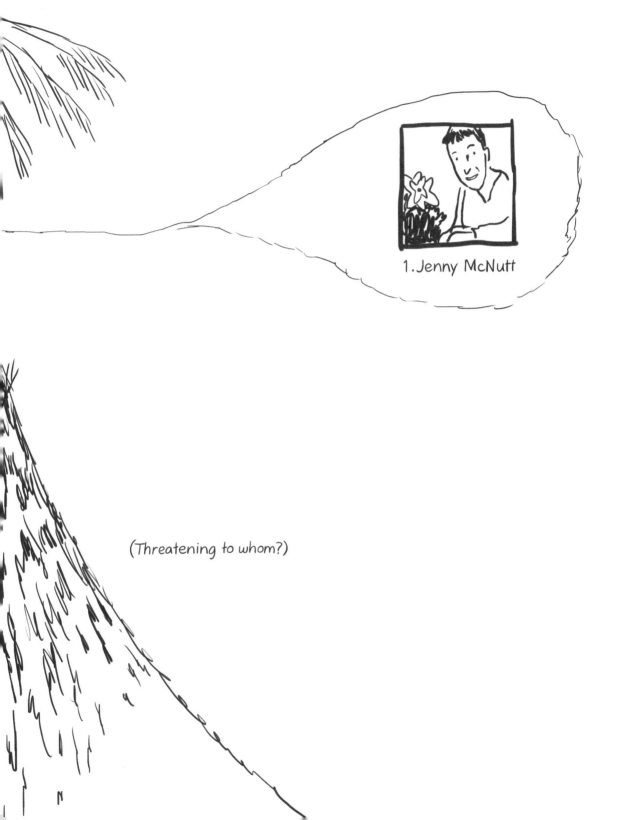

1.Jenny McNutt

(Threatening to whom?)

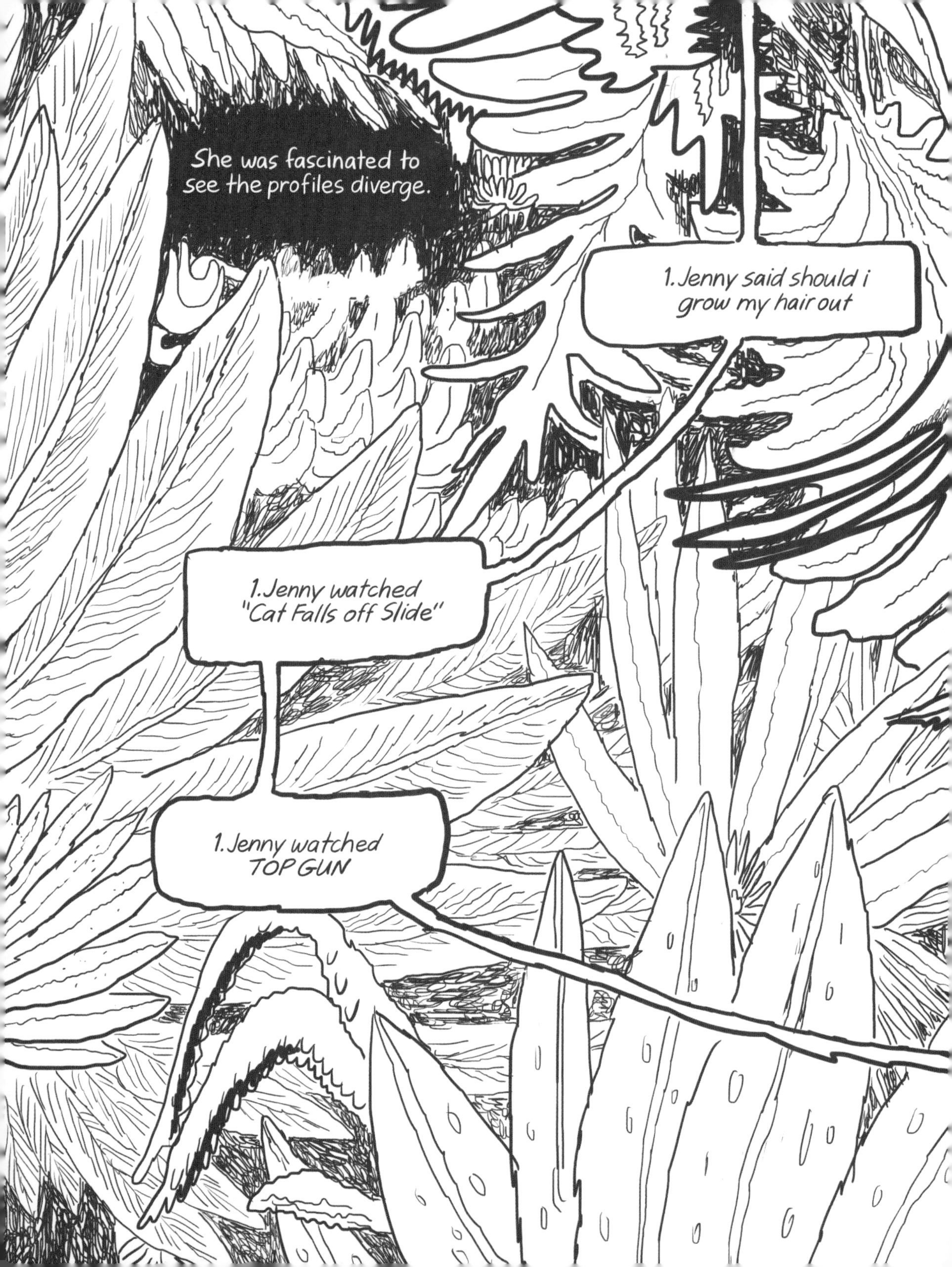
She was fascinated to see the profiles diverge.
1. Jenny said should i grow my hair out
1. Jenny watched "Cat Falls off Slide"
1. Jenny watched TOP GUN

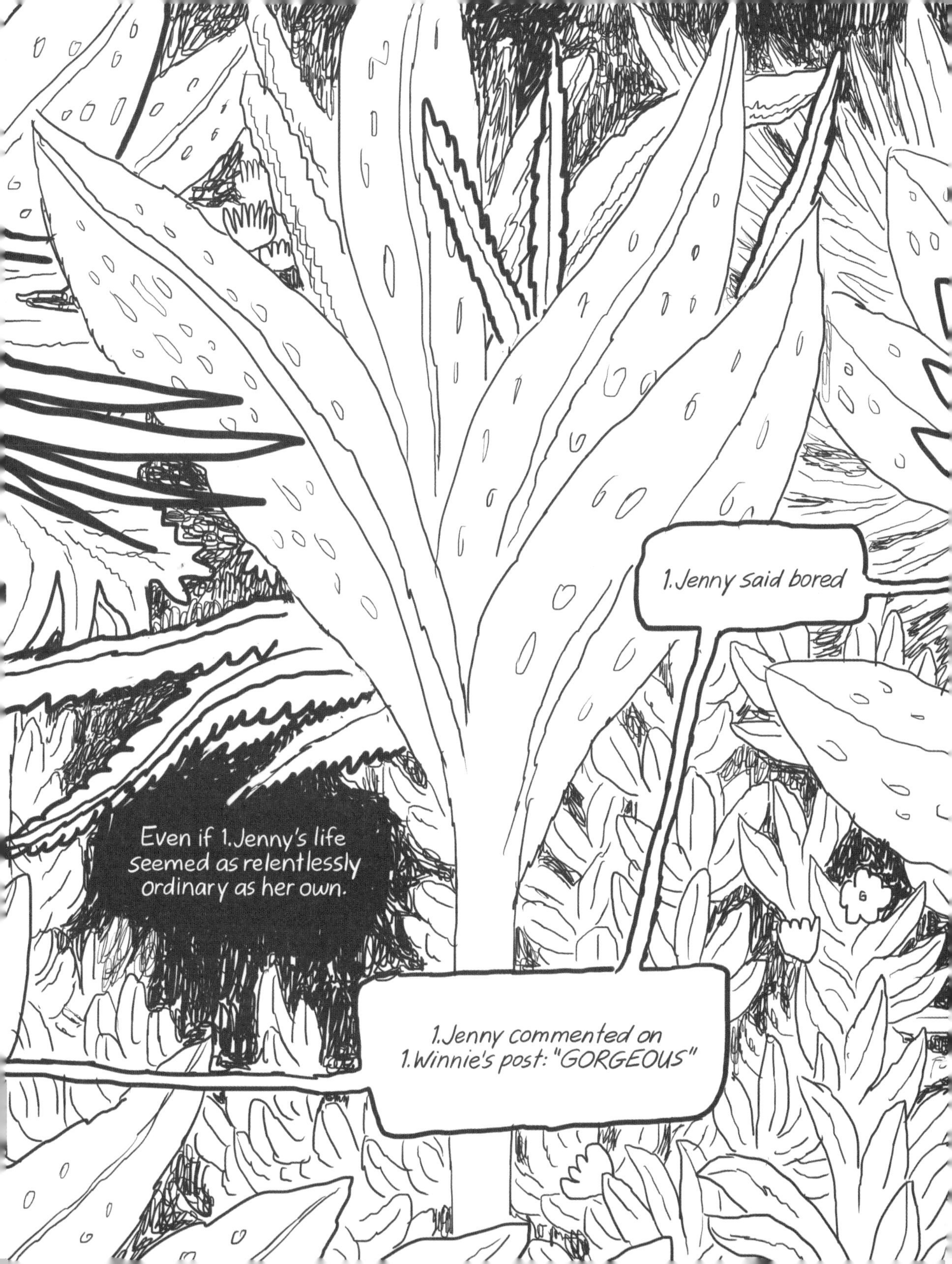
Even if 1.Jenny's life seemed as relentlessly ordinary as her own.
1.Jenny said bored
1.Jenny commented on 1.Winnie's post: "GORGEOUS"

That sweater.

1.Jenny did not look good in the blue sweater. The colour was fine but the fit was boxy and unflattering.

Did someone lend it to her? Had she, god forbid, bought it herself? Did 1.Jenny actually enjoy shopping?

Jenny thought about her own sweaters.

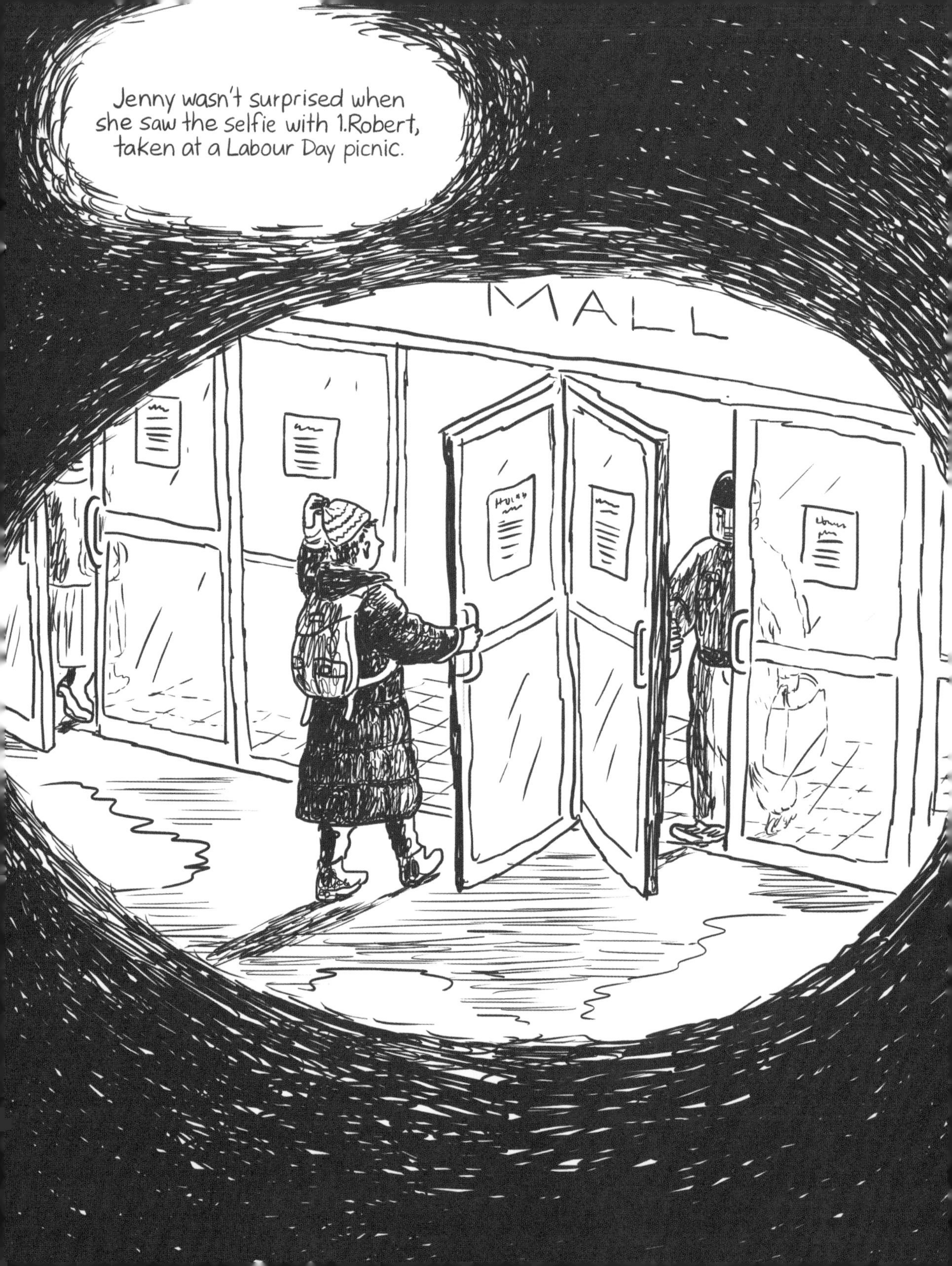
Jenny wasn't surprised when she saw the selfie with 1.Robert, taken at a Labour Day picnic.
MALL

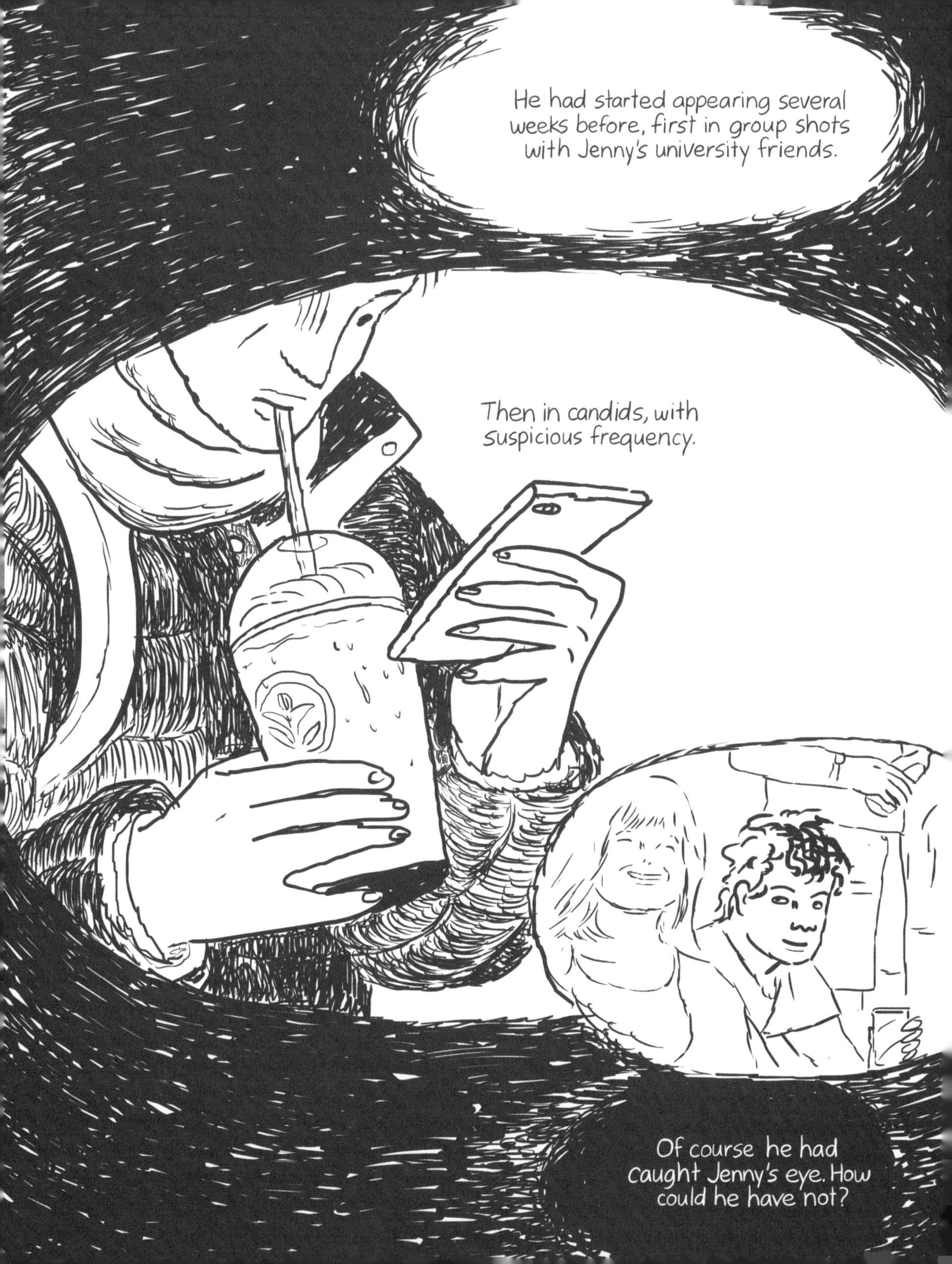
He had started appearing several weeks before, first in group shots with Jenny's university friends.
Then in candids, with suspicious frequency.
Of course he had caught Jenny's eye. How could he have not?

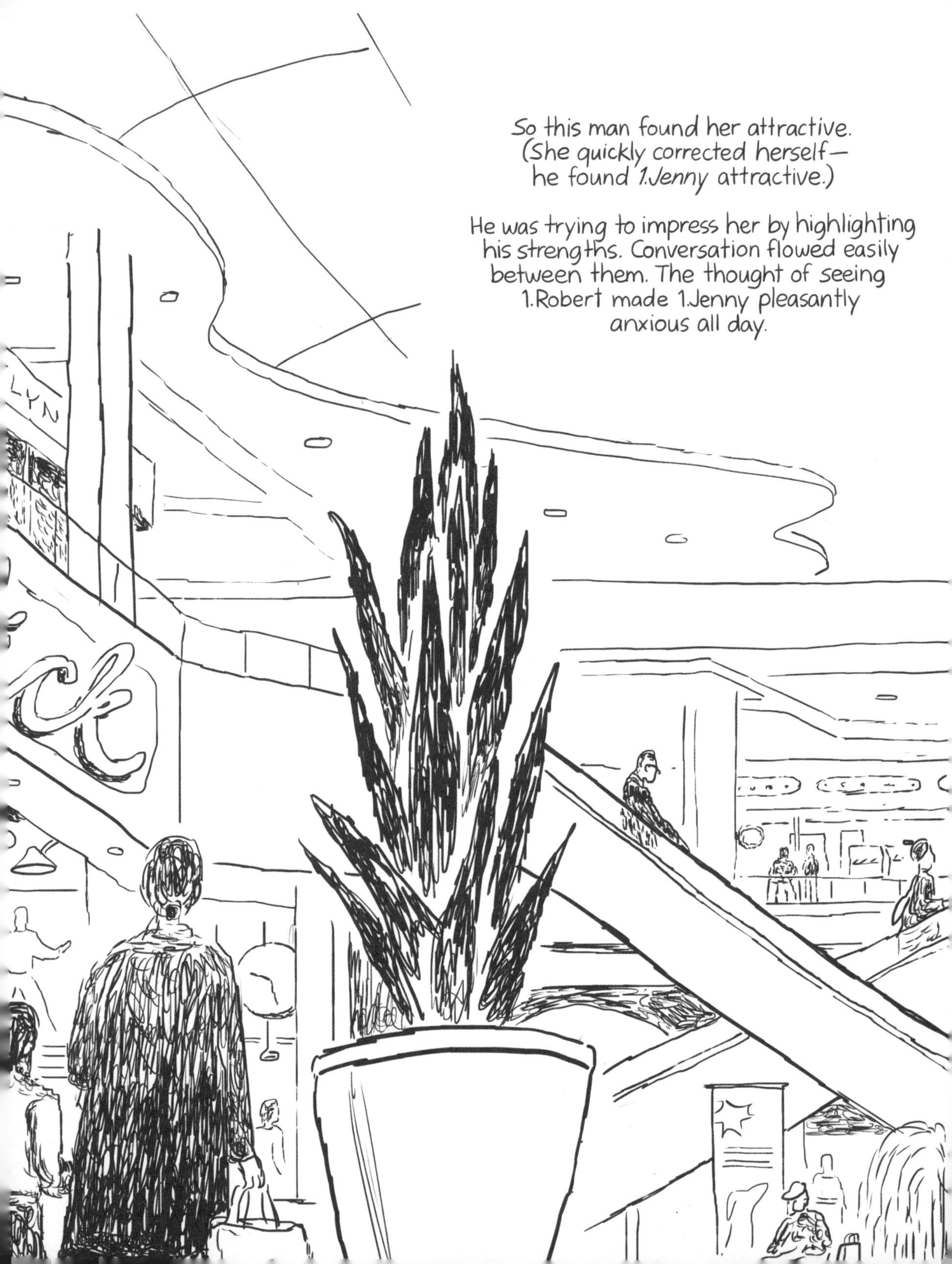
So this man found her attractive.
(She quickly corrected herself—
he found *1.Jenny* attractive.)
He was trying to impress her by highlighting his strengths. Conversation flowed easily between them. The thought of seeing 1.Robert made 1.Jenny pleasantly anxious all day.

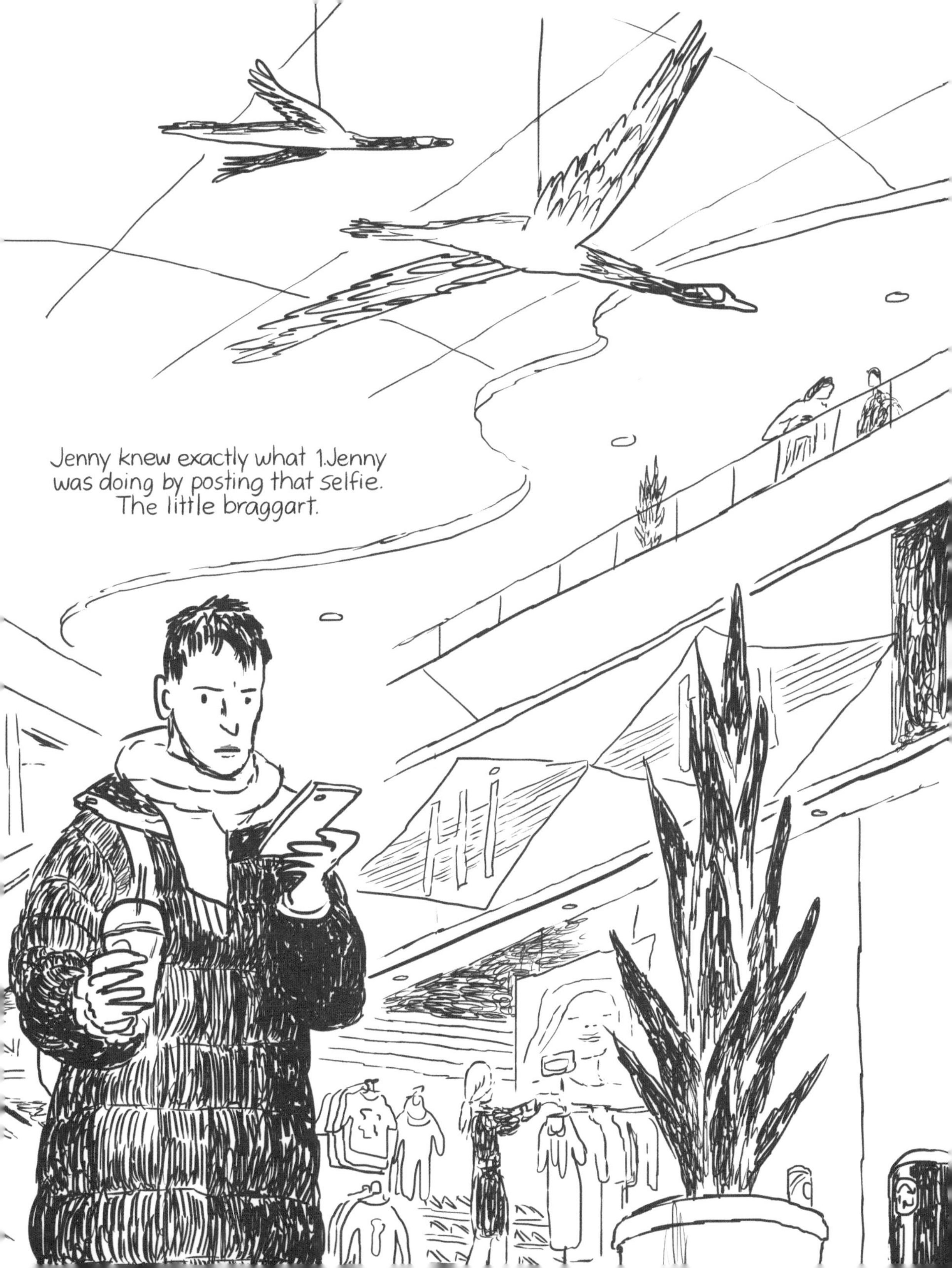
Jenny knew exactly what 1.Jenny was doing by posting that selfie. The little braggart.
Hi

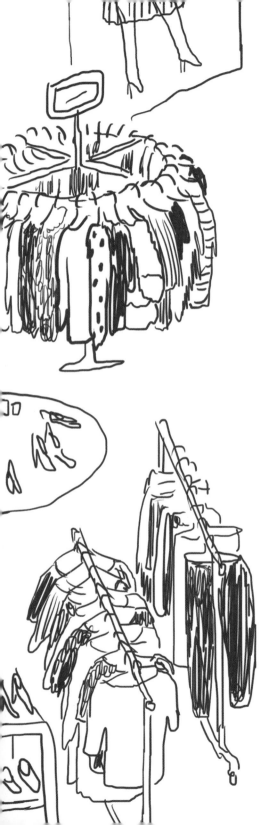

It was all so profoundly annoying.
Mostly because it made Jenny
think about O.

It was unbelievable that she had
once felt the same way towards
him, but at the same time, it was
very easy to conjure the memory.

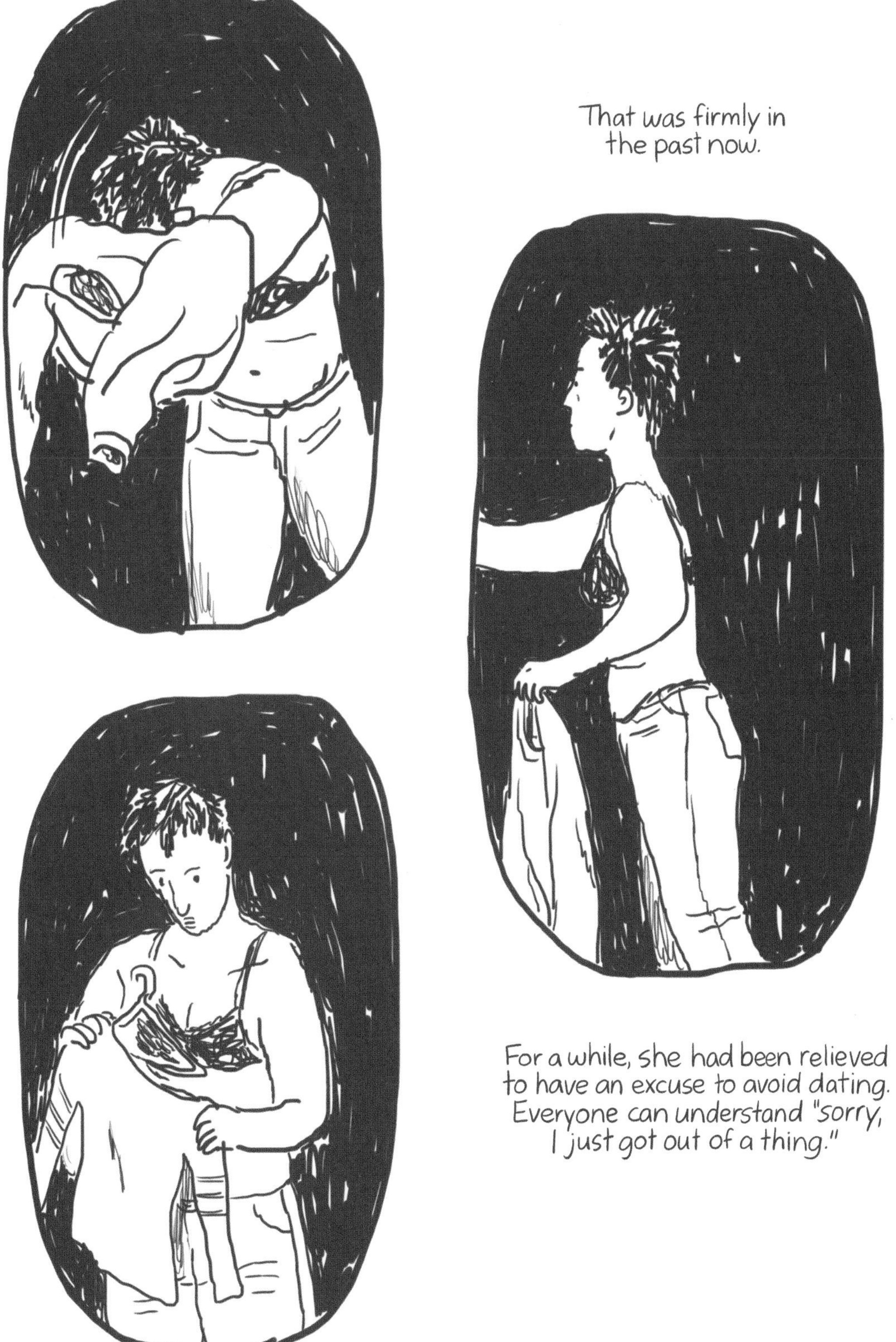
That was firmly in the past now.
For a while, she had been relieved to have an excuse to avoid dating. Everyone can understand "sorry, I just got out of a thing."

Now, though—Jenny
wasn't sure.

She felt acutely aware of some
sort of lost momentum.

Which was startling given that
she wasn't even aware she had
possessed said momentum in
the first place.

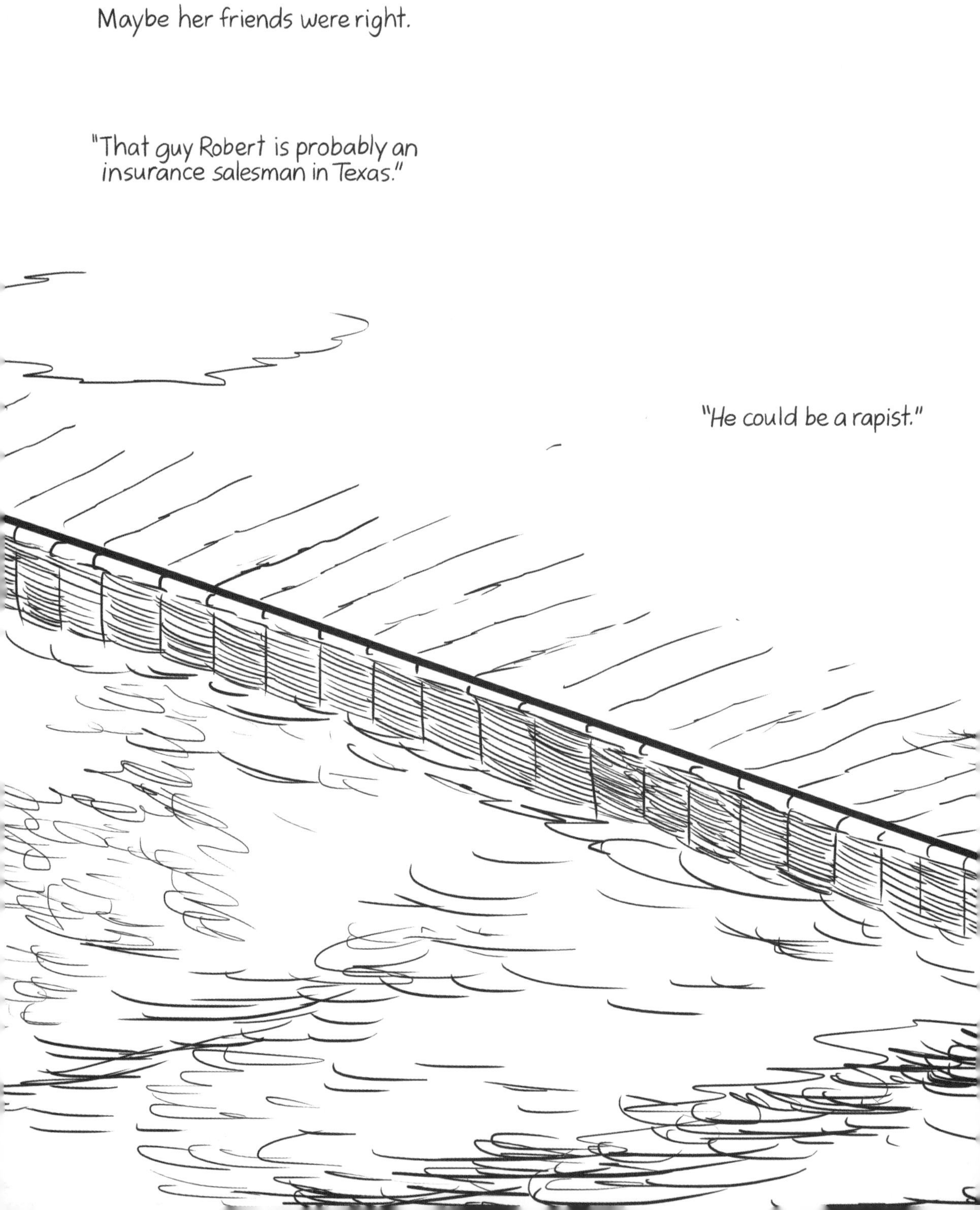
Maybe her friends were right.
"That guy Robert is probably an insurance salesman in Texas."
"He could be a rapist."

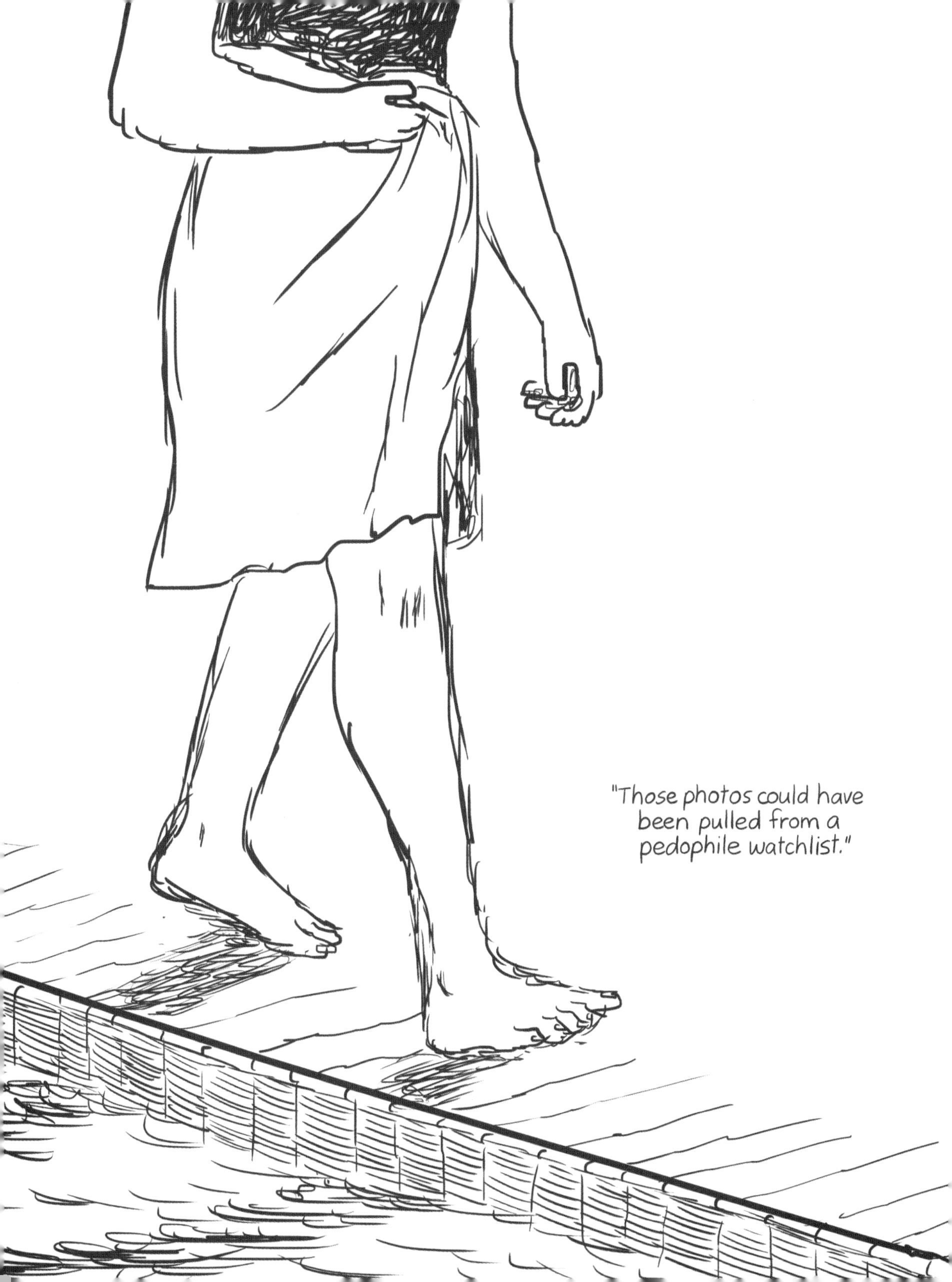
"Those photos could have been pulled from a pedophile watchlist."

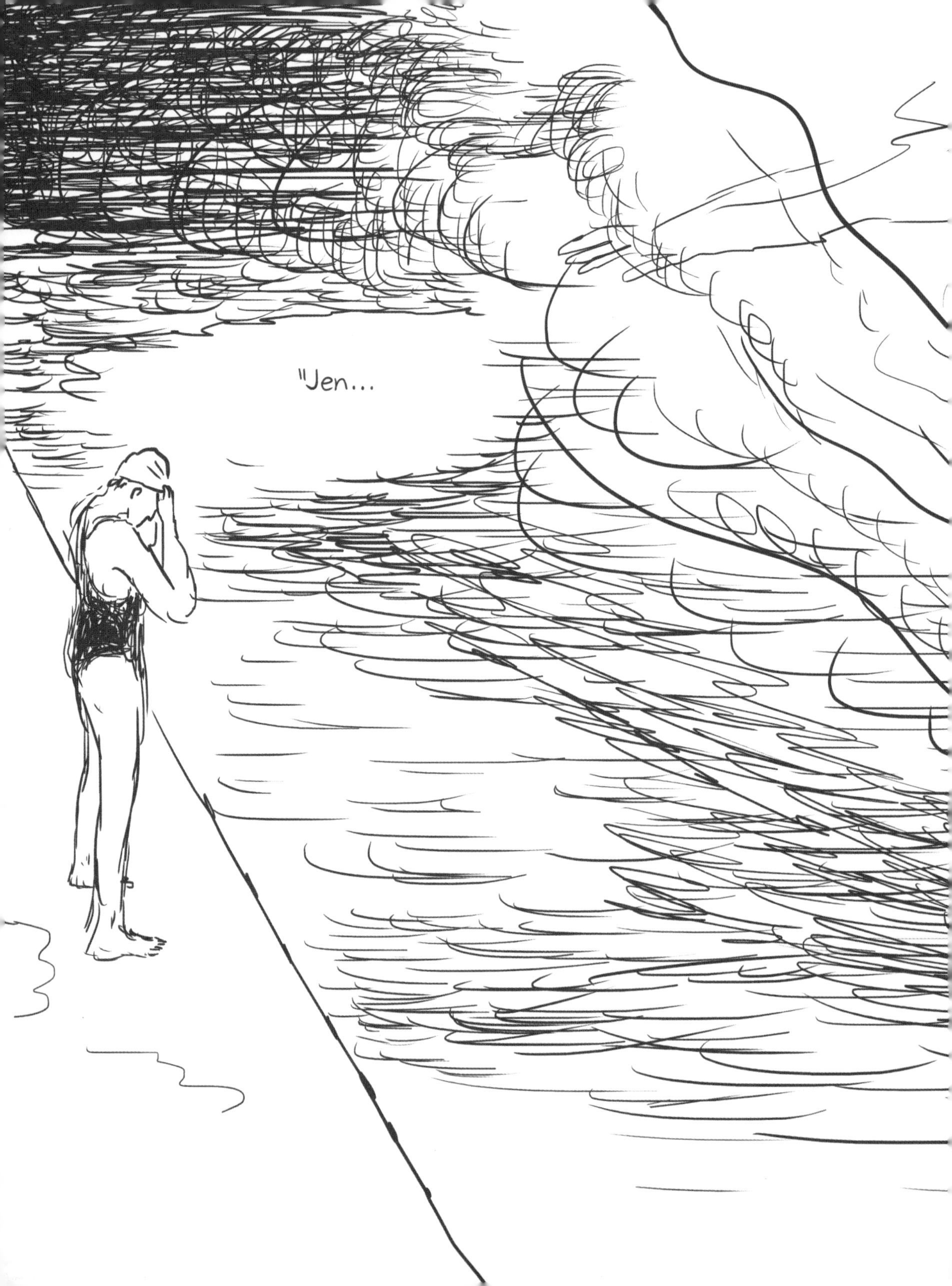
"Jen...

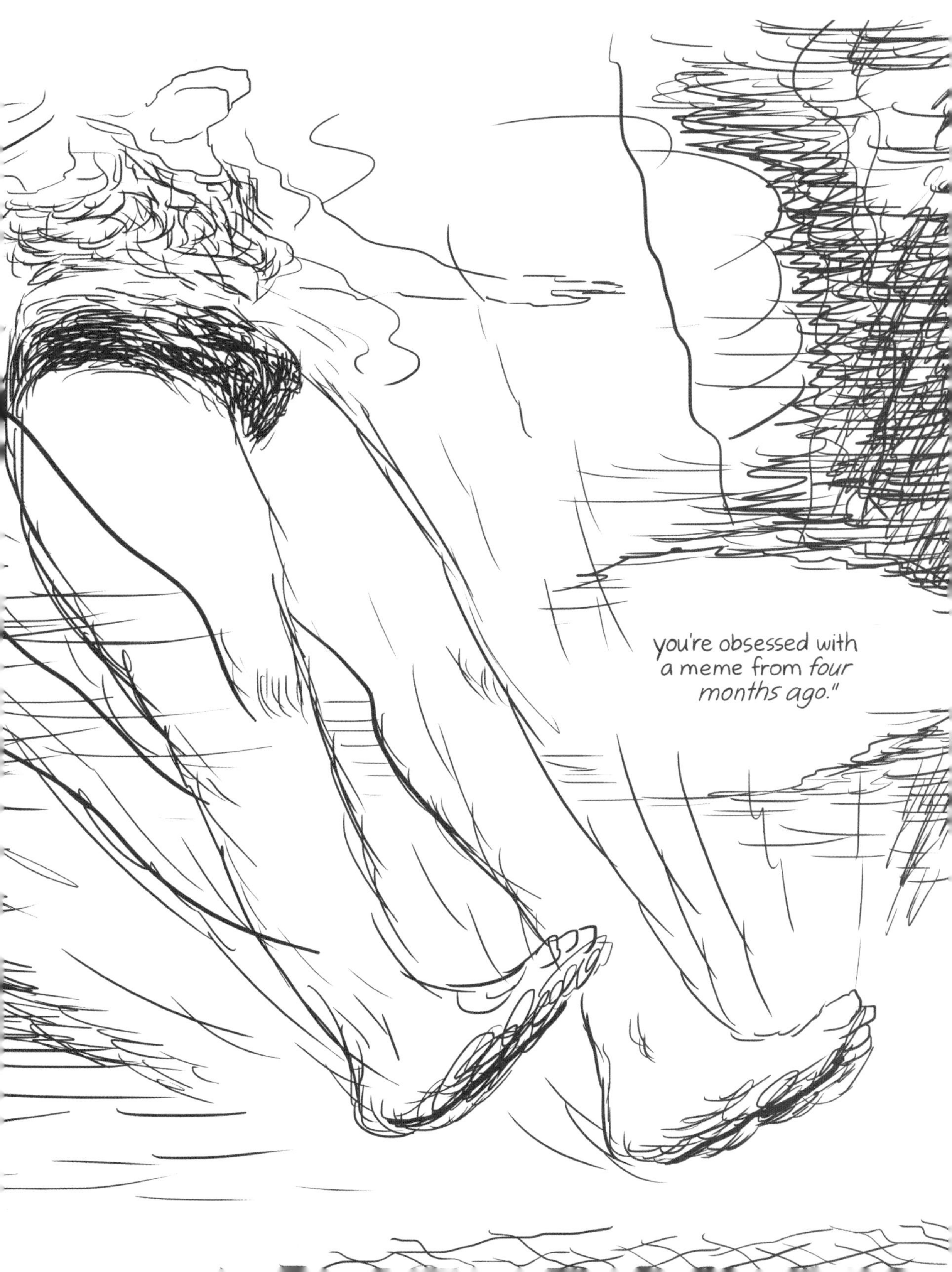
you're obsessed with a meme from *four* months ago."

Jenny had always wanted to try therapy and this seemed as good a time as any. The therapist was kind but Jenny sensed he was less interested in discussing the mirror profile than her family history.

Jenny explained that her family was almost freakishly normal, which the therapist made a note of.

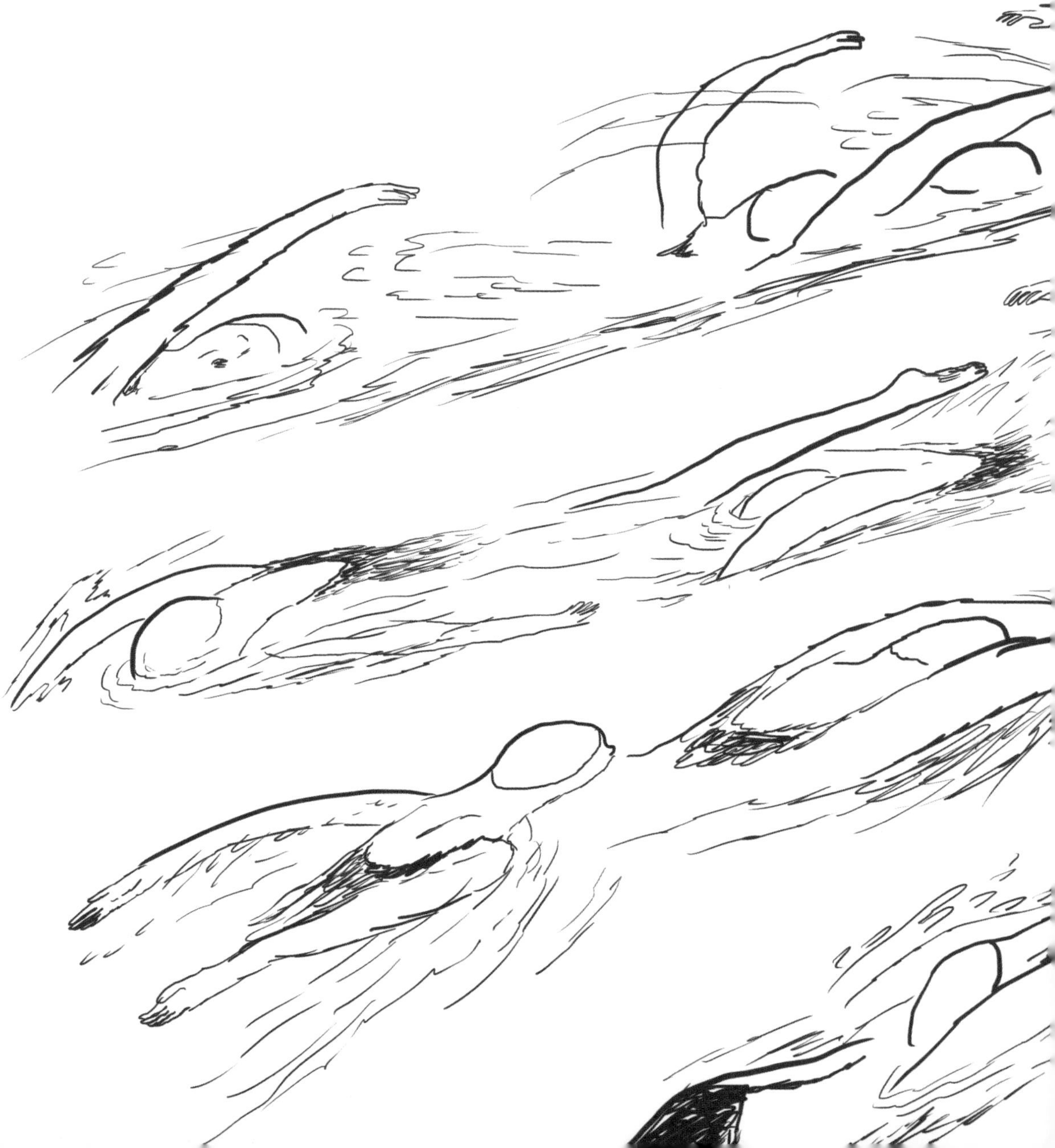

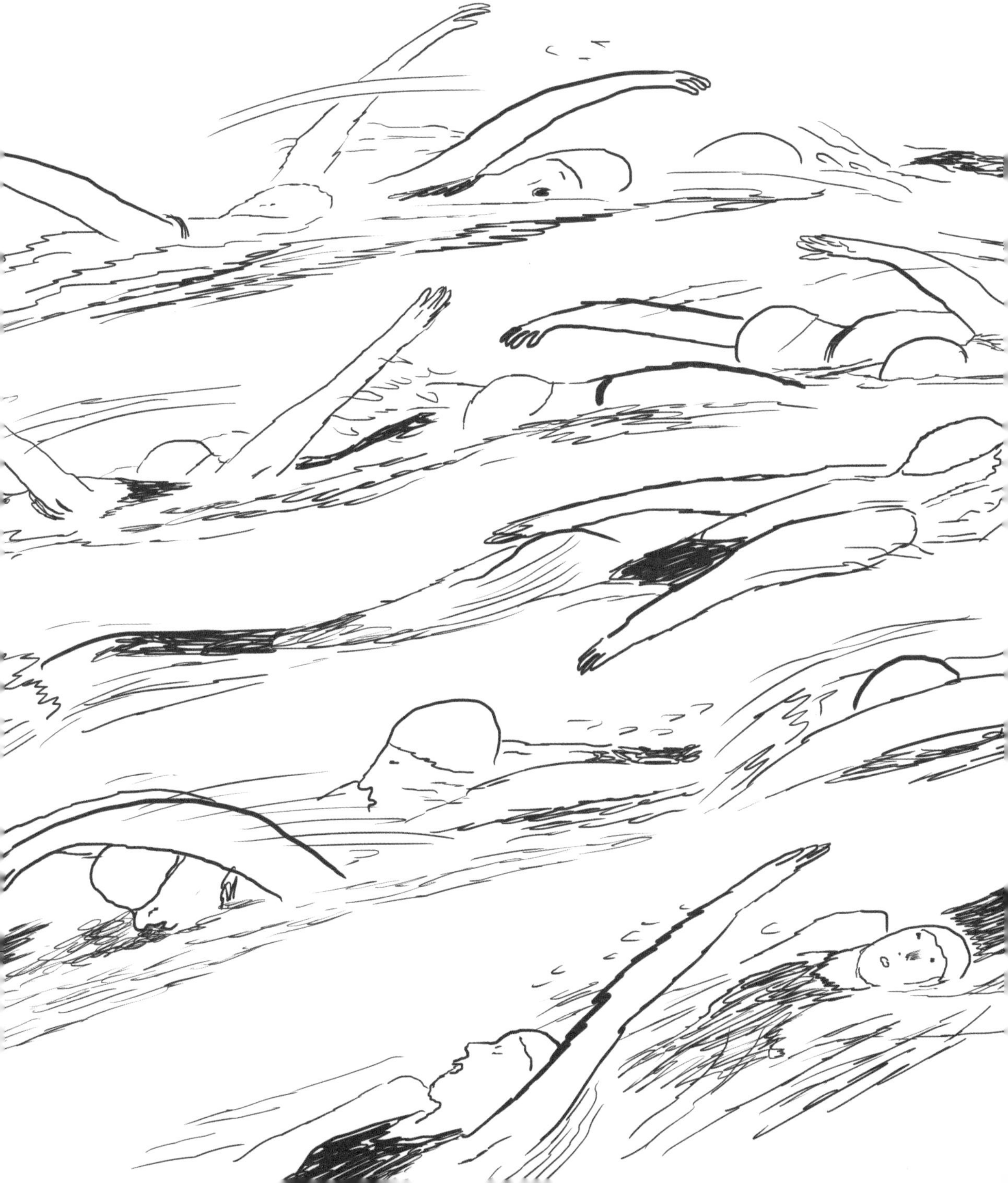

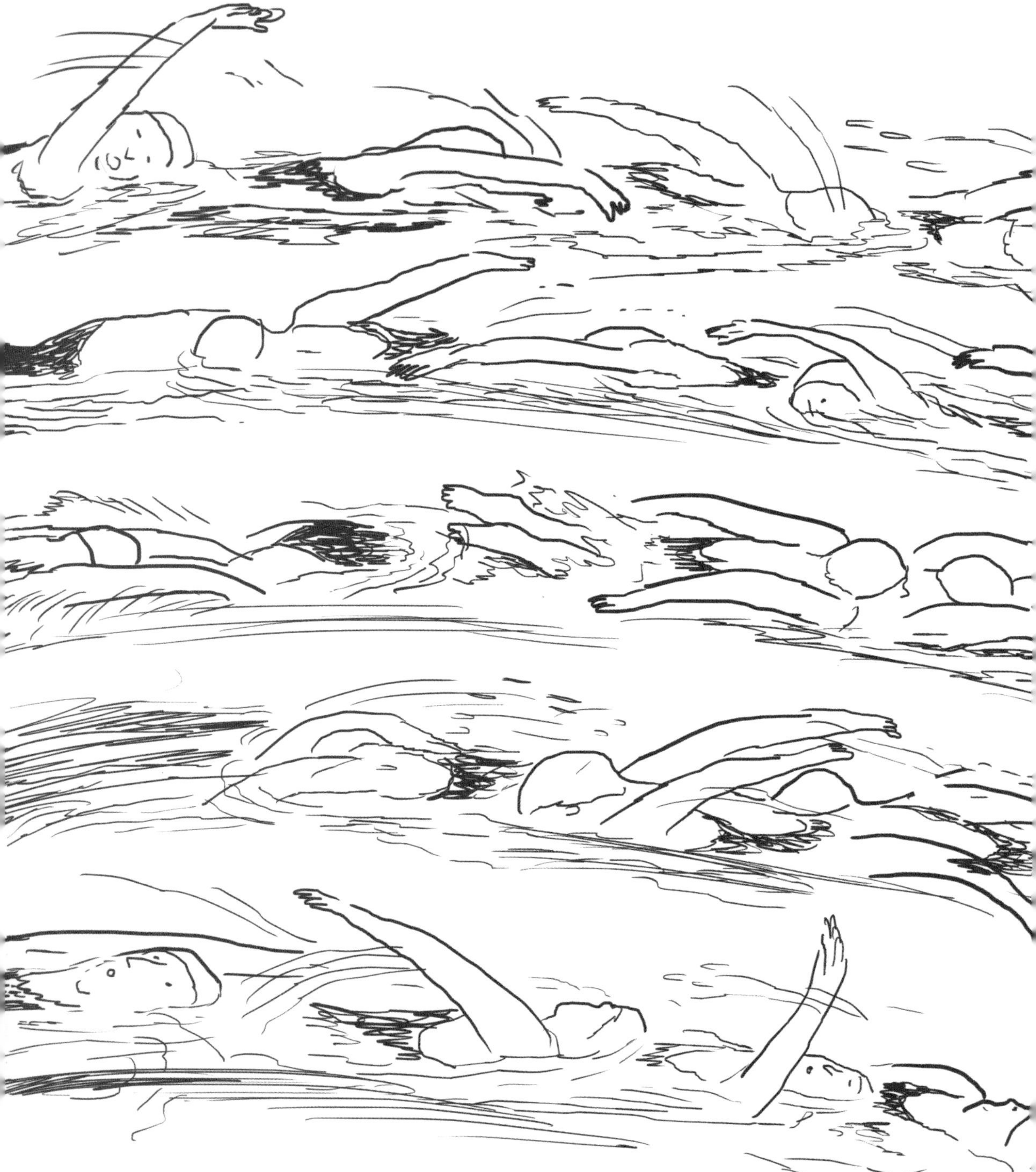

Jenny didn't let the discussion stray too far from the mirror profile. "Whether it's 'real' or not is irrelevant. The value of the profile is the response it provokes within you," sputtered the therapist, near the end of the session.

He suggested Jenny take up an activity wherein she couldn't use her phone, like ceramics or swimming.

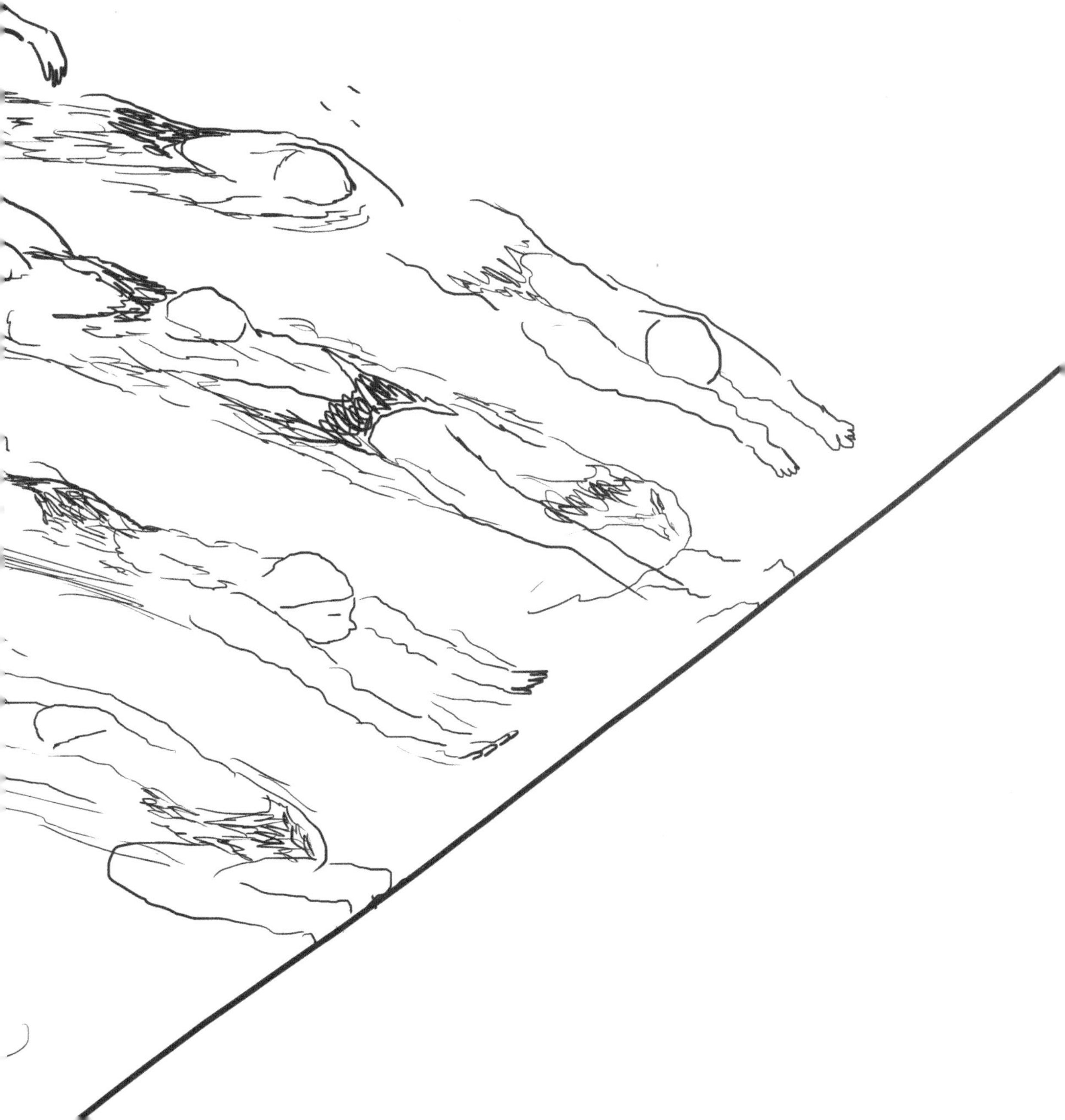

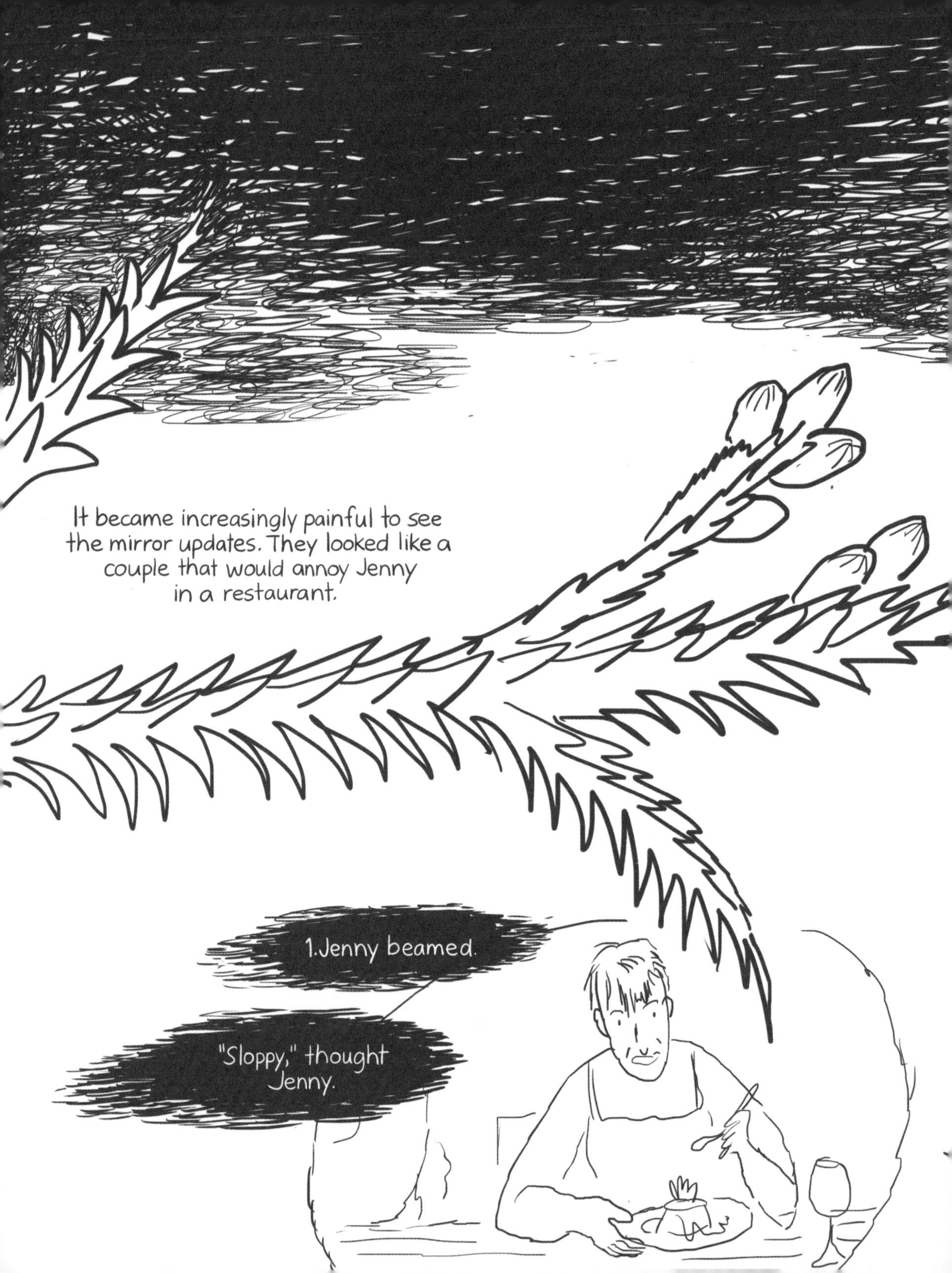
It became increasingly painful to see the mirror updates. They looked like a couple that would annoy Jenny in a restaurant.
1.Jenny beamed.
"Sloppy," thought Jenny.

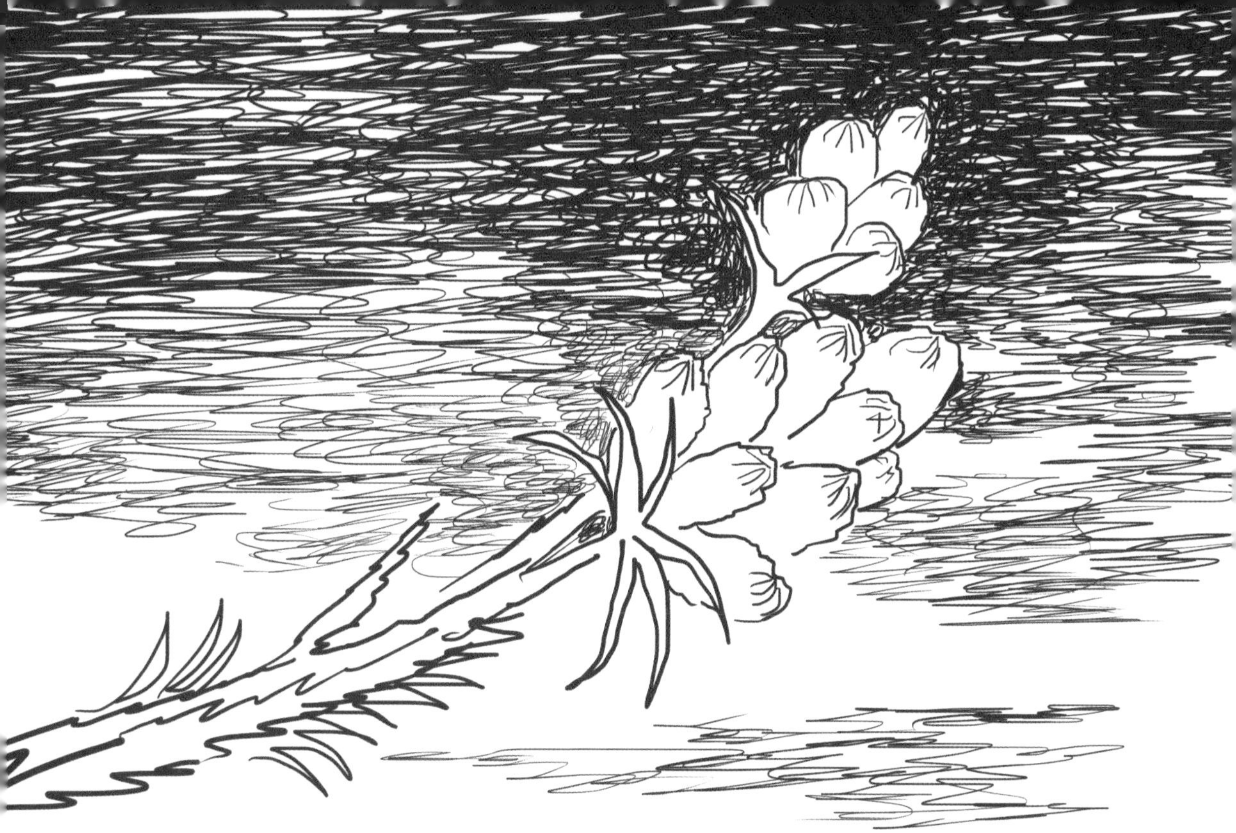

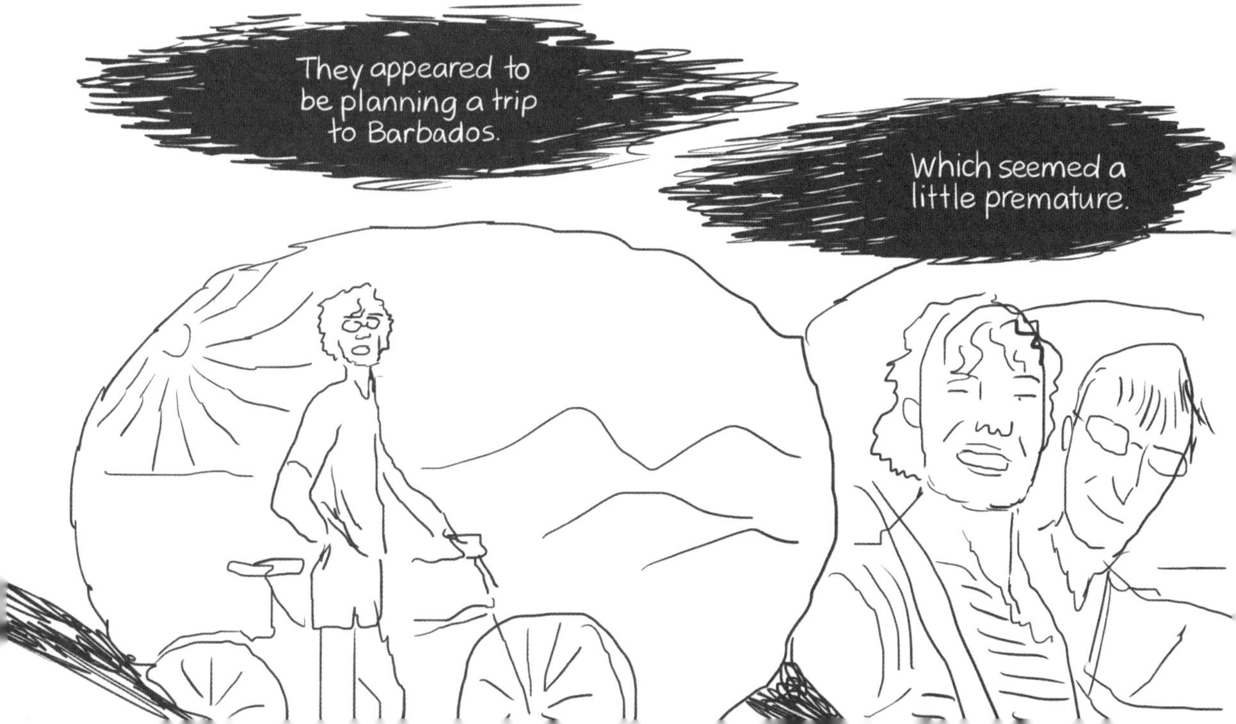
They appeared to be planning a trip to Barbados.
Which seemed a little premature.

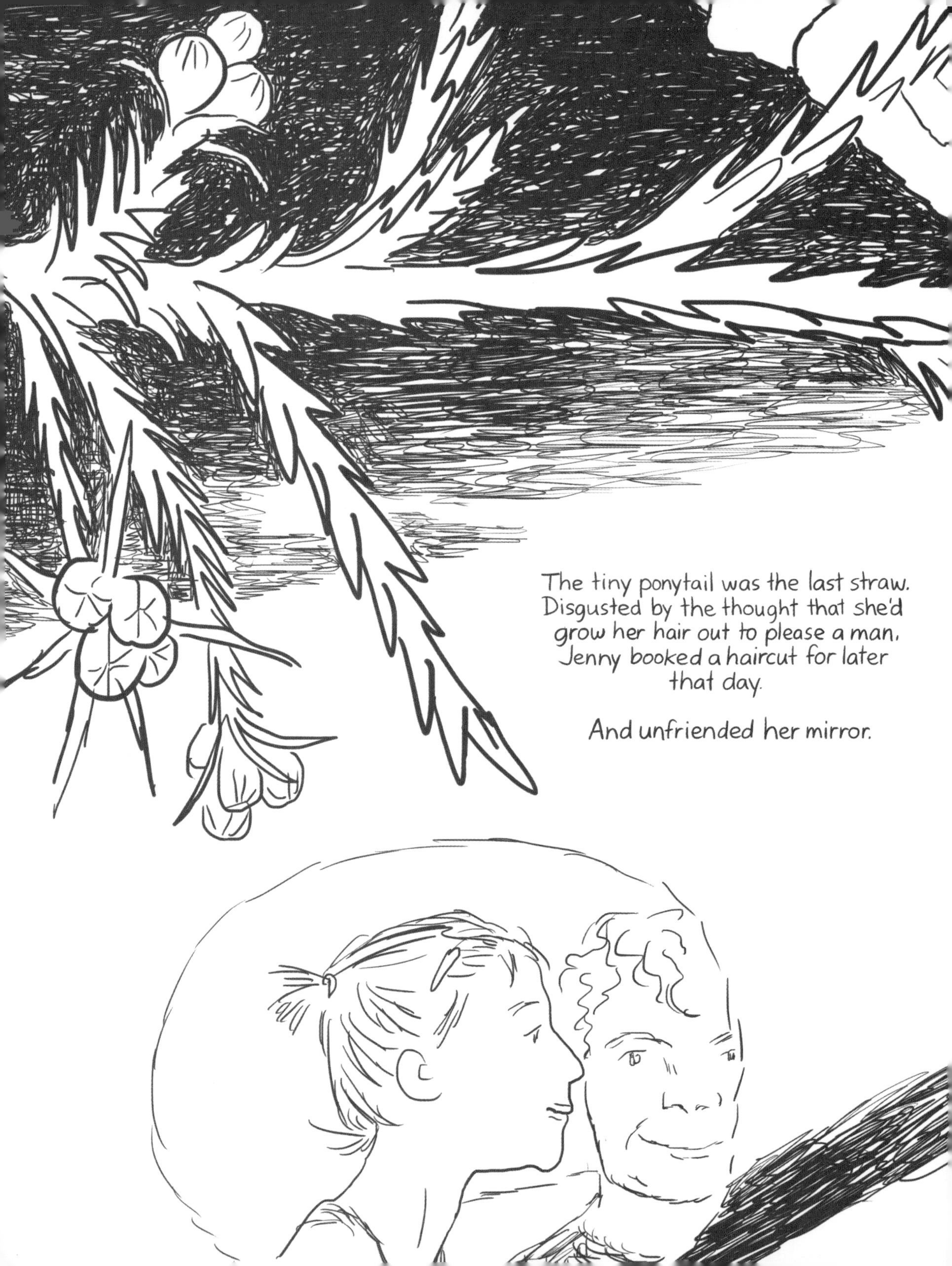
The tiny ponytail was the last straw. Disgusted by the thought that she'd grow her hair out to please a man, Jenny booked a haircut for later that day.
And unfriended her mirror.

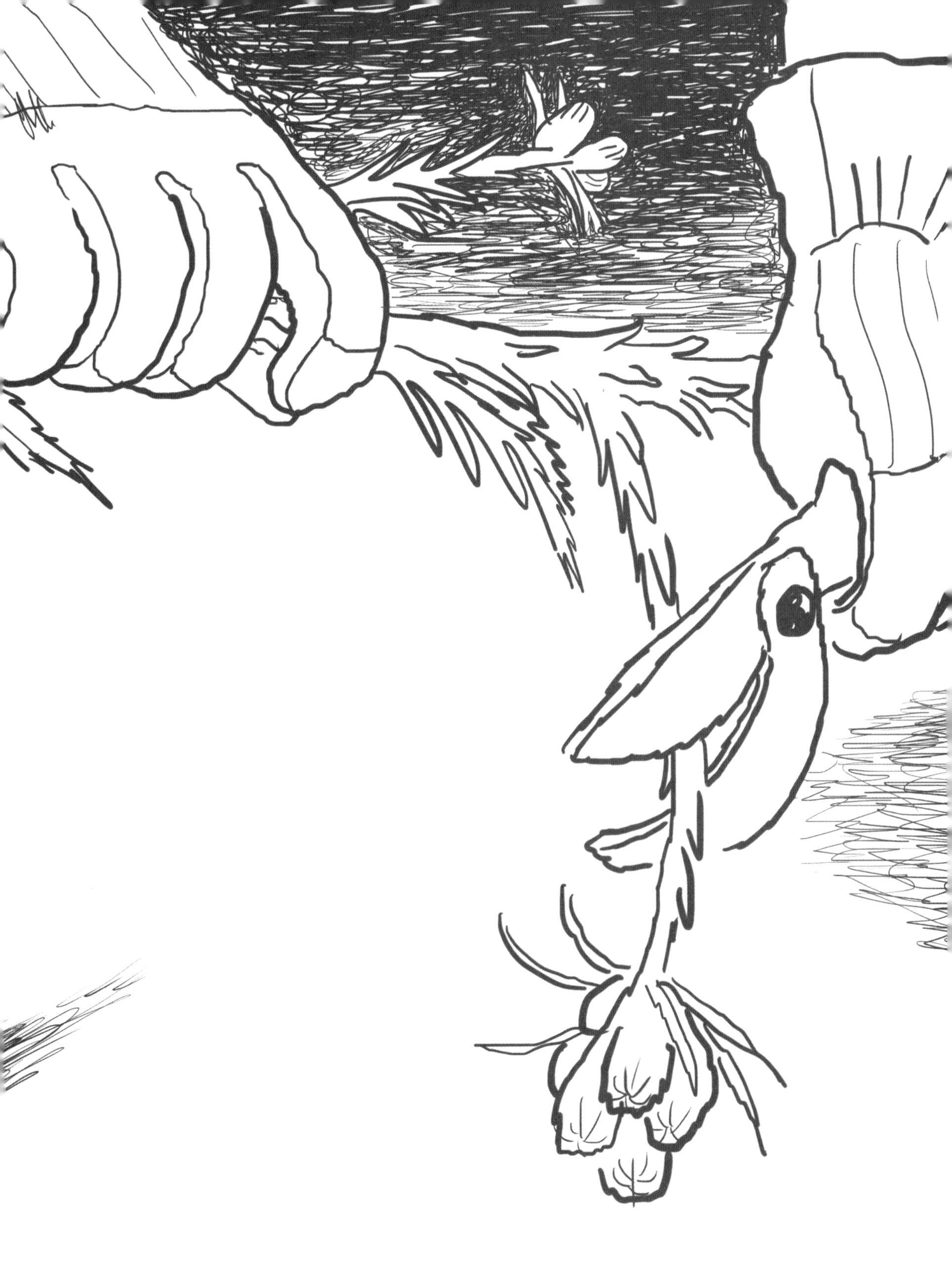

The poinsettias arrived, officially
ushering in Christmas at the nursery.

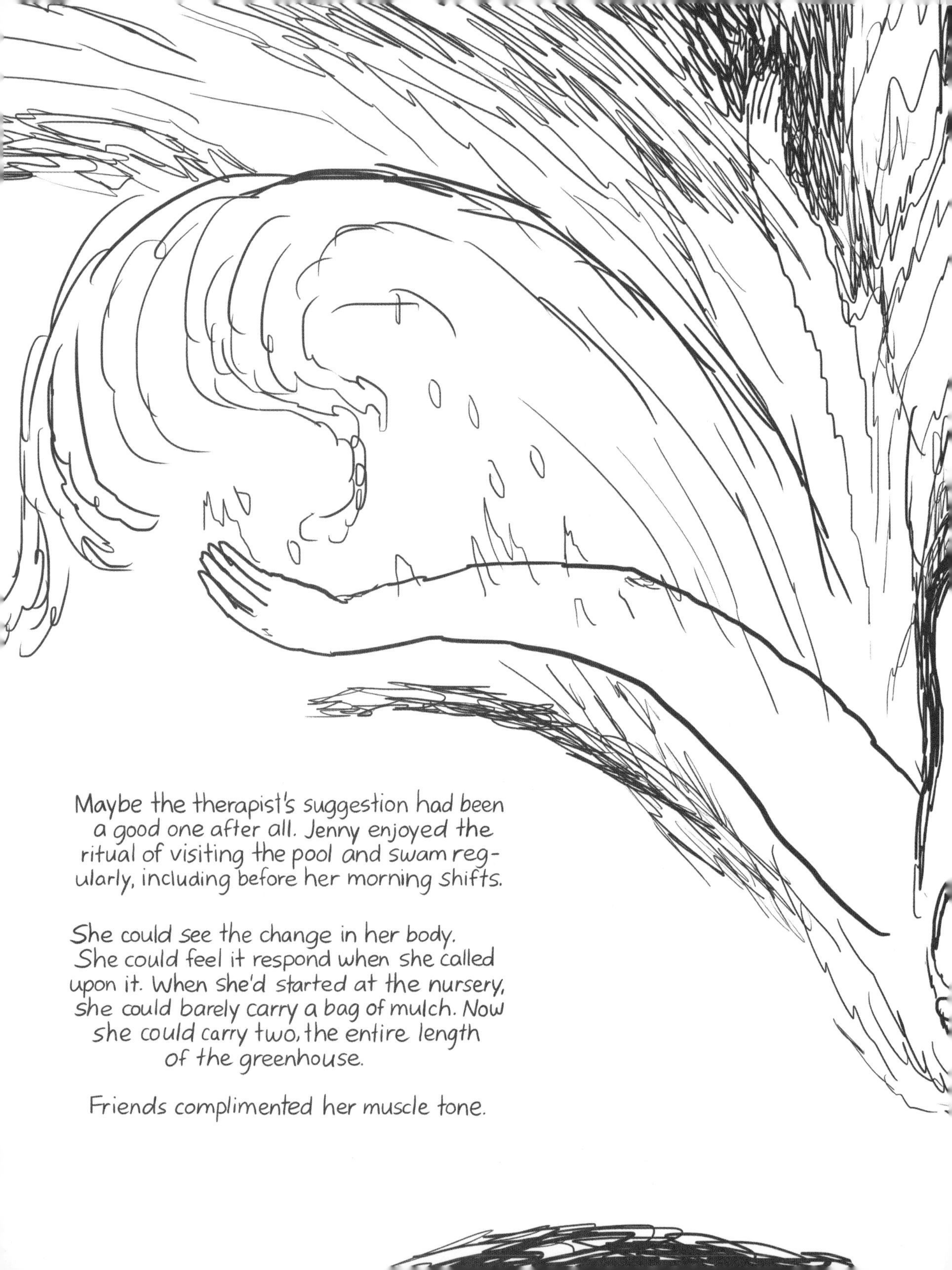

Maybe the therapist's suggestion had been a good one after all. Jenny enjoyed the ritual of visiting the pool and swam regularly, including before her morning shifts.

She could see the change in her body. She could feel it respond when she called upon it. When she'd started at the nursery, she could barely carry a bag of mulch. Now she could carry two, the entire length of the greenhouse.

Friends complimented her muscle tone.

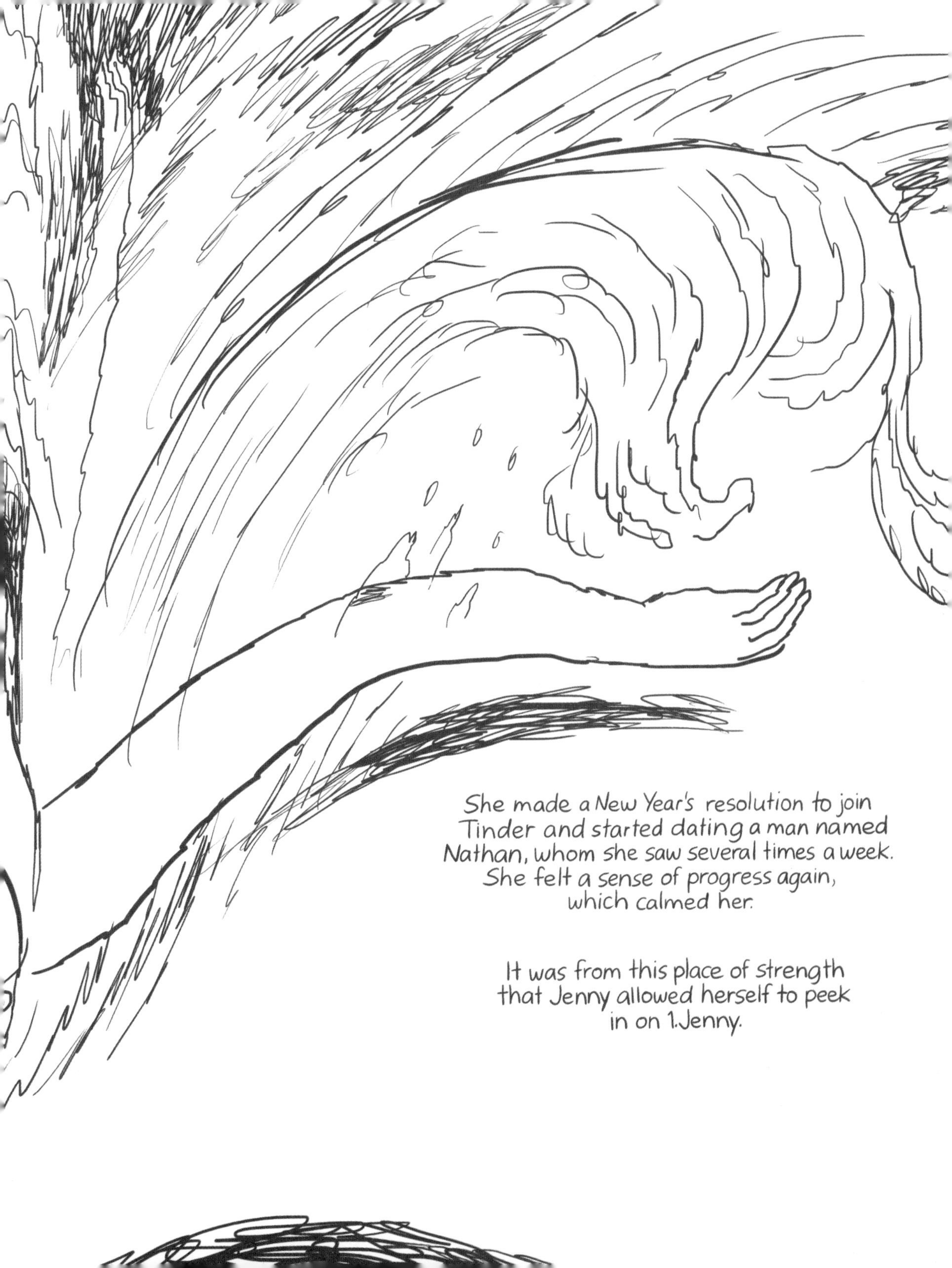
She made a New Year's resolution to join Tinder and started dating a man named Nathan, whom she saw several times a week. She felt a sense of progress again, which calmed her.
It was from this place of strength that Jenny allowed herself to peek in on 1.Jenny.

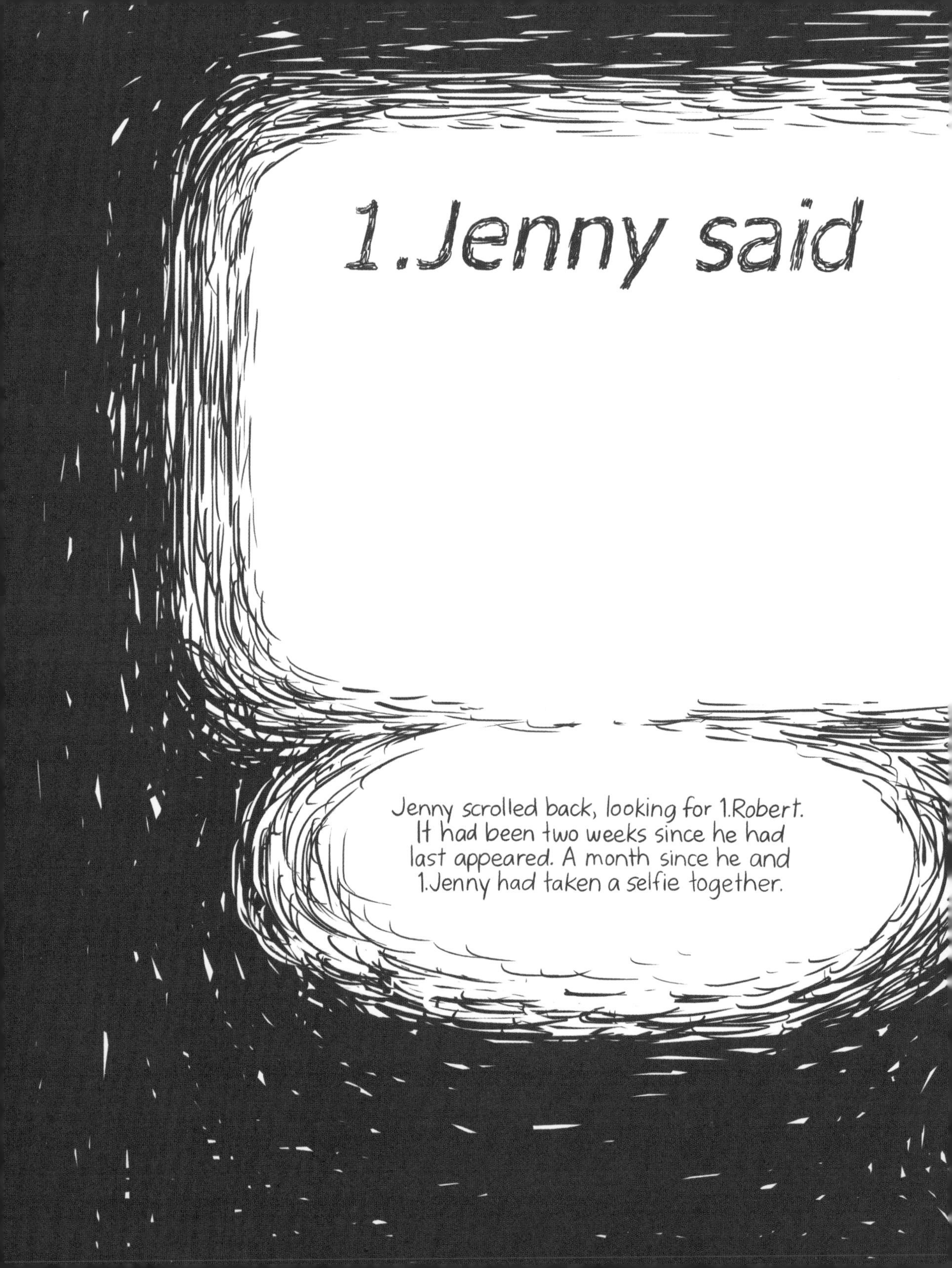
1.Jenny said
Jenny scrolled back, looking for 1.Robert. It had been two weeks since he had last appeared. A month since he and 1.Jenny had taken a selfie together.

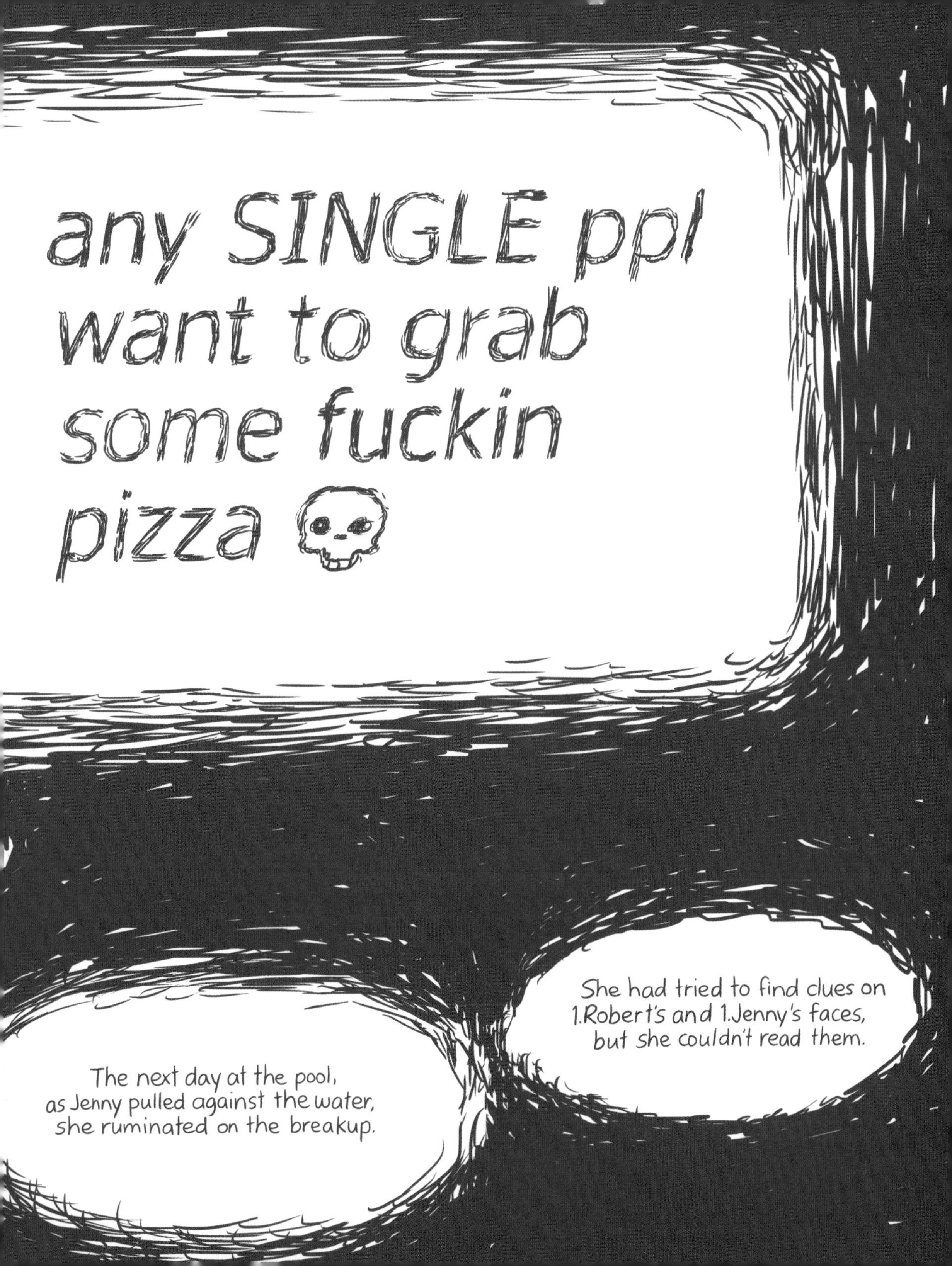
any SINGLE ppl want to grab some fuckin pizza
She had tried to find clues on 1.Robert's and 1.Jenny's faces, but she couldn't read them.
The next day at the pool, as Jenny pulled against the water, she ruminated on the breakup.

Jenny felt victorious. Also terrible—
—she was well aware that her delight equated
to 1.Jenny's misery. That made her bad.
Still, she achieved a personal best in the
pool that morning.

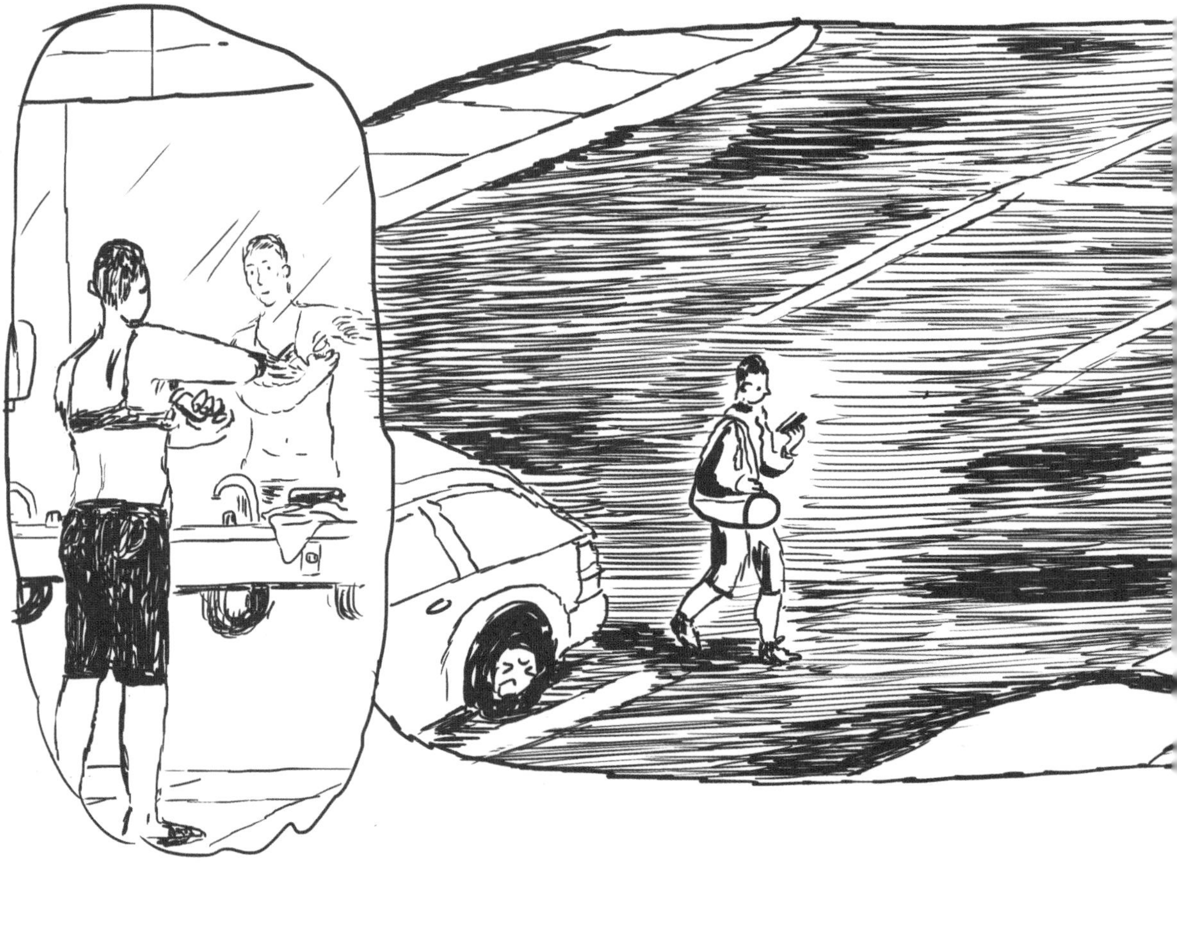

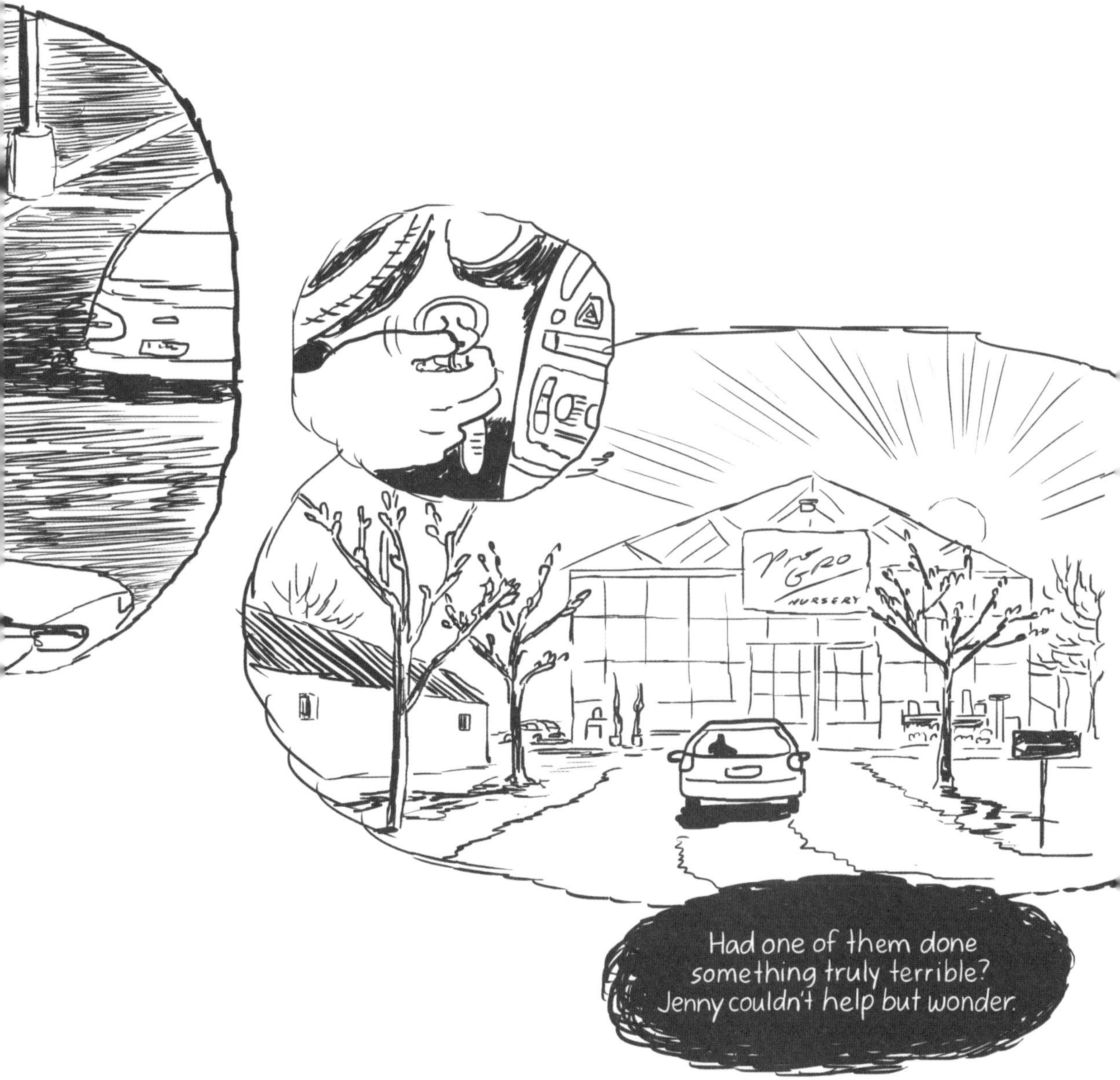
NURSERY
Had one of them done something truly terrible? Jenny couldn't help but wonder.

Probably not. Most breakups
are pretty mundane.

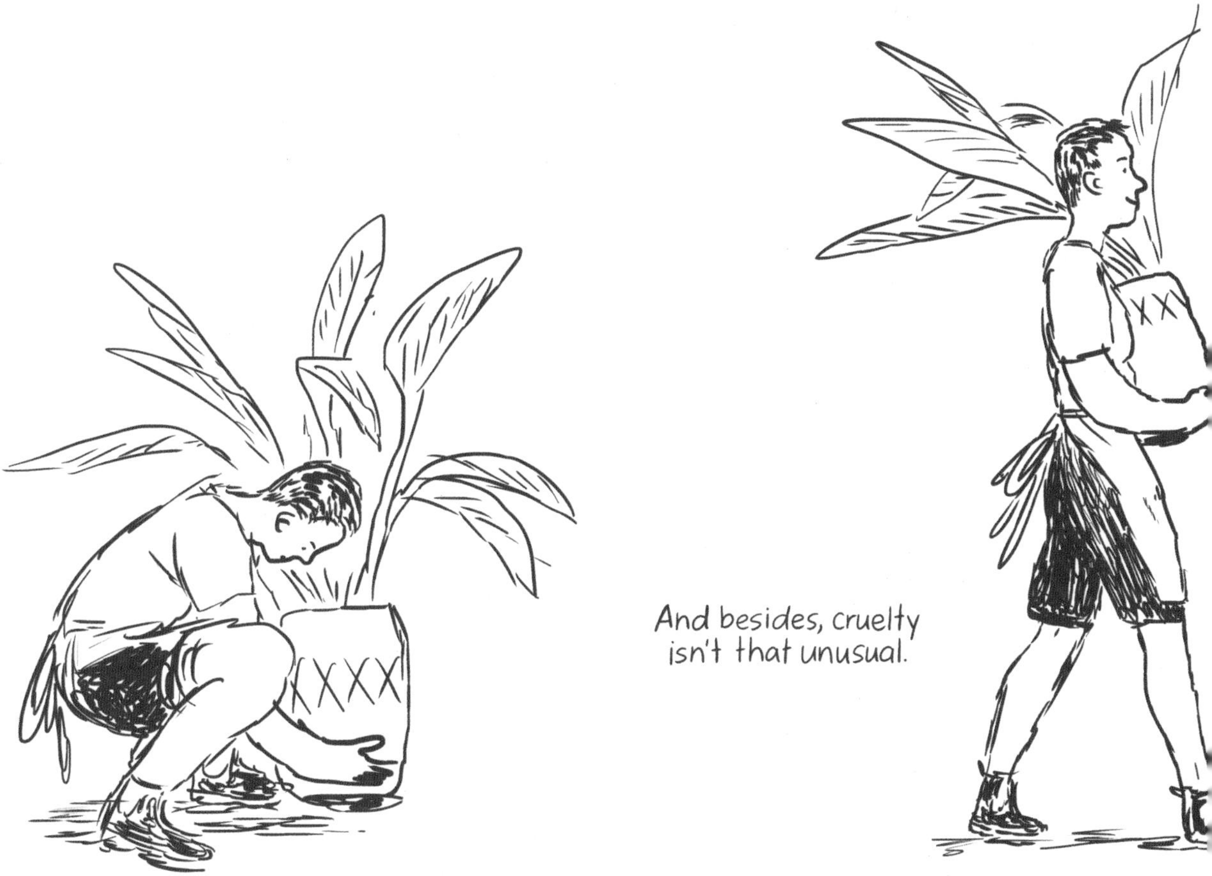
And besides, cruelty isn't that unusual.

HALF LIFE

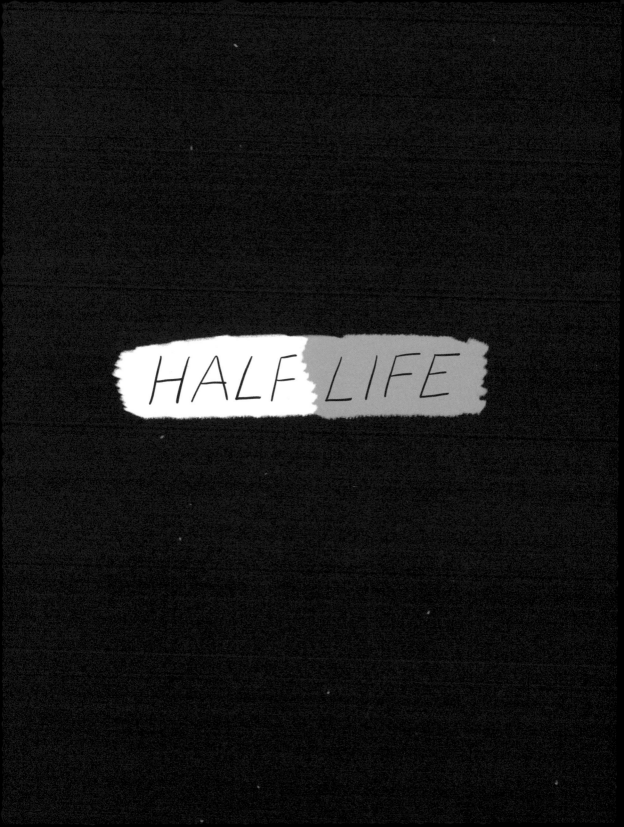

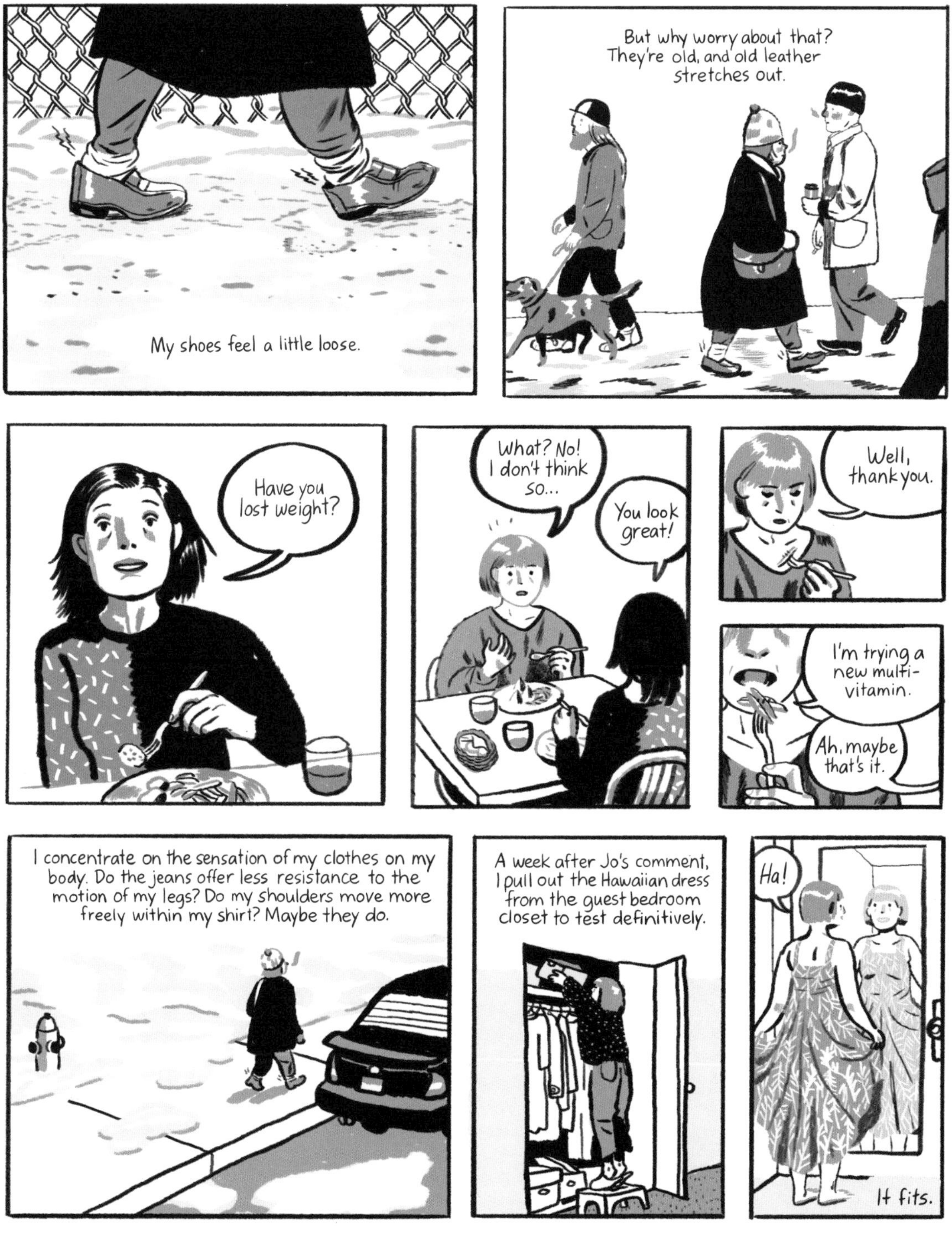

My shoes feel a little loose.
But why worry about that? They're old, and old leather stretches out.
Have you lost weight?
What? No! I don't think so...
You look great!
Well, thank you.
I'm trying a new multi-vitamin.
Ah, maybe that's it.
I concentrate on the sensation of my clothes on my body. Do the jeans offer less resistance to the motion of my legs? Do my shoulders move more freely within my shirt? Maybe they do.
A week after Jo's comment, I pull out the Hawaiian dress from the guest bedroom closet to test definitively.
Ha!
It fits.

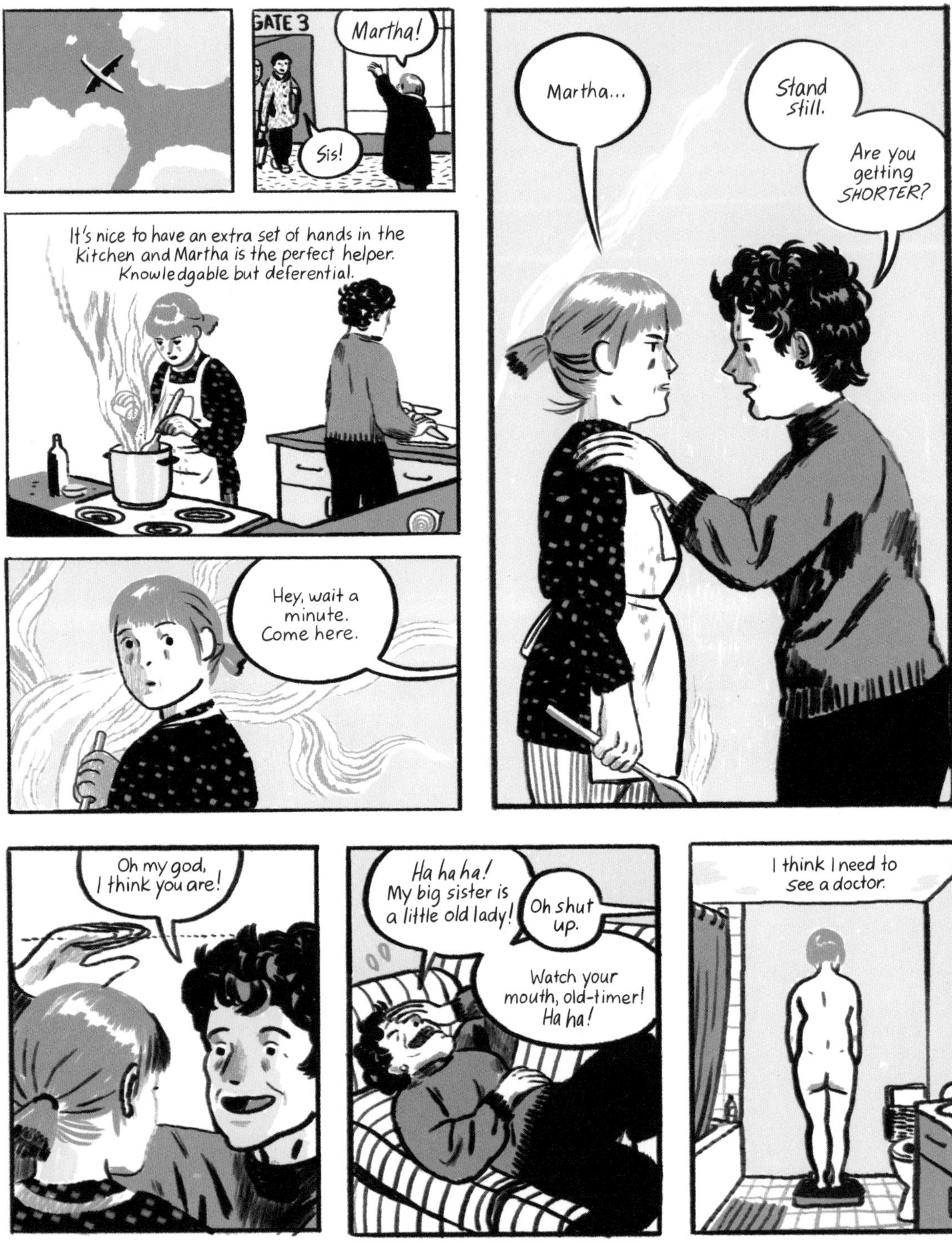
GATE 3
Martha!
Sis!
Martha...
Stand still.
Are you getting SHORTER?
It's nice to have an extra set of hands in the kitchen and Martha is the perfect helper. Knowledgable but deferential.
Hey, wait a minute. Come here.
Oh my god, I think you are!
Ha ha ha! My big sister is a little old lady!
Oh shut up.
Watch your mouth, old-timer! Ha ha!
I think I need to see a doctor.

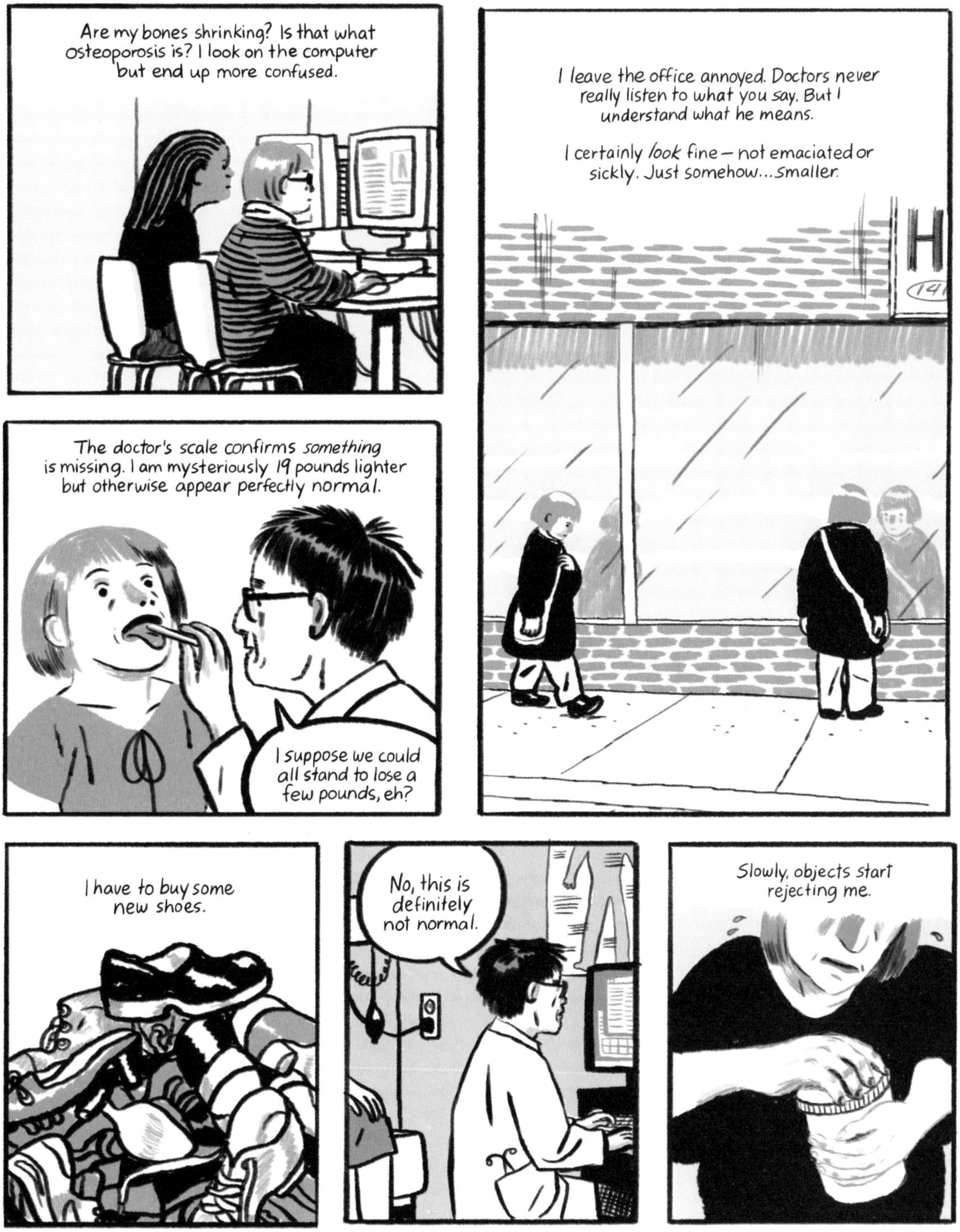
Are my bones shrinking? Is that what osteoporosis is? I look on the computer but end up more confused.
The doctor's scale confirms *something* is missing. I am mysteriously 19 pounds lighter but otherwise appear perfectly normal.
I suppose we could all stand to lose a few pounds, eh?
I leave the office annoyed. Doctors never really listen to what you say. But I understand what he means.
I certainly *look* fine — not emaciated or sickly. Just somehow... smaller.
I have to buy some new shoes.
No, this is definitely not normal.
Slowly, objects start rejecting me.

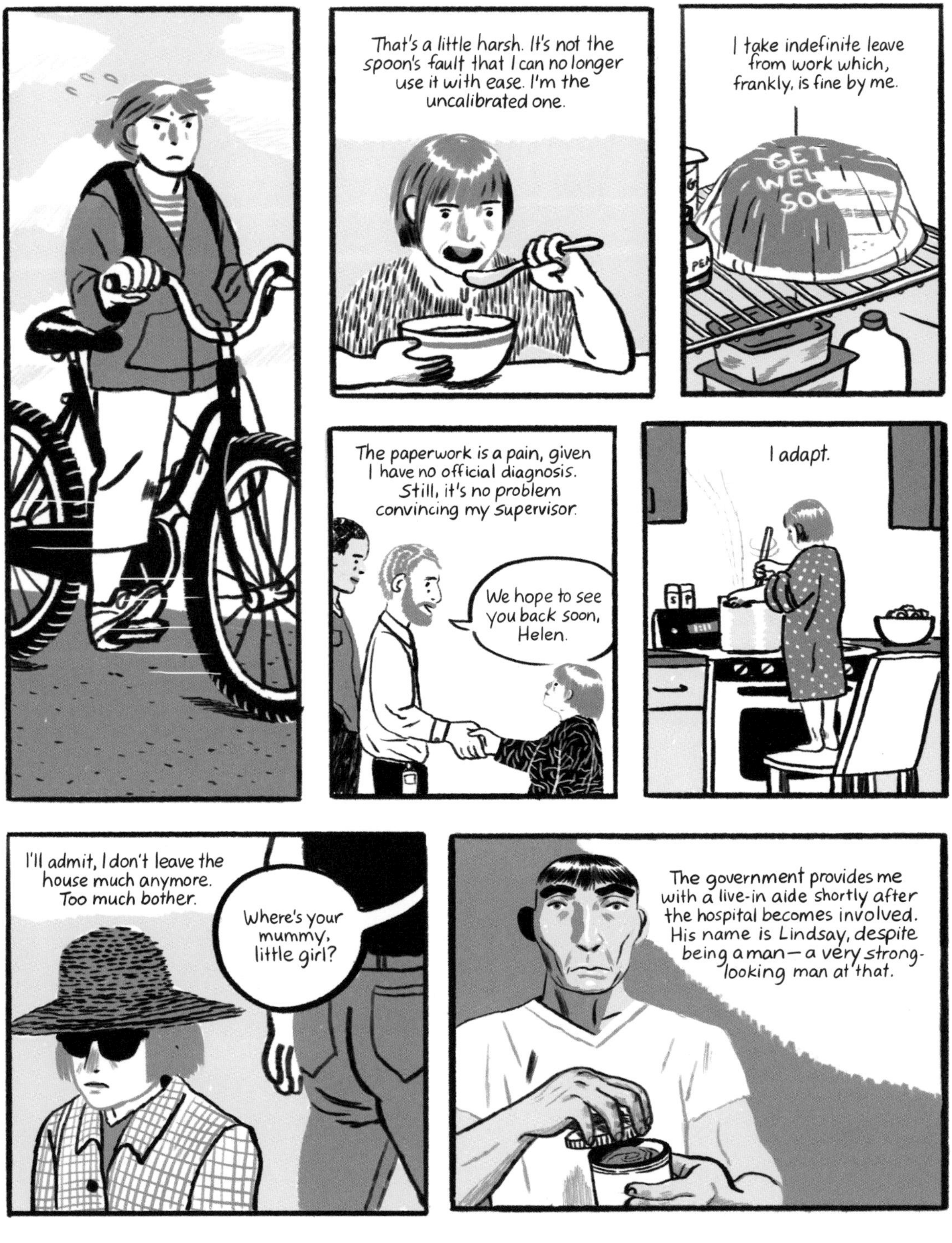
That's a little harsh. It's not the spoon's fault that I can no longer use it with ease. I'm the uncalibrated one.
I take indefinite leave from work which, frankly, is fine by me.
GET WEL SOO
The paperwork is a pain, given I have no official diagnosis. Still, it's no problem convincing my supervisor.
We hope to see you back soon, Helen.
I adapt.
I'll admit, I don't leave the house much anymore. Too much bother.
Where's your mummy, little girl?
The government provides me with a live-in aide shortly after the hospital becomes involved. His name is Lindsay, despite being a man—a very strong-looking man at that.

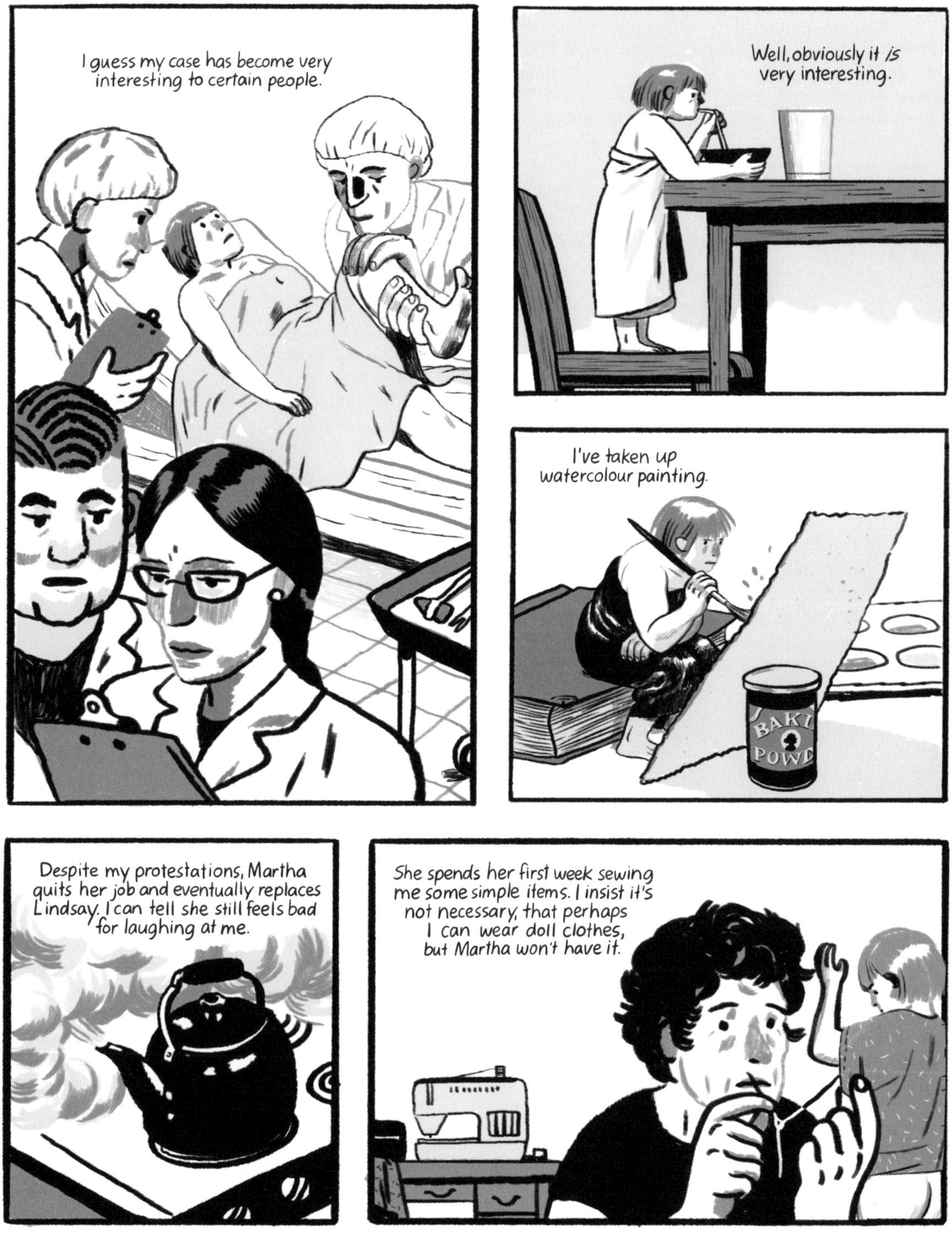

I guess my case has become very interesting to certain people.
Well, obviously it *is* very interesting.
I've taken up watercolour painting.
BAKI POWD
Despite my protestations, Martha quits her job and eventually replaces Lindsay. I can tell she still feels bad for laughing at me.
She spends her first week sewing me some simple items. I insist it's not necessary, that perhaps I can wear doll clothes, but Martha won't have it.

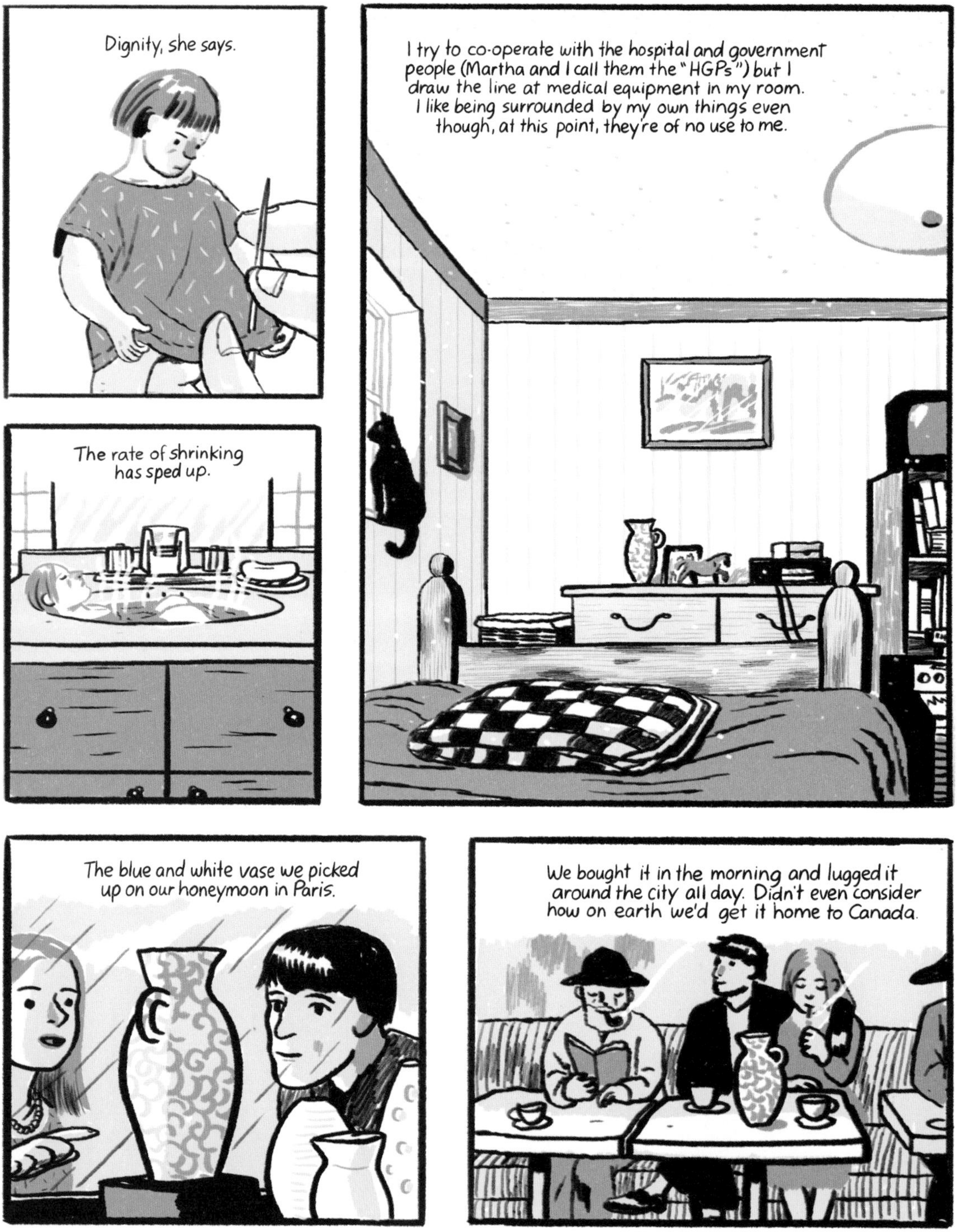

Dignity, she says.
I try to co-operate with the hospital and government people (Martha and I call them the "HGPs") but I draw the line at medical equipment in my room. I like being surrounded by my own things even though, at this point, they're of no use to me.
The rate of shrinking has sped up.
The blue and white vase we picked up on our honeymoon in Paris.
We bought it in the morning and lugged it around the city all day. Didn't even consider how on earth we'd get it home to Canada.

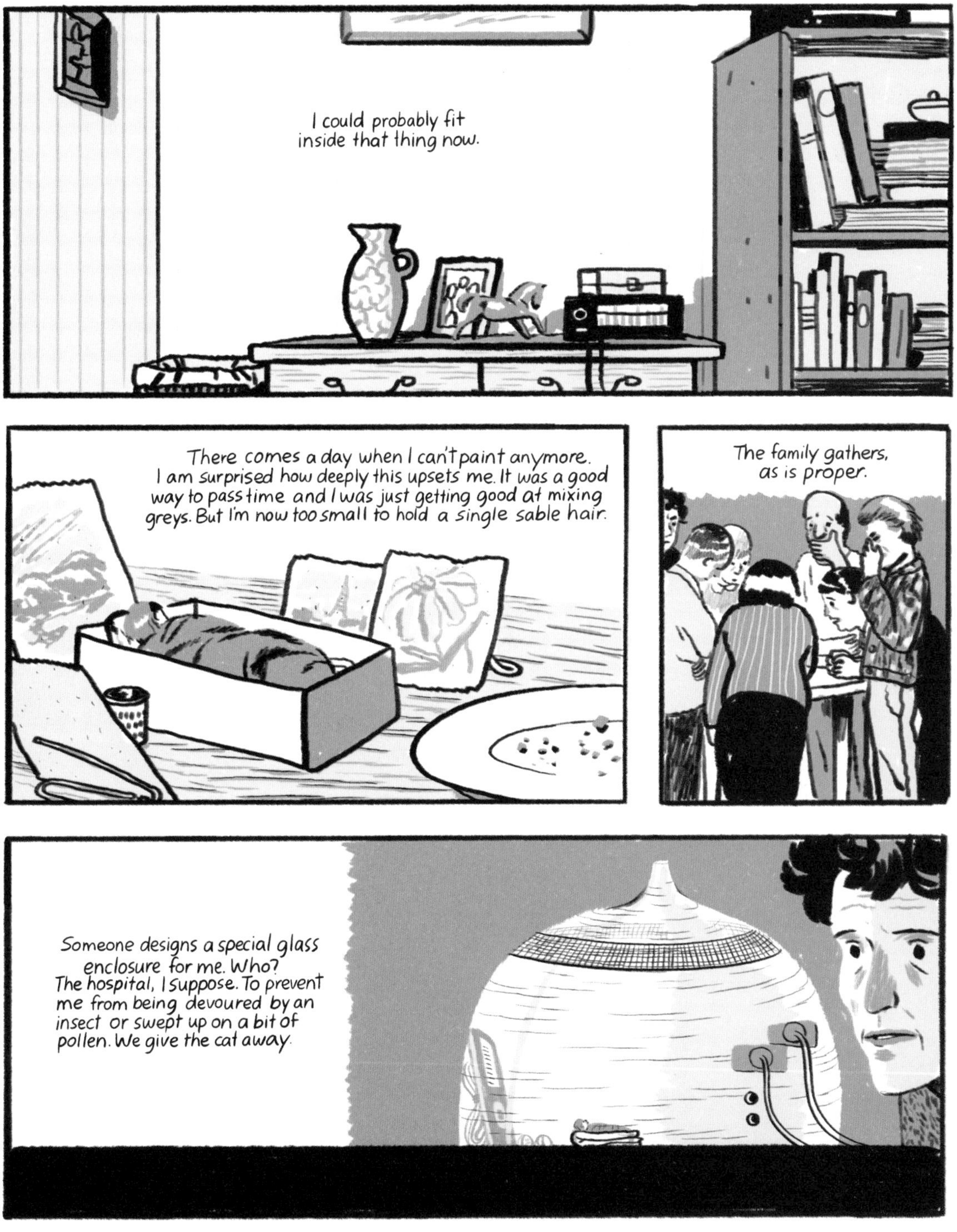
I could probably fit inside that thing now.
There comes a day when I can't paint anymore. I am surprised how deeply this upsets me. It was a good way to pass time and I was just getting good at mixing greys. But I'm now too small to hold a single sable hair.
The family gathers, as is proper.
Someone designs a special glass enclosure for me. Who? The hospital, I suppose. To prevent me from being devoured by an insect or swept up on a bit of pollen. We give the cat away.

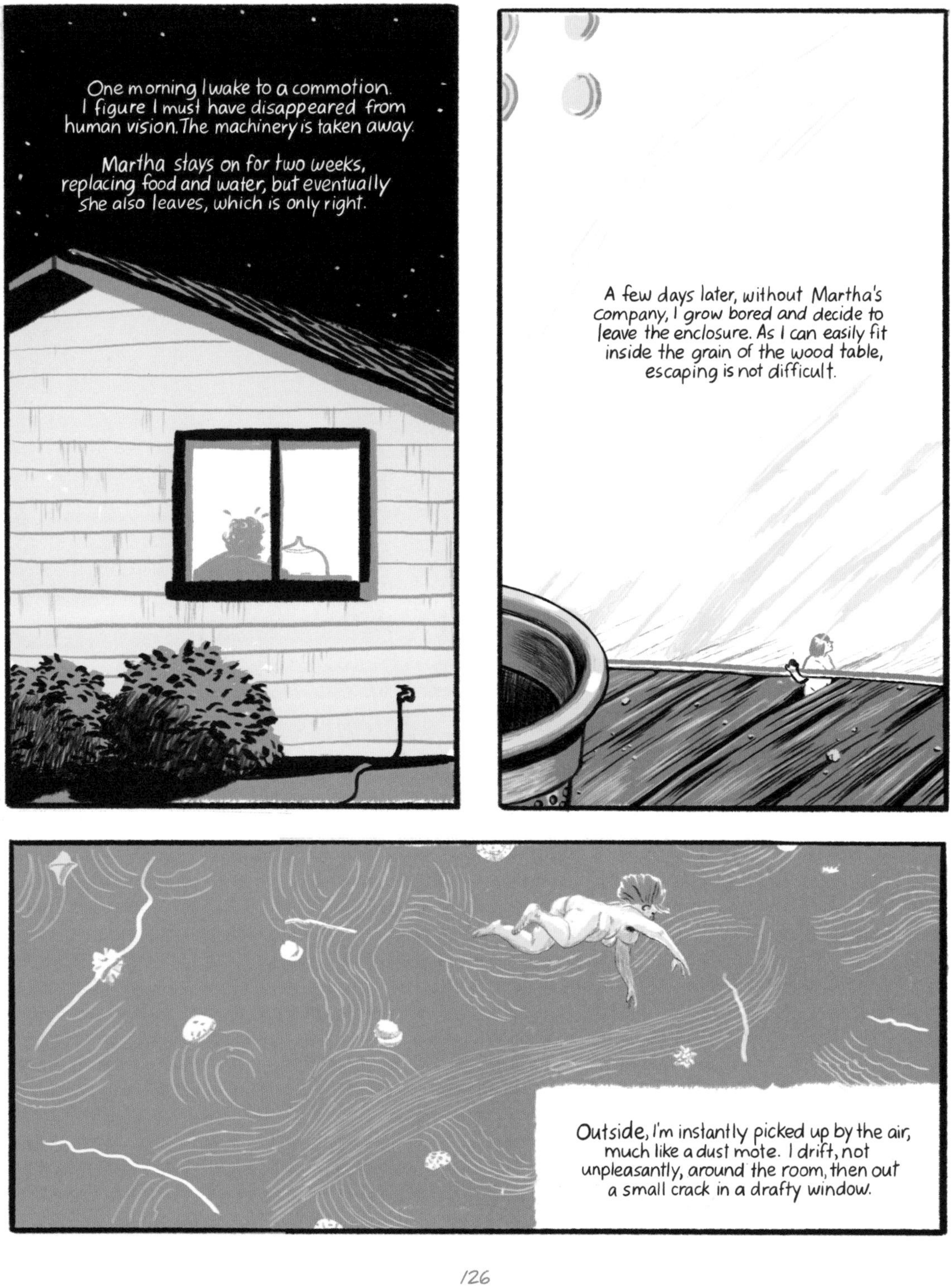
One morning I wake to a commotion. I figure I must have disappeared from human vision. The machinery is taken away.
Martha stays on for two weeks, replacing food and water, but eventually she also leaves, which is only right.
A few days later, without Martha's company, I grow bored and decide to leave the enclosure. As I can easily fit inside the grain of the wood table, escaping is not difficult.
Outside, I'm instantly picked up by the air, much like a dust mote. I drift, not unpleasantly, around the room, then out a small crack in a drafty window.

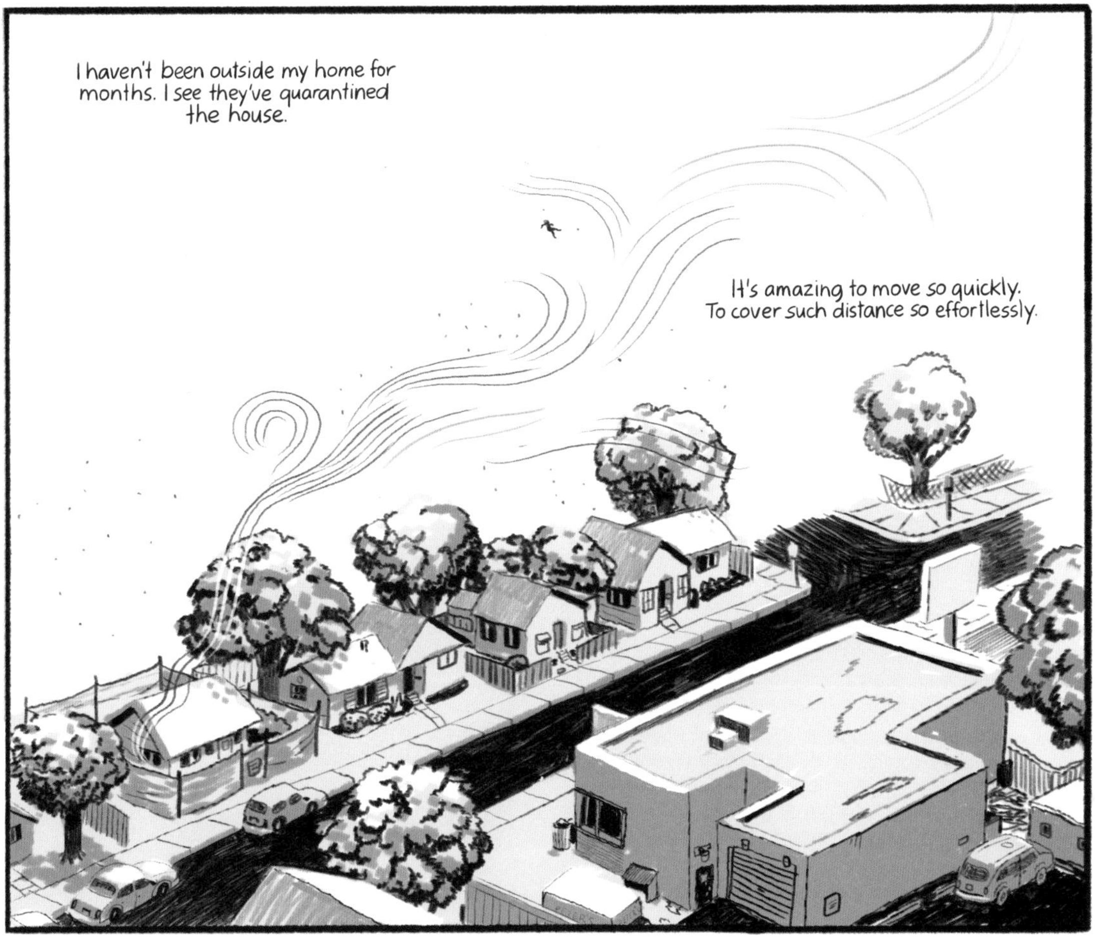
I haven't been outside my home for months. I see they've quarantined the house.
It's amazing to move so quickly. To cover such distance so effortlessly.

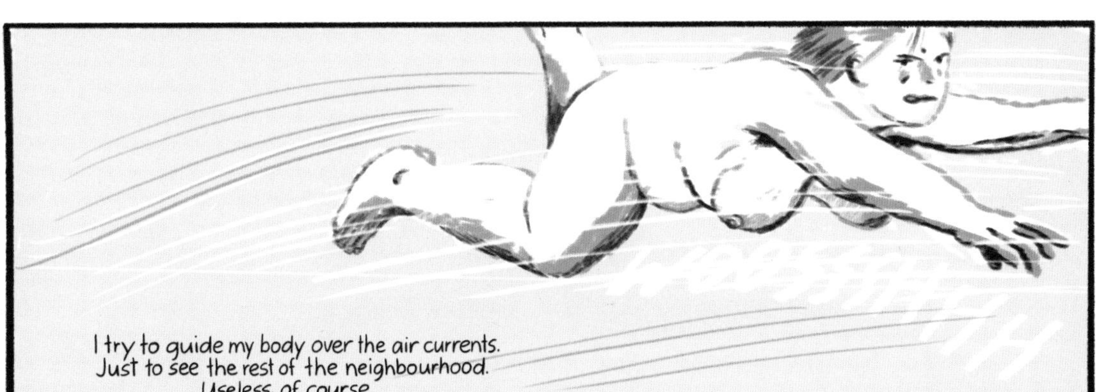
I try to guide my body over the air currents. Just to see the rest of the neighbourhood. Useless, of course.

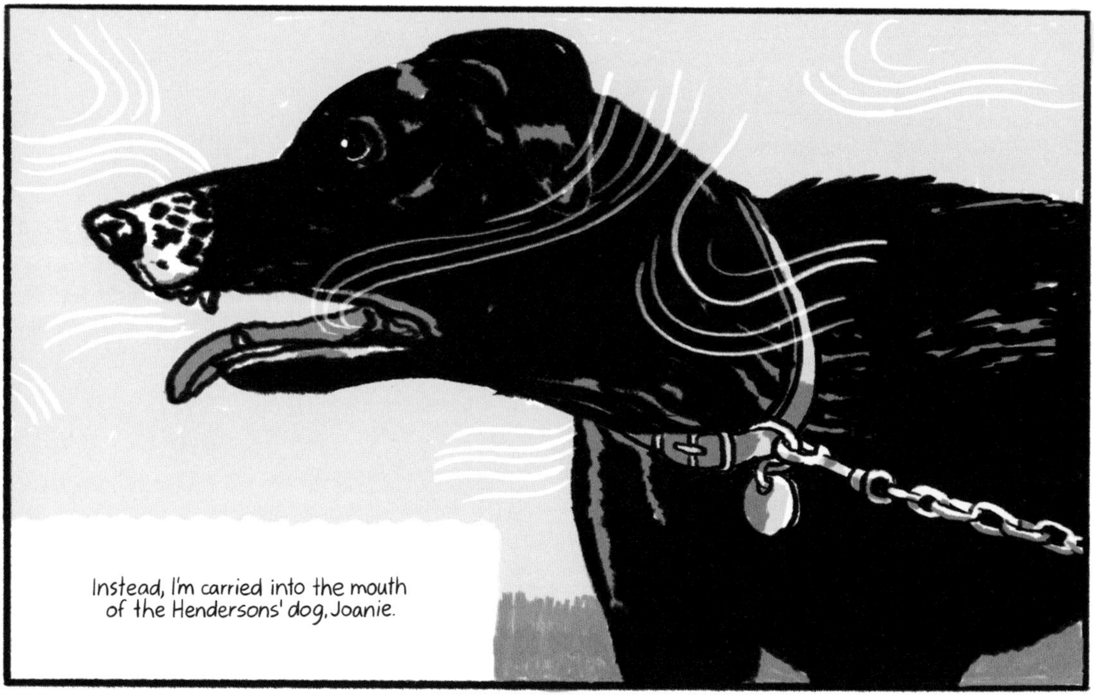
Instead, I'm carried into the mouth of the Hendersons' dog, Joanie.

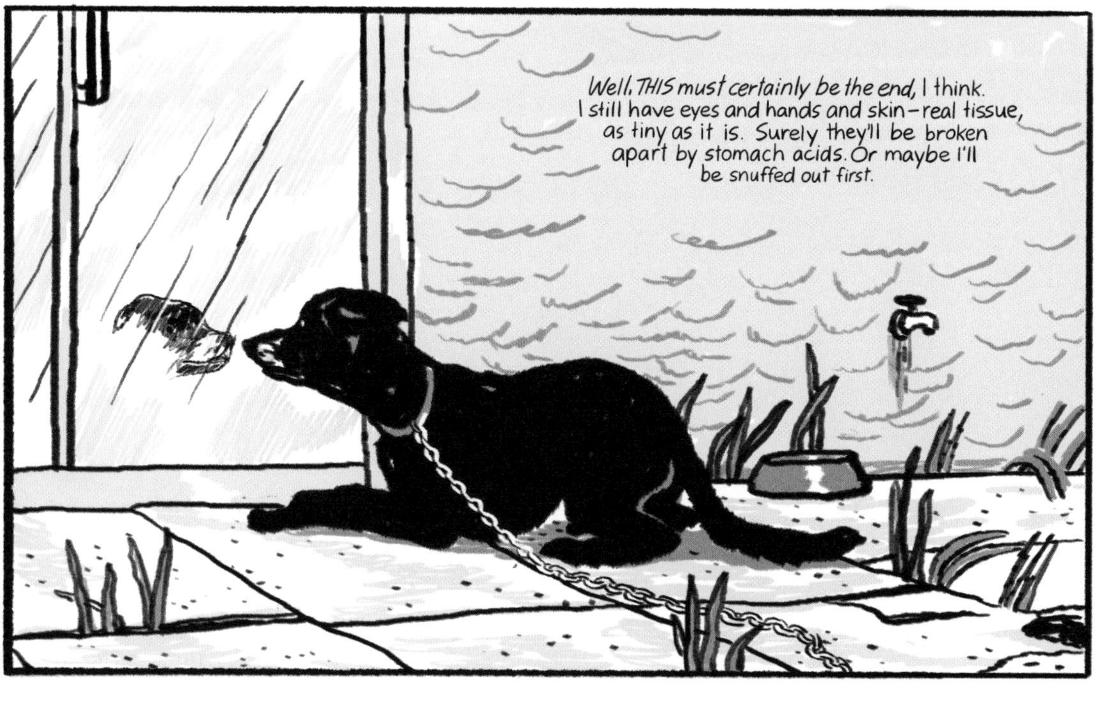
Well, THIS must certainly be the end, I think. I still have eyes and hands and skin—real tissue, as tiny as it is. Surely they'll be broken apart by stomach acids. Or maybe I'll be snuffed out first.

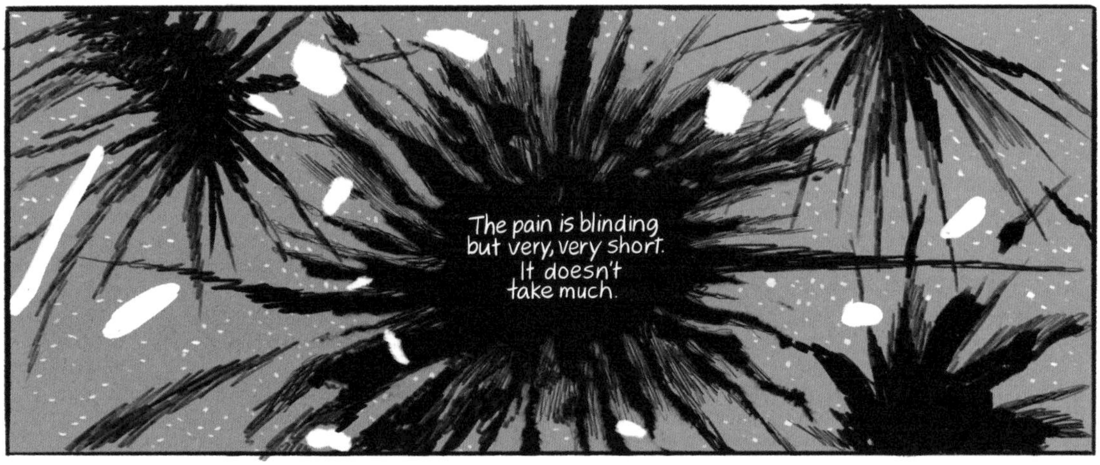
The pain is blinding but very, very short. It doesn't take much.

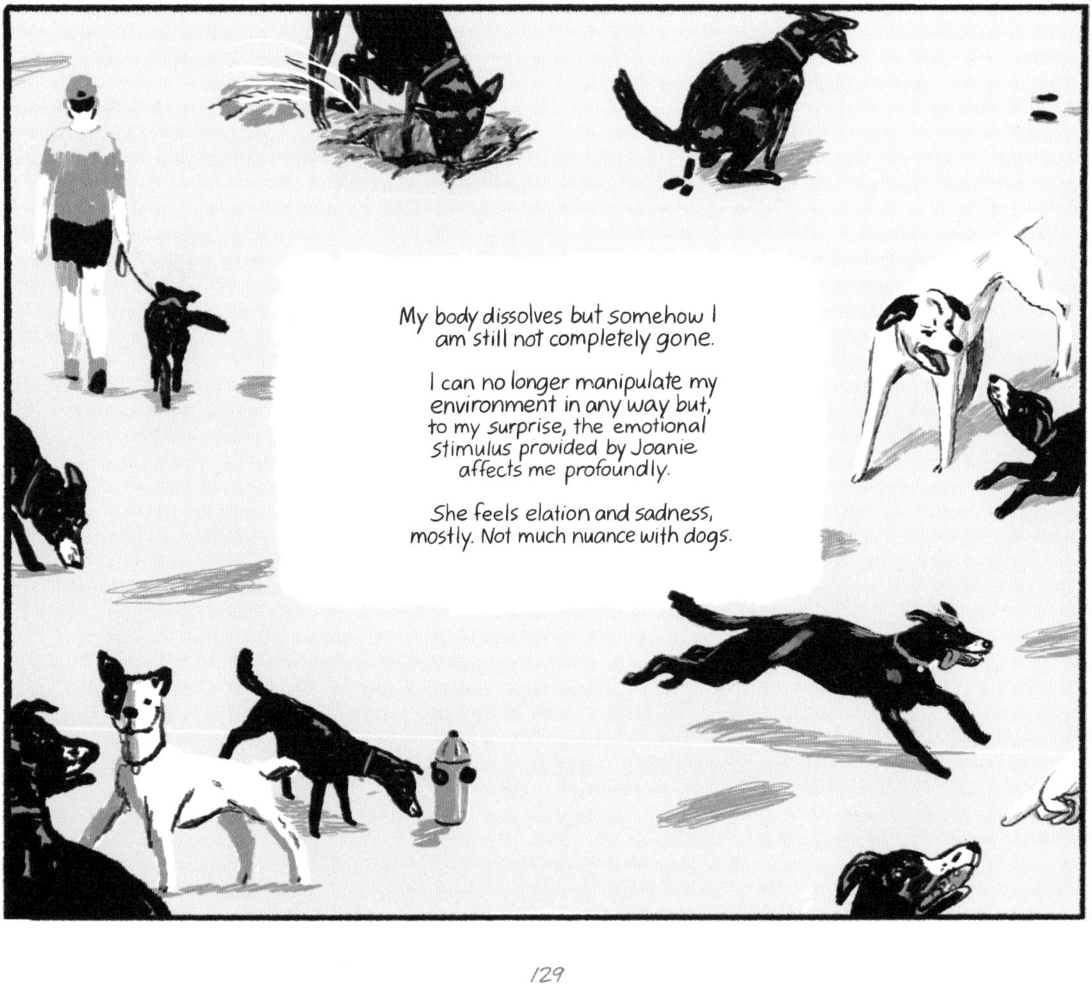
My body dissolves but somehow I am still not completely gone.
I can no longer manipulate my environment in any way but, to my surprise, the emotional stimulus provided by Joanie affects me profoundly.
She feels elation and sadness, mostly. Not much nuance with dogs.

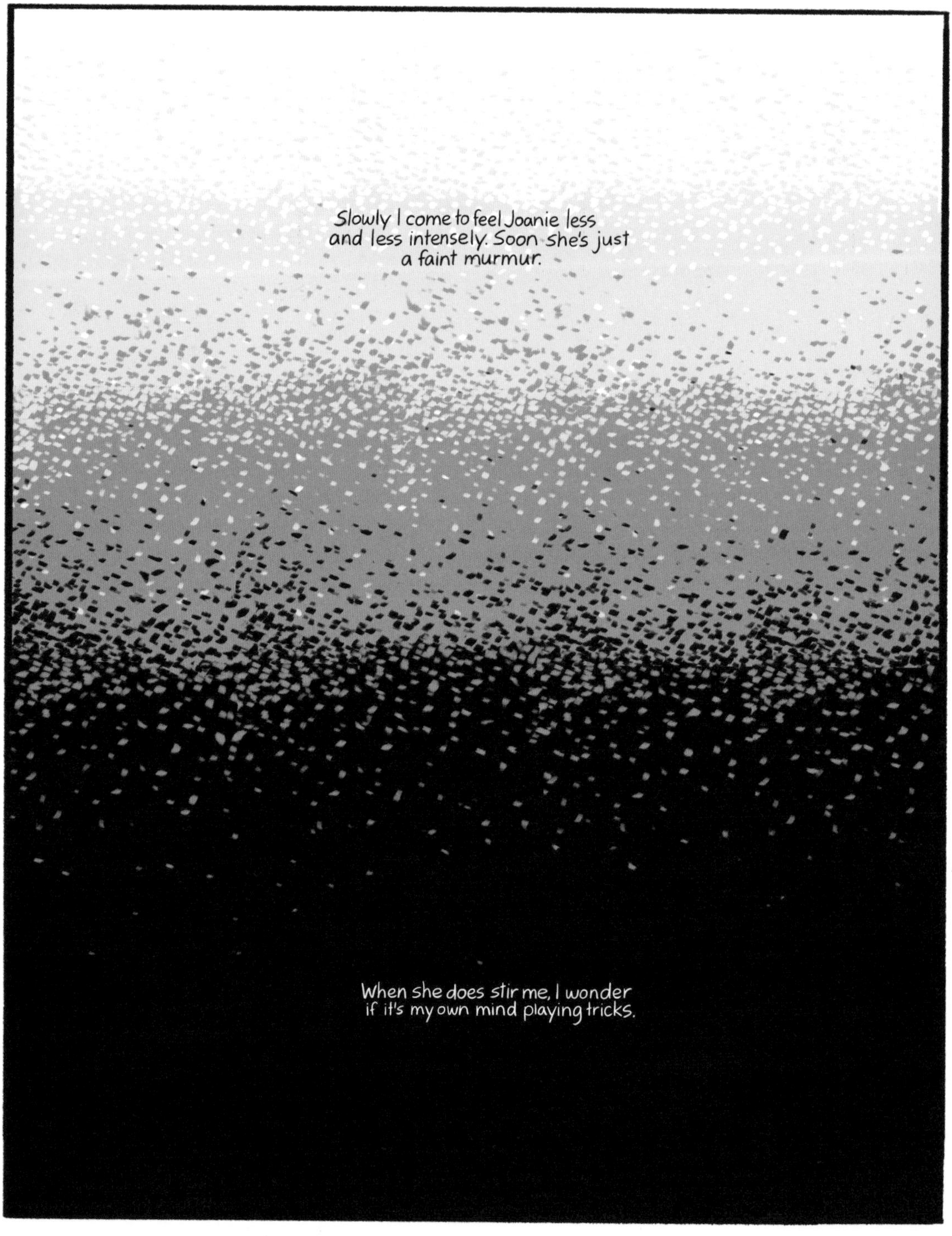
Slowly I come to feel Joanie less and less intensely. Soon she's just a faint murmur.
When she does stir me, I wonder if it's my own mind playing tricks.

Darla!

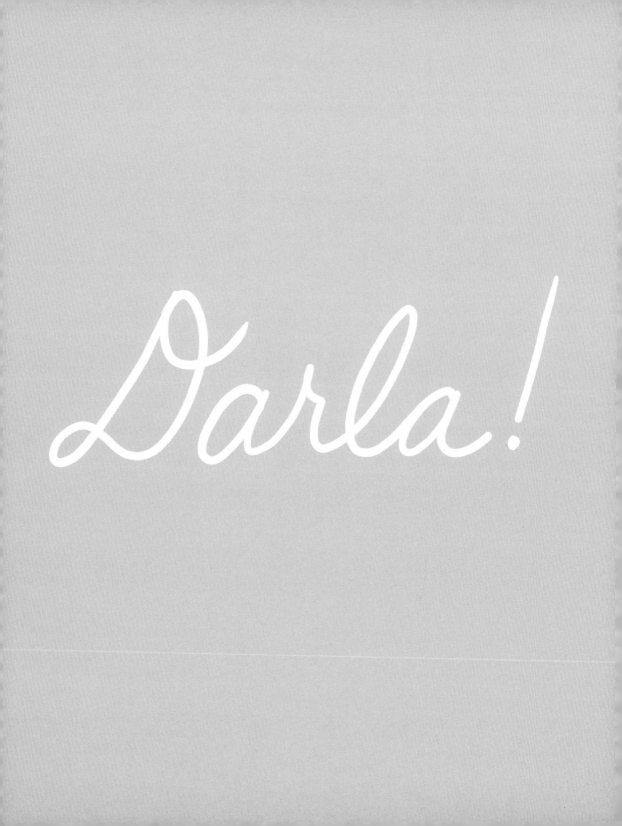

Perhaps it was a flawed idea in retrospect.

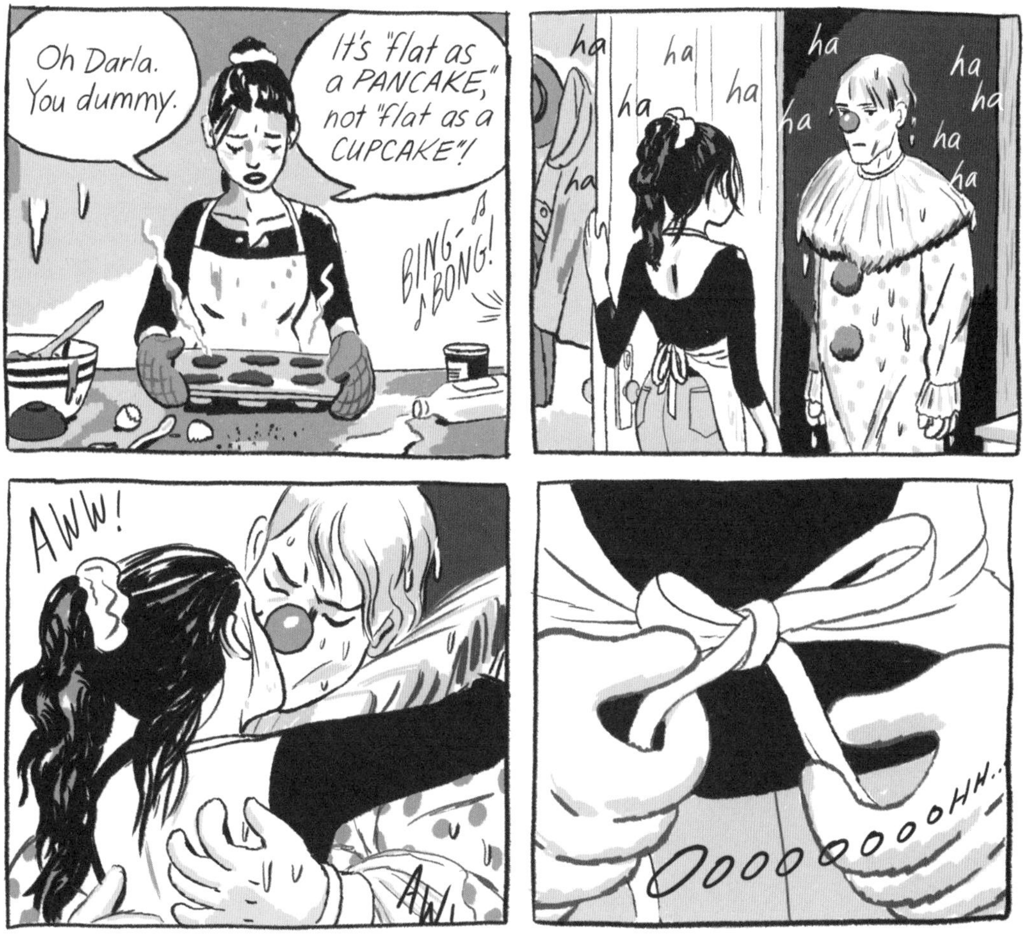

Oh Darla. You dummy.
It's "flat as a PANCAKE," not "flat as a CUPCAKE"!
BING-BONG!
ha ha ha ha ha ha ha ha ha ha ha
AWW!
AW!
OOOOOOOOOOHH...

It was a different time.
You could never make something like it now.
The whole culture has become so chickenshit.

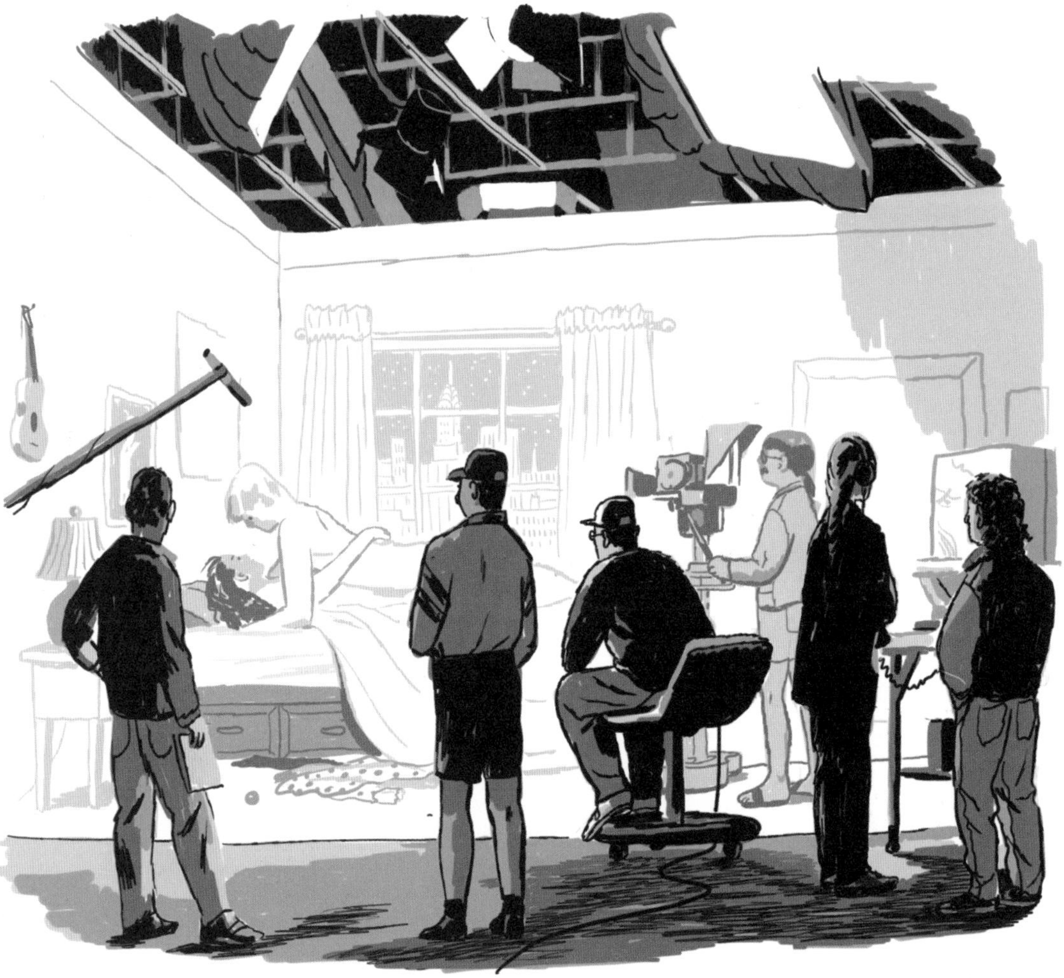

The idea of a sitcom-porno was conceived by me and Ron Frances, who I'd met in the writers' room of "Stages," which had been canned the previous year.

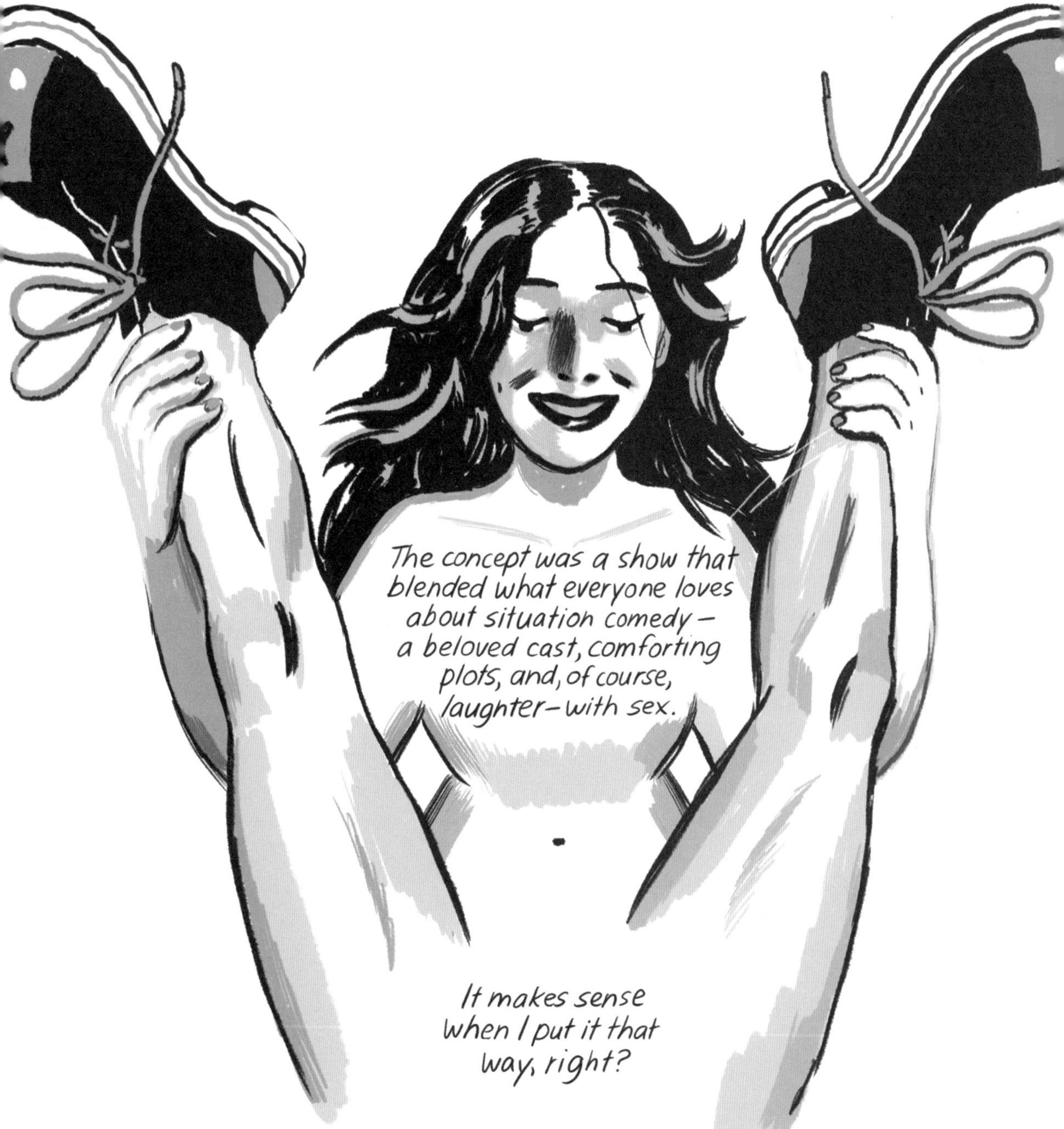
The concept was a show that blended what everyone loves about situation comedy — a beloved cast, comforting plots, and, of course, laughter — with sex.
It makes sense when I put it that way, right?

Well, what can I say.
It was the '90s and we were
doing a lot of cocaine.

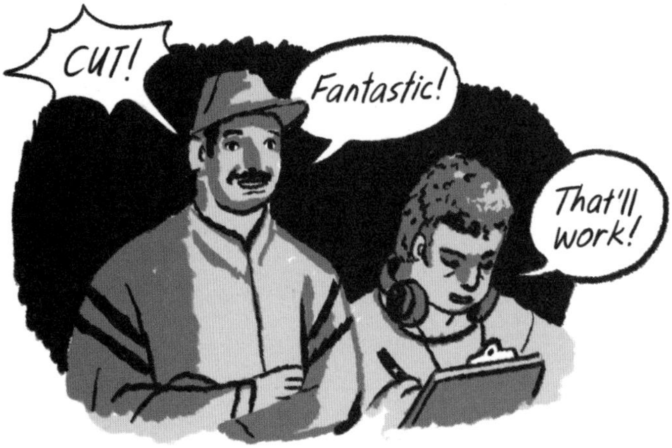
CUT!
Fantastic!
That'll work!

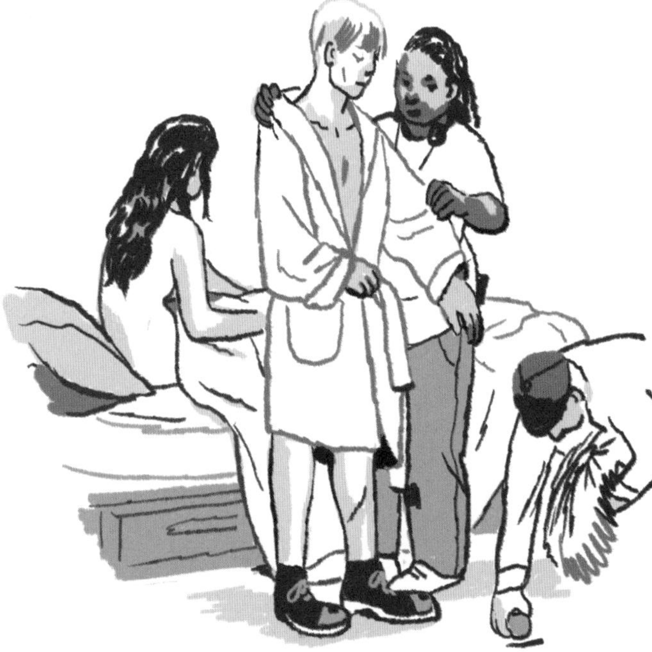

God, those shoots were fun.
We could not stop laughing.

Darla Nakamura starred as Darla, a young Midwestern single just arrived in New York City.

♪(theme music)♪
♪(theme music)♪
♪(theme music)♪

Growing up, the excitement of the big city. You know the story. You love it!

Of course, she gets into lots of adventures...

and a few tight spots. Haha.

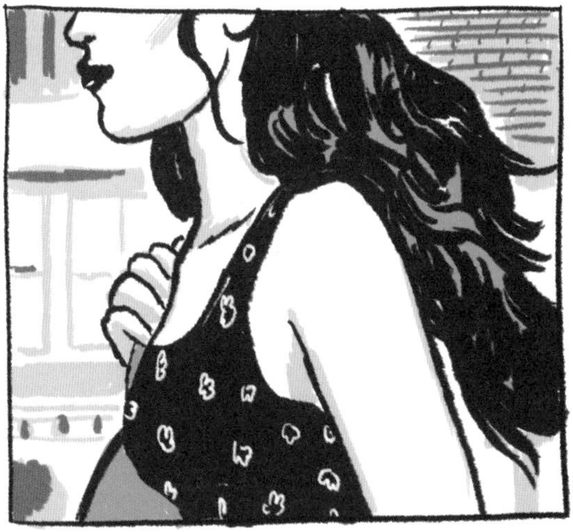

It was really sexy stuff. Though, all in all, pretty tame. Darla, both the character and the real girl, was wholesome. We were aiming for a general audience.

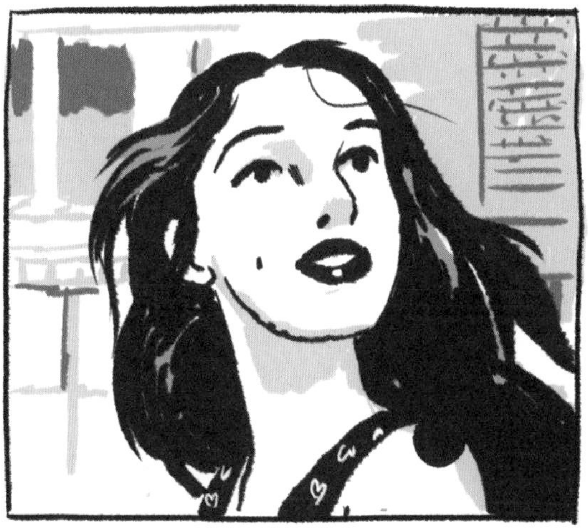

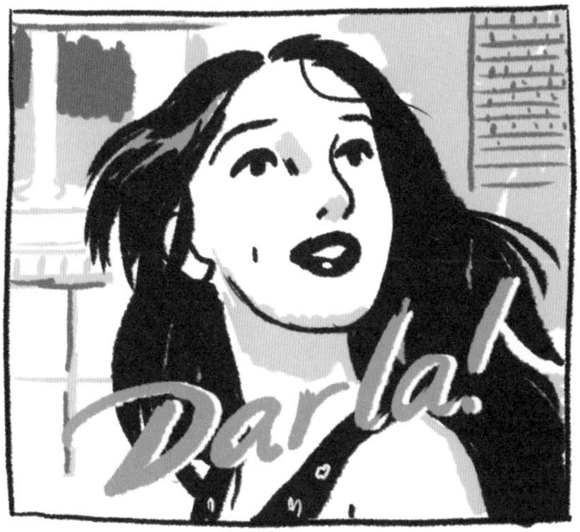
Darla!

Everyone thought Darla Nakamura was going to be a real star.

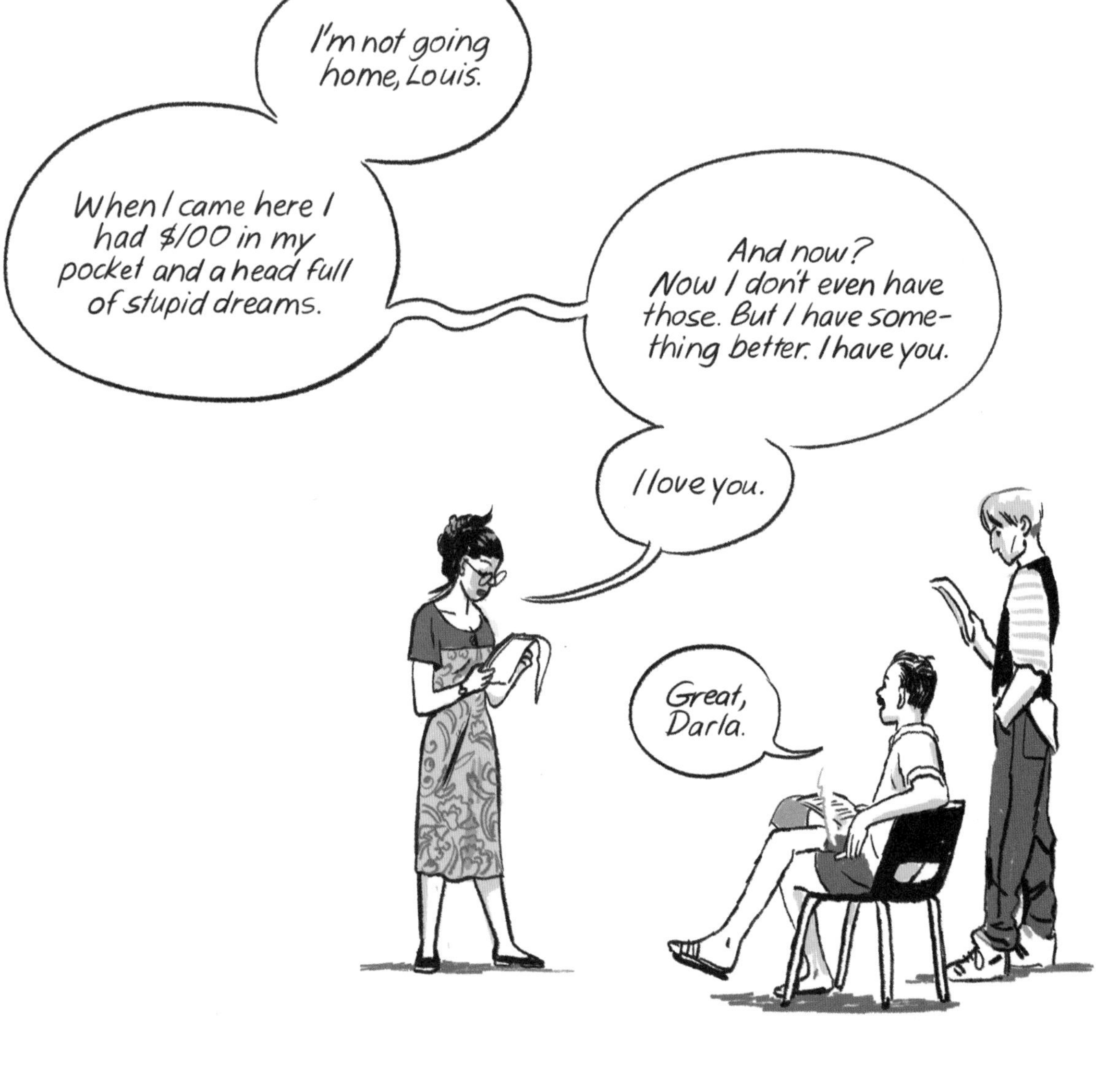
I'm not going home, Louis.
When I came here I had $100 in my pocket and a head full of stupid dreams.
And now? Now I don't even have those. But I have something better. I have you.
I love you.
Great, Darla.

The pilot was not well-received. We managed to squeak into production anyway, after Ron and I agreed to work on the script.

In my opinion, it hardly mattered. Interest was through the roof. People were very curious.

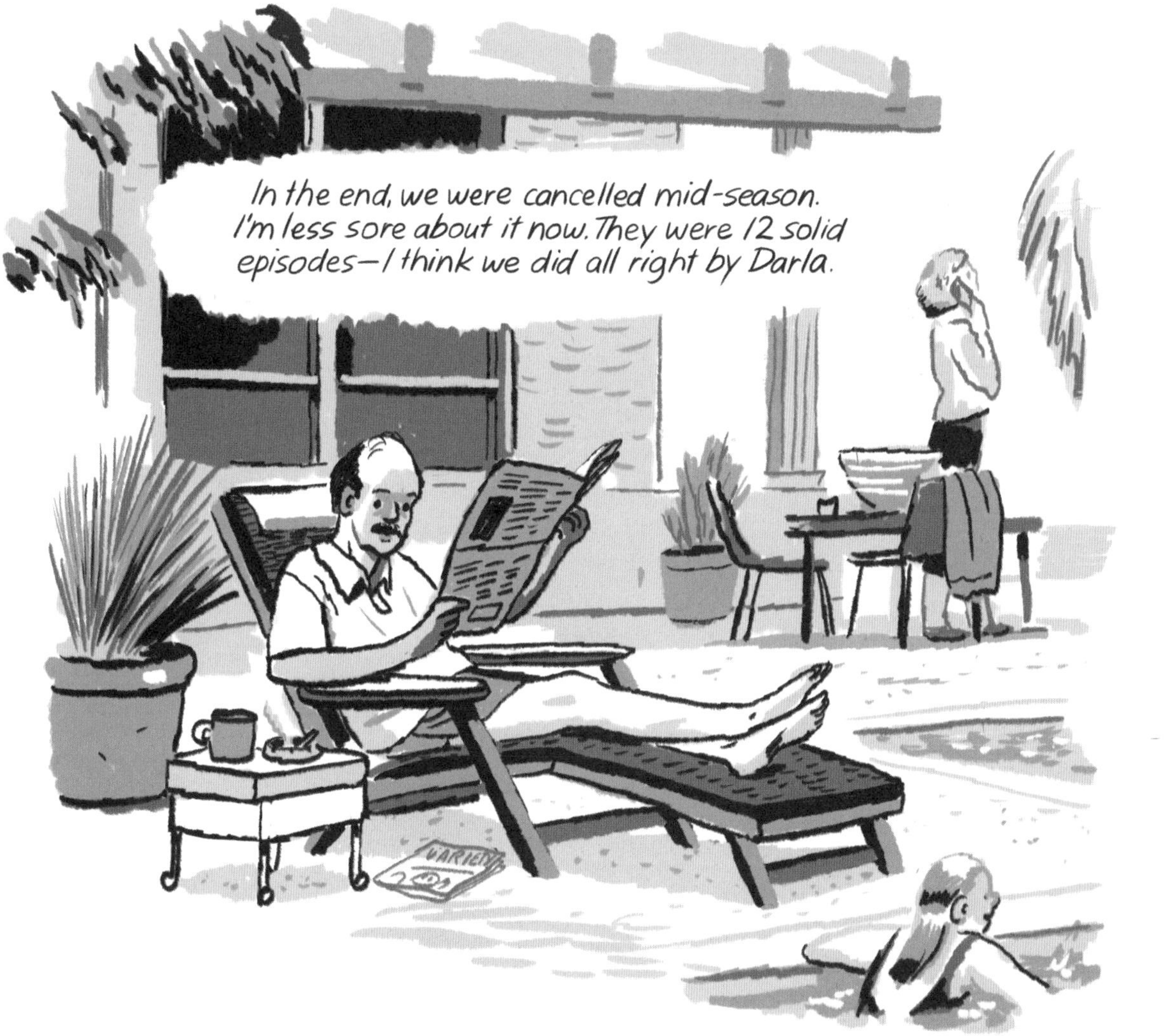
In the end, we were cancelled mid-season. I'm less sore about it now. They were 12 solid episodes—I think we did all right by Darla.

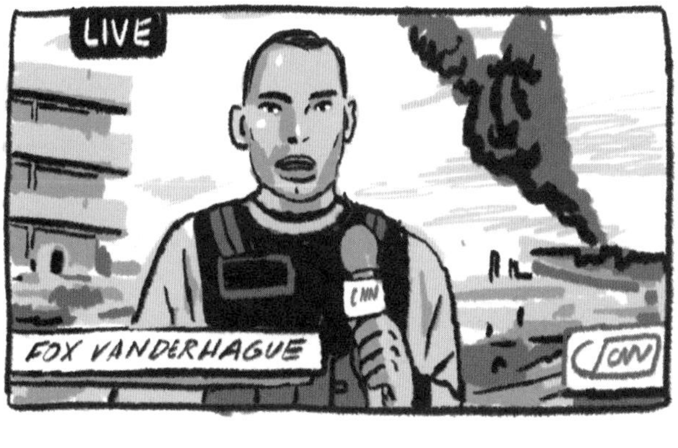
LIVE
FOX VANDERHAGUE
CNN

Hey, I bet you didn't know we have famous alumni! Fox Vanderhague played Fabian in episode four.

We had plans to extend his role later in the season. Alas.

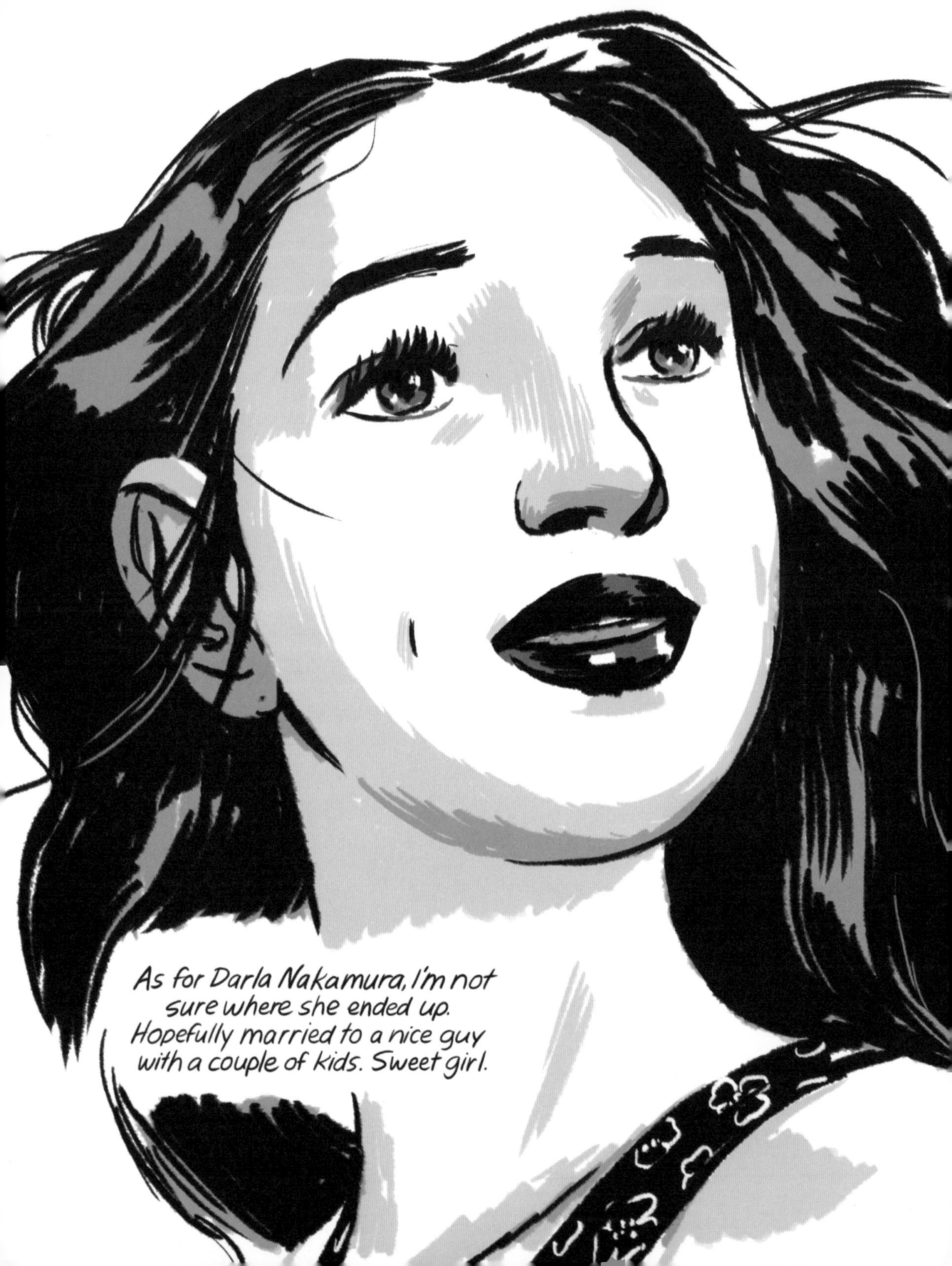
As for Darla Nakamura, I'm not sure where she ended up. Hopefully married to a nice guy with a couple of kids. Sweet girl.

A few years ago, someone uploaded the series onto Google and we got a little attention online.

I'm tickled people are connecting with the show. I even get asked to go to fan conferences sometimes.

Fans of what, I'm not sure exactly. Maybe the Internet in general.

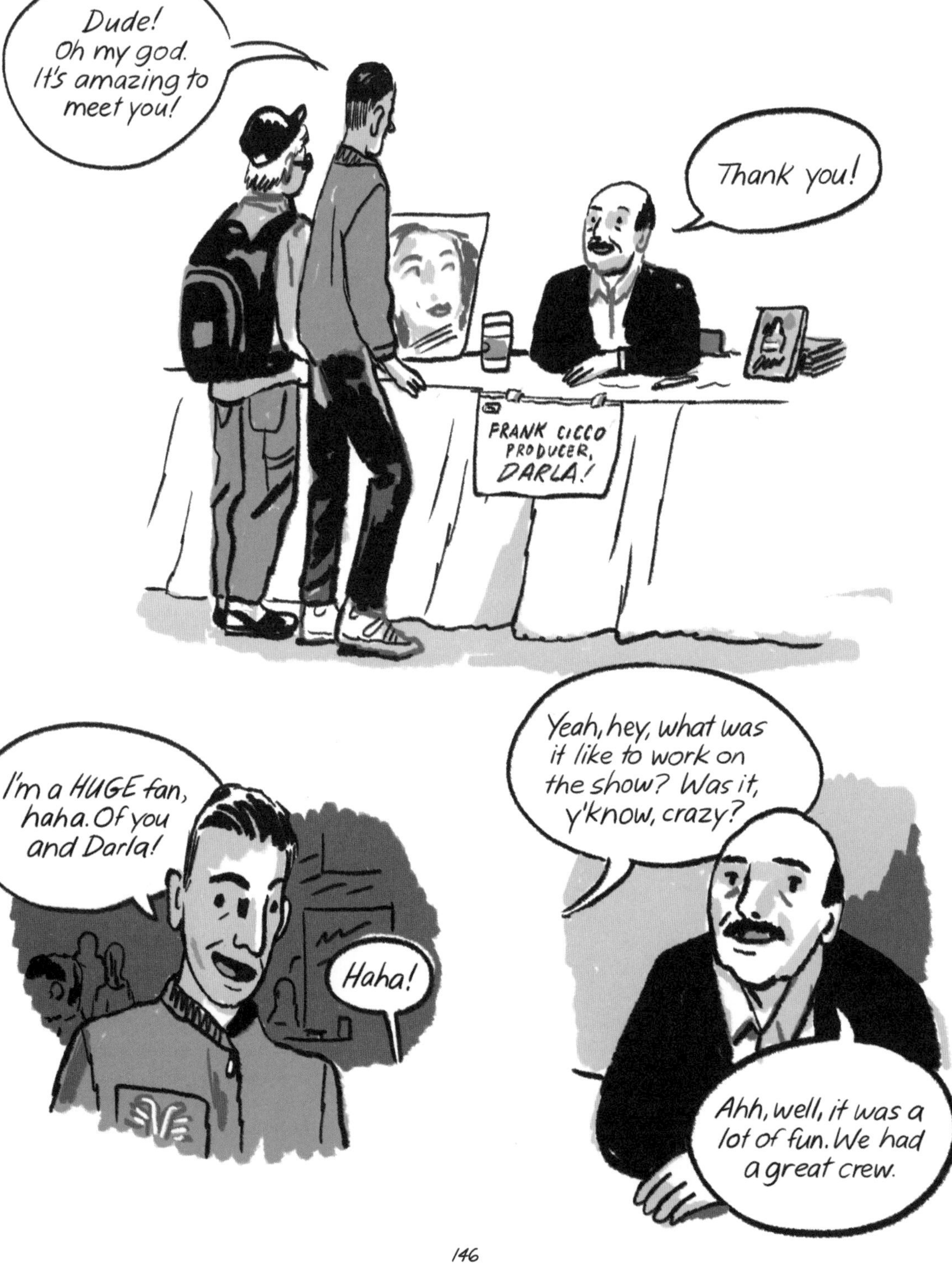
Dude! Oh my god. It's amazing to meet you!
Thank you!
FRANK CICCO PRODUCER, DARLA!
I'm a HUGE fan, haha. Of you and Darla!
Haha!
Yeah, hey, what was it like to work on the show? Was it, y'know, crazy?
Ahh, well, it was a lot of fun. We had a great crew.

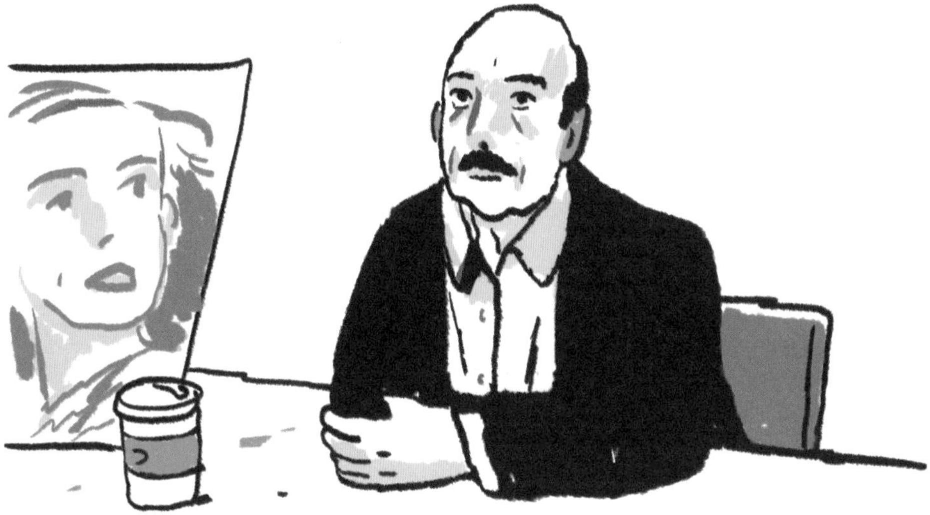

Don't get me wrong, I'm grateful. I can't say I relate to the kids I meet, however. I don't like some of what they say about "Darla".

Maybe it's their attitude. A little too snide, too winky-winky.

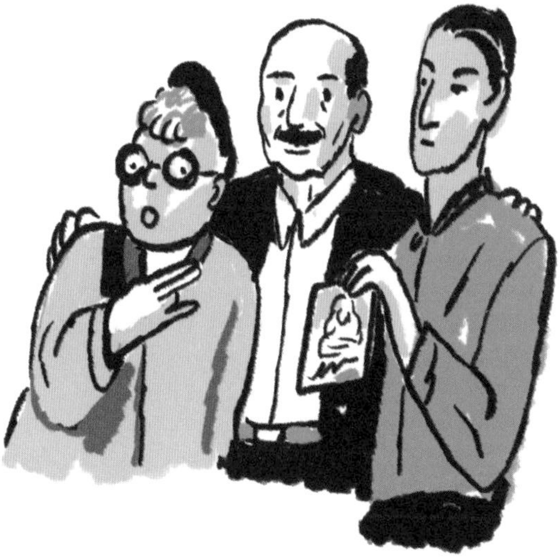

I never thought we were making high art, but we put a lot of heart into that show.

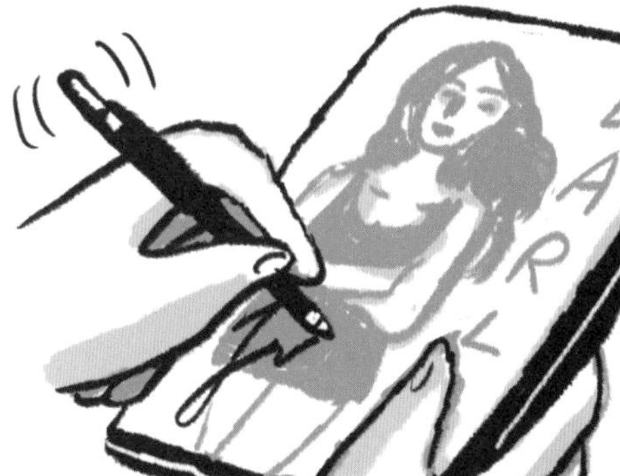
DARL

There's nothing wrong with being sincere.

bedbug

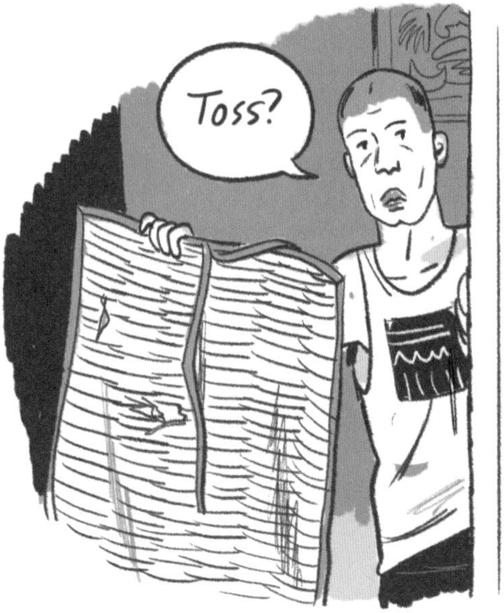
Toss?

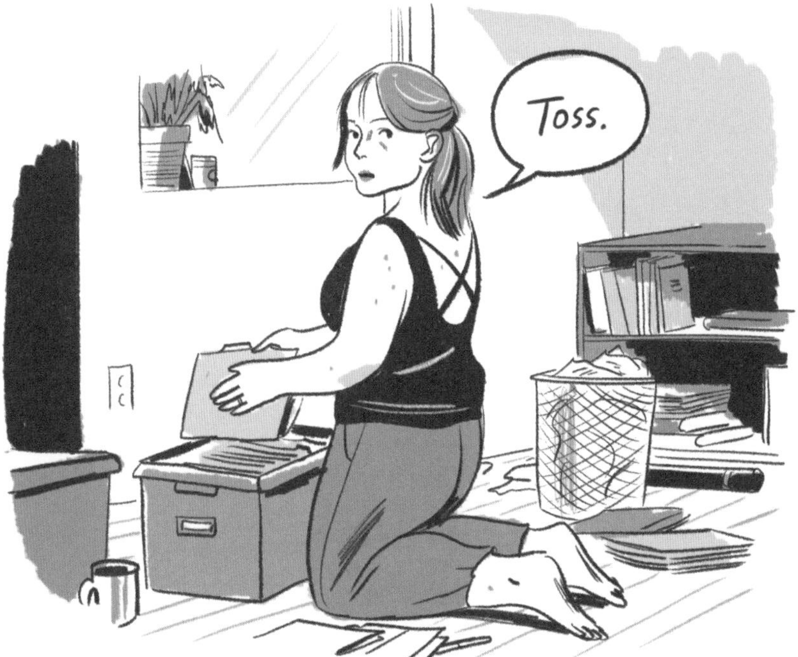
Toss.

I got bitten first, on my lower leg. We assumed mosquitos—Jeremy closed the bedroom window. But soon, we both had bites in the tell-tale rows.

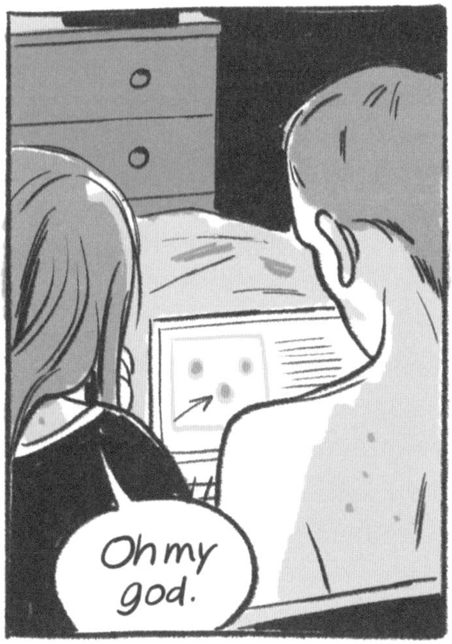
Oh my god.

We stripped the bed. No sign, not even a hollow molted shell. The Internet said that was common, though.

We couldn't tell our coworkers. People treat you like you have Ebola, not that I blame them. But I swear, we were being responsible.

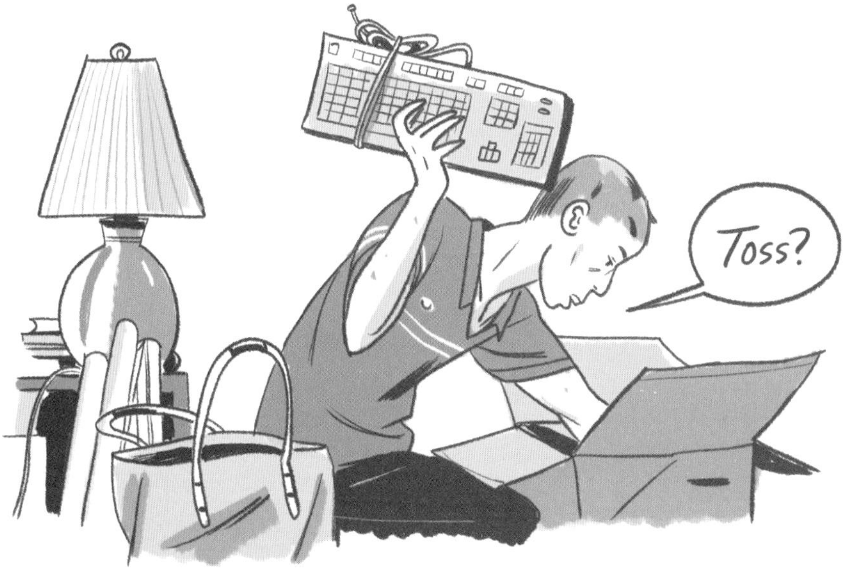
Toss?

Despite the warming weather, we continued to wear pants and long-sleeved shirts whenever we weren't home.

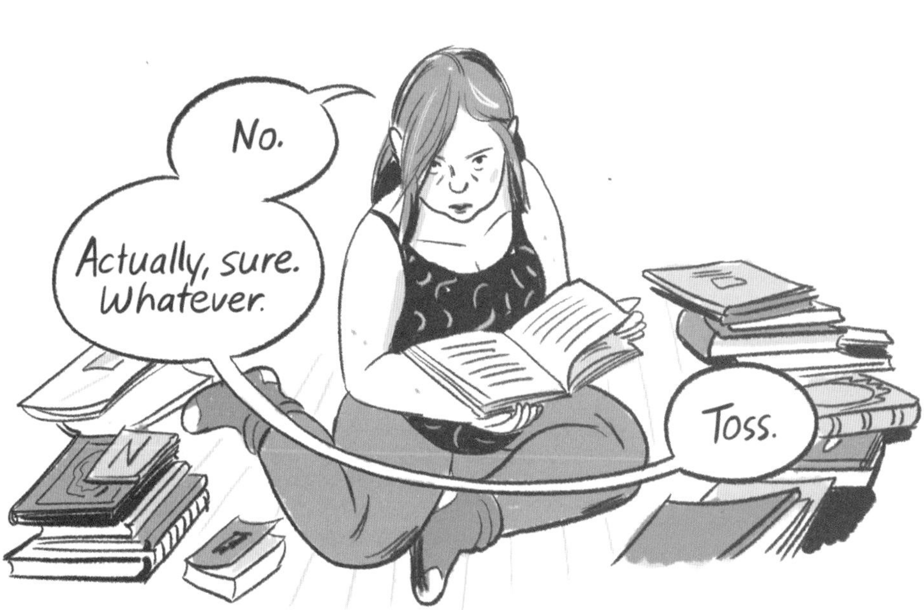
No.
Actually, sure. Whatever.
Toss.

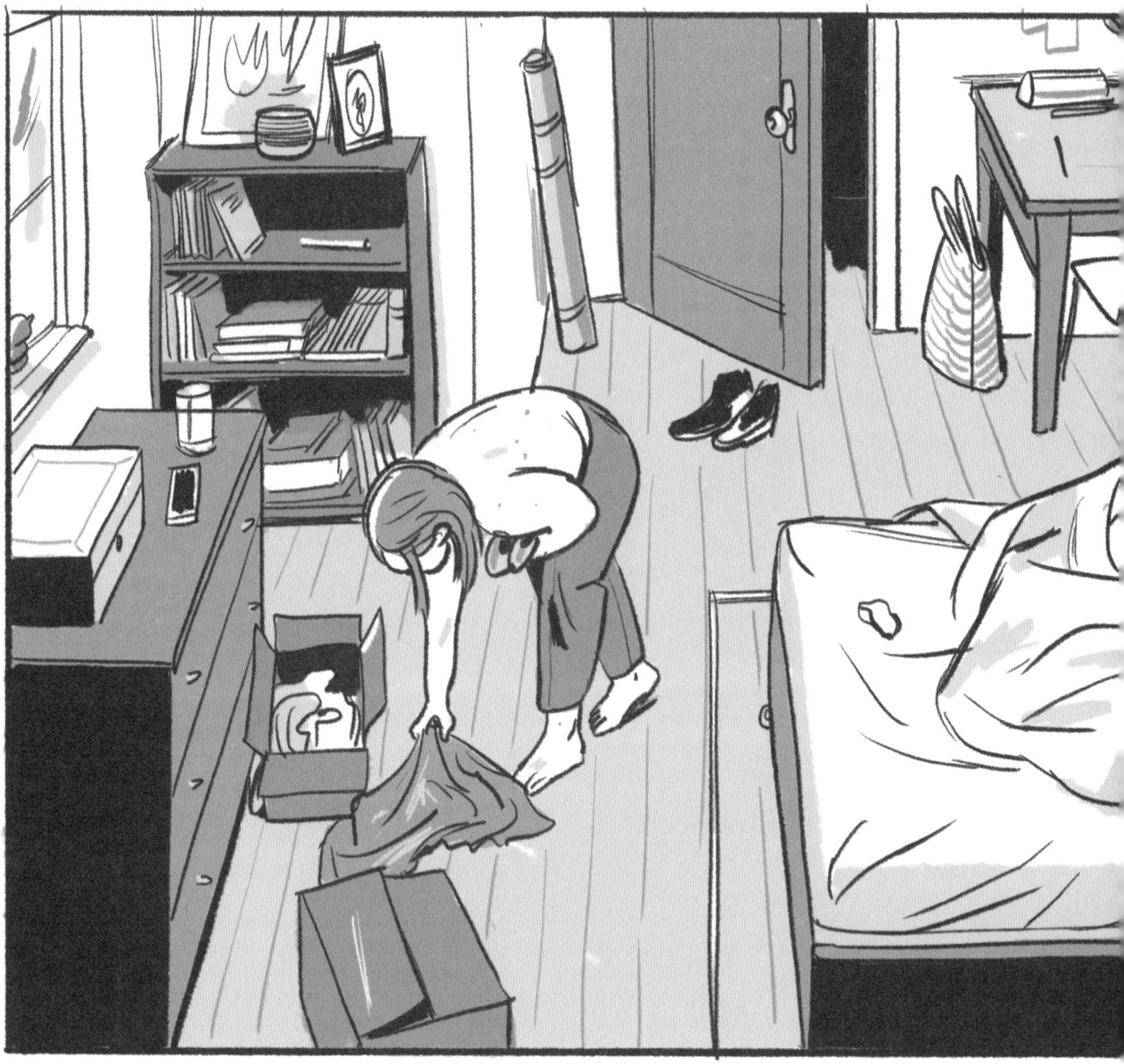

Where could we have gotten them? Neither of us had travelled recently. We hadn't had a houseguest in over a year.

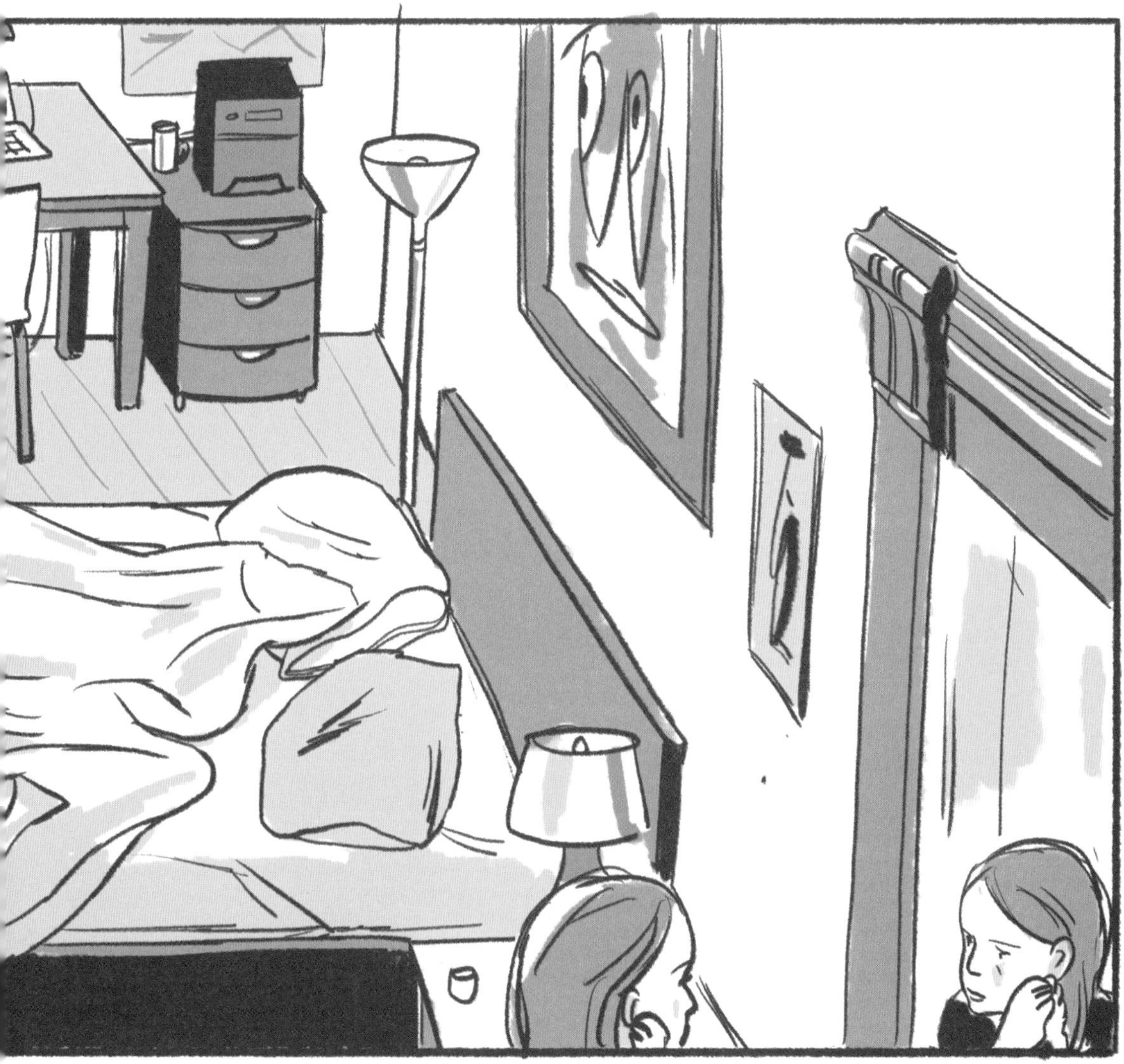

They're everywhere now, though.
Fancy hotels, park benches, train
seats. It's impossible to know for sure.

Greg was a T.A. in my English 111-8 class.
We usually fucked at his shitty apartment near campus, but sometimes other places too.
Only after he graduated, of course.

I'm not stupid.

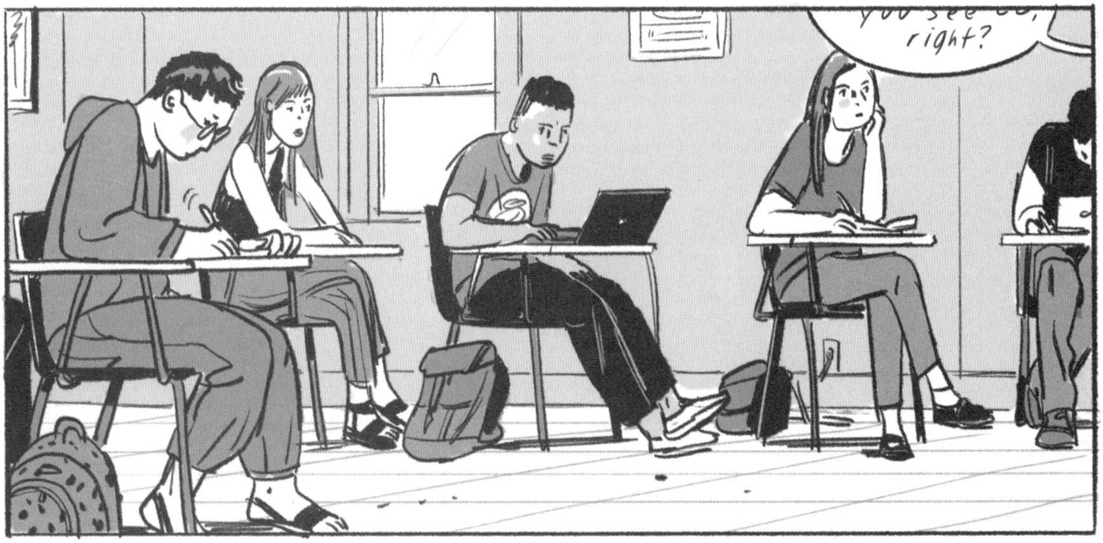
right?

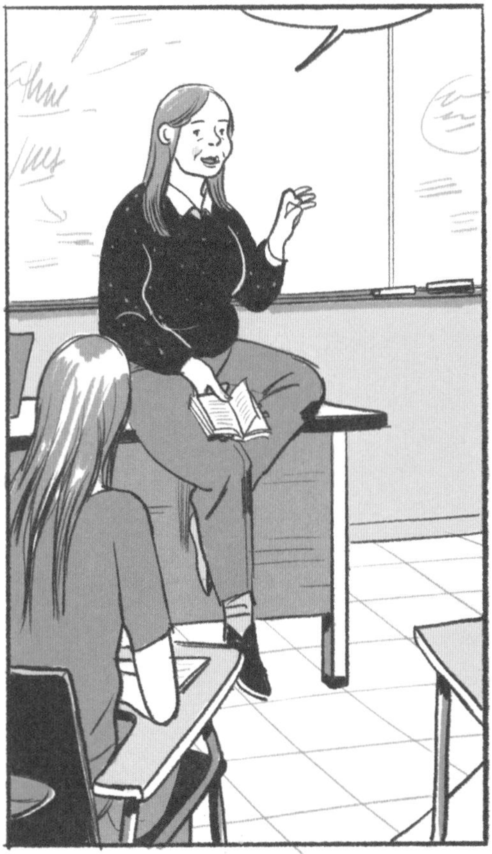

Well, I mean I'm not stupid in that I would never jeopardize my career by messing around with a student like that. Obviously I'm a fucking idiot.

The reasons why are really complicated.

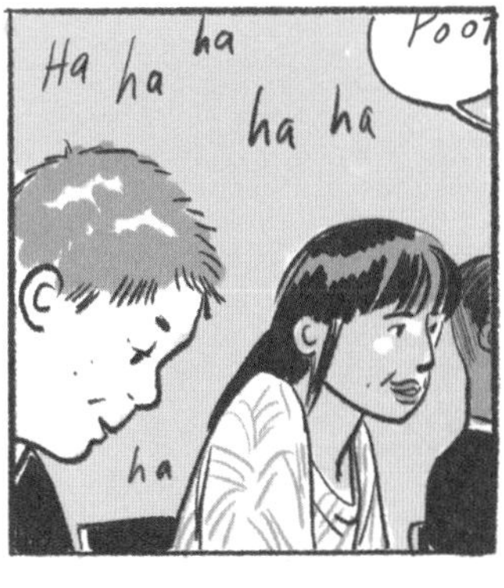
Ha ha
ha
ha ha
ha

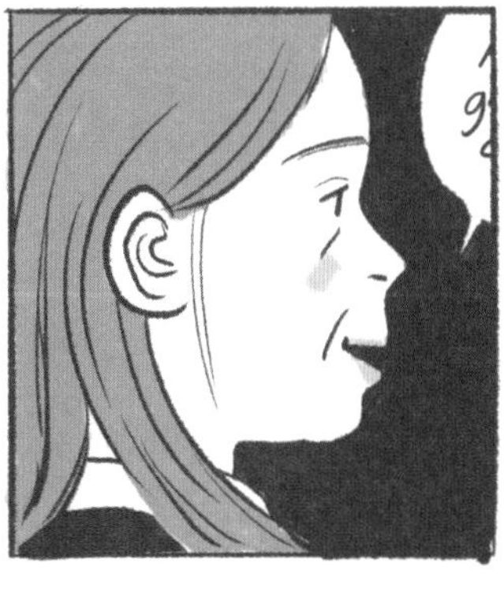

That's not true. The reasons are very cliché, and therefore embarrassing.

I should probably say that I was unfulfilled. That I was not engaging my "whole" self.

That my husband and I stopped having "new experiences."

When I put it that way, don't I sound so reasonable?

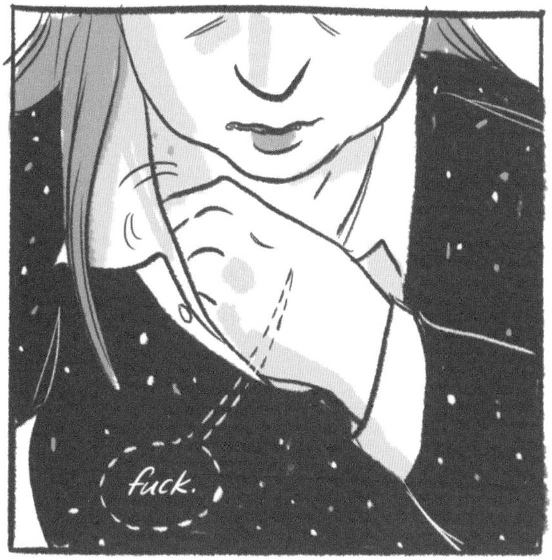
fuck.

I was bored.

So, not so complicated after all, I guess.

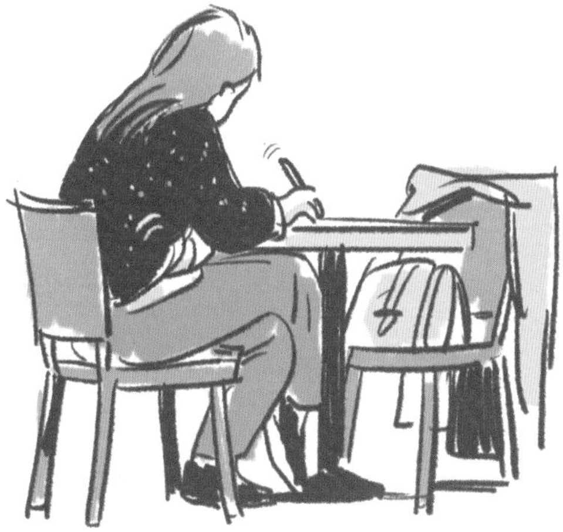

I'm not saying that I deserve to not be bored or whatever.

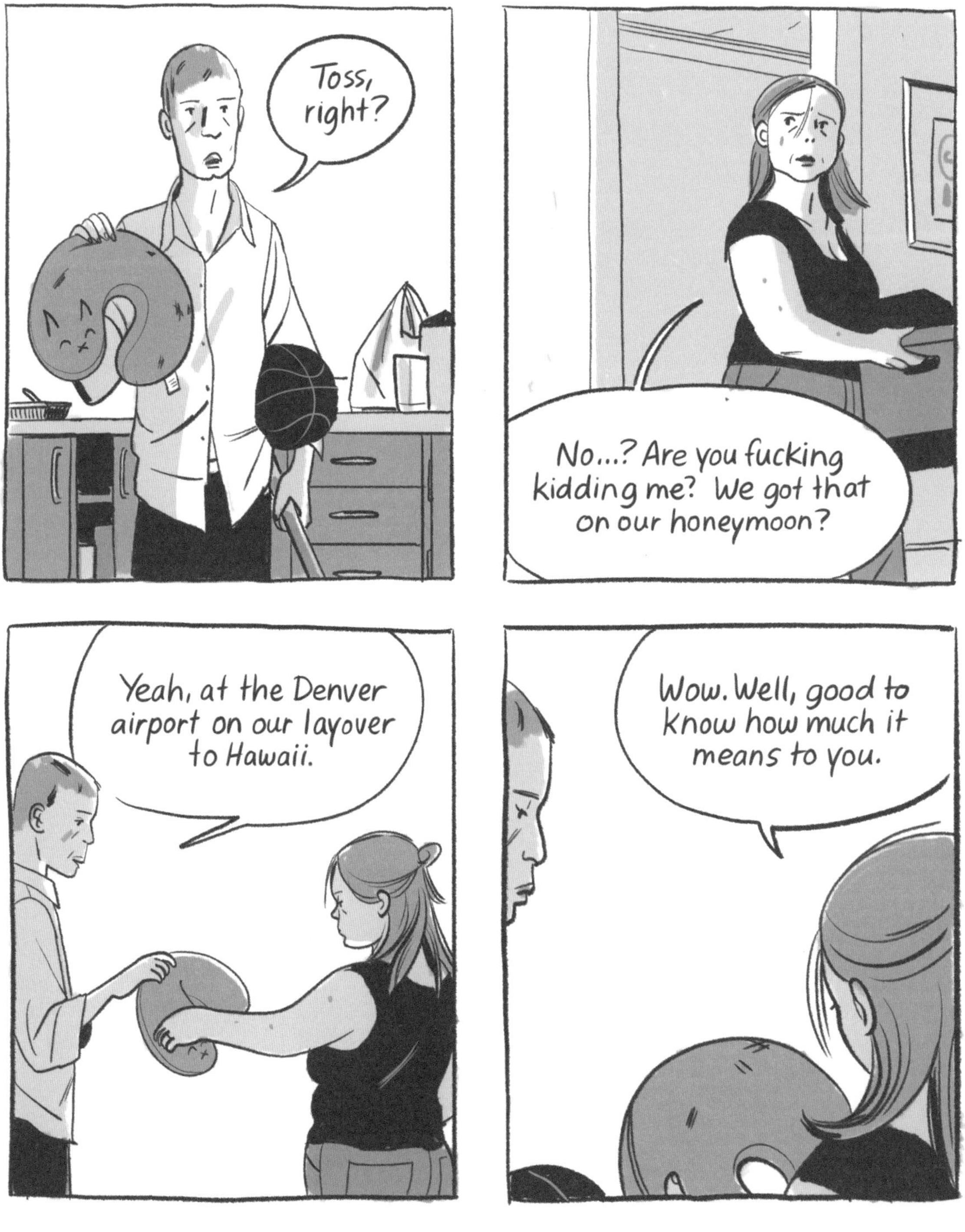
Toss, right?
No...? Are you fucking kidding me? We got that on our honeymoon?
Yeah, at the Denver airport on our layover to Hawaii.
Wow. Well, good to know how much it means to you.

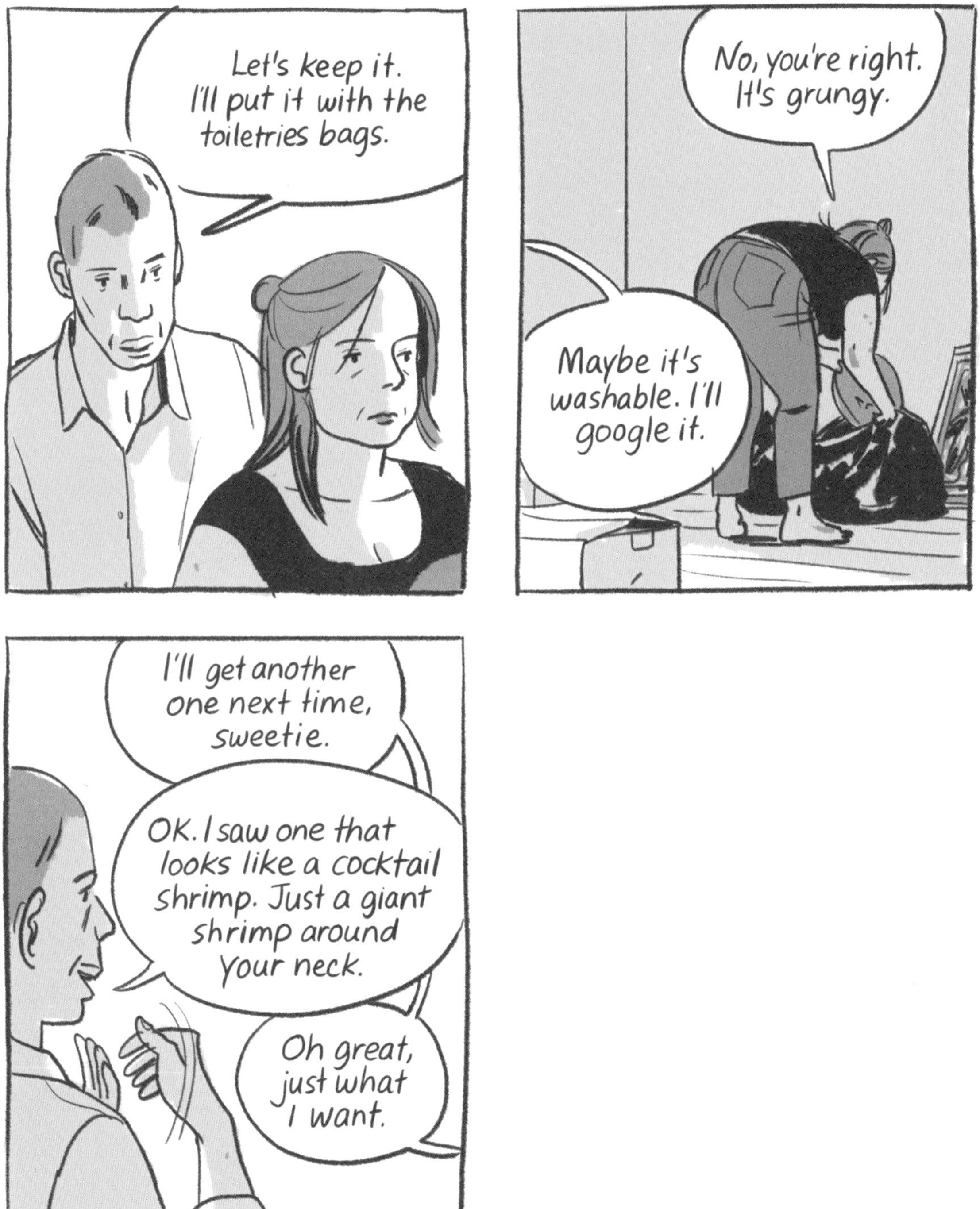
Let's keep it. I'll put it with the toiletries bags.
No, you're right. It's grungy.
Maybe it's washable. I'll google it.
I'll get another one next time, sweetie.
OK. I saw one that looks like a cocktail shrimp. Just a giant shrimp around your neck.
Oh great, just what I want.

Two months after ending it
with Greg, I feel a little better.

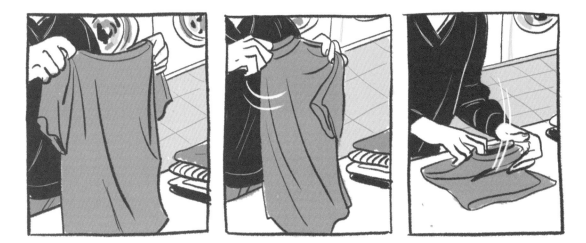

Don't worry. Deep down, where it actually counts, I'm surely
rotting away. Doing irreversible damage to... something.

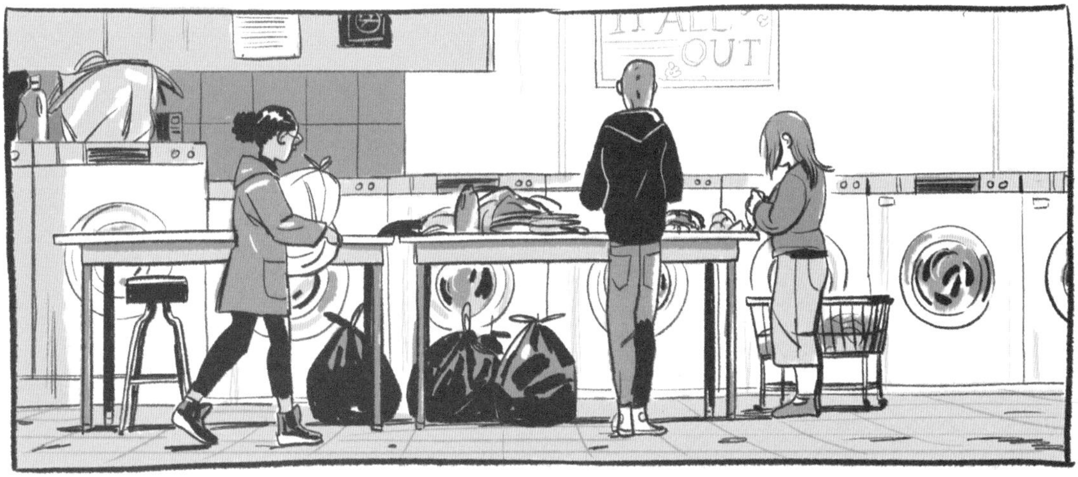

No, I just feel less edgy.
I'm good with that for now.

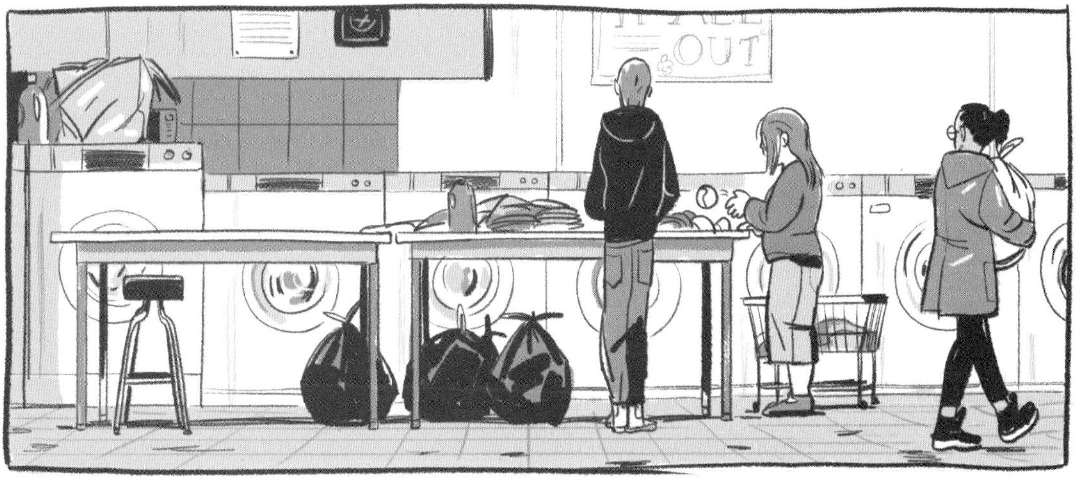

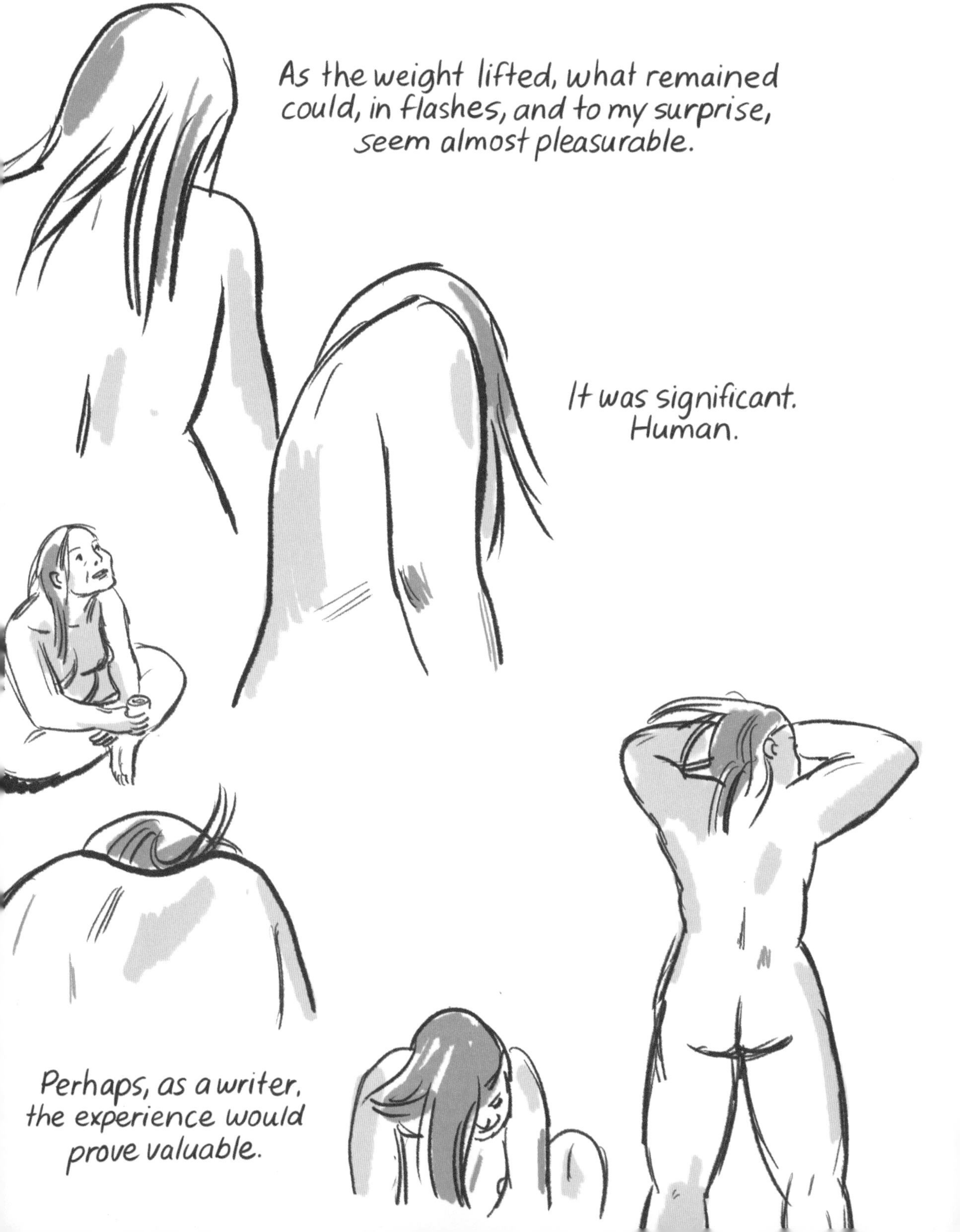
As the weight lifted, what remained could, in flashes, and to my surprise, seem almost pleasurable.
It was significant. Human.
Perhaps, as a writer, the experience would prove valuable.

My first novel, about a young woman who returns to her hometown after living abroad, had been described by a few reviewers as a little thin. I dismissed the critique as sexist.

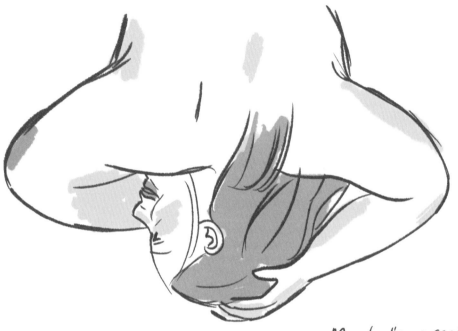

Maybe I'm a sociopath.

Only a narcissist would call
herself a sociopath.

OK, with the sniffer dog,
fumigation pod, boxes,
mattress... $4,000.

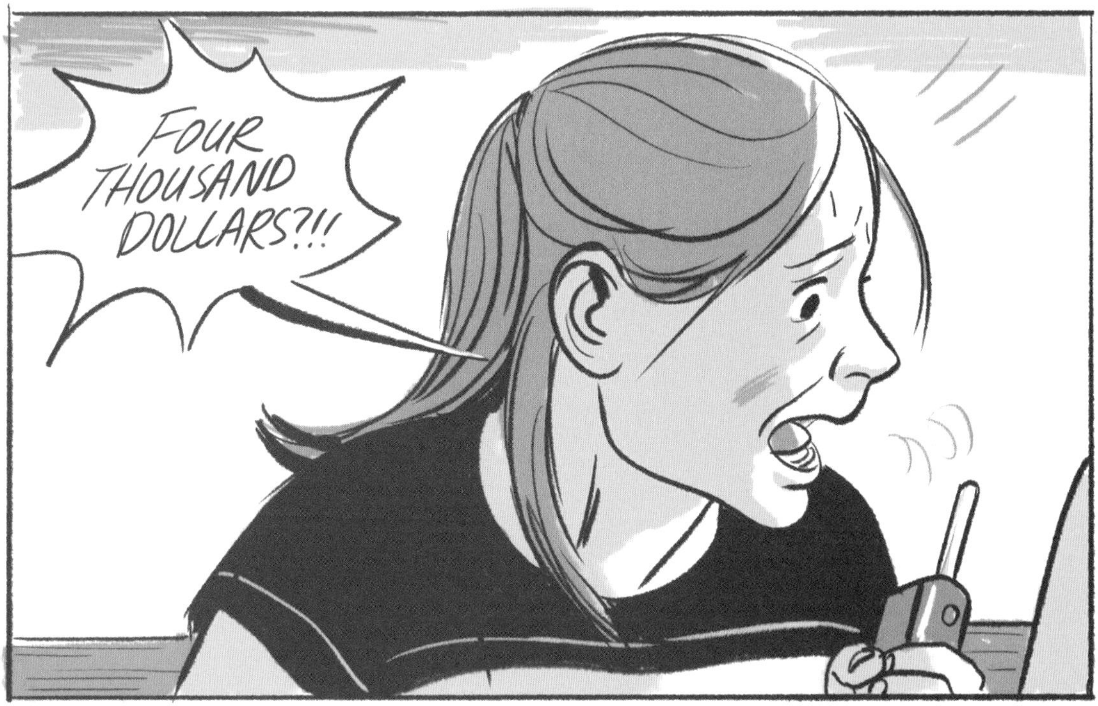
FOUR THOUSAND DOLLARS?!!

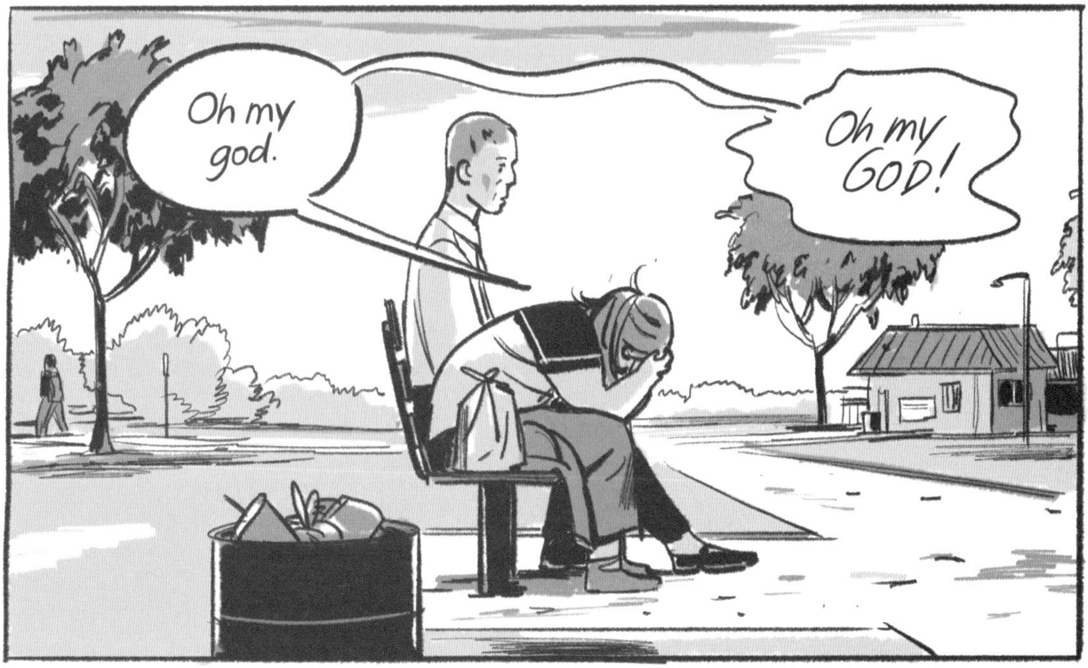
Oh my god.
Oh my GOD!

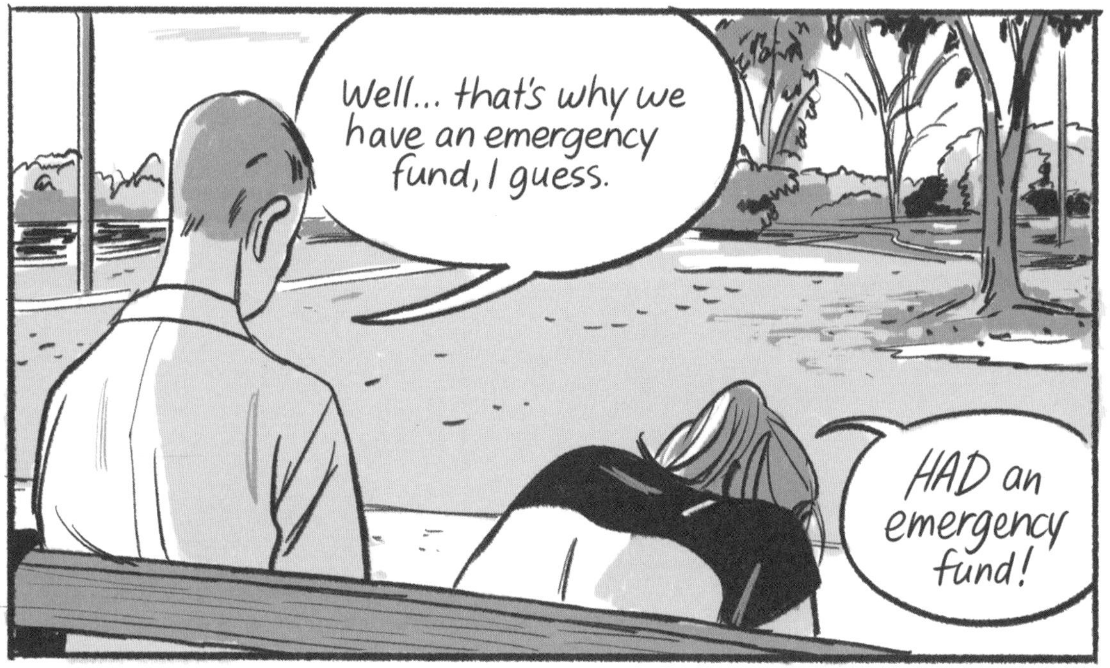
Well... that's why we have an emergency fund, I guess.
HAD an emergency fund!

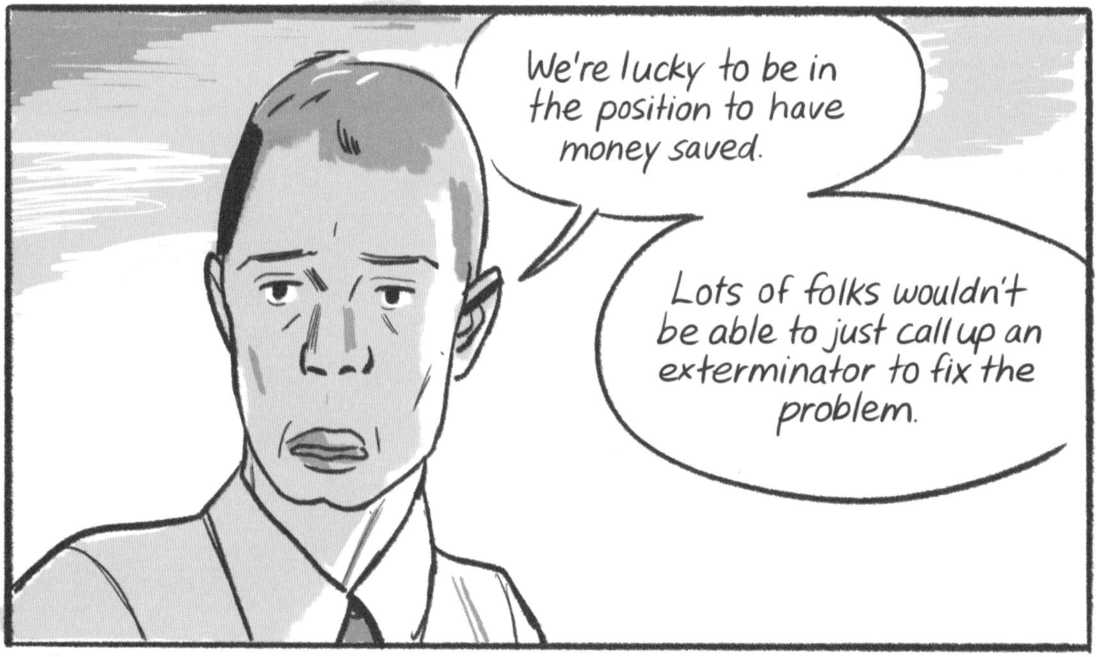
We're lucky to be in the position to have money saved.
Lots of folks wouldn't be able to just call up an exterminator to fix the problem.

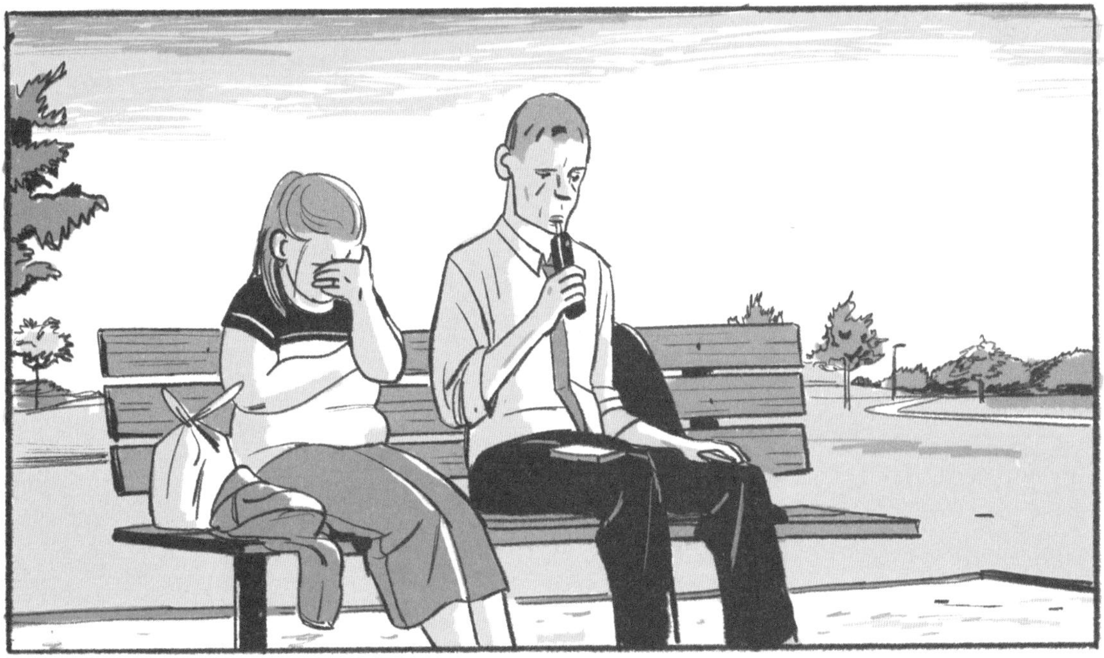

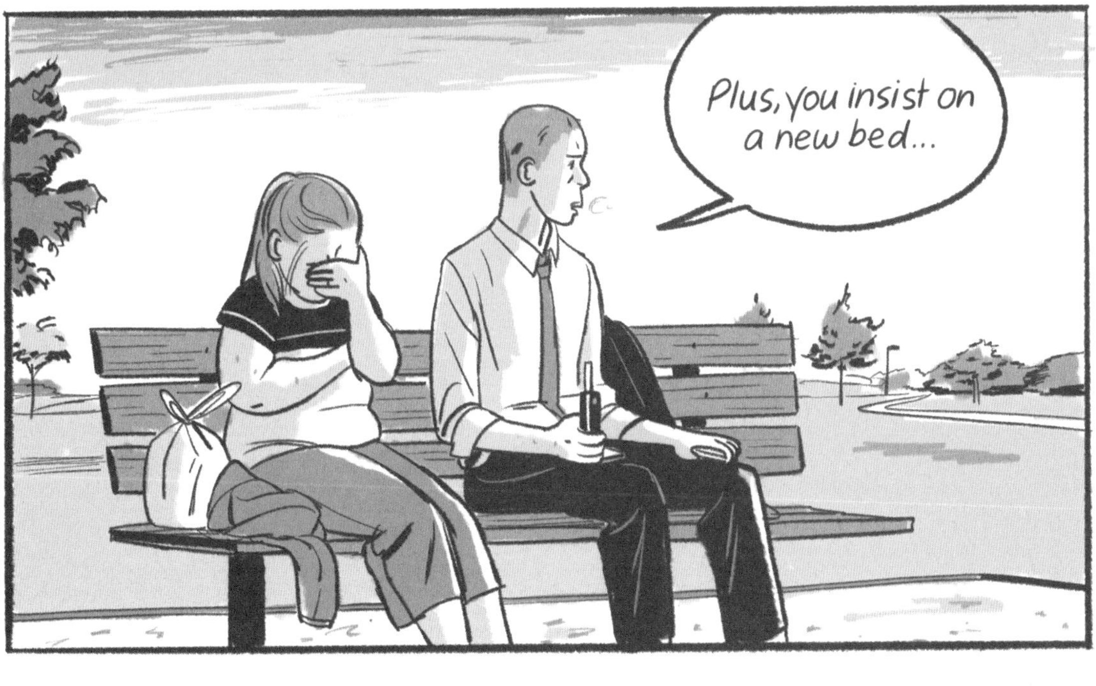
Plus, you insist on a new bed...

After we drove the mattress to the dump, we stopped for pizza. The place was shitty, as was the pizza, but it wasn't our apartment, so it felt safe and clean.

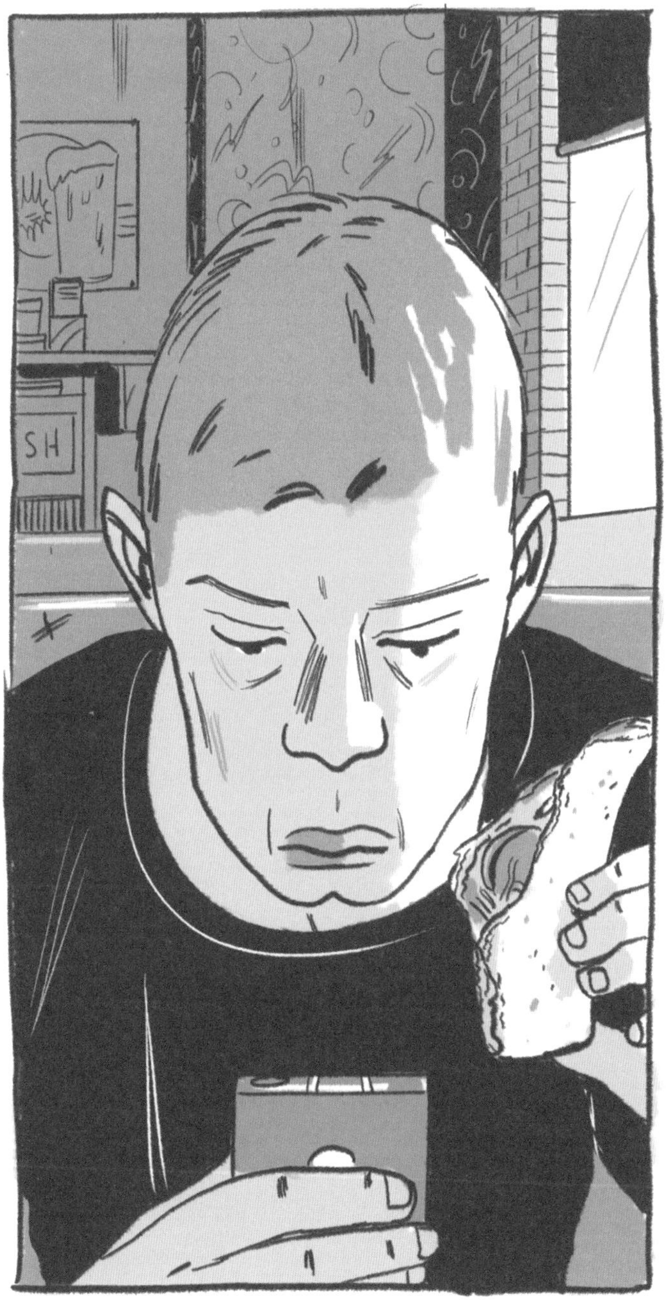
SH

We were exhausted.
Jeremy's face was so worn.
I'm sure mine was too.

Something about staring
at the stitching of a throw
pillow can really make
you crazy.

When I was in the thing with Greg, the rules didn't apply to me anymore. In fact, I saw my life more clearly than I had before. It looked flat. Small. I could see all its edges.

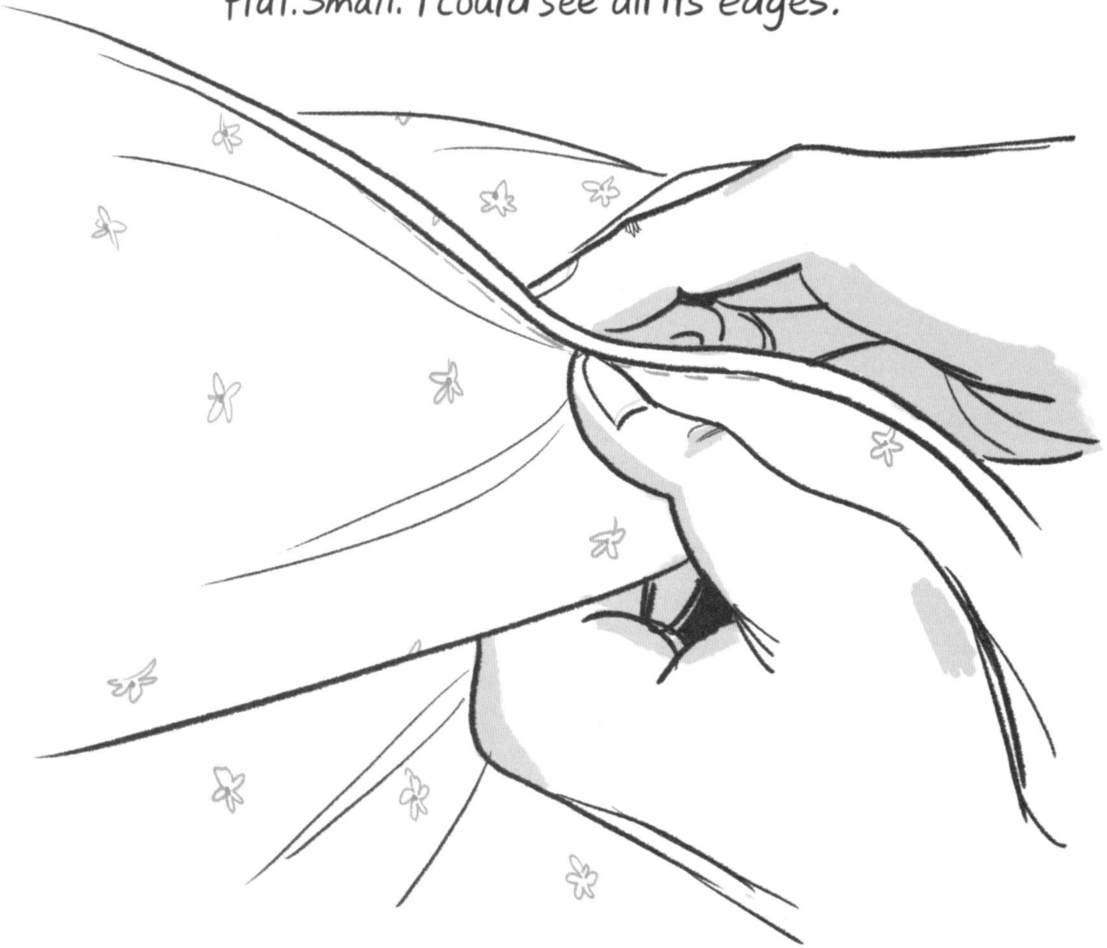

It was a trick. Of perception or hormones or whatever. I knew it then, and now, thank god.

I still miss it though.

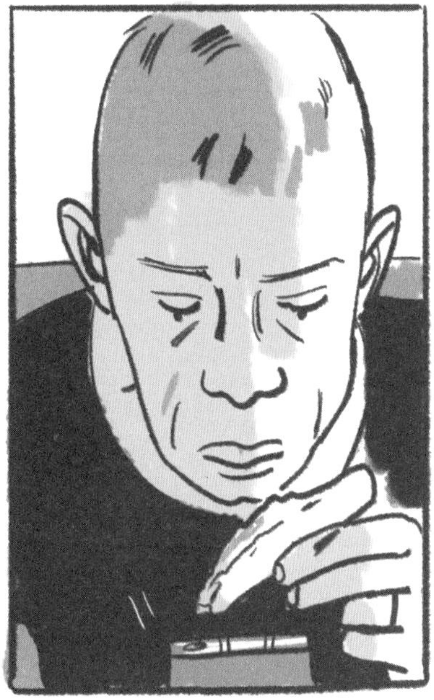

I was sure that image of Jeremy in the pizza place would stay with me my whole life.

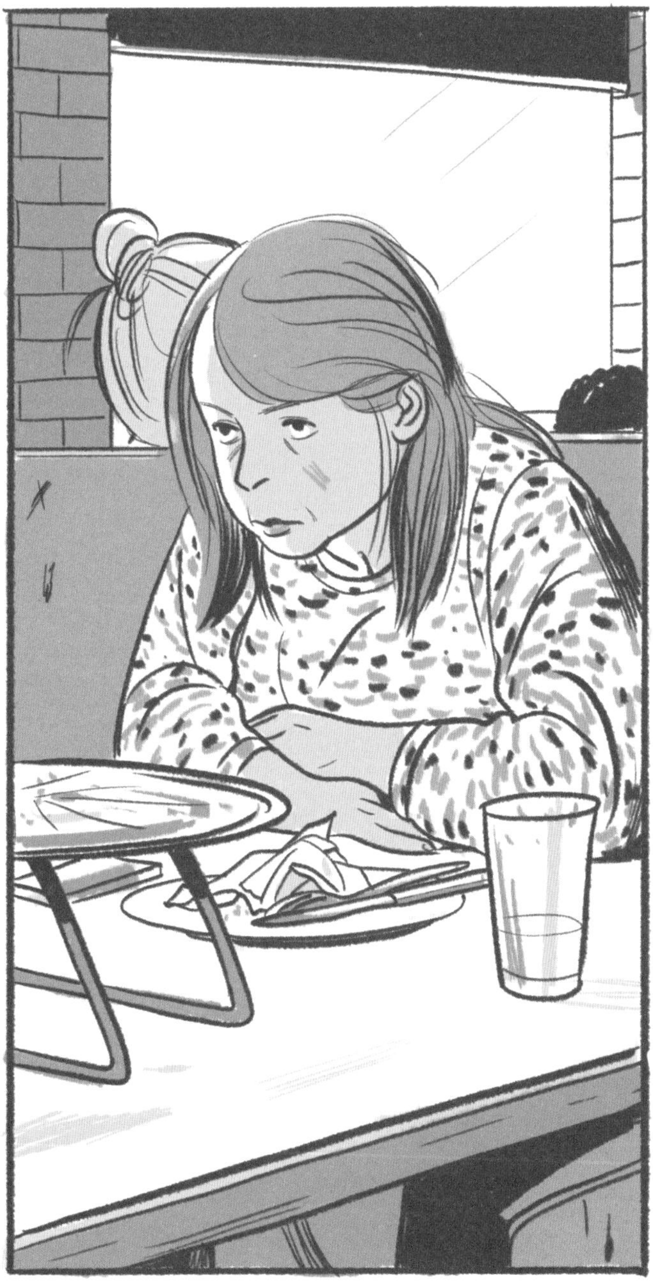

I tried to imprint it on my brain, just in case.

As I watched the movers load the last of our
belongings into the truck to be fumigated,
I could feel my body unclench.

Our home, compact and
stripped of excess.

These were the essentials:
useful, meaningful, or both.
And soon, clean.

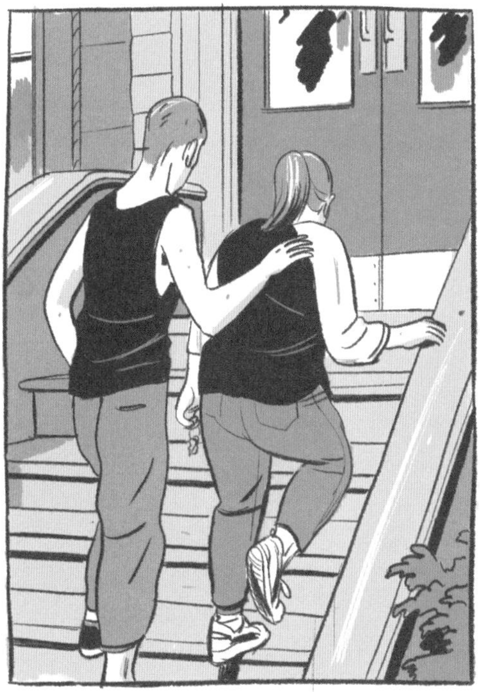

Jeremy is such a good person. And I am too. Not as good as Jeremy, but OK.

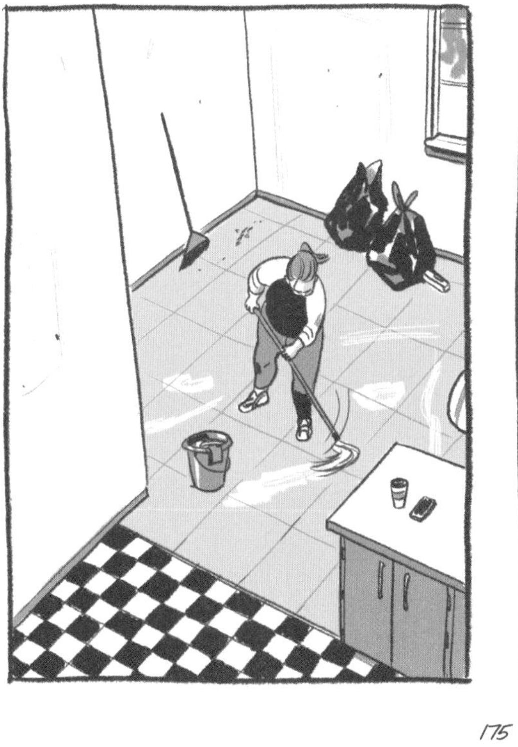

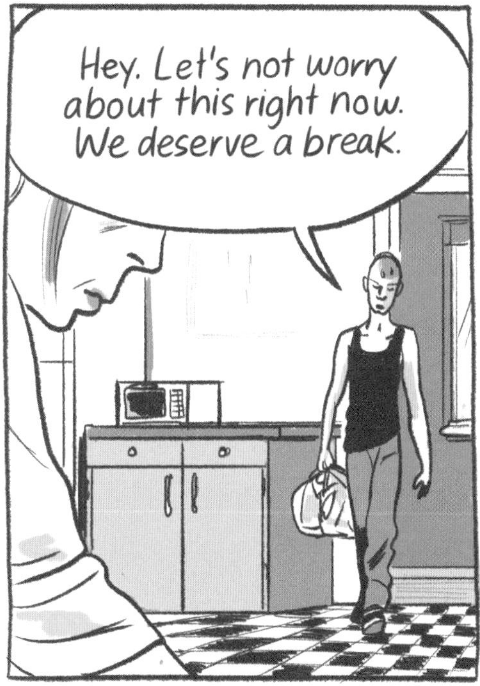
Hey. Let's not worry about this right now. We deserve a break.

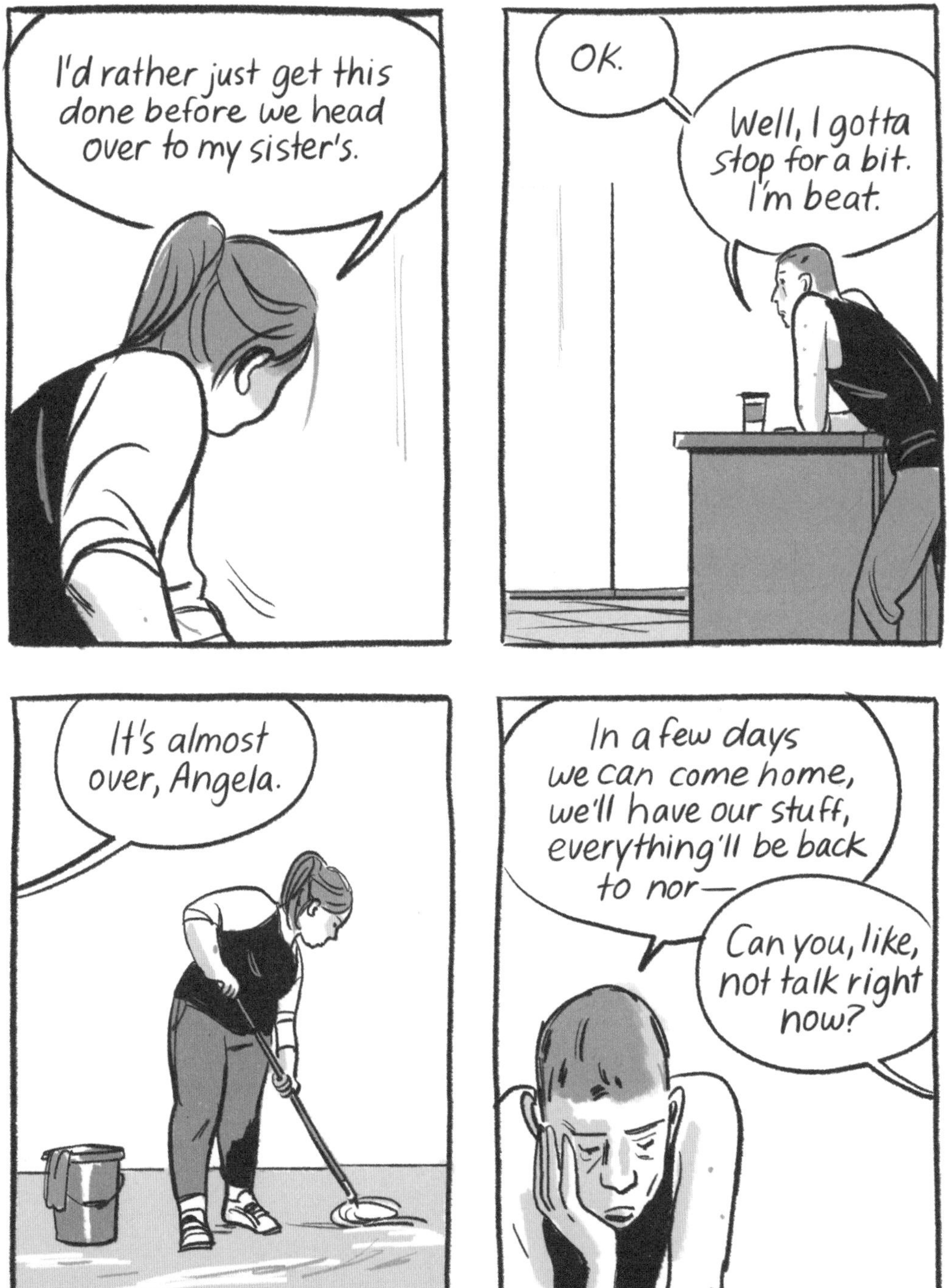
I'd rather just get this done before we head over to my sister's.
OK.
Well, I gotta stop for a bit. I'm beat.
It's almost over, Angela.
In a few days we can come home, we'll have our stuff, everything'll be back to nor—
Can you, like, not talk right now?

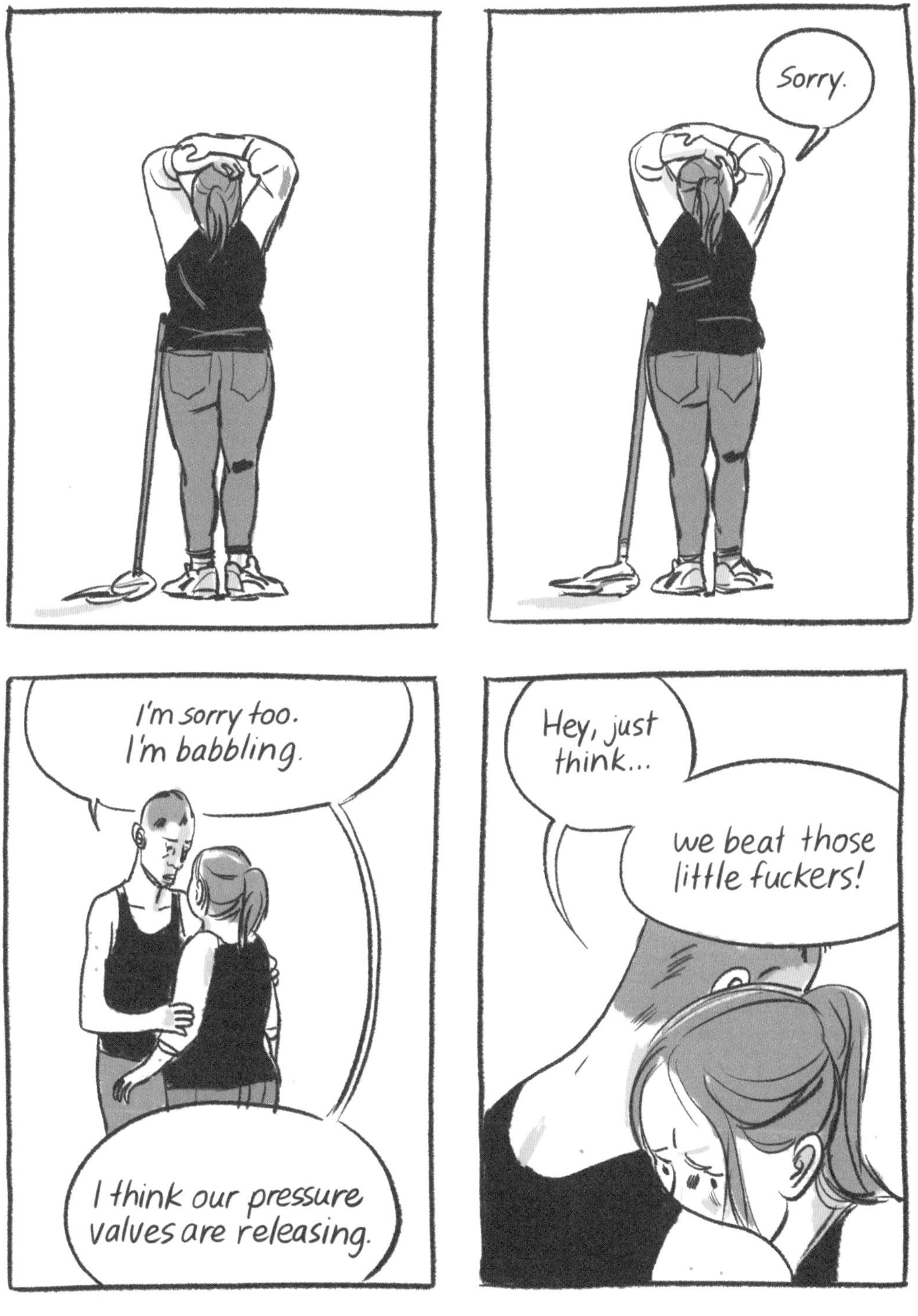
Sorry.
I'm sorry too. I'm babbling.
I think our pressure valves are releasing.
Hey, just think...
we beat those little fuckers!

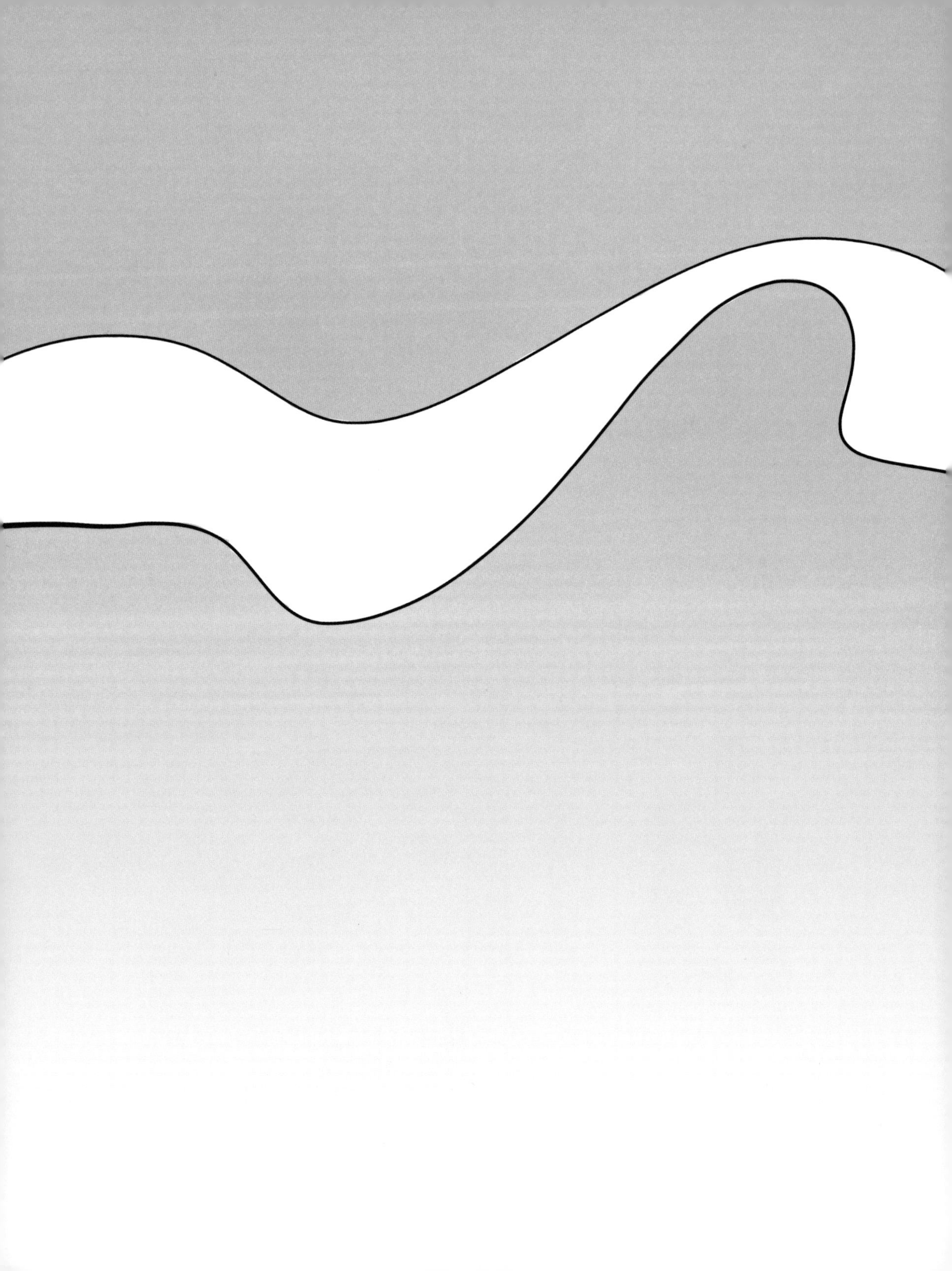

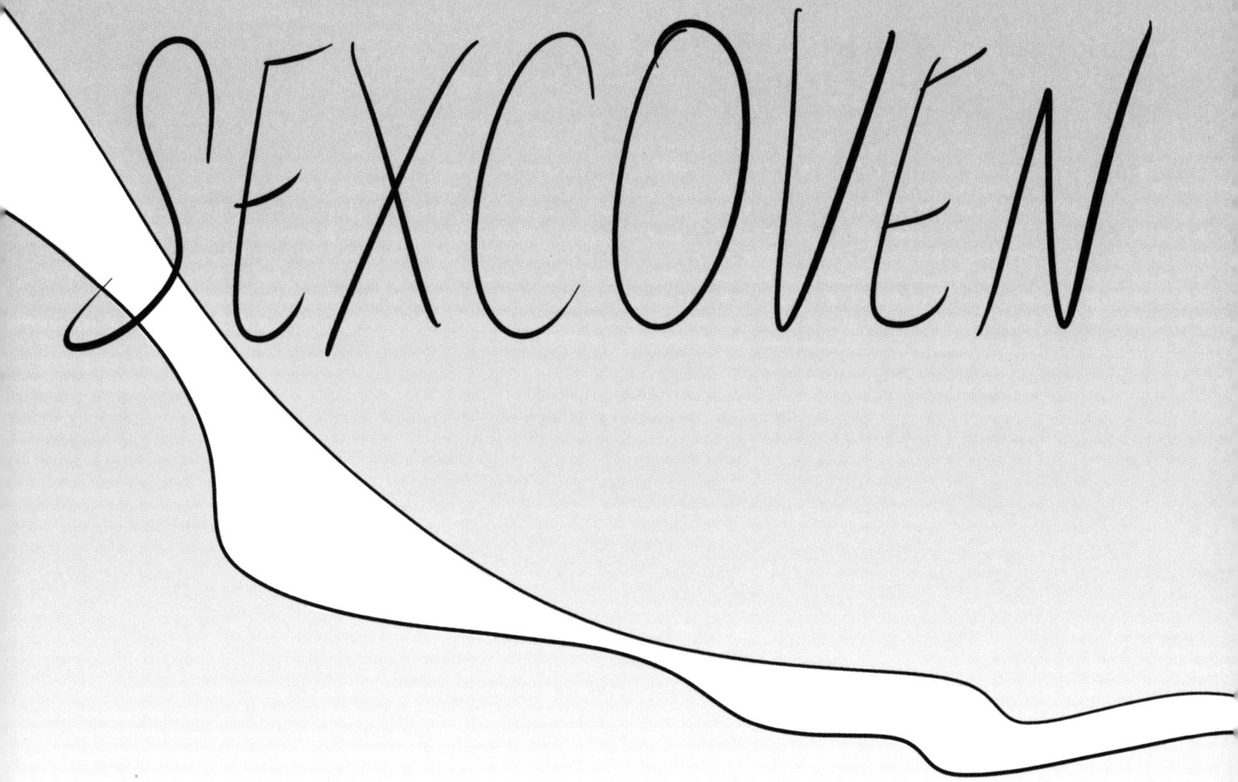
SEXCOVEN

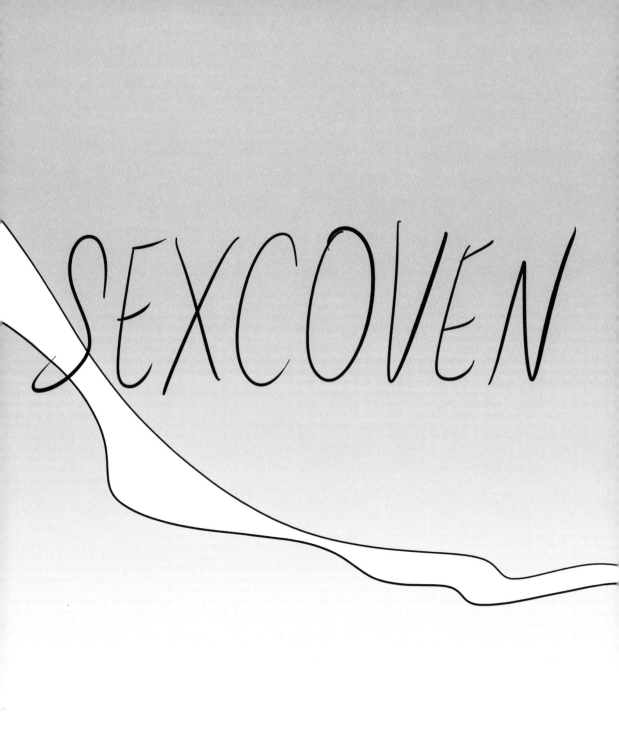

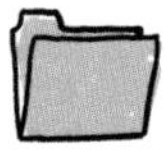

untitled folder

The file was uploaded July 26, 1996.

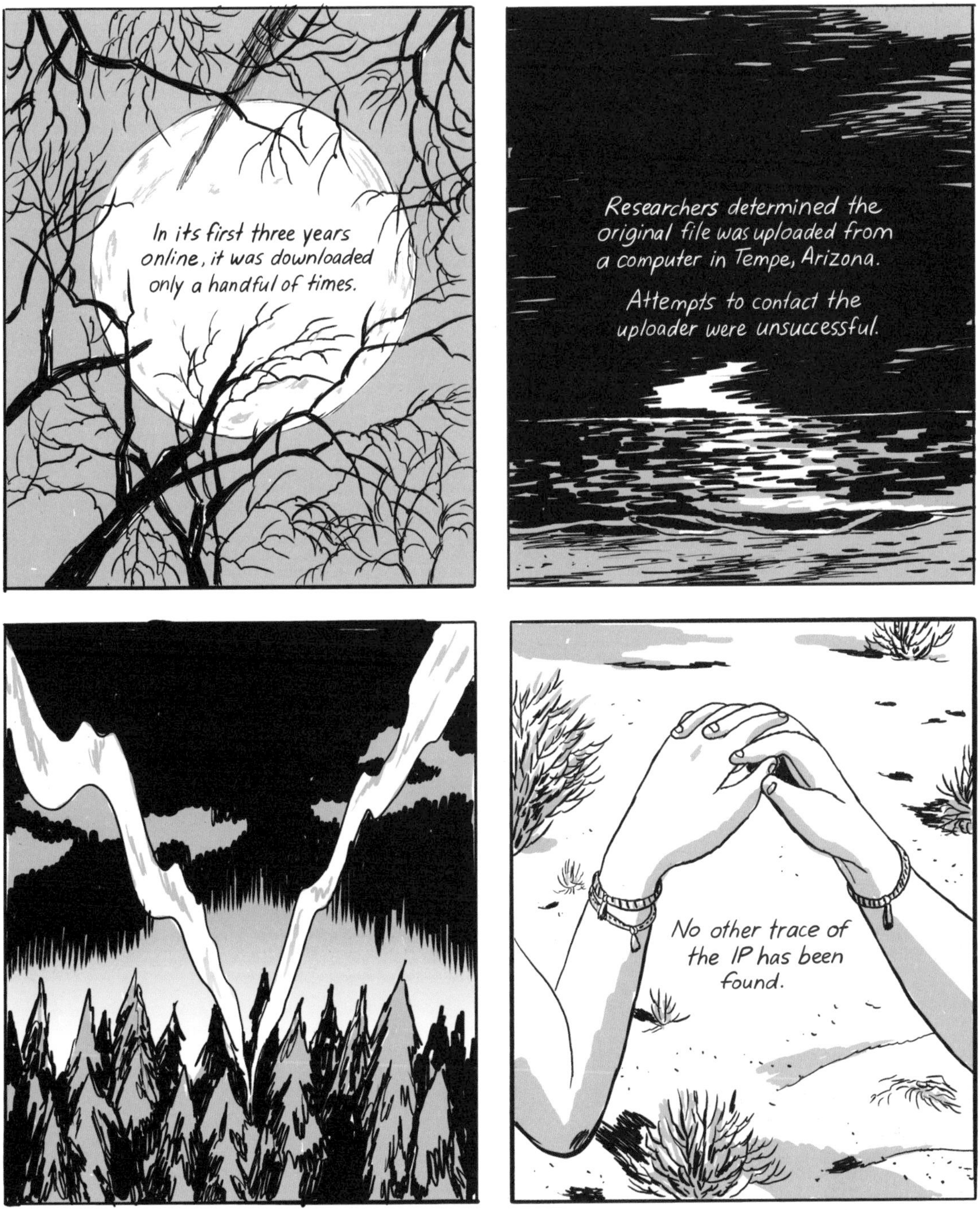
In its first three years online, it was downloaded only a handful of times.
Researchers determined the original file was uploaded from a computer in Tempe, Arizona.
Attempts to contact the uploader were unsuccessful.
No other trace of the IP has been found.

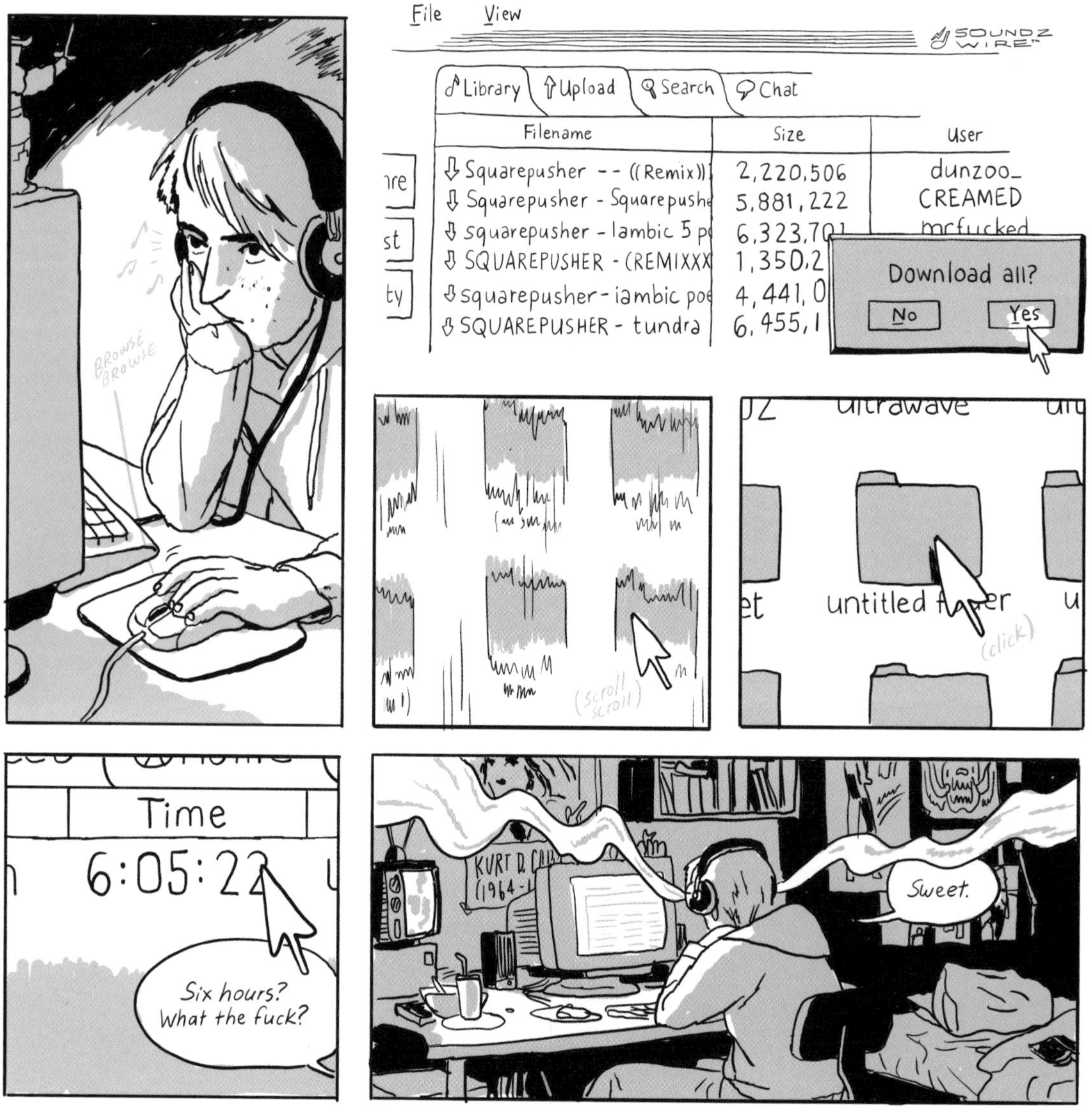
File View
SOUNDZ WIRE
Library
Upload
Search
Chat
Filename
Size
User
Squarepusher -- ((Remix))
2,220,506
dunzoo_
Squarepusher - Squarepushe
5,881,222
CREAMED
squarepusher - lambic 5 p
SQUAREPUSHER - (REMIXXX
squarepusher - iambic poe
SQUAREPUSHER - tundra
Download all?
No
Yes
BROWSE BROWSE
(scroll scroll)
ultrawave
(click)
Time
6:05:22
Six hours? What the fuck?
Sweet.

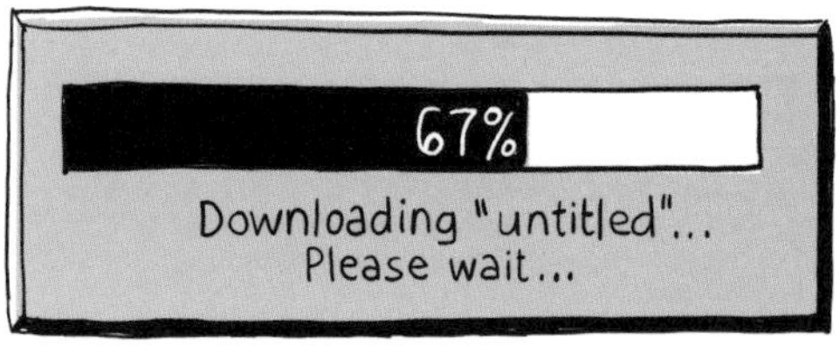
67%
Downloading "untitled"...
Please wait...

In early 1999, a user named _EyeOfTheKush found the folder on the music-sharing site SoundzWire. It contained a single mp3, also untitled.

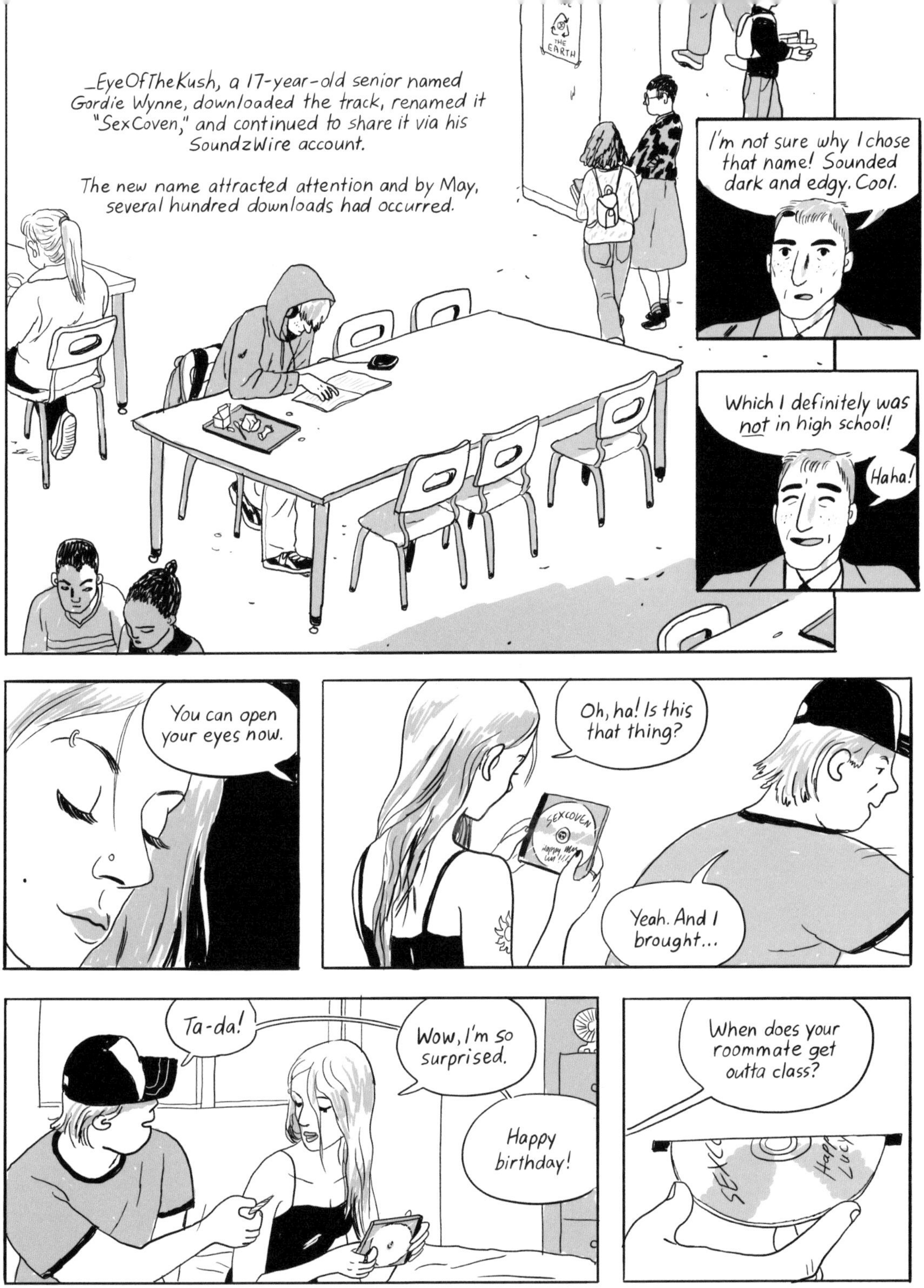
_EyeOfTheKush, a 17-year-old senior named Gordie Wynne, downloaded the track, renamed it "SexCoven," and continued to share it via his SoundzWire account.
The new name attracted attention and by May, several hundred downloads had occurred.
THE EARTH
I'm not sure why I chose that name! Sounded dark and edgy. Cool.
Which I definitely was not in high school!
Haha!
You can open your eyes now.
Oh, ha! Is this that thing?
SEXCOVEN
Yeah. And I brought...
Ta-da!
Wow, I'm so surprised.
Happy birthday!
When does your roommate get outta class?

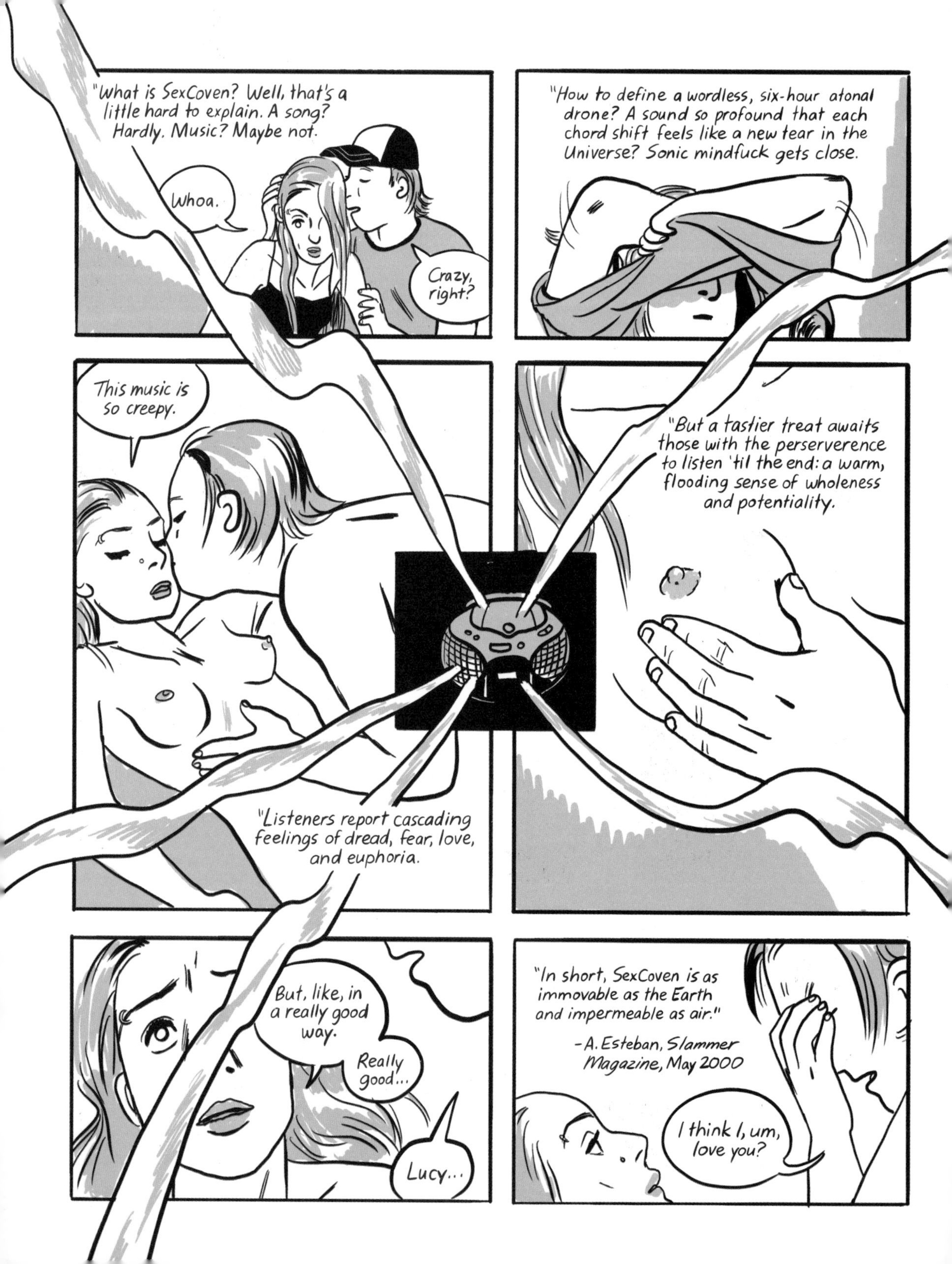

"What is SexCoven? Well, that's a little hard to explain. A song? Hardly. Music? Maybe not.
Whoa.
Crazy, right?
"How to define a wordless, six-hour atonal drone? A sound so profound that each chord shift feels like a new tear in the Universe? Sonic mindfuck gets close.
This music is so creepy.
"But a tastier treat awaits those with the perserverence to listen 'til the end: a warm, flooding sense of wholeness and potentiality.
"Listeners report cascading feelings of dread, fear, love, and euphoria.
But, like, in a really good way.
Really good...
Lucy...
"In short, SexCoven is as immovable as the Earth and impermeable as air."
-A. Esteban, Slammer Magazine, May 2000
I think I, um, love you?

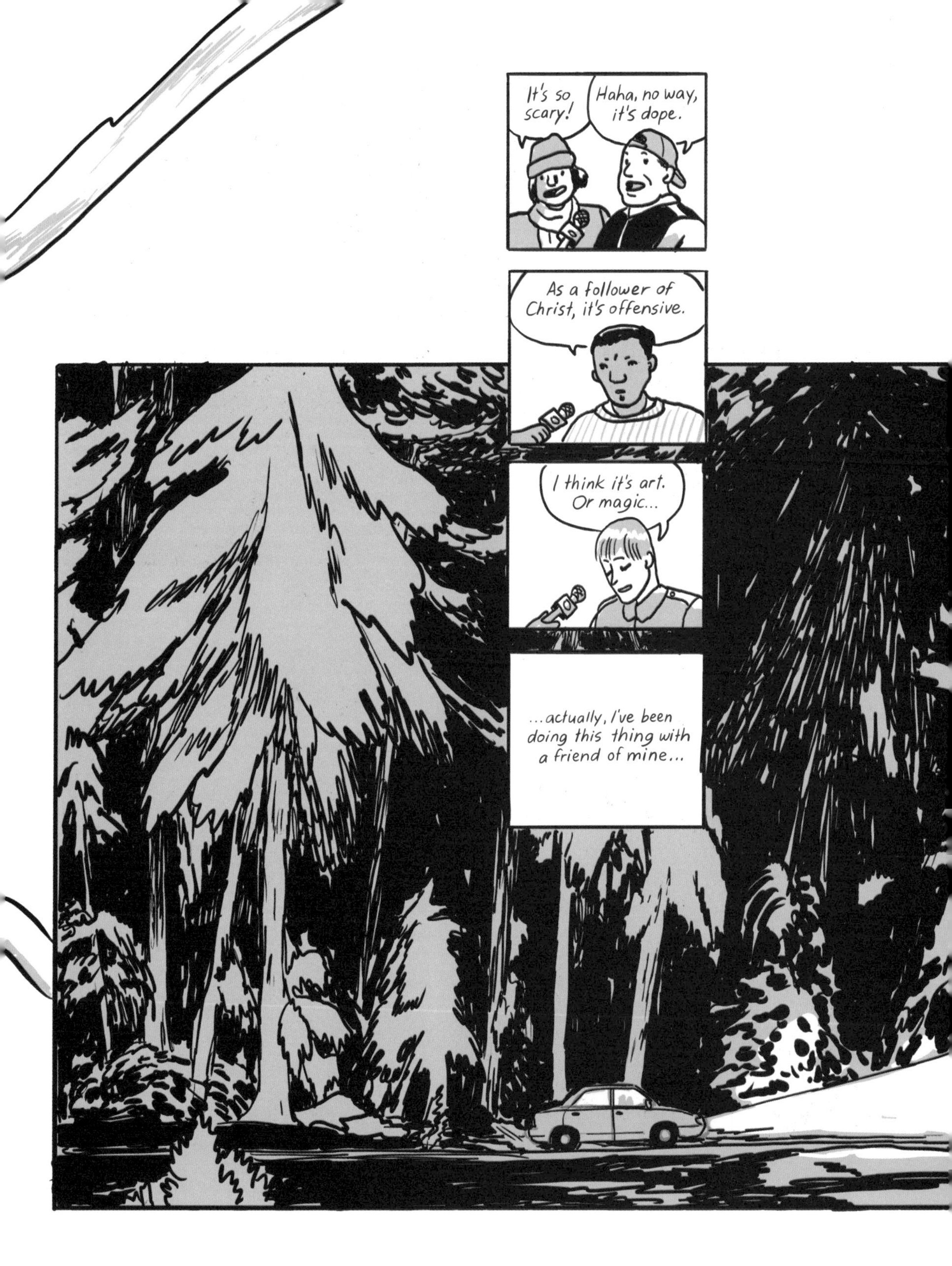
It's so scary!
Haha, no way, it's dope.
As a follower of Christ, it's offensive.
I think it's art. Or magic...
...actually, I've been doing this thing with a friend of mine...

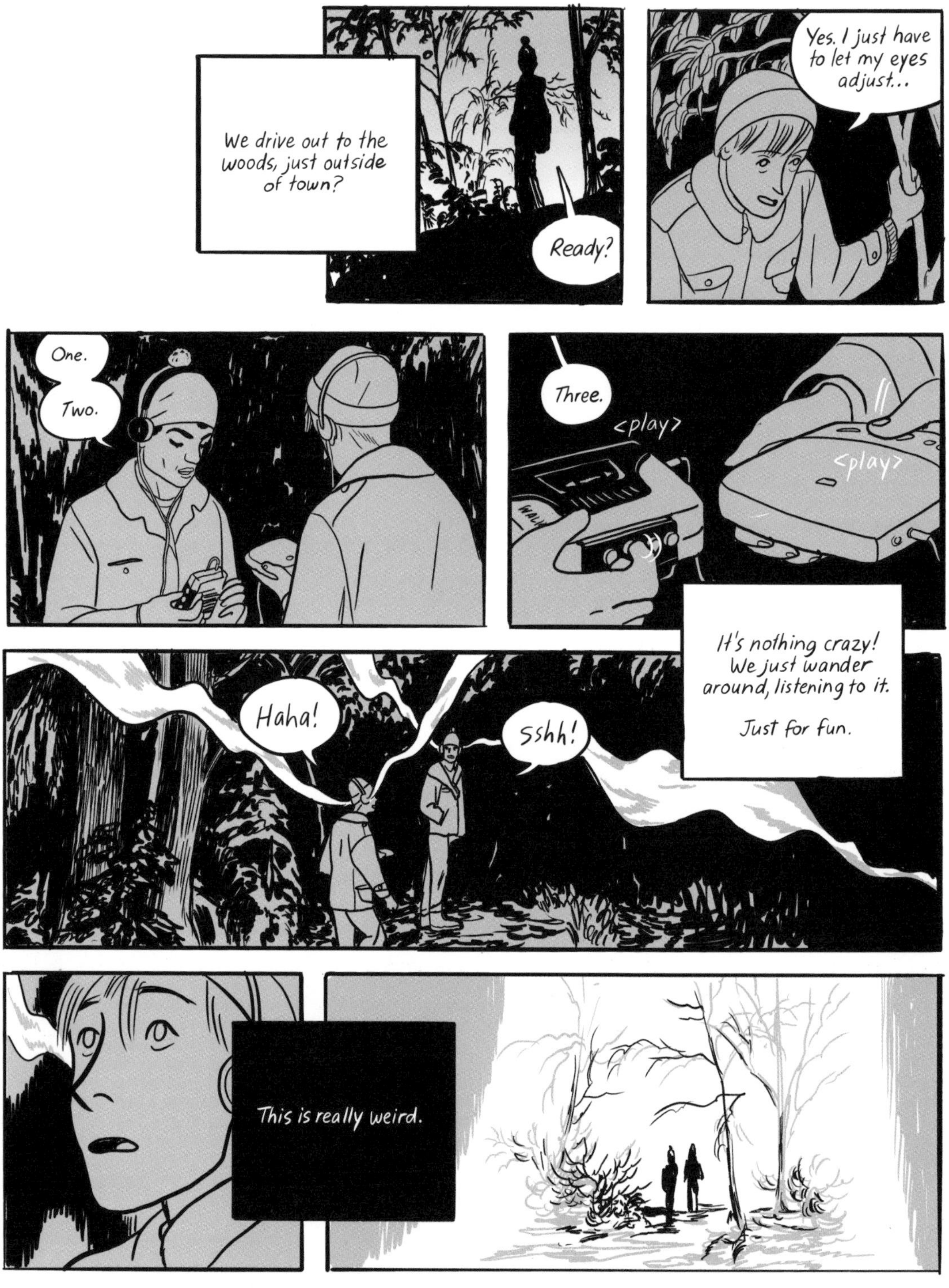
We drive out to the woods, just outside of town?
Ready?
Yes. I just have to let my eyes adjust...
One.
Two.
Three.
<play>
<play>
It's nothing crazy! We just wander around, listening to it.
Just for fun.
Haha!
Sshh!
This is really weird.

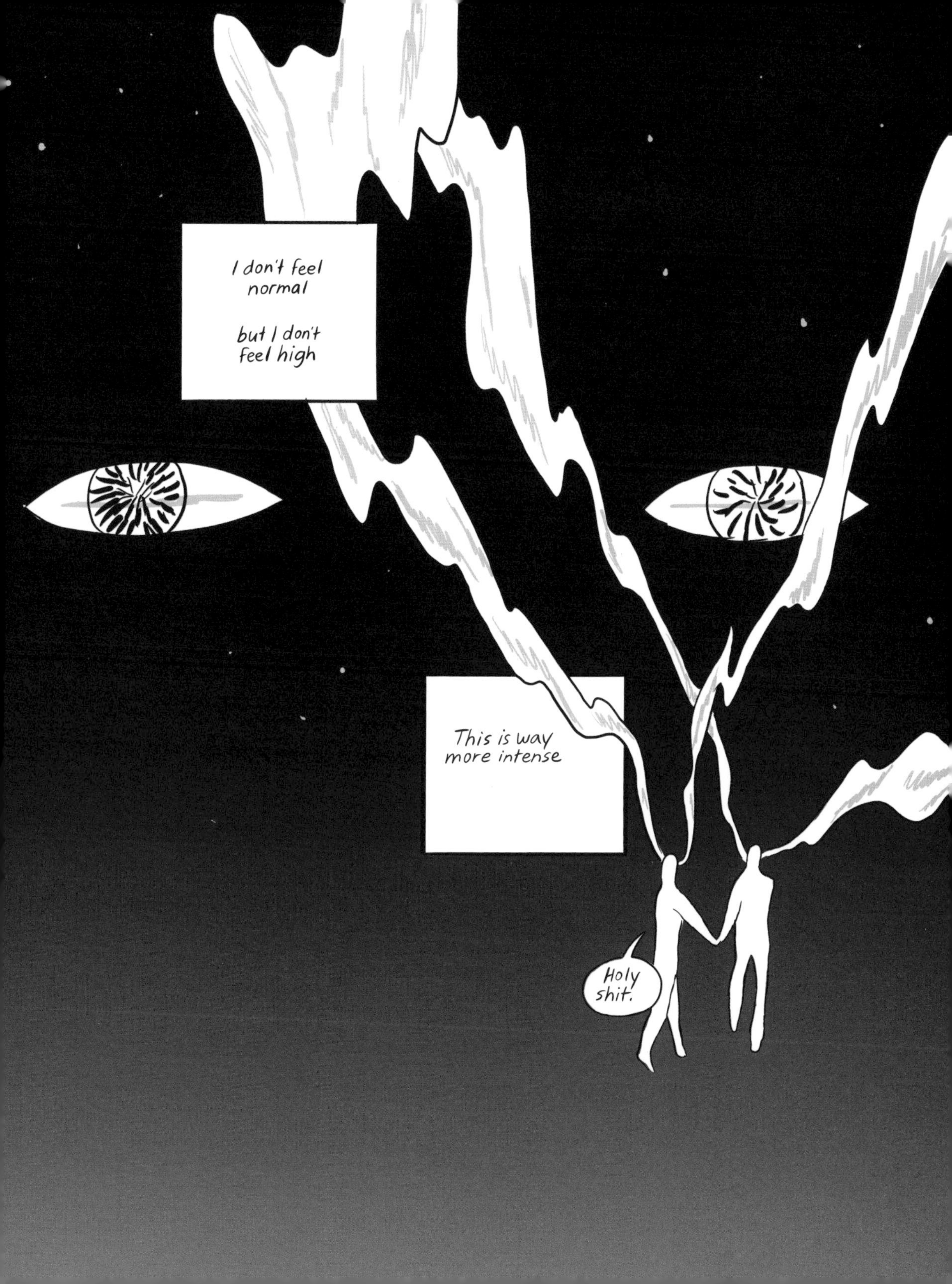
I don't feel normal

but I don't feel high
This is way more intense
Holy shit.

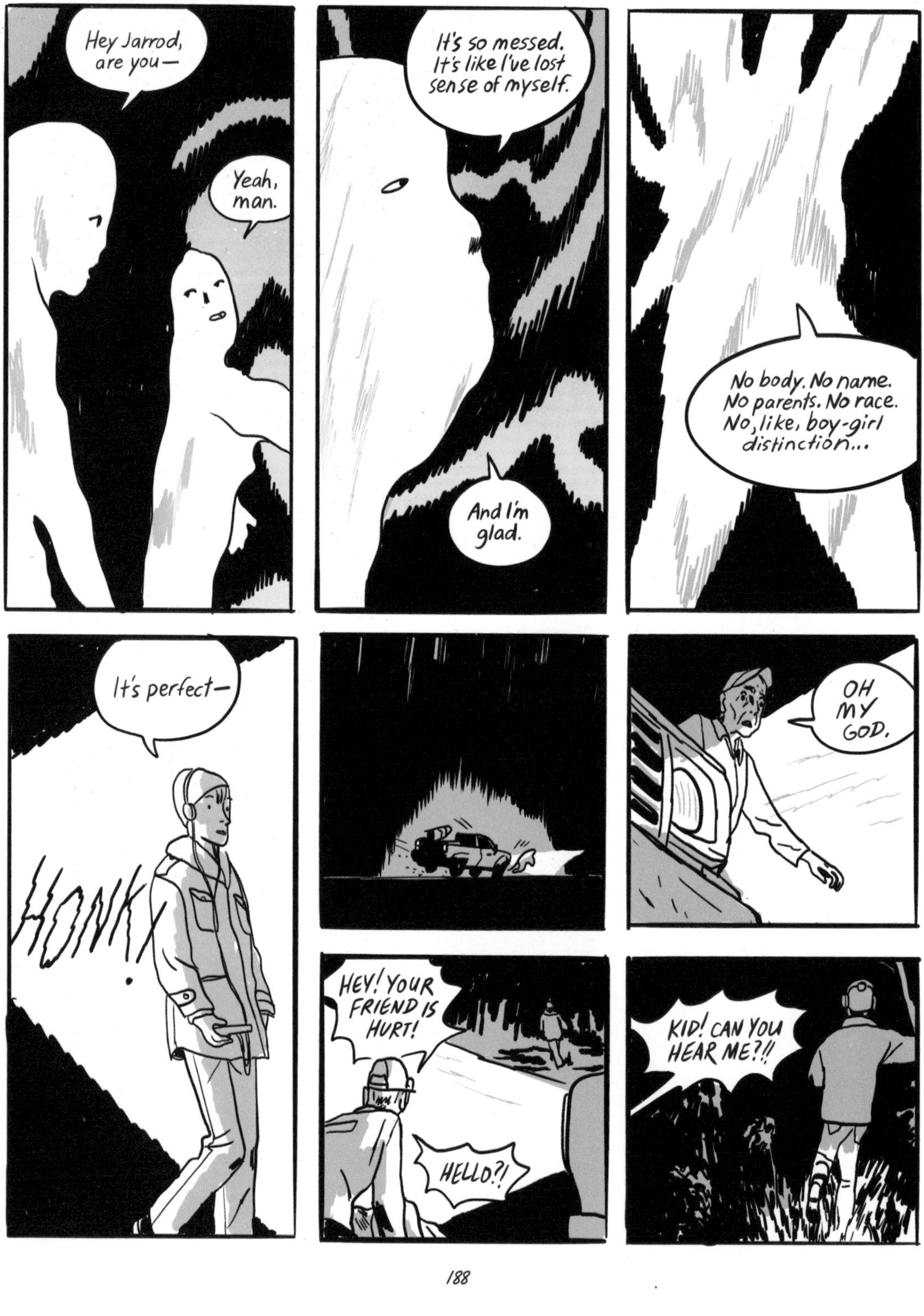
Hey Jarrod, are you—
Yeah, man.
It's so messed. It's like I've lost sense of myself.
And I'm glad.
No body. No name. No parents. No race. No, like, boy-girl distinction...
It's perfect—
HONK!
OH MY GOD.
HEY! YOUR FRIEND IS HURT!
HELLO?!
KID! CAN YOU HEAR ME?!!

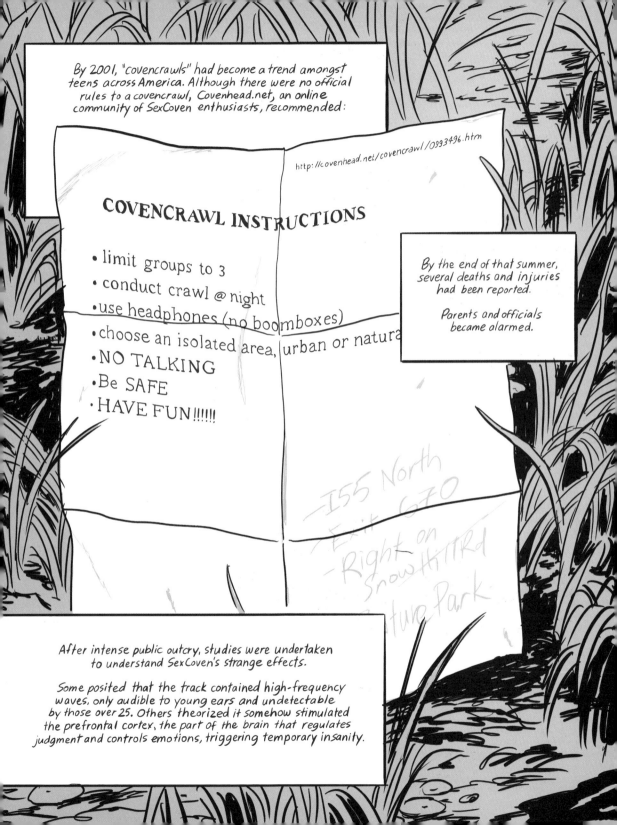

By 2001, "covencrawls" had become a trend amongst teens across America. Although there were no official rules to a covencrawl, Covenhead.net, an online community of SexCoven enthusiasts, recommended:

http://covenhead.net/covencrawl/0993496.htm

COVENCRAWL INSTRUCTIONS

- limit groups to 3
- conduct crawl @ night
- use headphones (no boomboxes)
- choose an isolated area, urban or natura
- NO TALKING
- Be SAFE
- HAVE FUN !!!!!!

By the end of that summer, several deaths and injuries had been reported.

Parents and officials became alarmed.

—I55 North
—Exit 670
—Right on Snow Hill Rd
...ture Park

After intense public outcry, studies were undertaken to understand SexCoven's strange effects.

Some posited that the track contained high-frequency waves, only audible to young ears and undetectable by those over 25. Others theorized it somehow stimulated the prefrontal cortex, the part of the brain that regulates judgment and controls emotions, triggering temporary insanity.

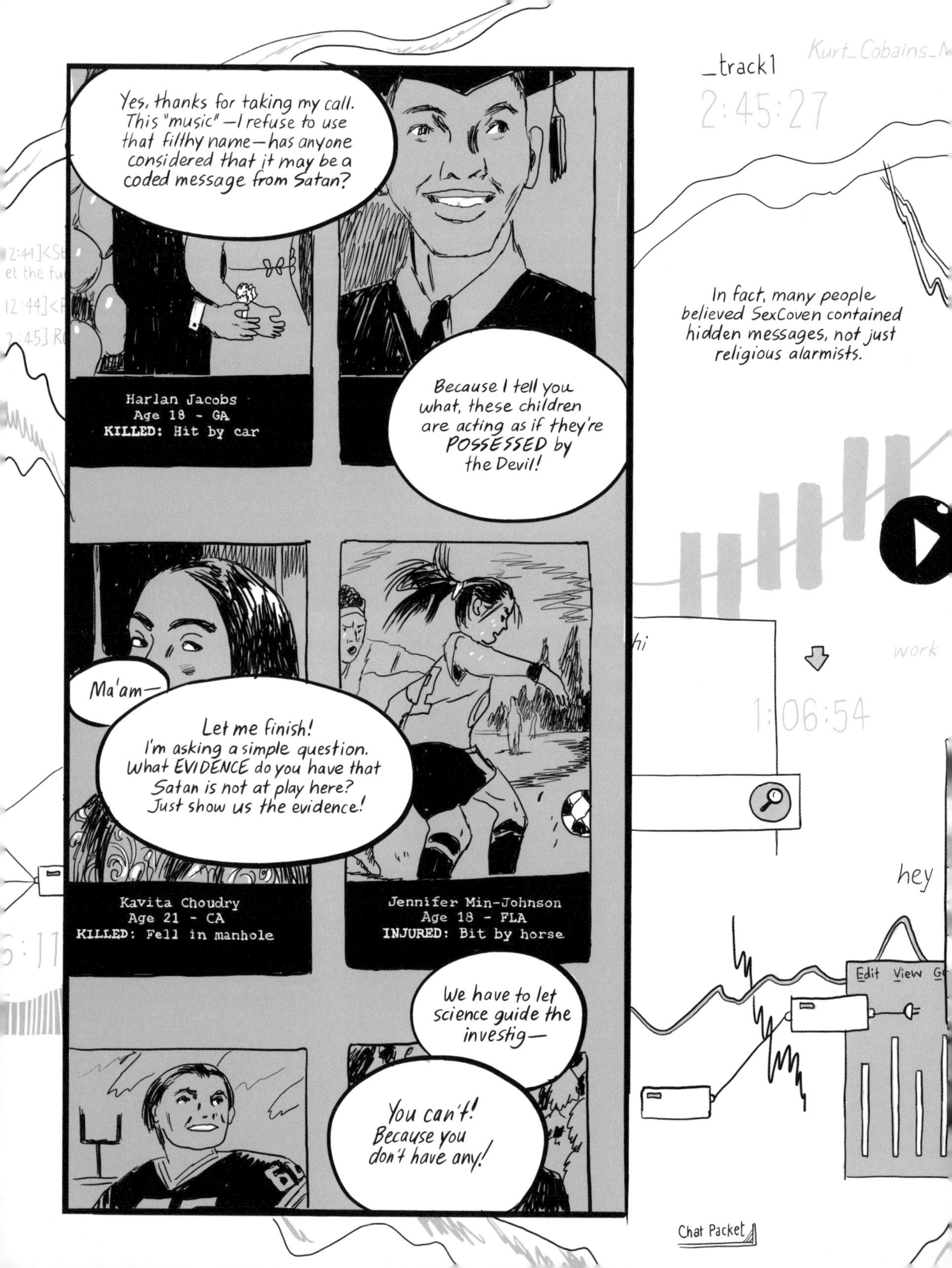

Yes, thanks for taking my call. This "music"—I refuse to use that filthy name—has anyone considered that it may be a coded message from Satan?
Harlan Jacobs
Age 18 - GA
KILLED: Hit by car
Because I tell you what, these children are acting as if they're POSSESSED by the Devil!
_track1
2:45:27
In fact, many people believed SexCoven contained hidden messages, not just religious alarmists.
Ma'am—
Let me finish! I'm asking a simple question. What EVIDENCE do you have that Satan is not at play here? Just show us the evidence!
Kavita Choudry
Age 21 - CA
KILLED: Fell in manhole
Jennifer Min-Johnson
Age 18 - FLA
INJURED: Bit by horse
hi
work
1:06:54
hey
We have to let science guide the investig—
You can't! Because you don't have any!
Edit View
Chat Packet

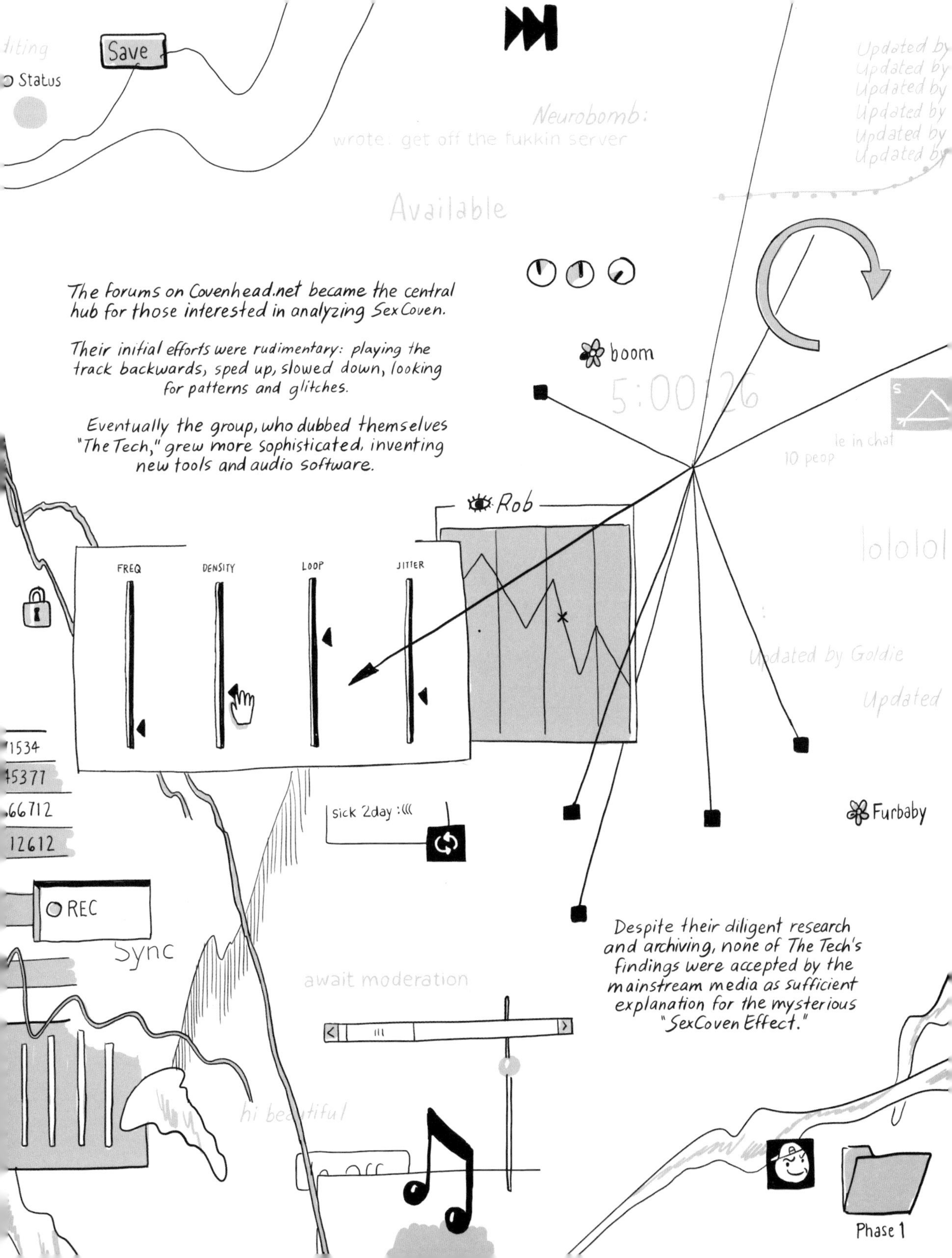
Save
Status
Neurobomb:
wrote: get off the fukkin server
Updated by
Updated by
Updated by
Updated by
Updated by
Updated by
Available
The forums on Covenhead.net became the central hub for those interested in analyzing SexCoven.
Their initial efforts were rudimentary: playing the track backwards, sped up, slowed down, looking for patterns and glitches.
Eventually the group, who dubbed themselves "The Tech," grew more sophisticated, inventing new tools and audio software.
boom
5:00 26
le in chat
10 peop
Rob
lololol
FREQ
DENSITY
LOOP
JITTER
Updated by Goldie
Updated
sick 2day :(((
Furbaby
REC
Sync
await moderation
Despite their diligent research and archiving, none of The Tech's findings were accepted by the mainstream media as sufficient explanation for the mysterious "SexCoven Effect."
hi beautiful
Phase 1

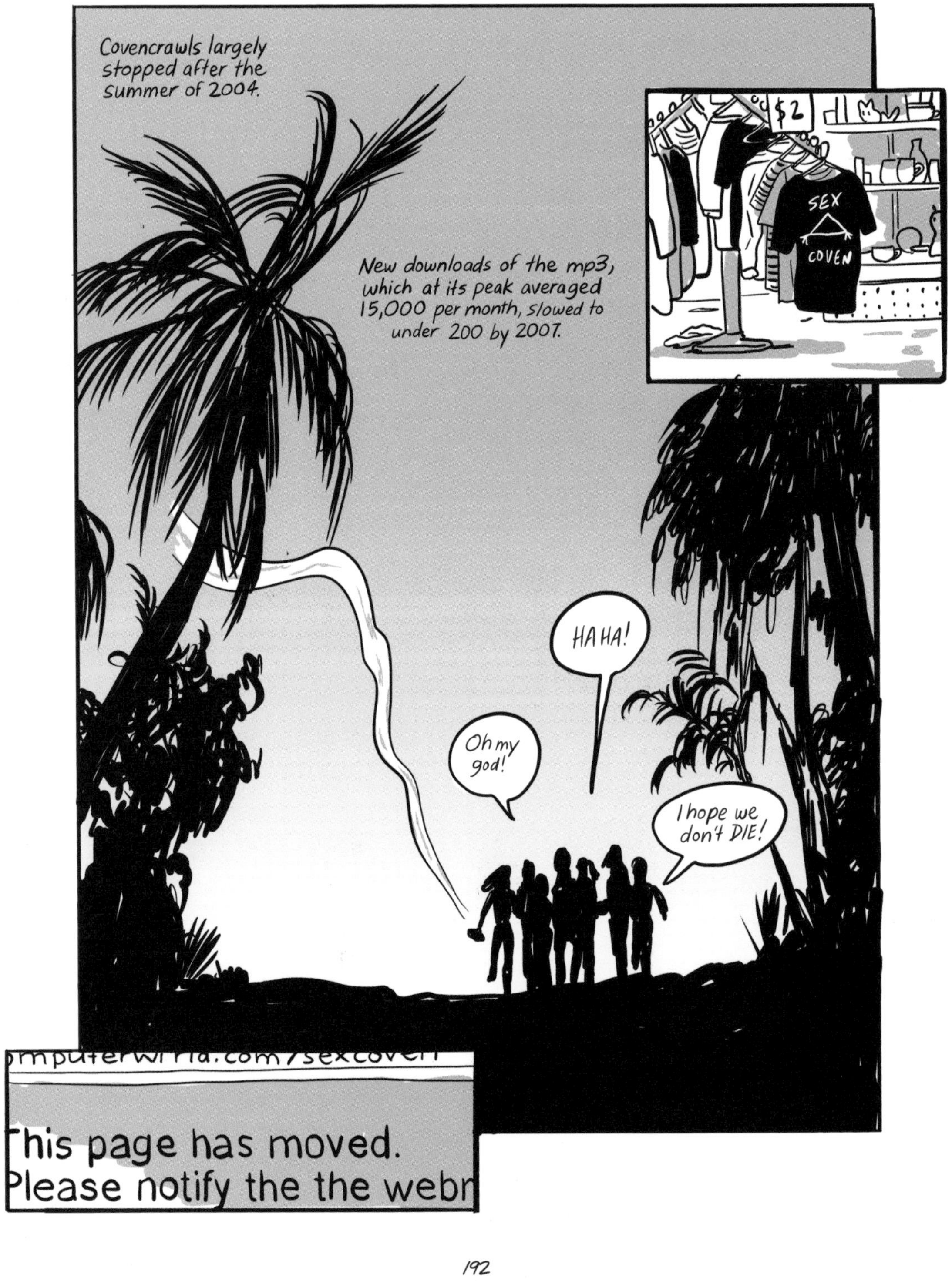
Covencrawls largely stopped after the summer of 2004.
$2
SEX
COVEN
New downloads of the mp3, which at its peak averaged 15,000 per month, slowed to under 200 by 2007.
HA HA!
Oh my god!
I hope we don't DIE!
This page has moved.
Please notify the the webr

Even many of The Tech drifted away from the community, usually after college.

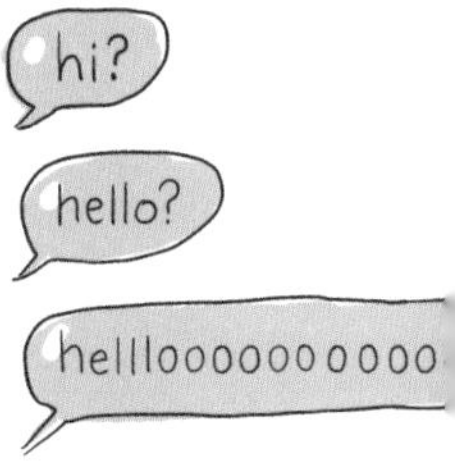
hi?
hello?
helllooooooooooo

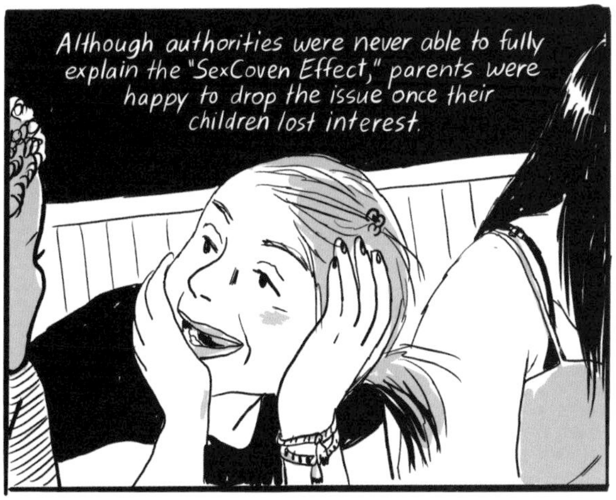
Although authorities were never able to fully explain the "SexCoven Effect," parents were happy to drop the issue once their children lost interest.

In 2010, The Tech that remained, most in their late twenties, moved their operations off the Covenhead.net forums to an unsearchable network.

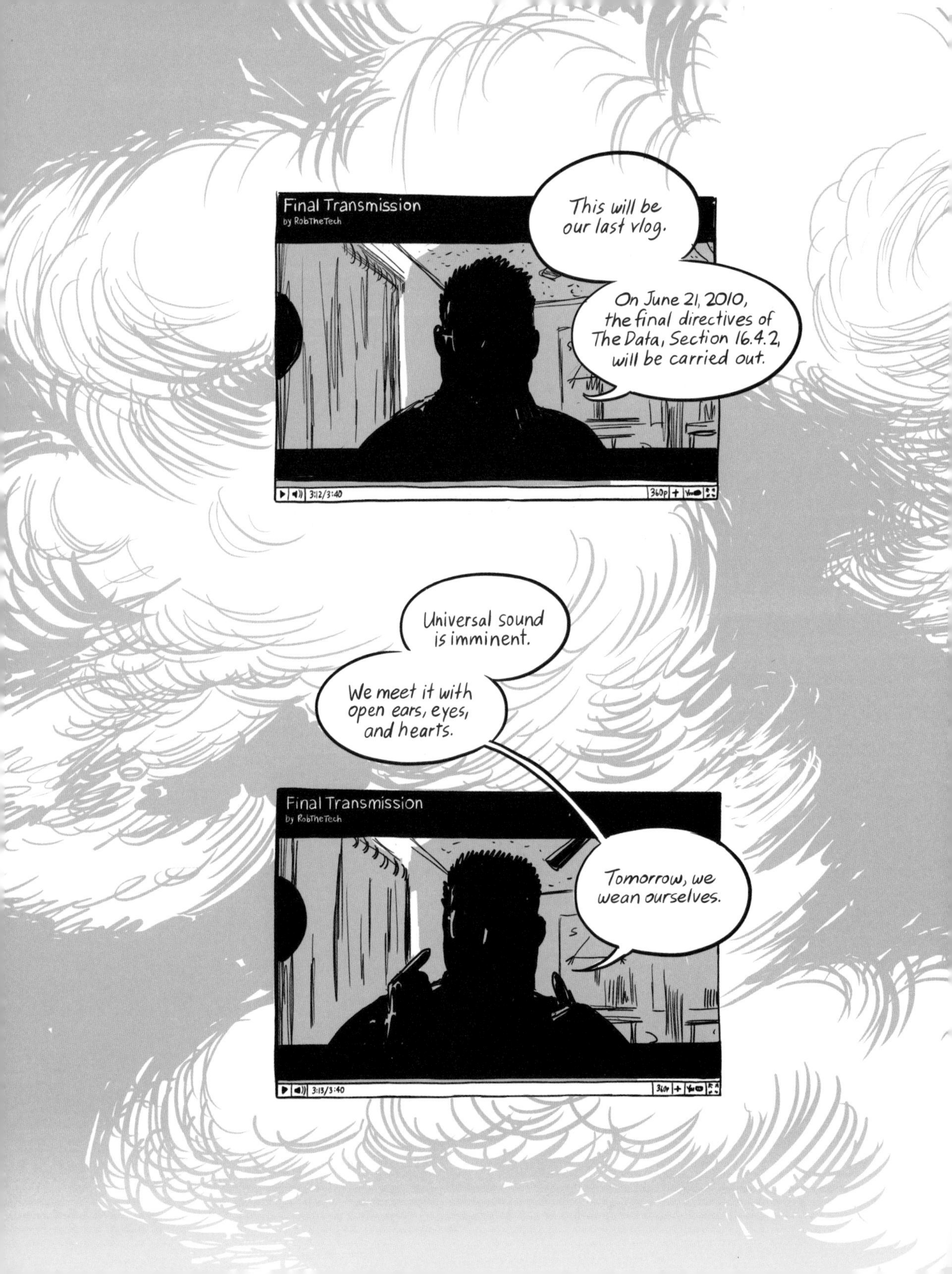
Final Transmission
by RobTheTech
This will be our last vlog.
On June 21, 2010, the final directives of The Data, Section 16.4.2, will be carried out.
3:12/3:40
360p
Universal sound is imminent.
We meet it with open ears, eyes, and hearts.
Final Transmission
by RobTheTech
Tomorrow, we wean ourselves.
3:13/3:40

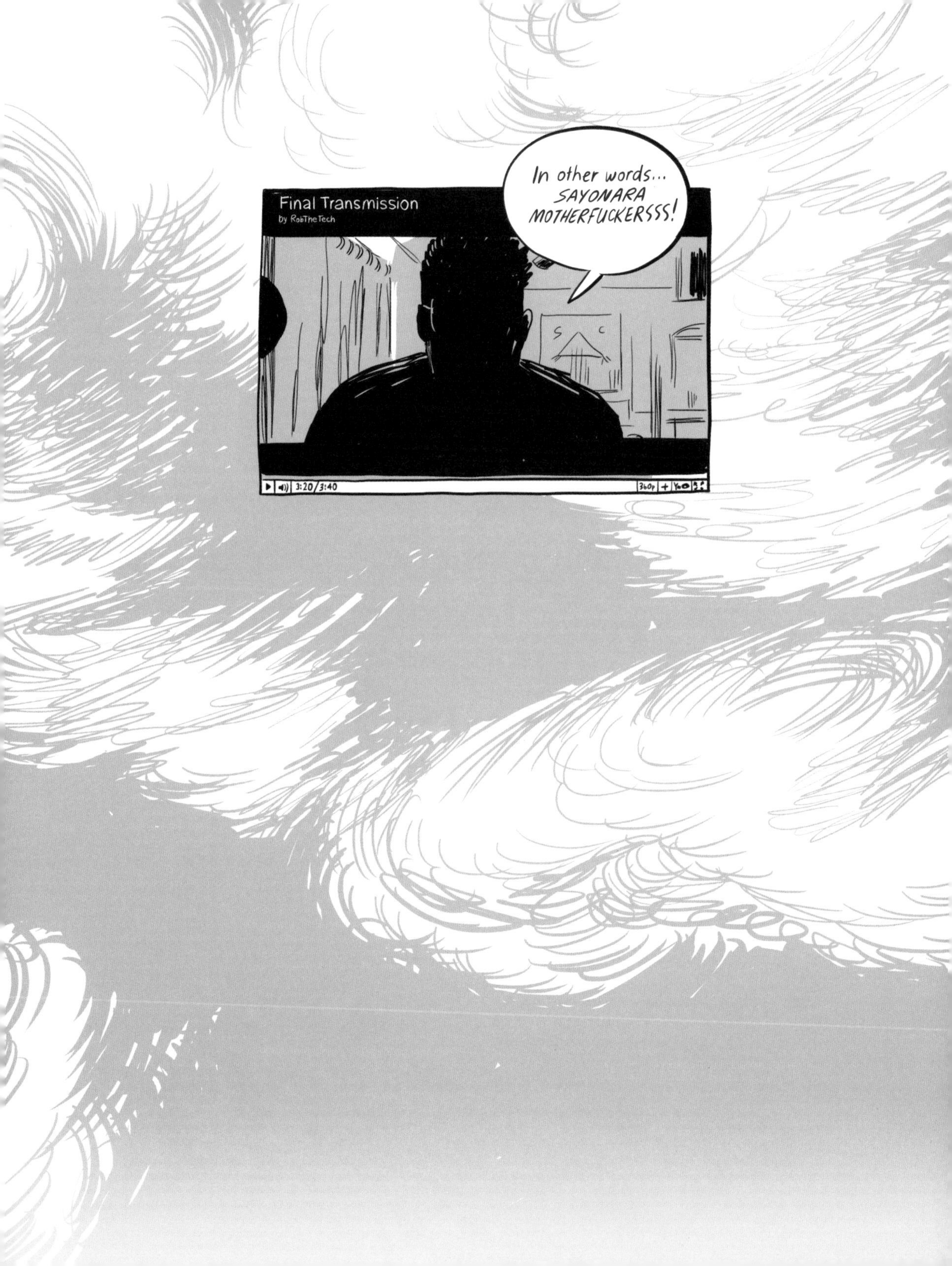

Final Transmission
by RobTheTech
In other words... SAYONARA MOTHERFUCKERSSS!
3:20/3:40
360p

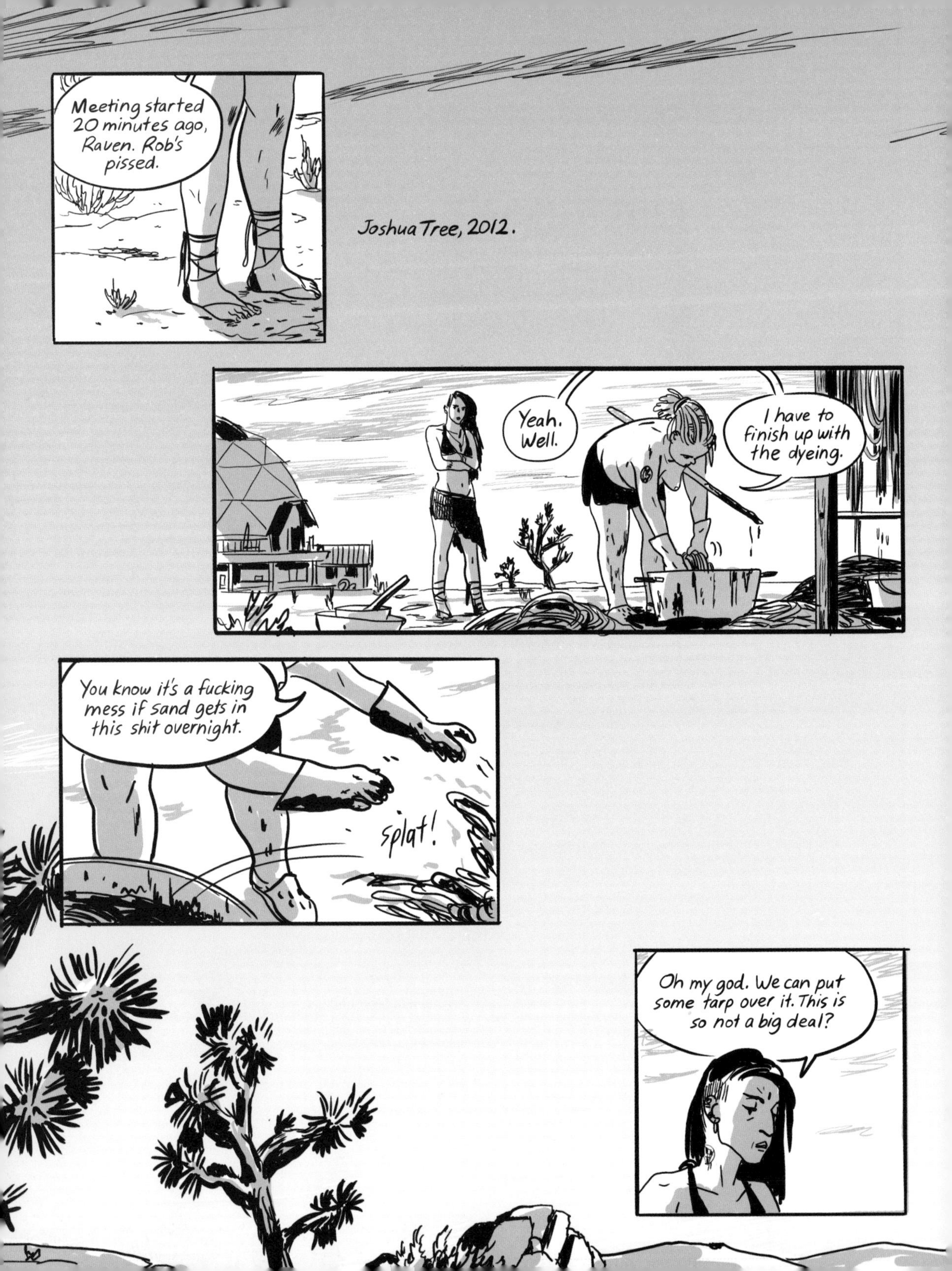
Meeting started 20 minutes ago, Raven. Rob's pissed.
Joshua Tree, 2012.
Yeah. Well.
I have to finish up with the dyeing.
You know it's a fucking mess if sand gets in this shit overnight.
splat!
Oh my god. We can put some tarp over it. This is so not a big deal?

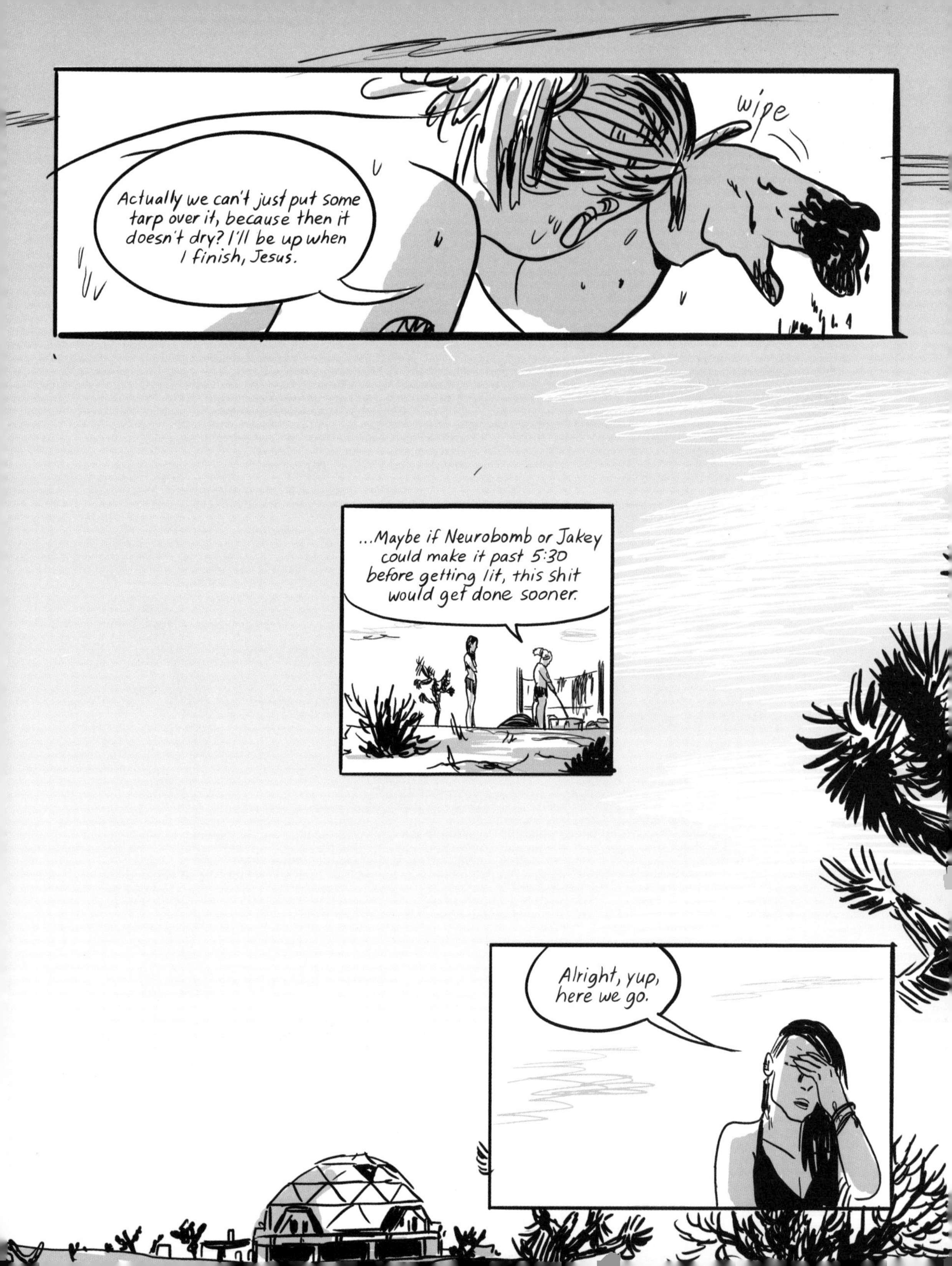
wipe
Actually we can't just put some tarp over it, because then it doesn't dry? I'll be up when I finish, Jesus.
...Maybe if Neurobomb or Jakey could make it past 5:30 before getting lit, this shit would get done sooner.
Alright, yup, here we go.

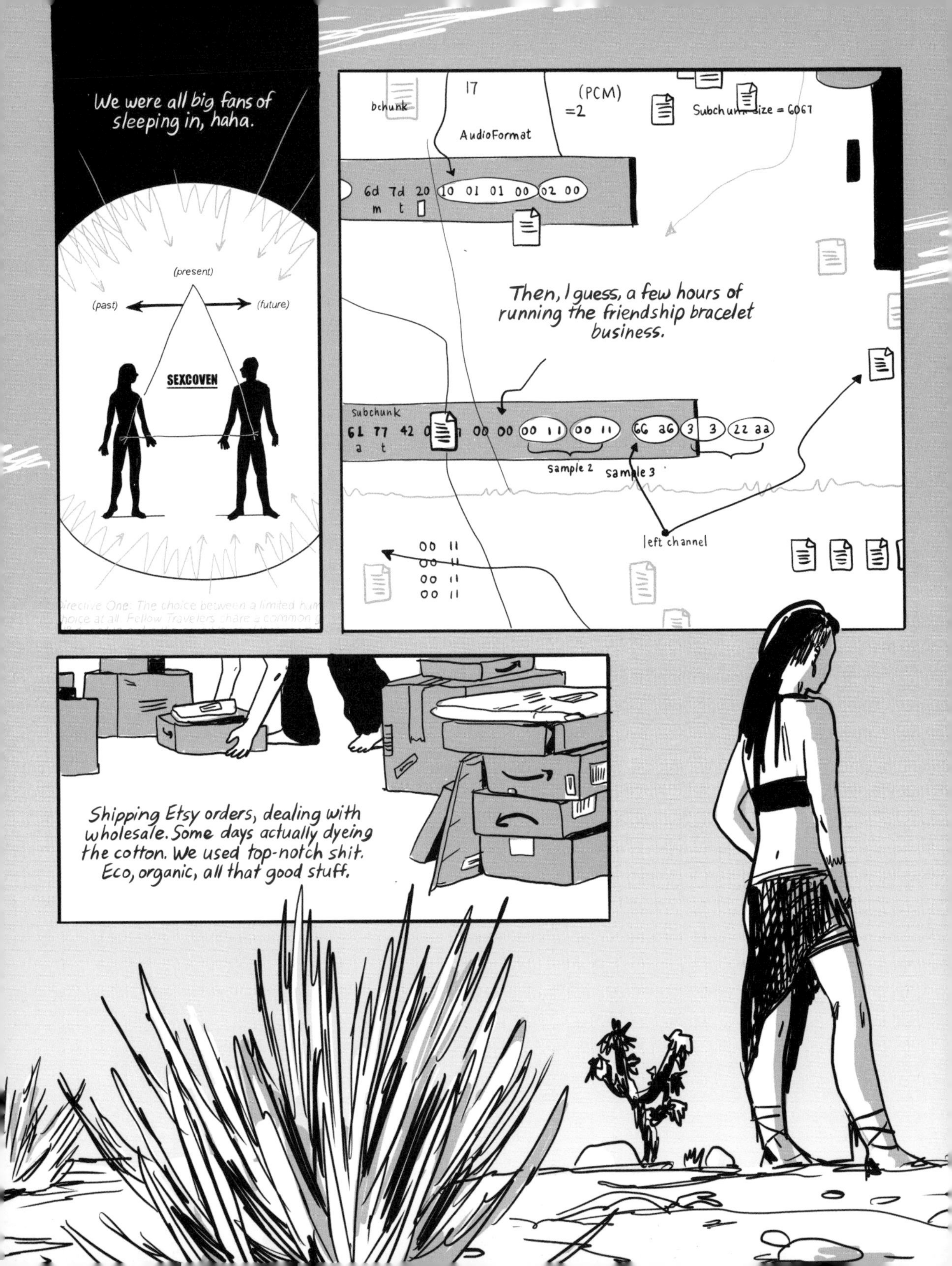
We were all big fans of sleeping in, haha.
(present)
(past)
(future)
SEXCOVEN
17
(PCM)
=2
bchunk
AudioFormat
Subchunk size = 6067
6d 7d 20 10 01 01 00 02 00
m t
Then, I guess, a few hours of running the friendship bracelet business.
subchunk
sample 2
sample 3
left channel
00 11
00 11
00 11
00 11
Shipping Etsy orders, dealing with wholesale. Some days actually dyeing the cotton. We used top-notch shit. Eco, organic, all that good stuff.

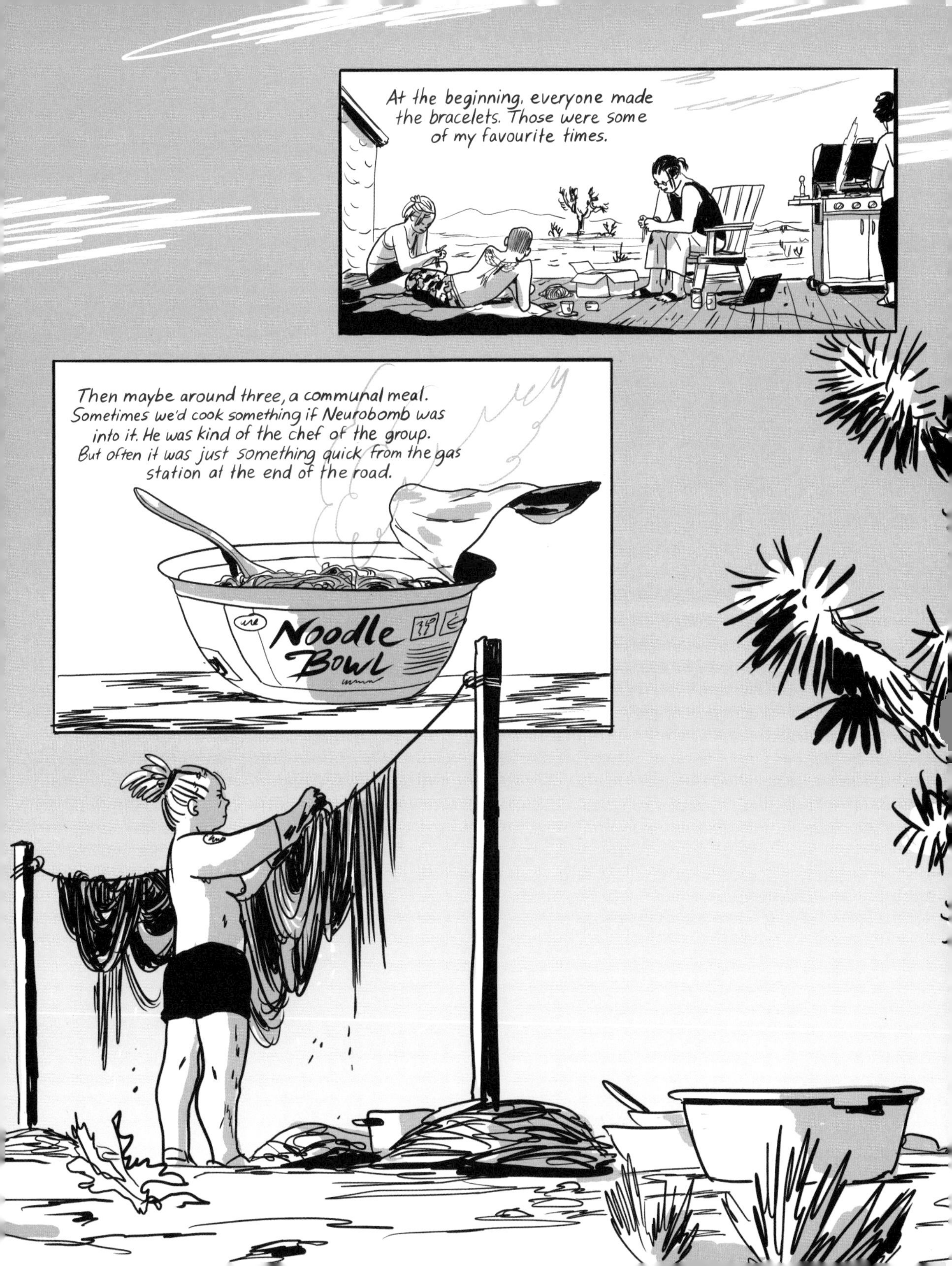
At the beginning, everyone made the bracelets. Those were some of my favourite times.
Then maybe around three, a communal meal. Sometimes we'd cook something if Neurobomb was into it. He was kind of the chef of the group. But often it was just something quick from the gas station at the end of the road.
Noodle Bowl

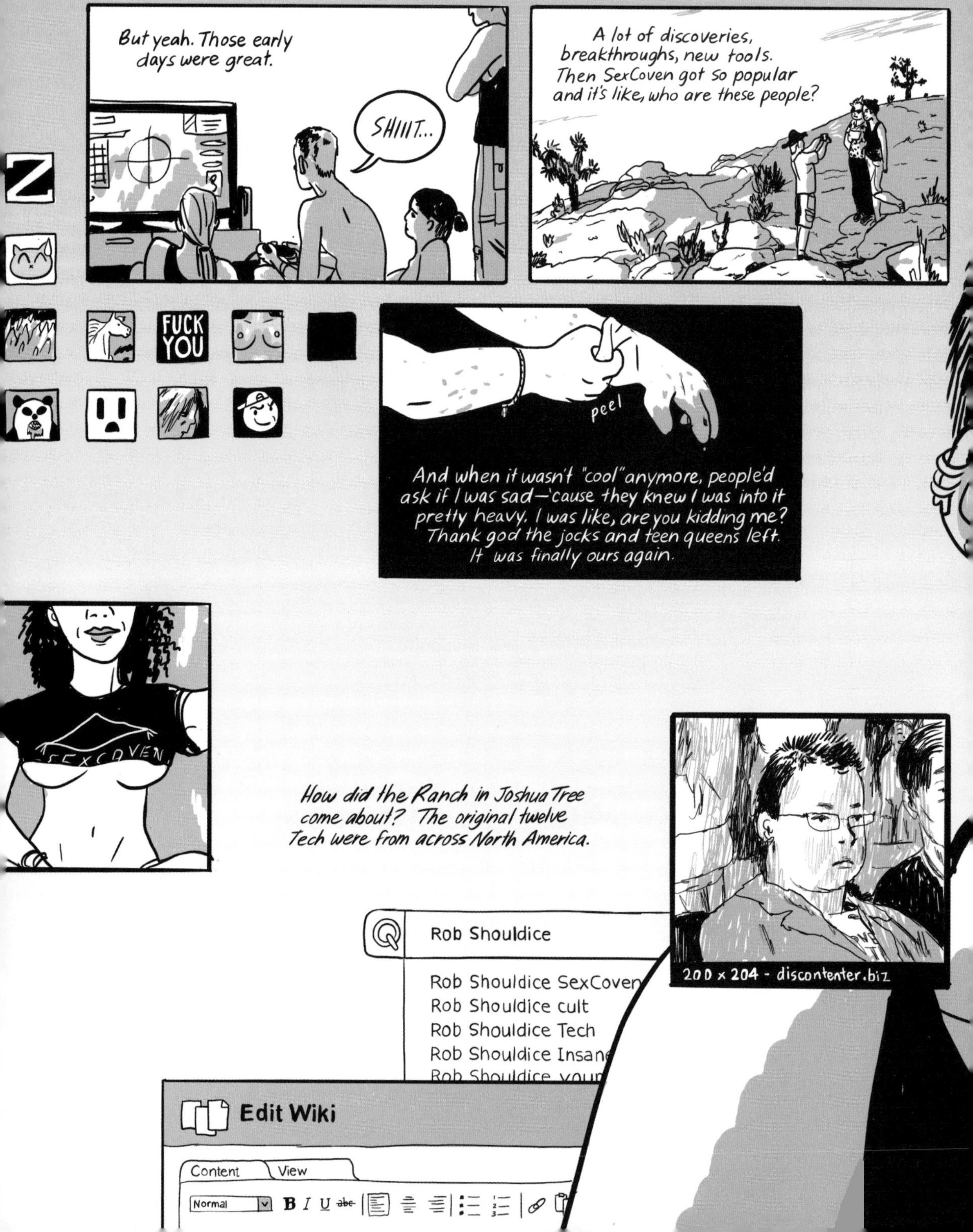
But yeah. Those early days were great.
SHIIIT...
A lot of discoveries, breakthroughs, new tools. Then SexCoven got so popular and it's like, who are these people?
FUCK YOU
peel
And when it wasn't "cool" anymore, people'd ask if I was sad—'cause they knew I was into it pretty heavy. I was like, are you kidding me? Thank god the jocks and teen queens left. It was finally ours again.
SEXCOVEN
How did the Ranch in Joshua Tree come about? The original twelve Tech were from across North America.
Rob Shouldice
Rob Shouldice SexCoven
Rob Shouldice cult
Rob Shouldice Tech
Rob Shouldice Insane
200 x 204 - discontenter.biz
Edit Wiki
Content
View
Normal
B I U abc

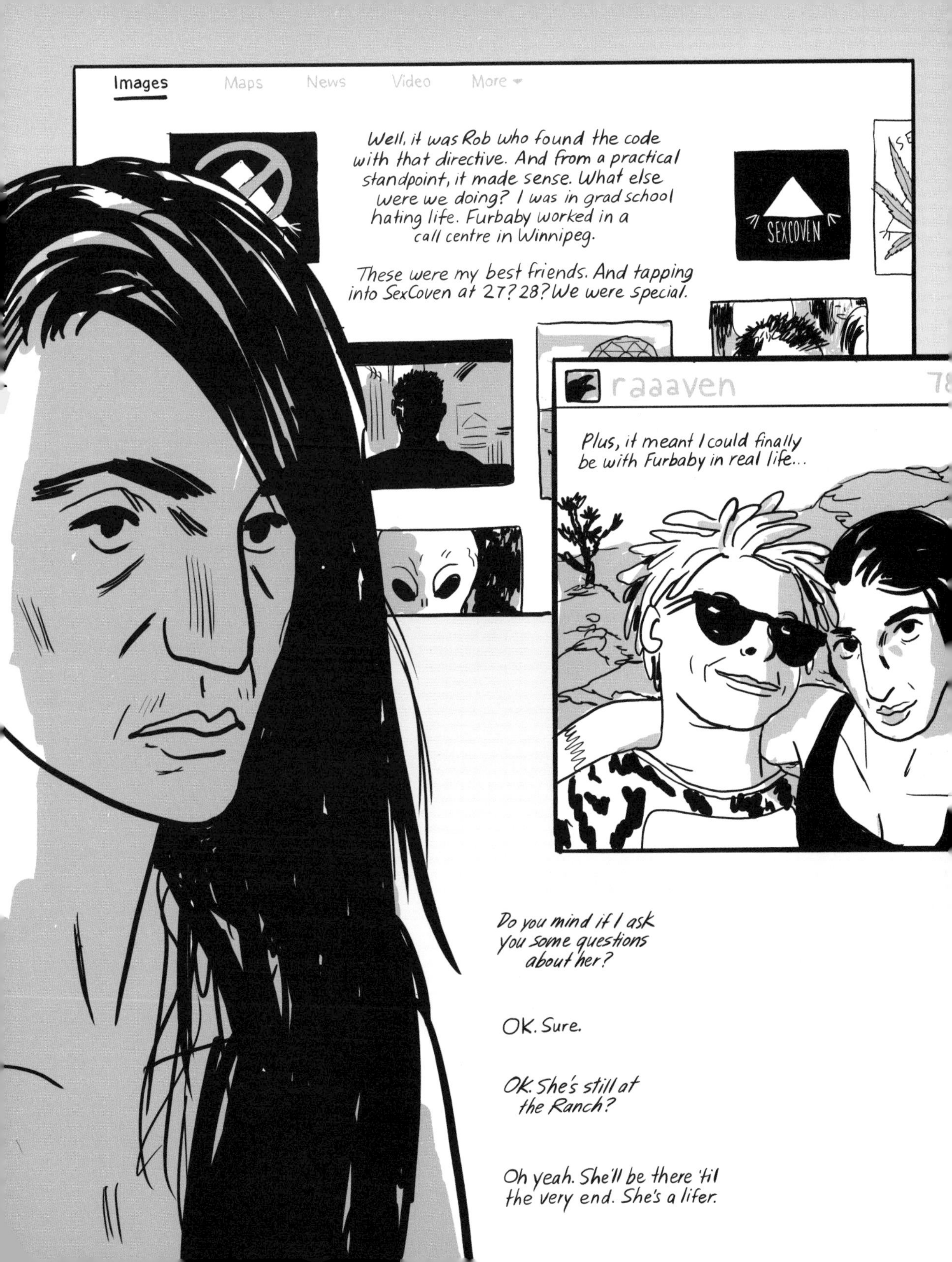
Images
Maps
News
Video
More
Well, it was Rob who found the code with that directive. And from a practical standpoint, it made sense. What else were we doing? I was in grad school hating life. Furbaby worked in a call centre in Winnipeg.
These were my best friends. And tapping into SexCoven at 27? 28? We were special.
SEXCOVEN
raaaven
Plus, it meant I could finally be with Furbaby in real life...
Do you mind if I ask you some questions about her?
OK. Sure.
OK. She's still at the Ranch?
Oh yeah. She'll be there 'til the very end. She's a lifer.

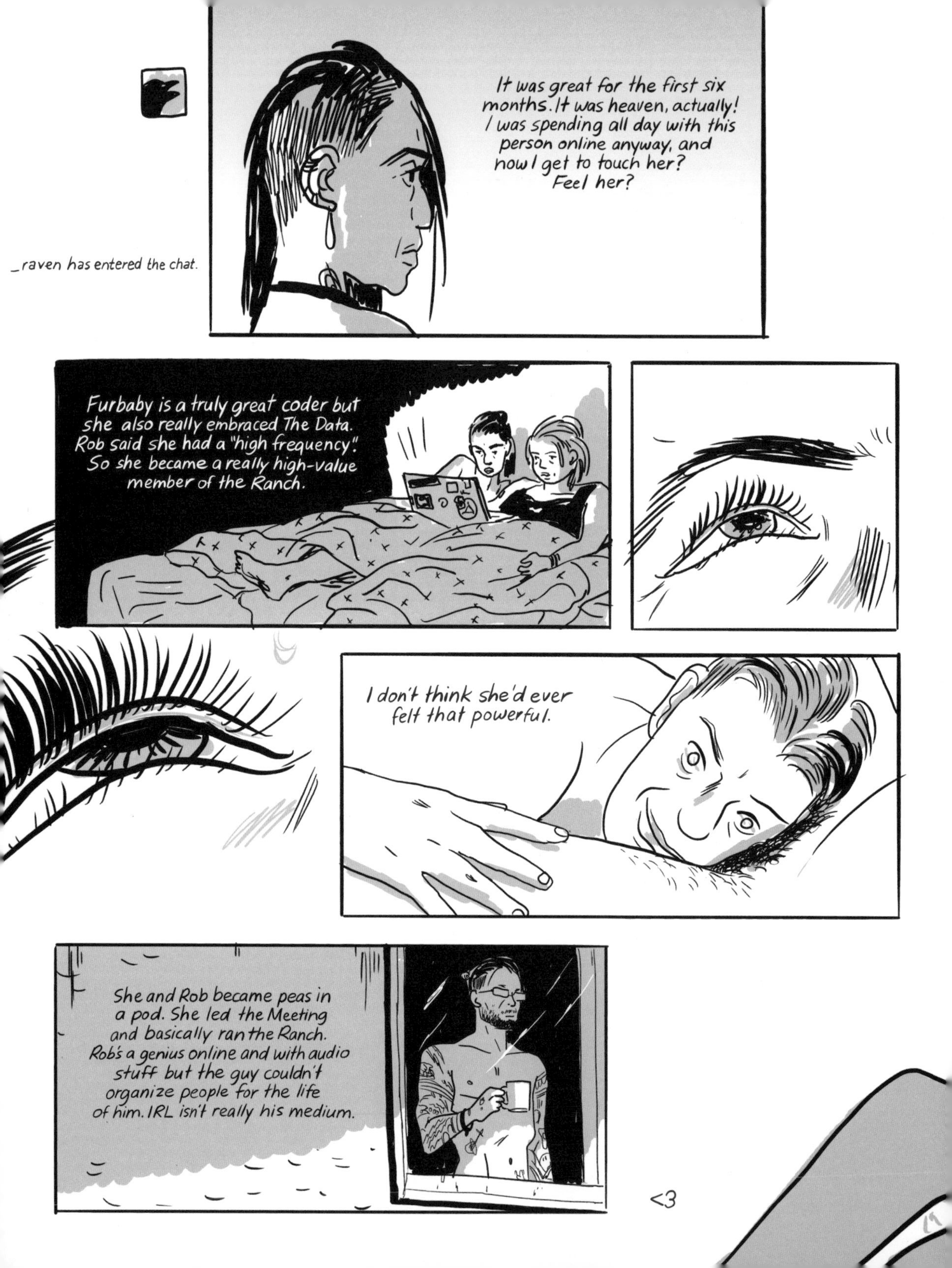

_raven has entered the chat.
It was great for the first six months. It was heaven, actually! I was spending all day with this person online anyway, and now I get to touch her? Feel her?
Furbaby is a truly great coder but she also really embraced The Data. Rob said she had a "high frequency". So she became a really high-value member of the Ranch.
I don't think she'd ever felt that powerful.
She and Rob became peas in a pod. She led the Meeting and basically ran the Ranch. Rob's a genius online and with audio stuff but the guy couldn't organize people for the life of him. IRL isn't really his medium.
<3

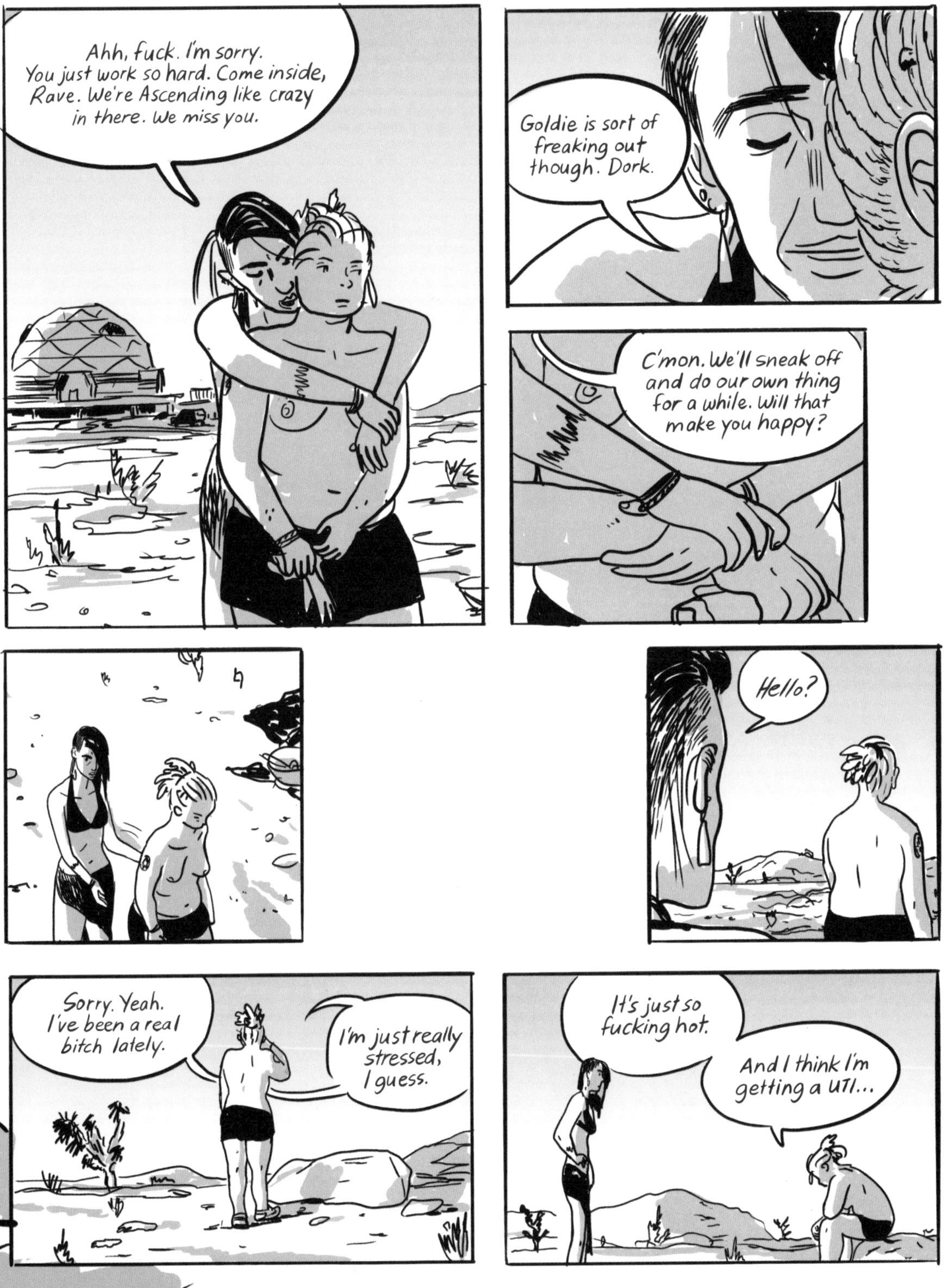
Ahh, fuck. I'm sorry. You just work so hard. Come inside, Rave. We're Ascending like crazy in there. We miss you.
Goldie is sort of freaking out though. Dork.
C'mon. We'll sneak off and do our own thing for a while. Will that make you happy?
Hello?
Sorry. Yeah. I've been a real bitch lately.
I'm just really stressed, I guess.
It's just so fucking hot.
And I think I'm getting a UTI...

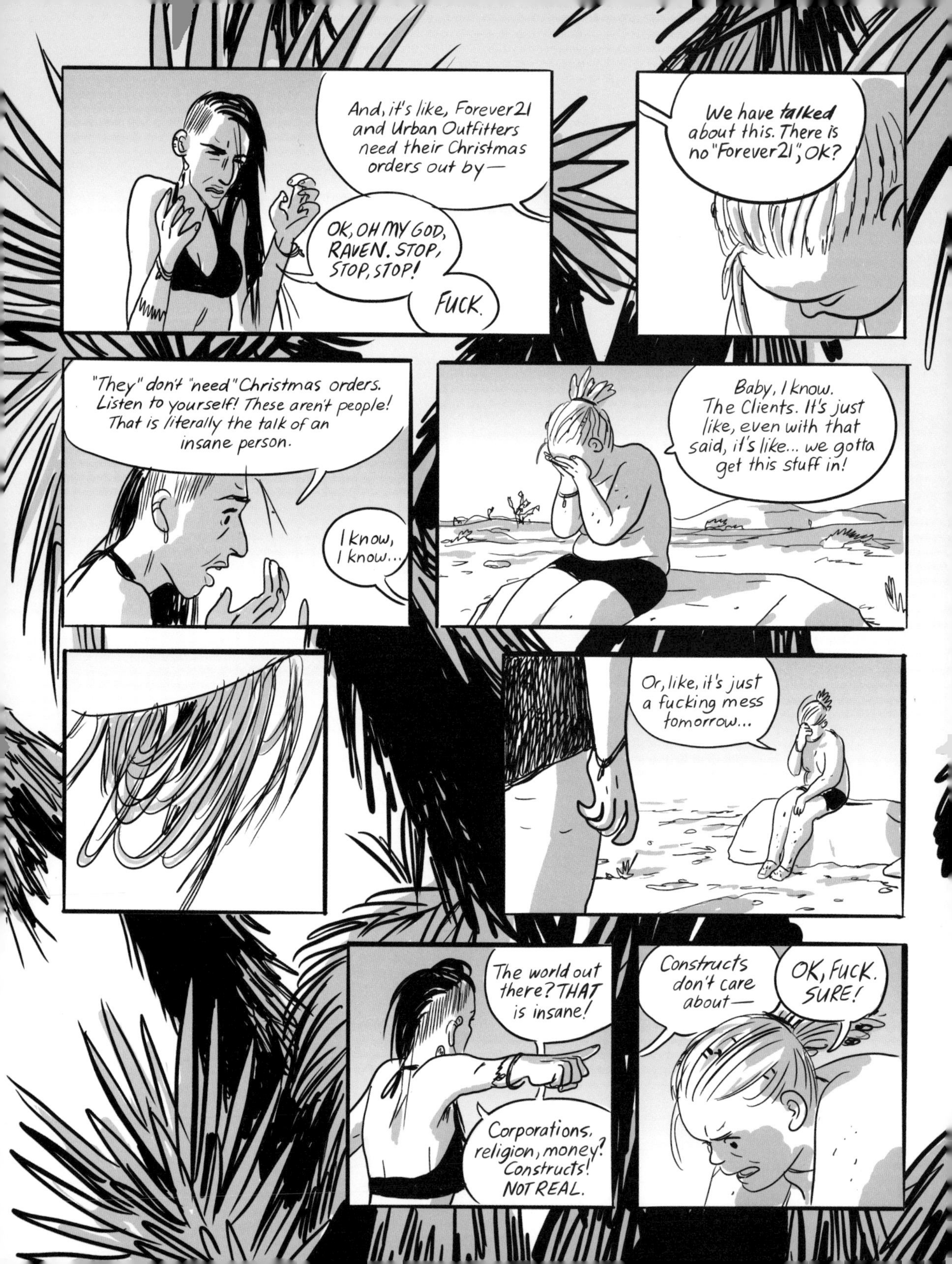

And, it's like, Forever21 and Urban Outfitters need their Christmas orders out by—
OK, OH MY GOD, RAVEN. STOP, STOP, STOP!
FUCK.
We have **talked** about this. There is no "Forever21," OK?
"They" don't "need" Christmas orders. Listen to yourself! These aren't people! That is literally the talk of an insane person.
I know, I know...
Baby, I know. The Clients. It's just like, even with that said, it's like... we gotta get this stuff in!
Or, like, it's just a fucking mess tomorrow...
The world out there? THAT is insane!
Corporations, religion, money? Constructs! NOT REAL.
Constructs don't care about—
OK, FUCK. SURE!

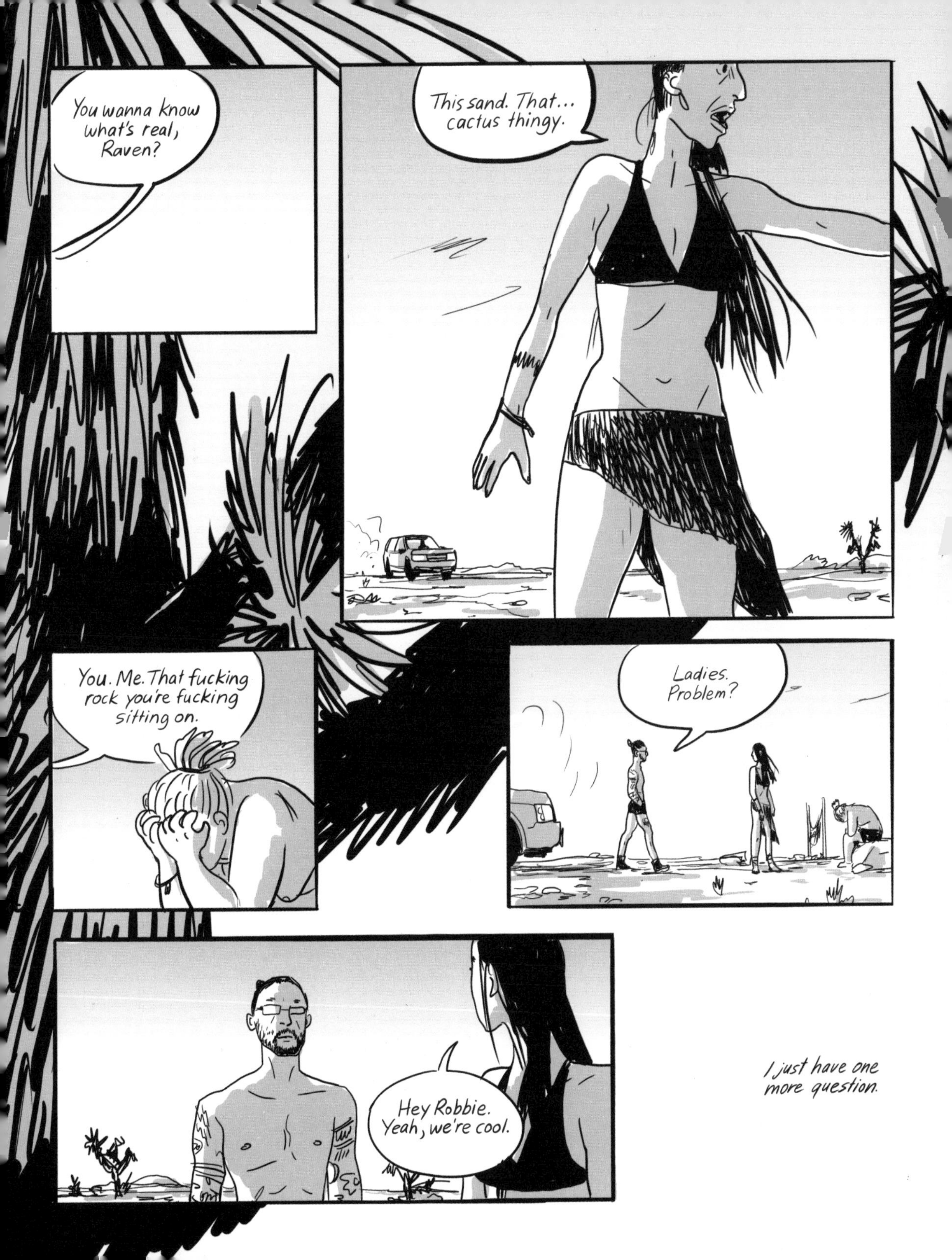
You wanna know what's real, Raven?
This sand. That... cactus thingy.
You. Me. That fucking rock you're fucking sitting on.
Ladies. Problem?
Hey Robbie. Yeah, we're cool.
I just have one more question.

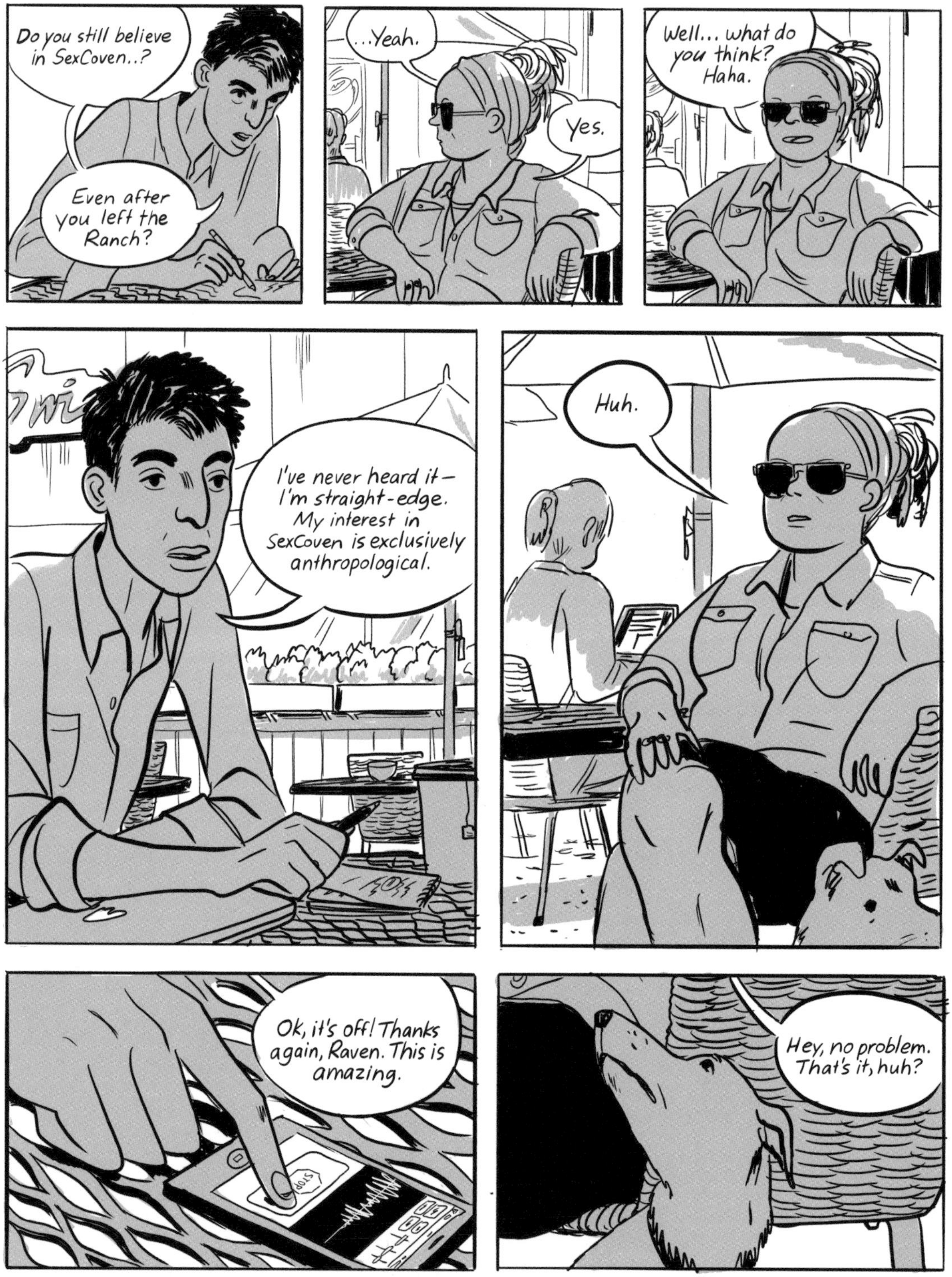
Do you still believe in SexCoven..?
Even after you left the Ranch?
...Yeah.
Yes.
Well... what do you think? Haha.
I've never heard it—I'm straight-edge. My interest in SexCoven is exclusively anthropological.
Huh.
Ok, it's off! Thanks again, Raven. This is amazing.
STOP
Hey, no problem. That's it, huh?

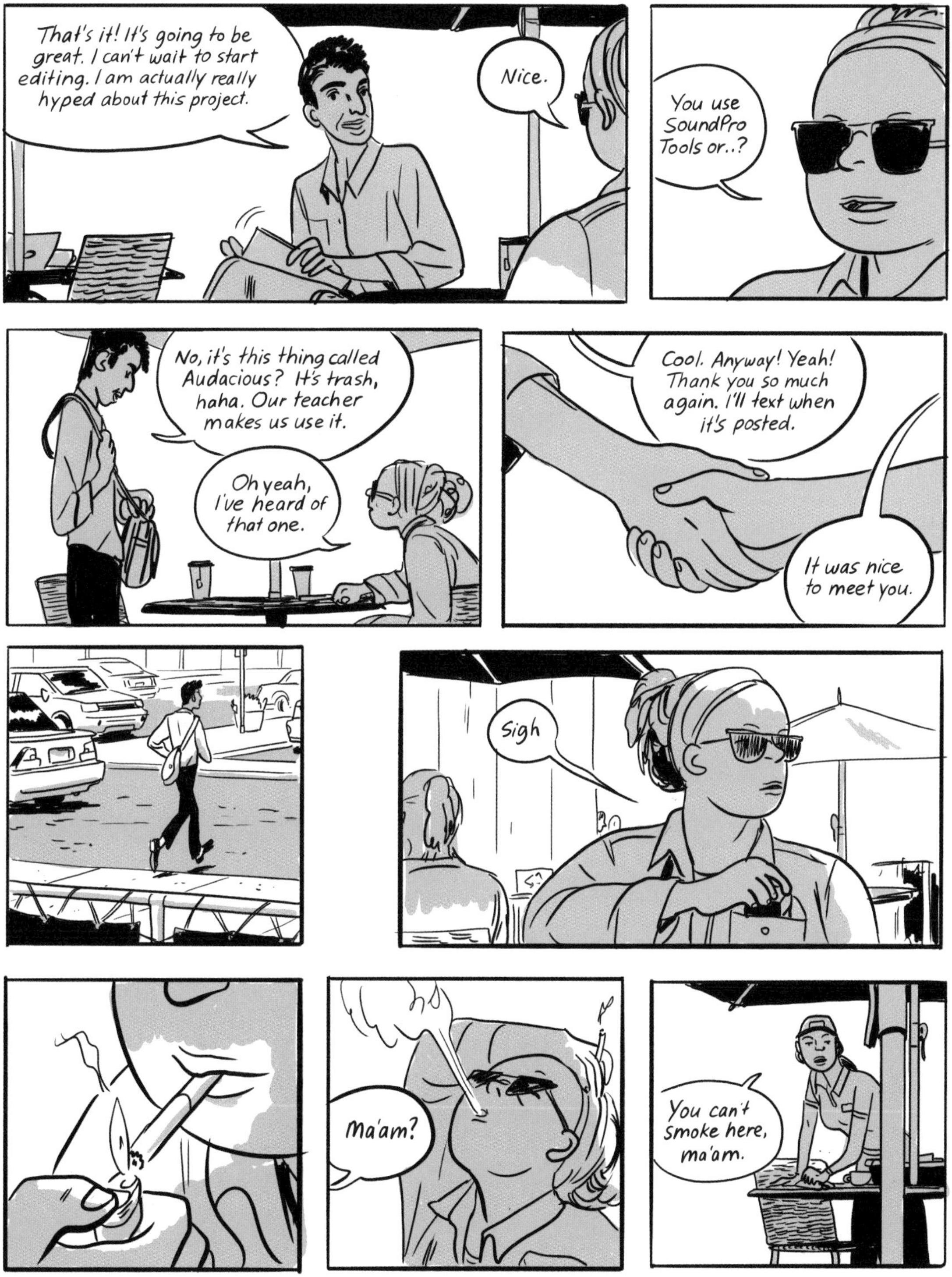

That's it! It's going to be great. I can't wait to start editing. I am actually really hyped about this project.
Nice.
You use SoundPro Tools or..?
No, it's this thing called Audacious? It's trash, haha. Our teacher makes us use it.
Oh yeah, I've heard of that one.
Cool. Anyway! Yeah! Thank you so much again. I'll text when it's posted.
It was nice to meet you.
Sigh
Ma'am?
You can't smoke here, ma'am.

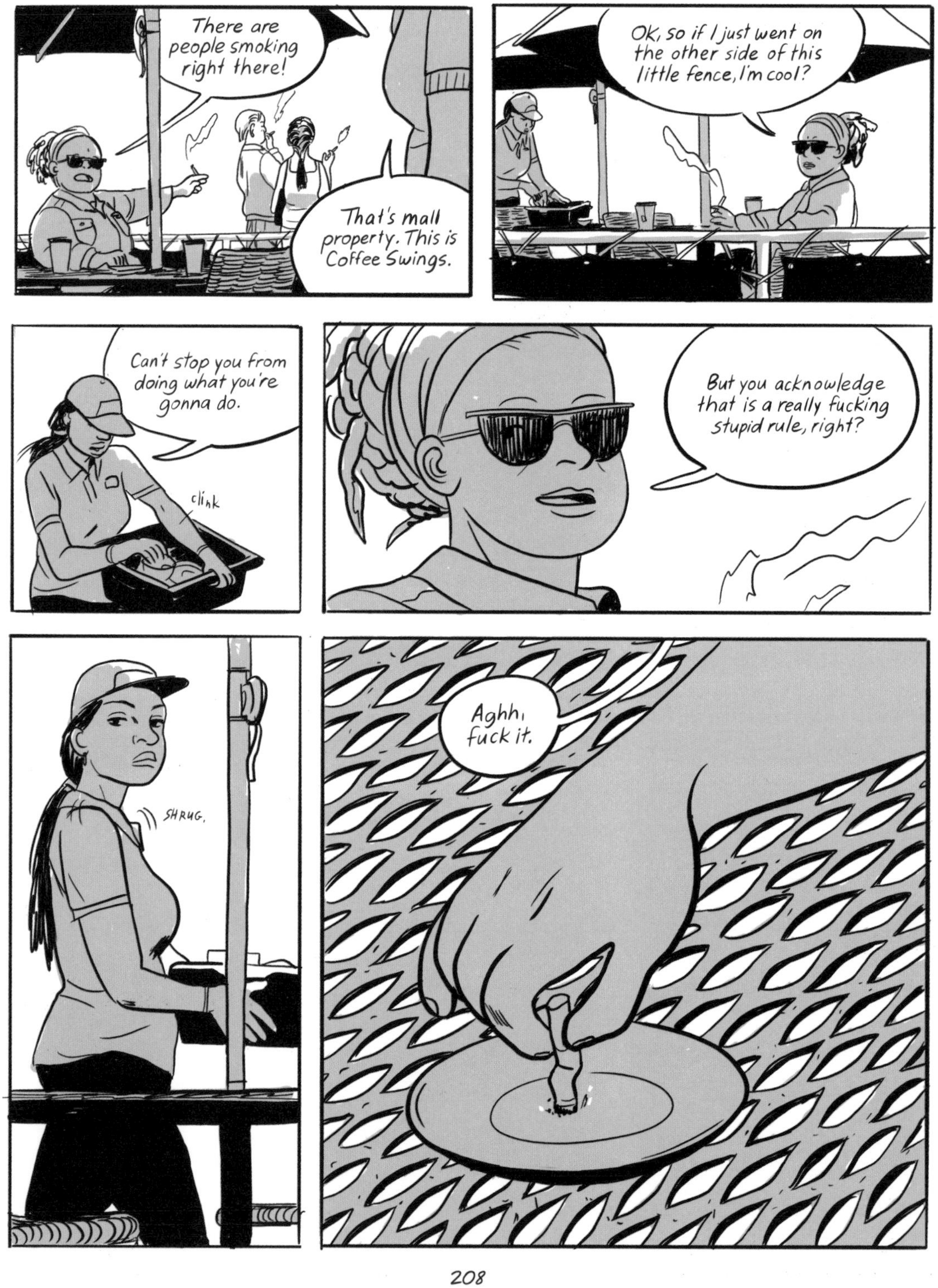
There are people smoking right there!
That's mall property. This is Coffee Swings.
Ok, so if I just went on the other side of this little fence, I'm cool?
Can't stop you from doing what you're gonna do.
clink
But you acknowledge that is a really fucking stupid rule, right?
SHRUG.
Aghh, fuck it.

BOUNDLESS

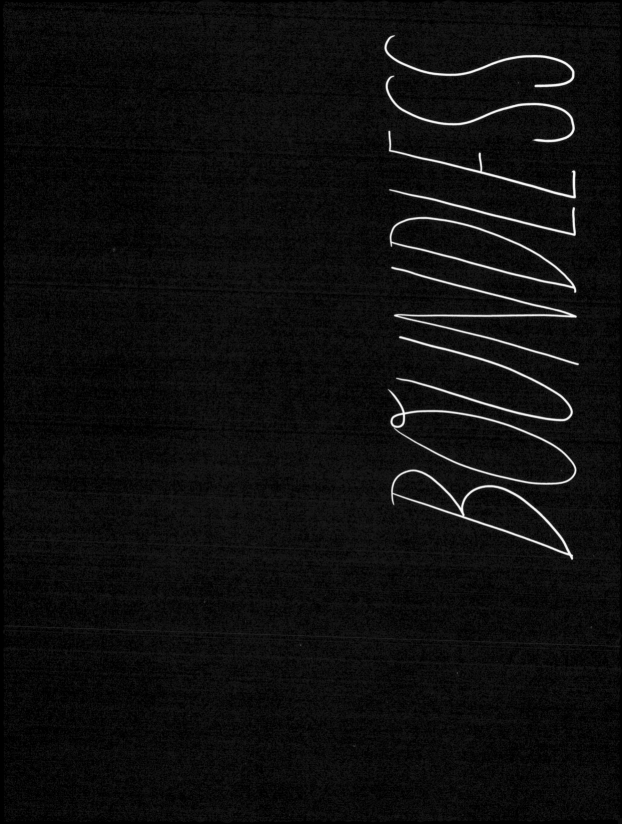

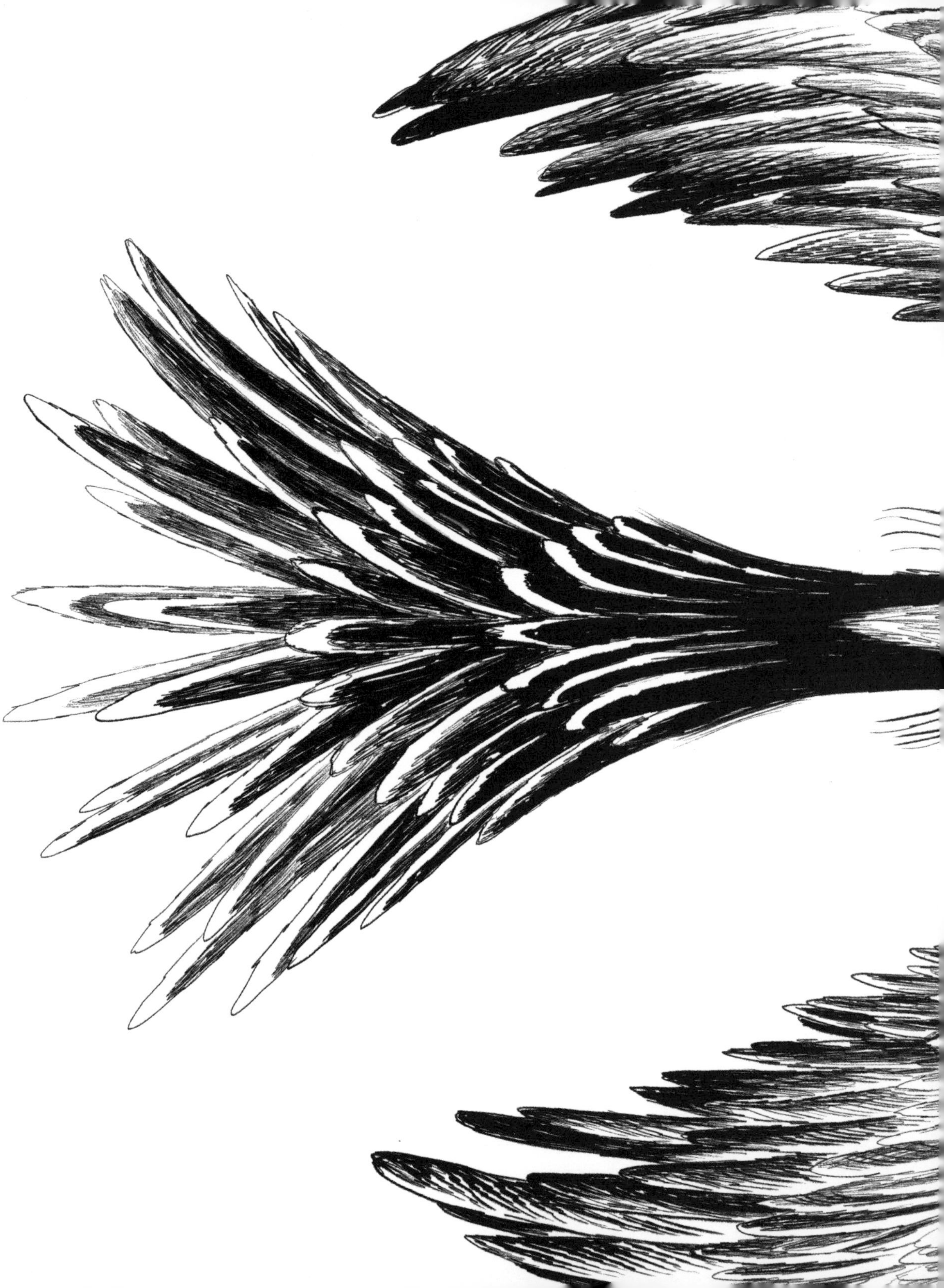

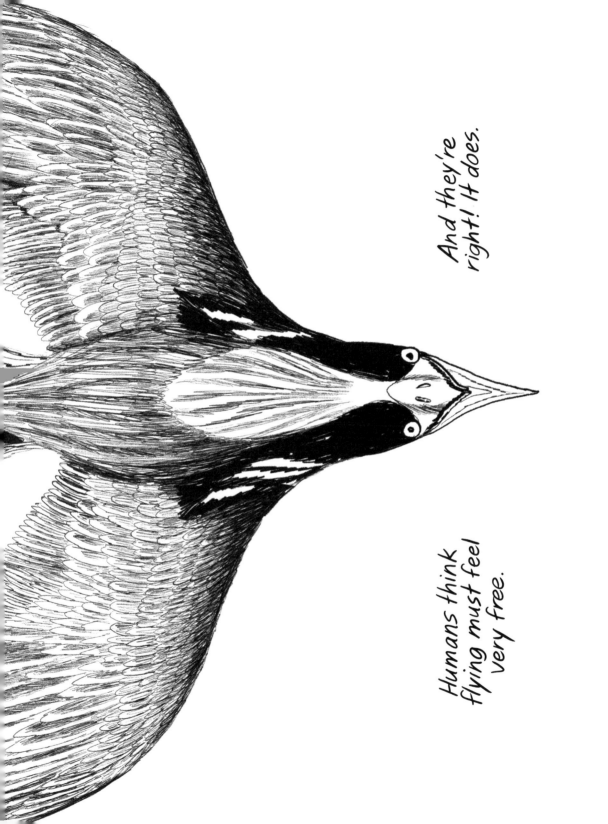

Humans think
flying must feel
very free.

And they're
right! It does.

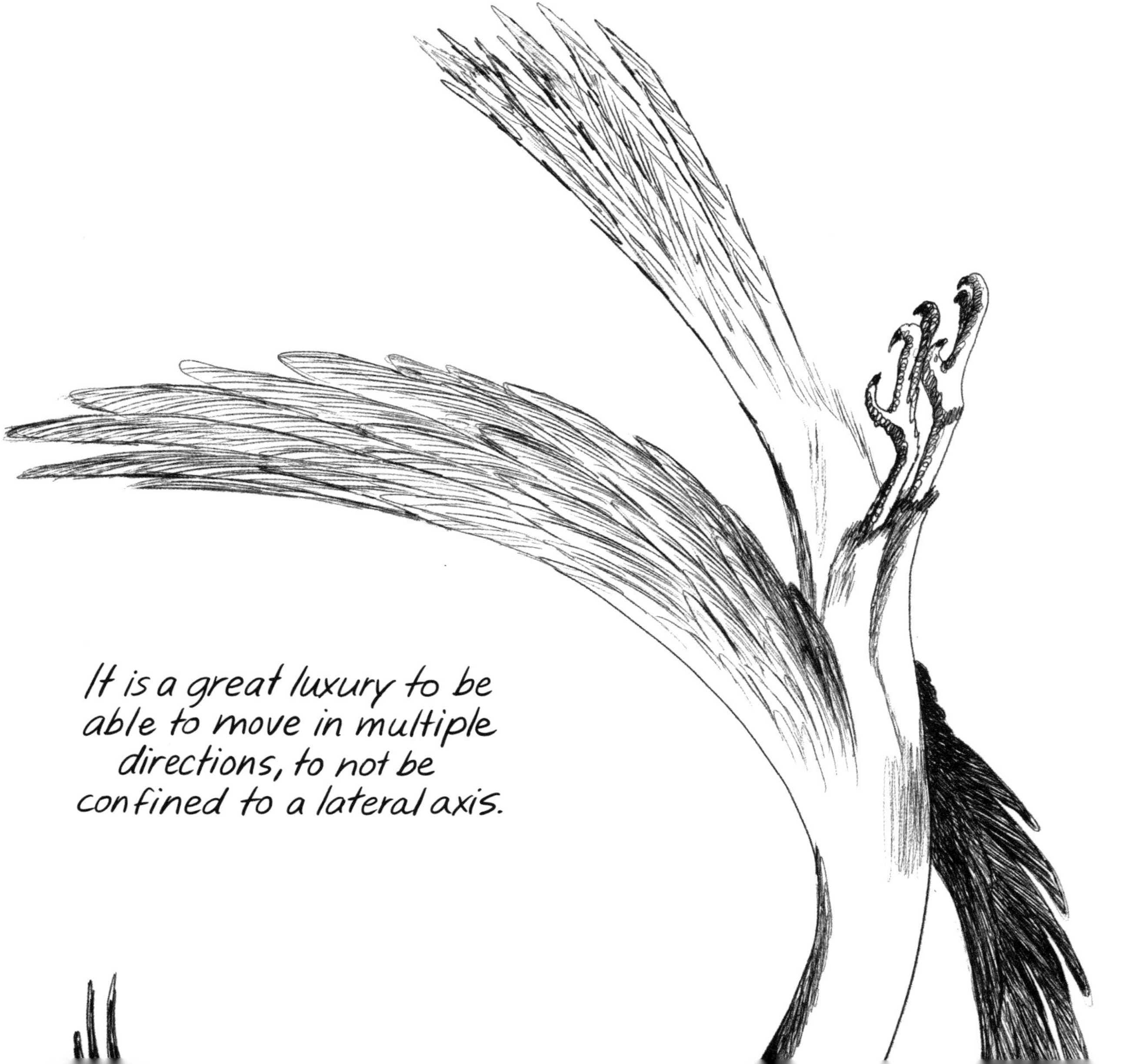
It is a great luxury to be
able to move in multiple
directions, to not be
confined to a lateral axis.

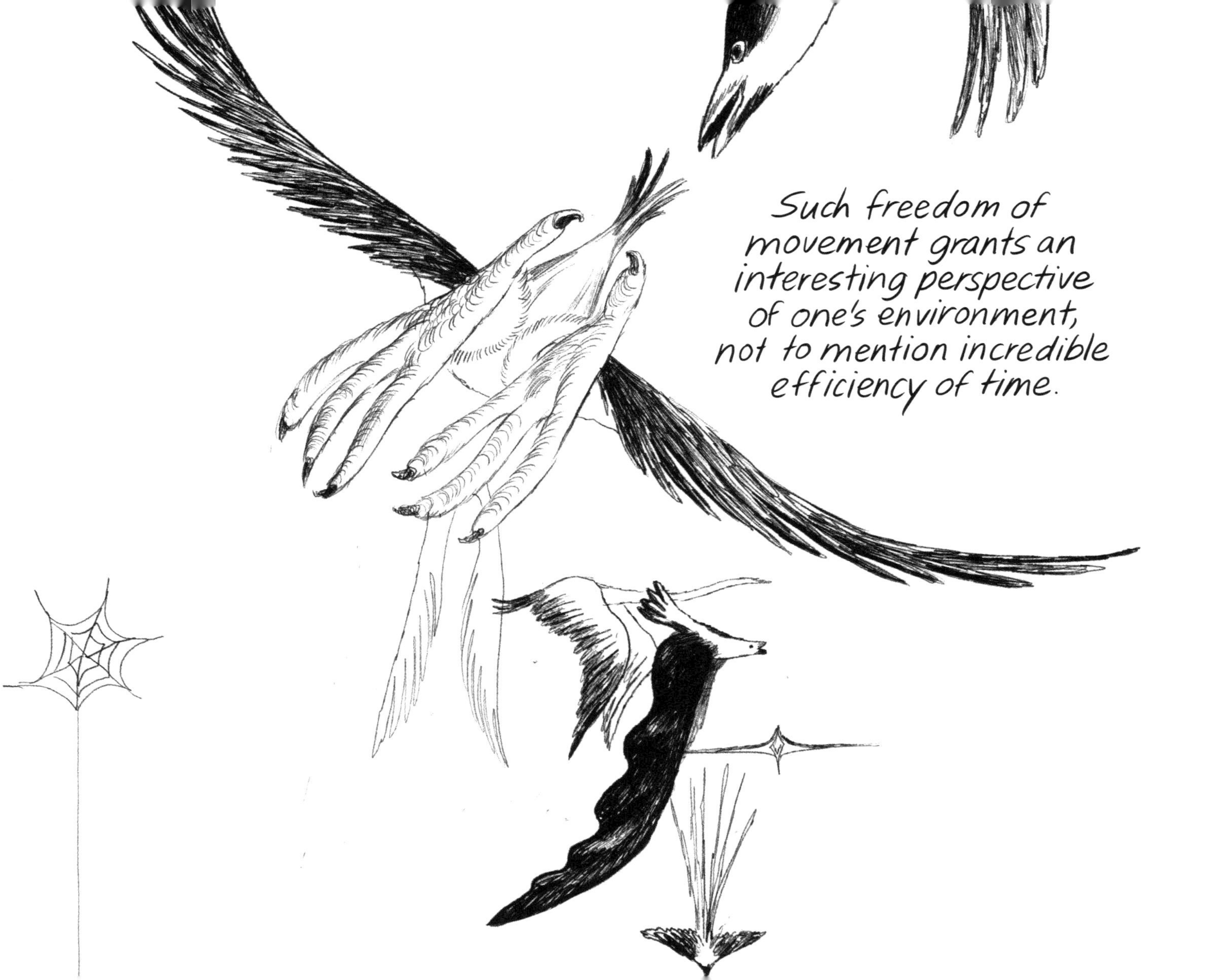
Such freedom of
movement grants an
interesting perspective
of one's environment,
not to mention incredible
efficiency of time.

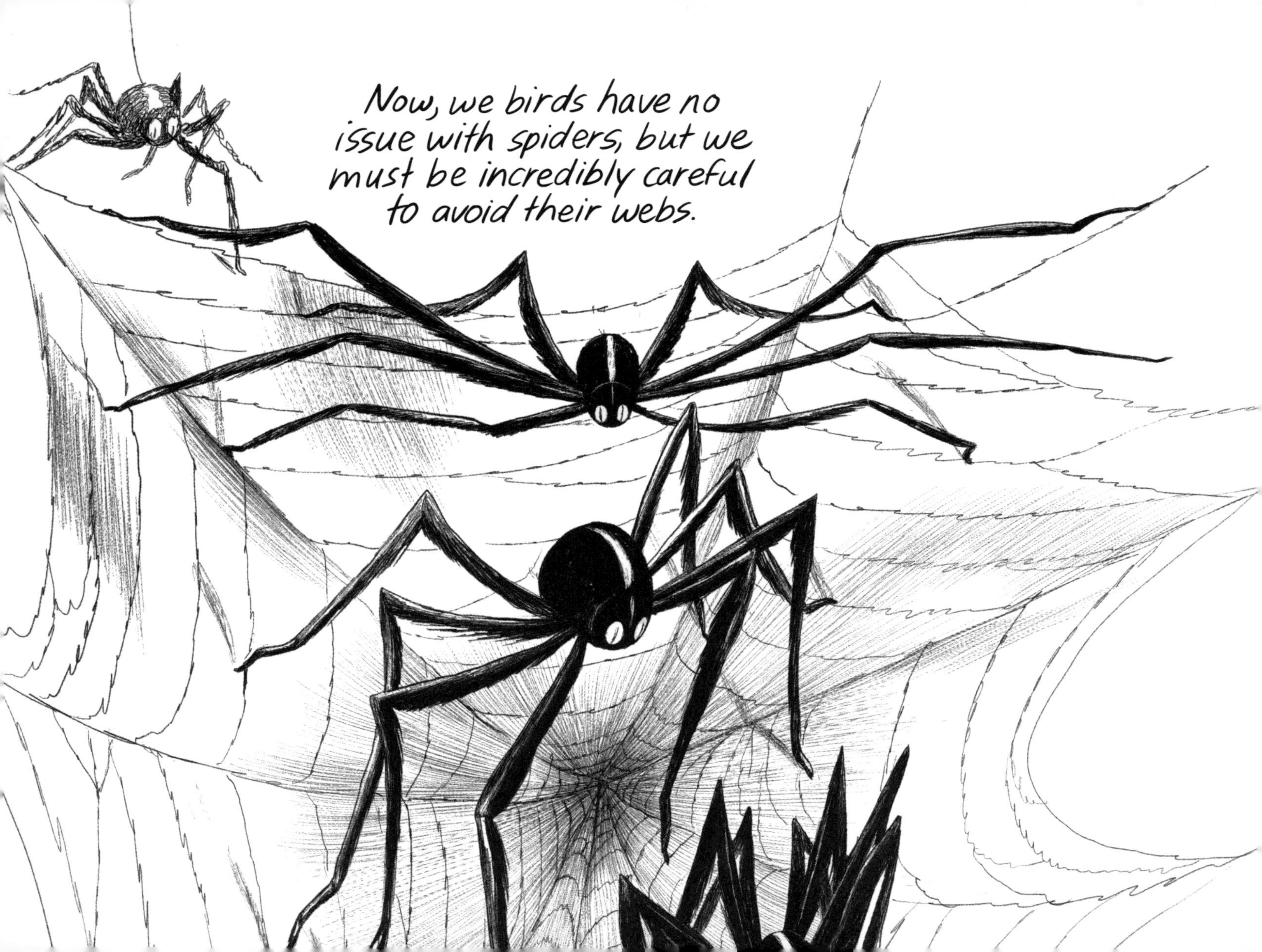
Now, we birds have no issue with spiders, but we must be incredibly careful to avoid their webs.

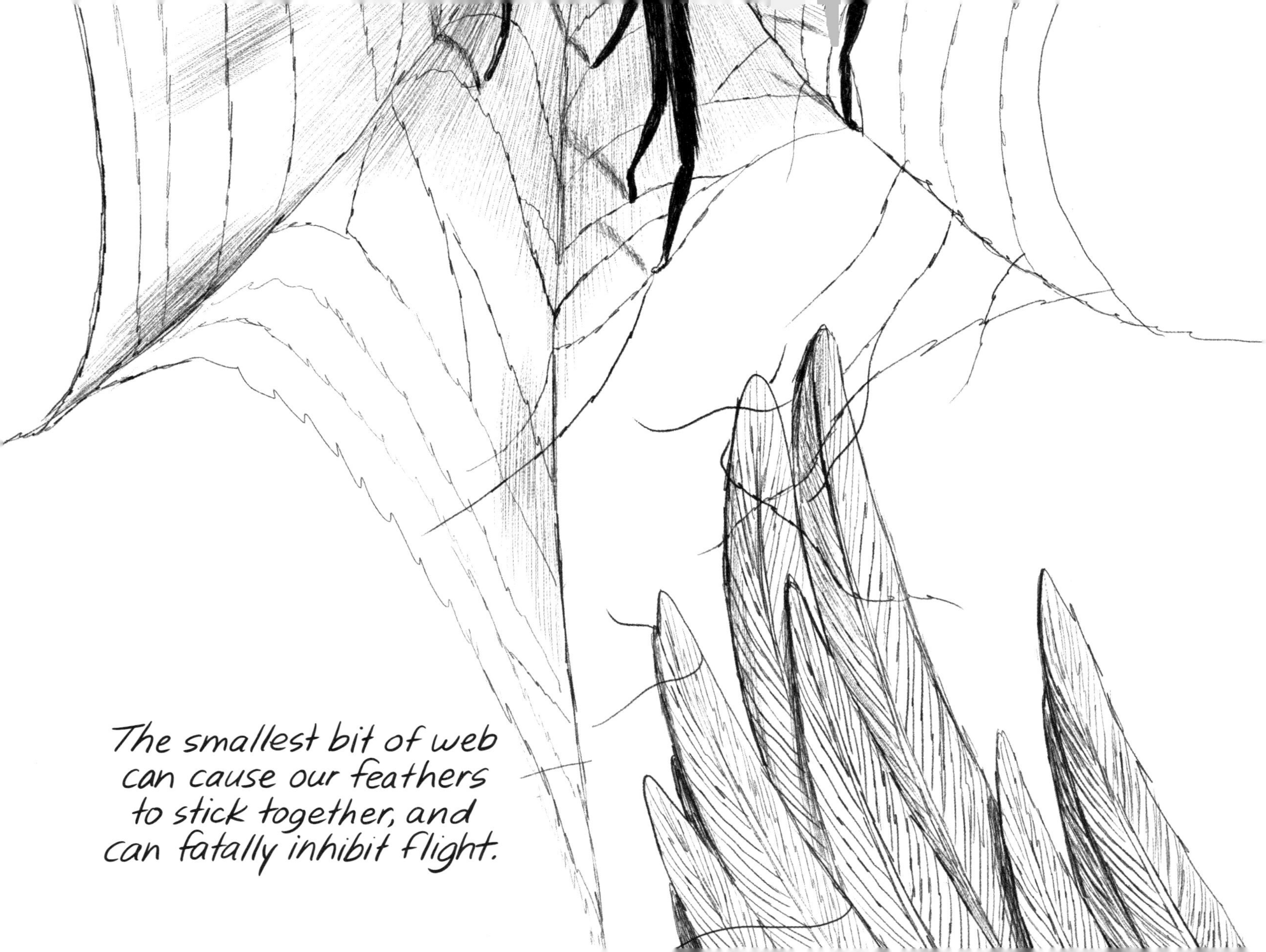
The smallest bit of web
can cause our feathers
to stick together, and
can fatally inhibit flight.

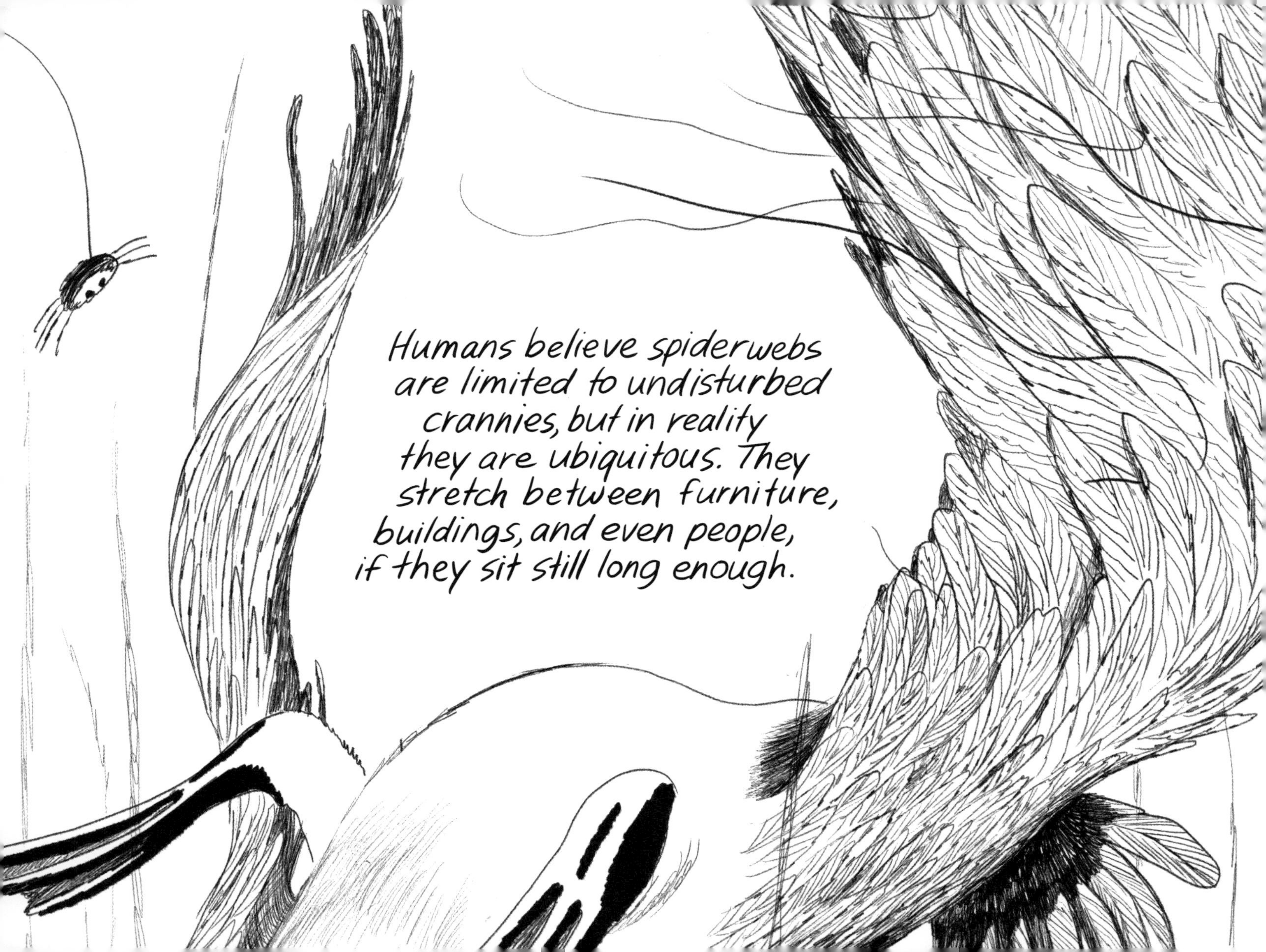
Humans believe spiderwebs are limited to undisturbed crannies, but in reality they are ubiquitous. They stretch between furniture, buildings, and even people, if they sit still long enough.

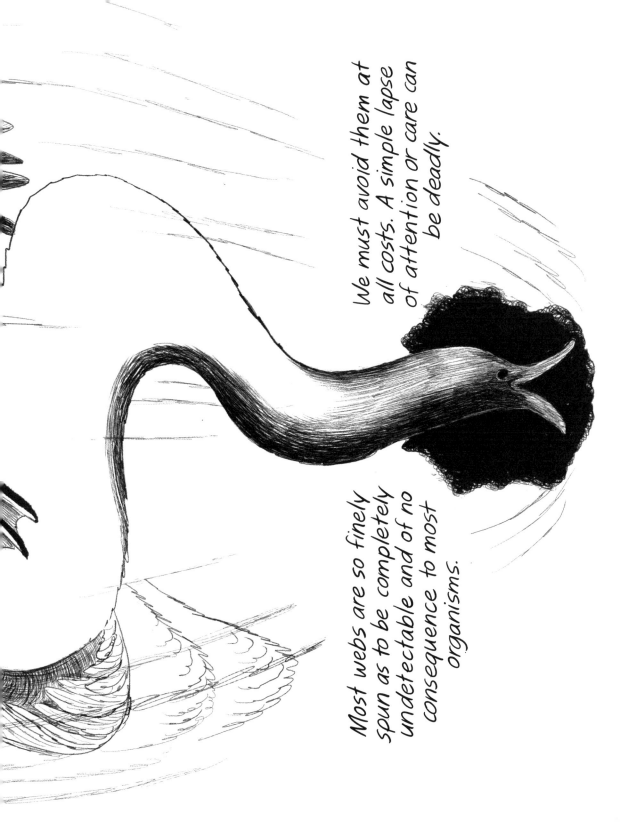

We must avoid them at all costs. A simple lapse of attention or care can be deadly.

Most webs are so finely spun as to be completely undetectable and of no consequence to most organisms.

While a younger bird can fly higher and faster, the older, more experienced bird can manoeuvre around webs with the most finesse and skill.

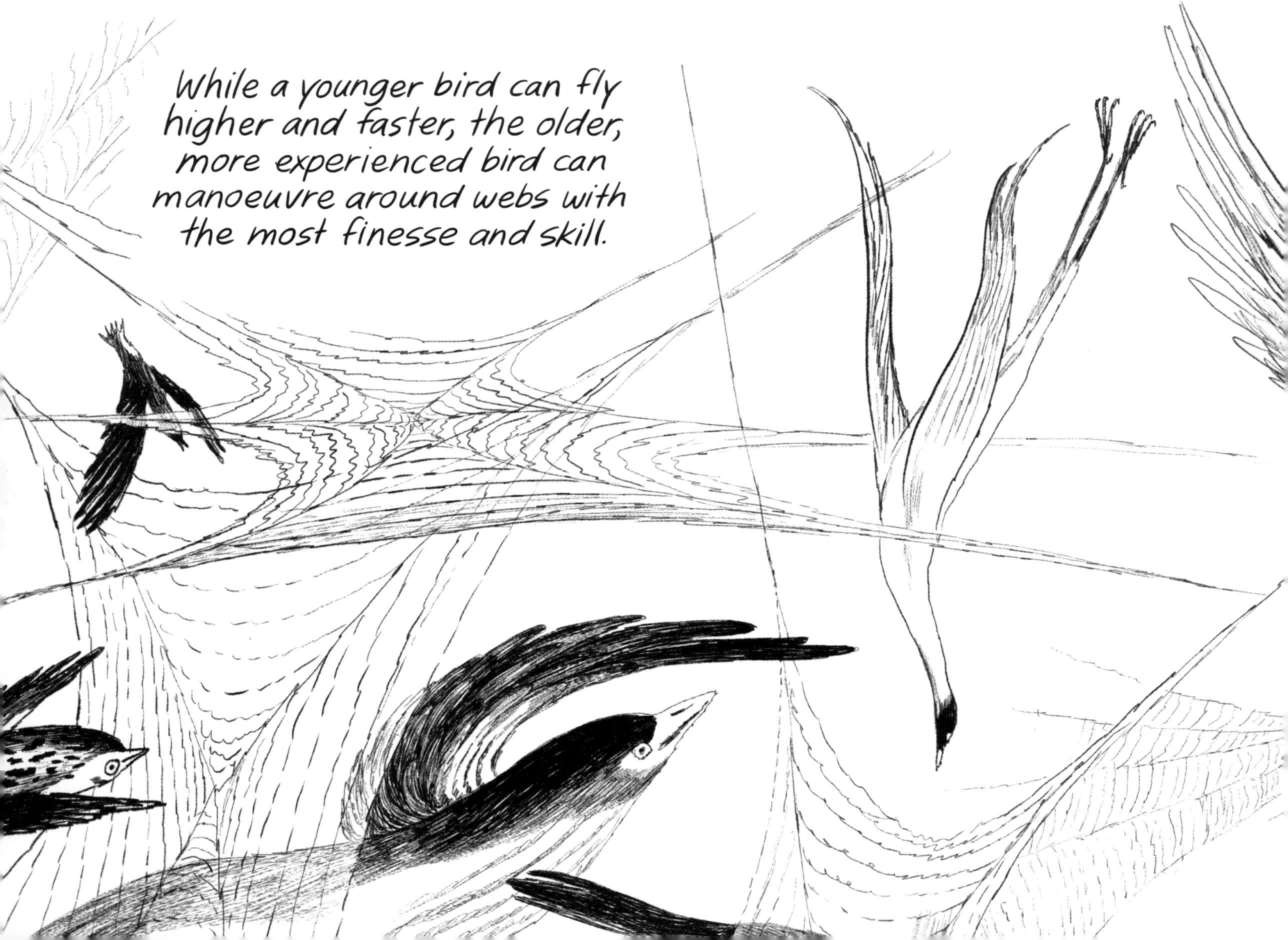

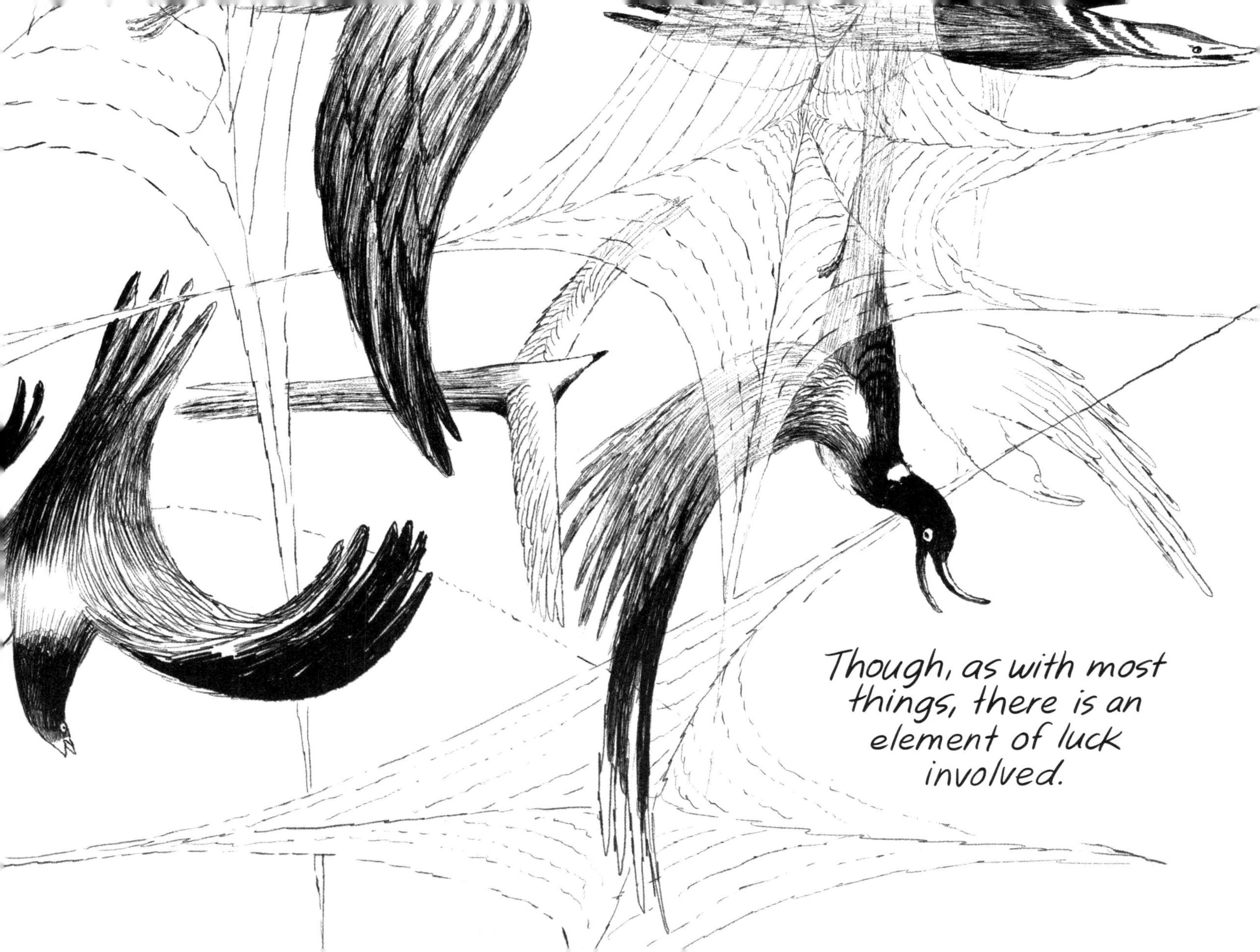
Though, as with most things, there is an element of luck involved.

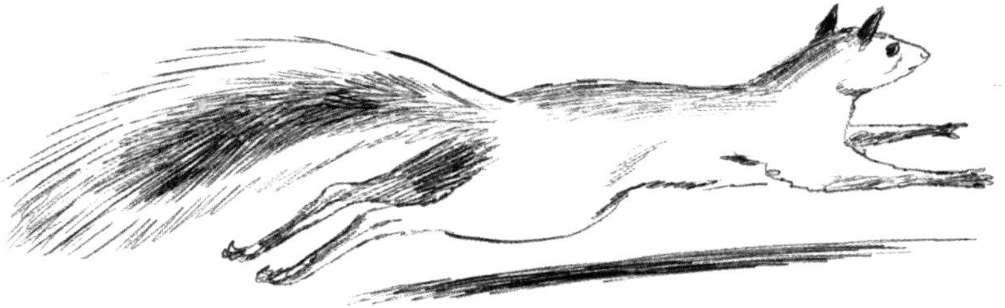

I move about the land
when and where I want.

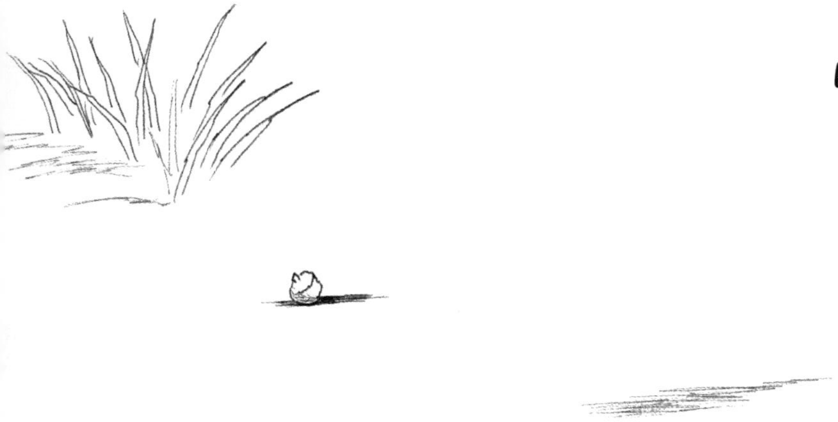

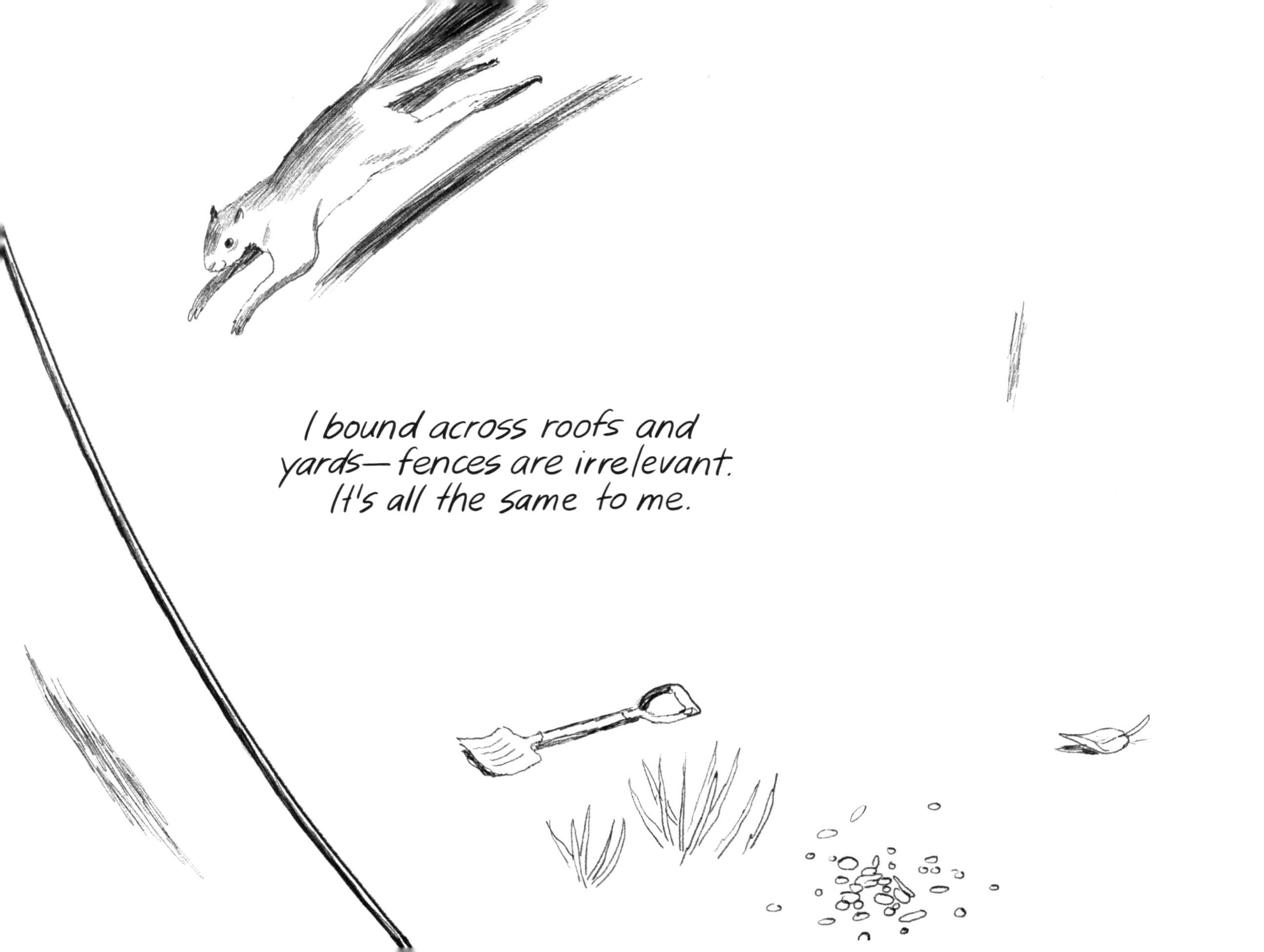
I bound across roofs and
yards—fences are irrelevant.
It's all the same to me.

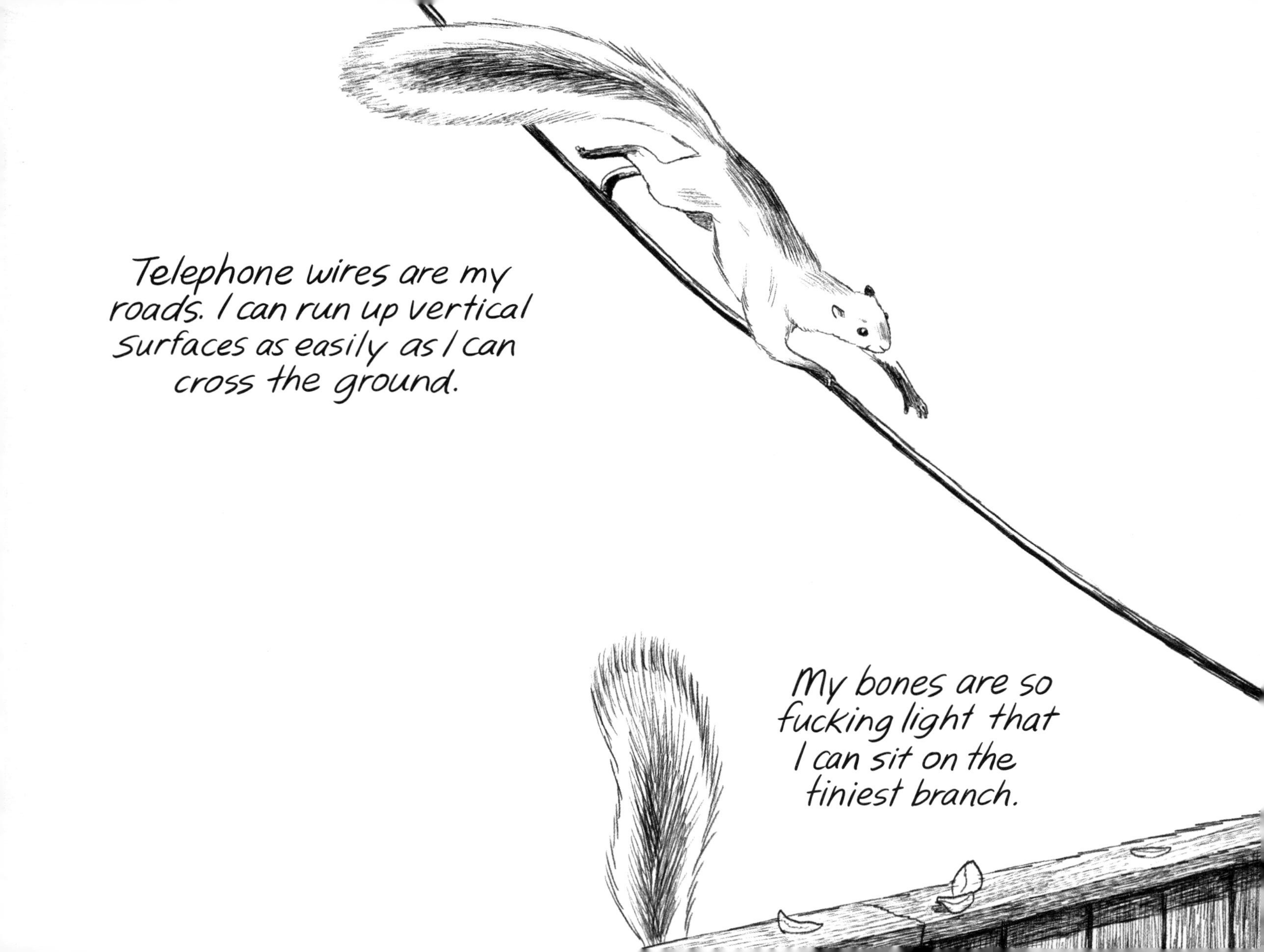
Telephone wires are my roads. I can run up vertical surfaces as easily as I can cross the ground.
My bones are so fucking light that I can sit on the finiest branch.

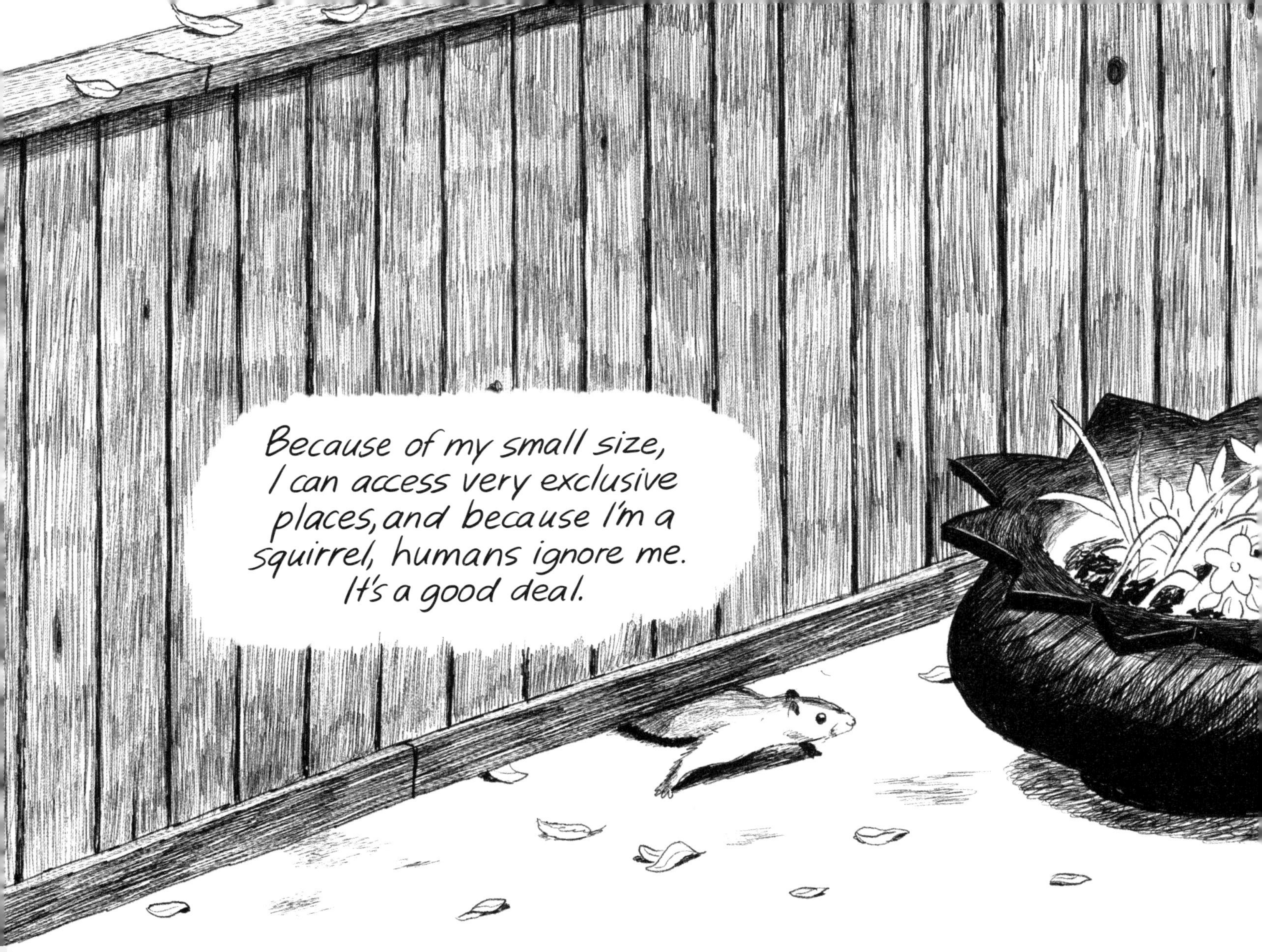
Because of my small size, I can access very exclusive places, and because I'm a squirrel, humans ignore me. It's a good deal.

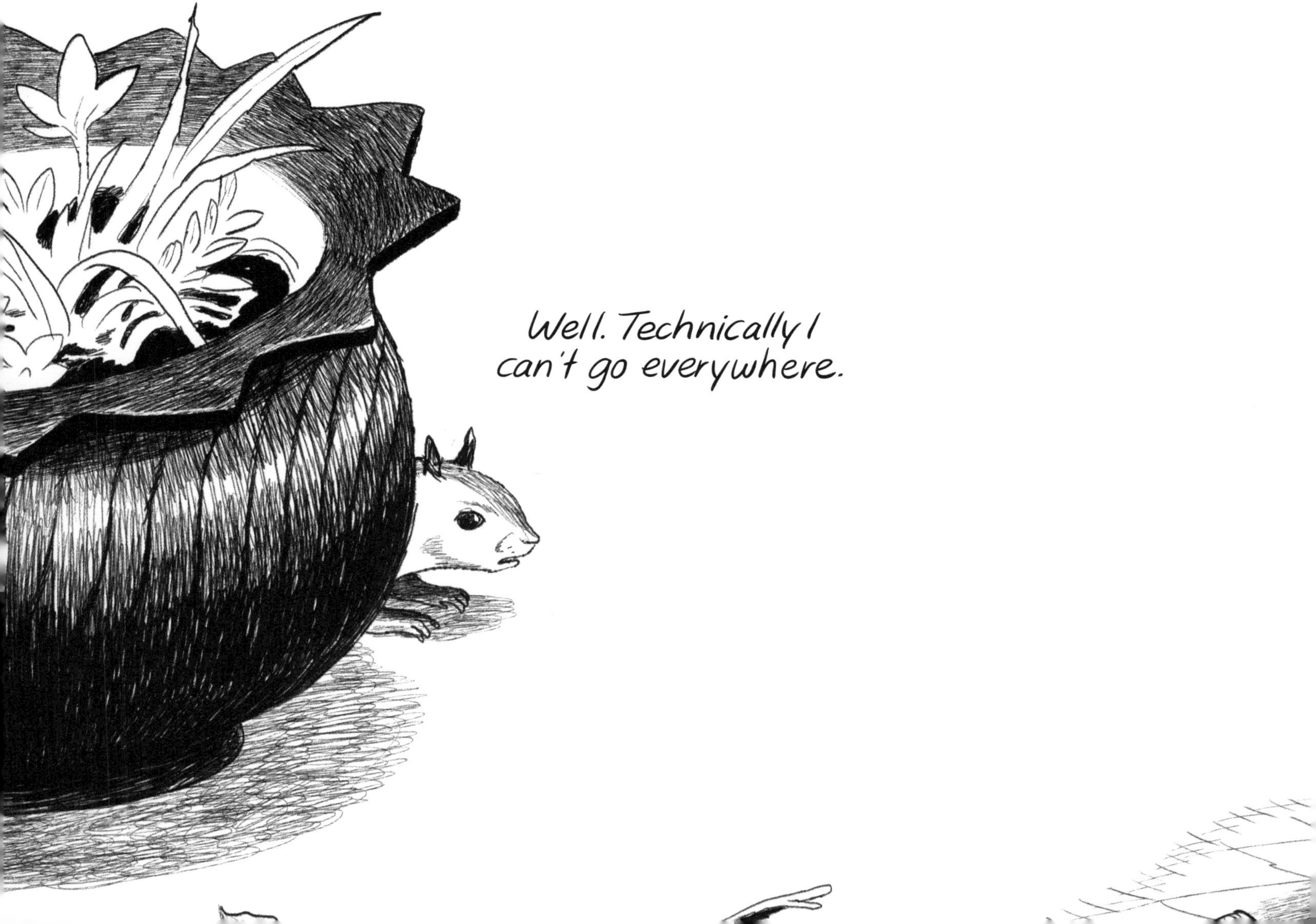
Well. Technically I can't go everywhere.

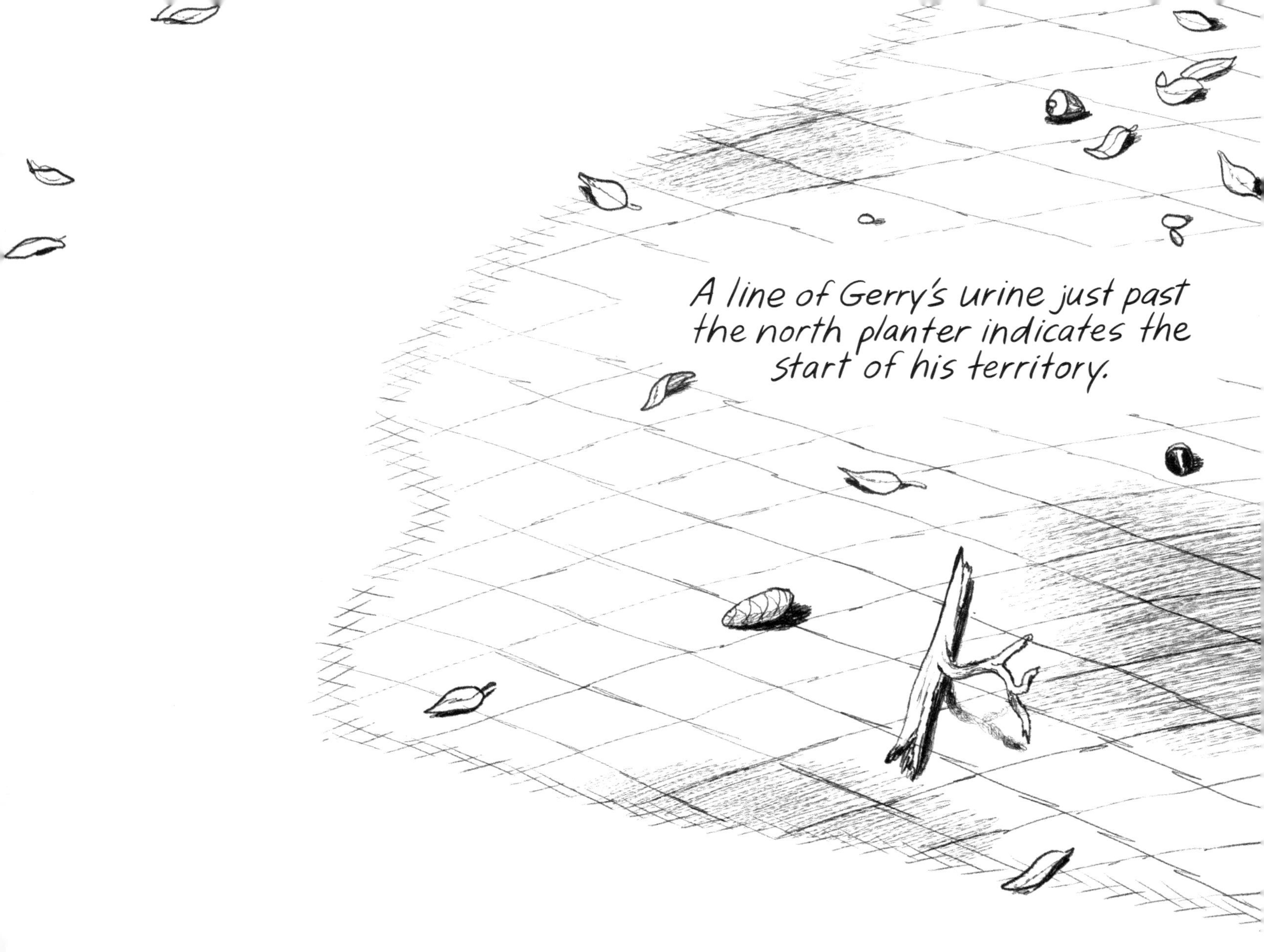
A line of Gerry's urine just past the north planter indicates the start of his territory.

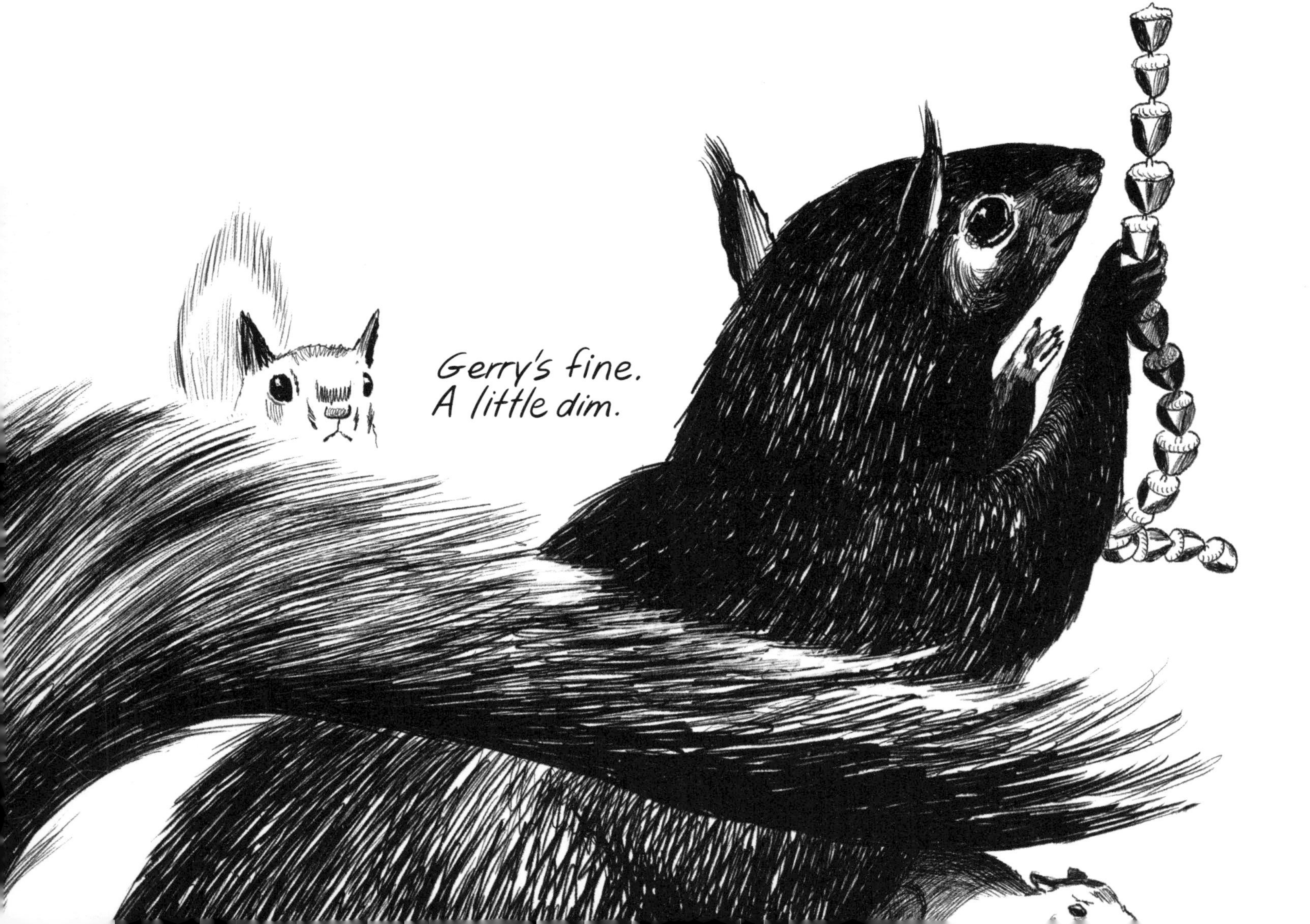
Gerry's fine.
A little dim.

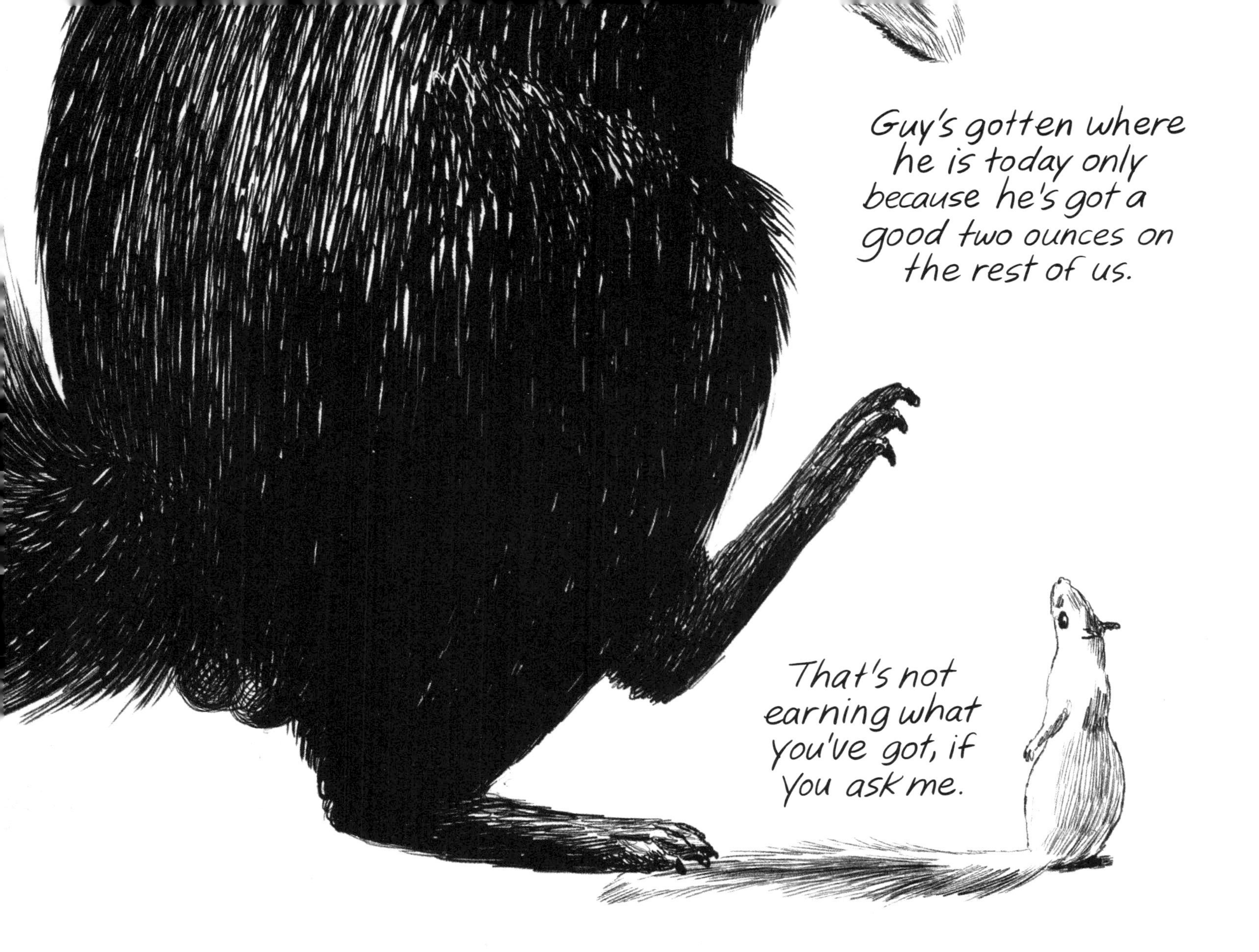
Guy's gotten where he is today only because he's got a good two ounces on the rest of us.
That's not earning what you've got, if you ask me.

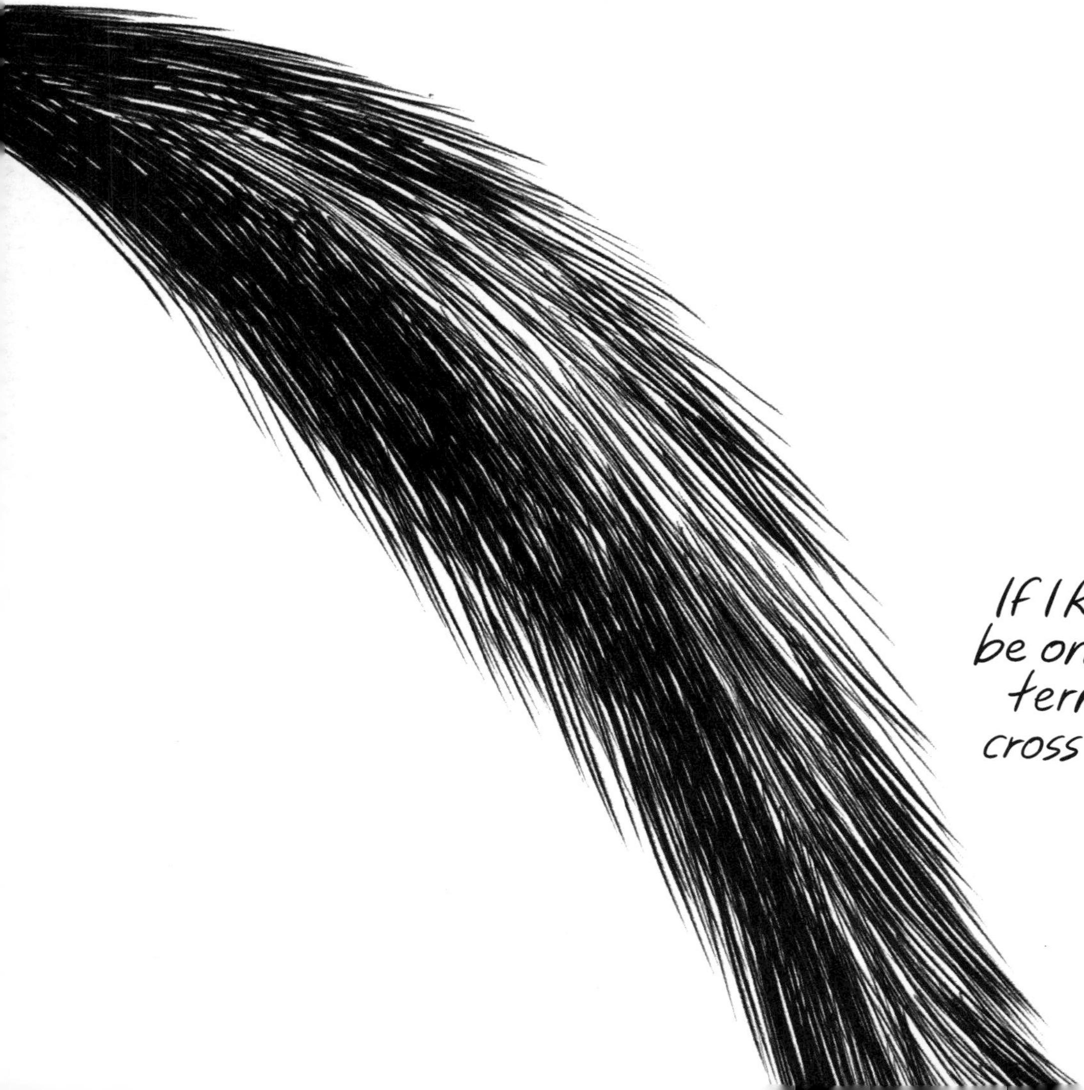

If I know Gerry's going to be on the other side of his territory, I'll occasionally cross the planter and snag a few acorns.

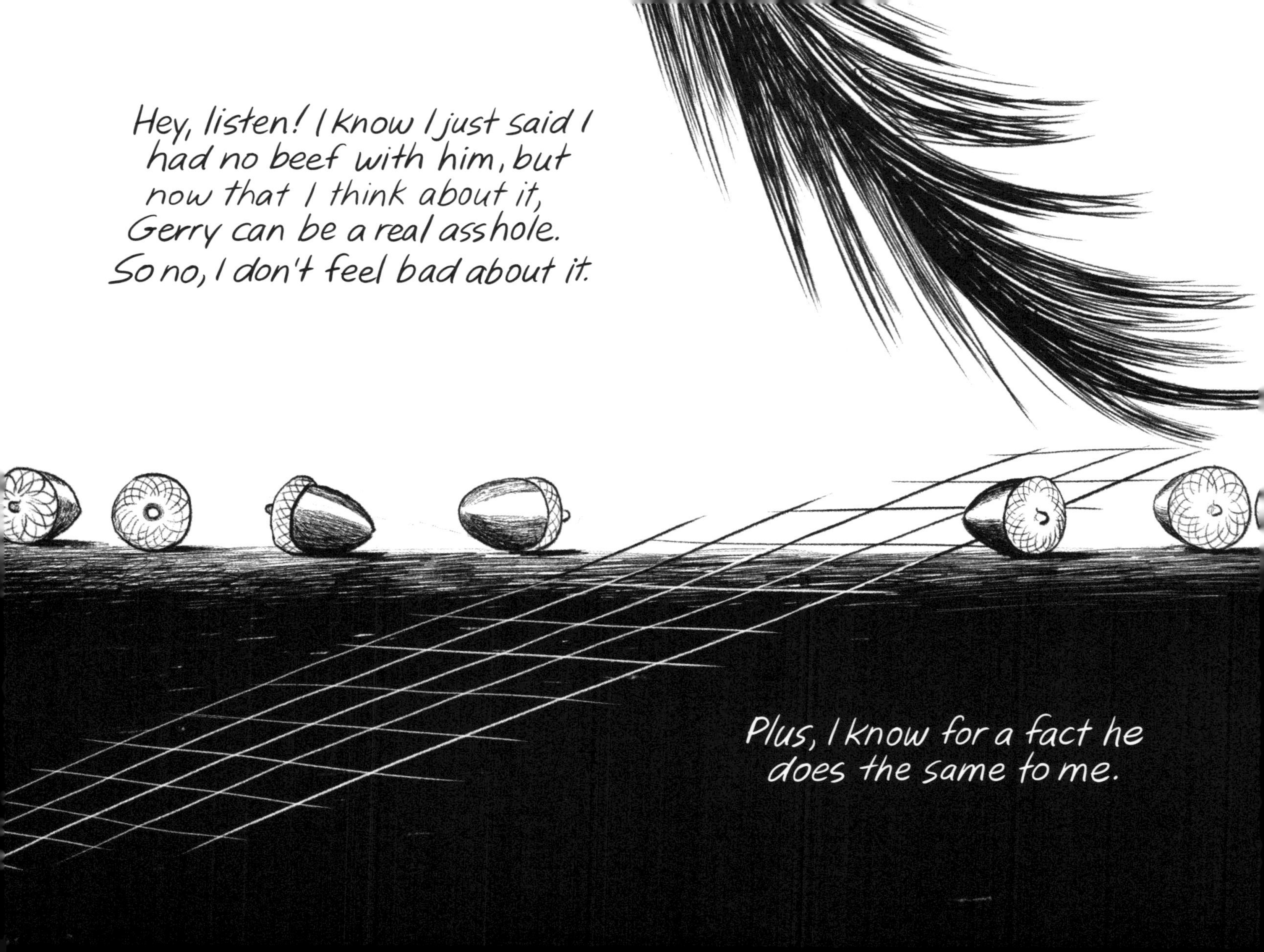
Hey, listen! I know I just said I had no beef with him, but now that I think about it, Gerry can be a real asshole. So no, I don't feel bad about it.
Plus, I know for a fact he does the same to me.

Ever since I was hatched,
I have known the universe
is a dangerous place.

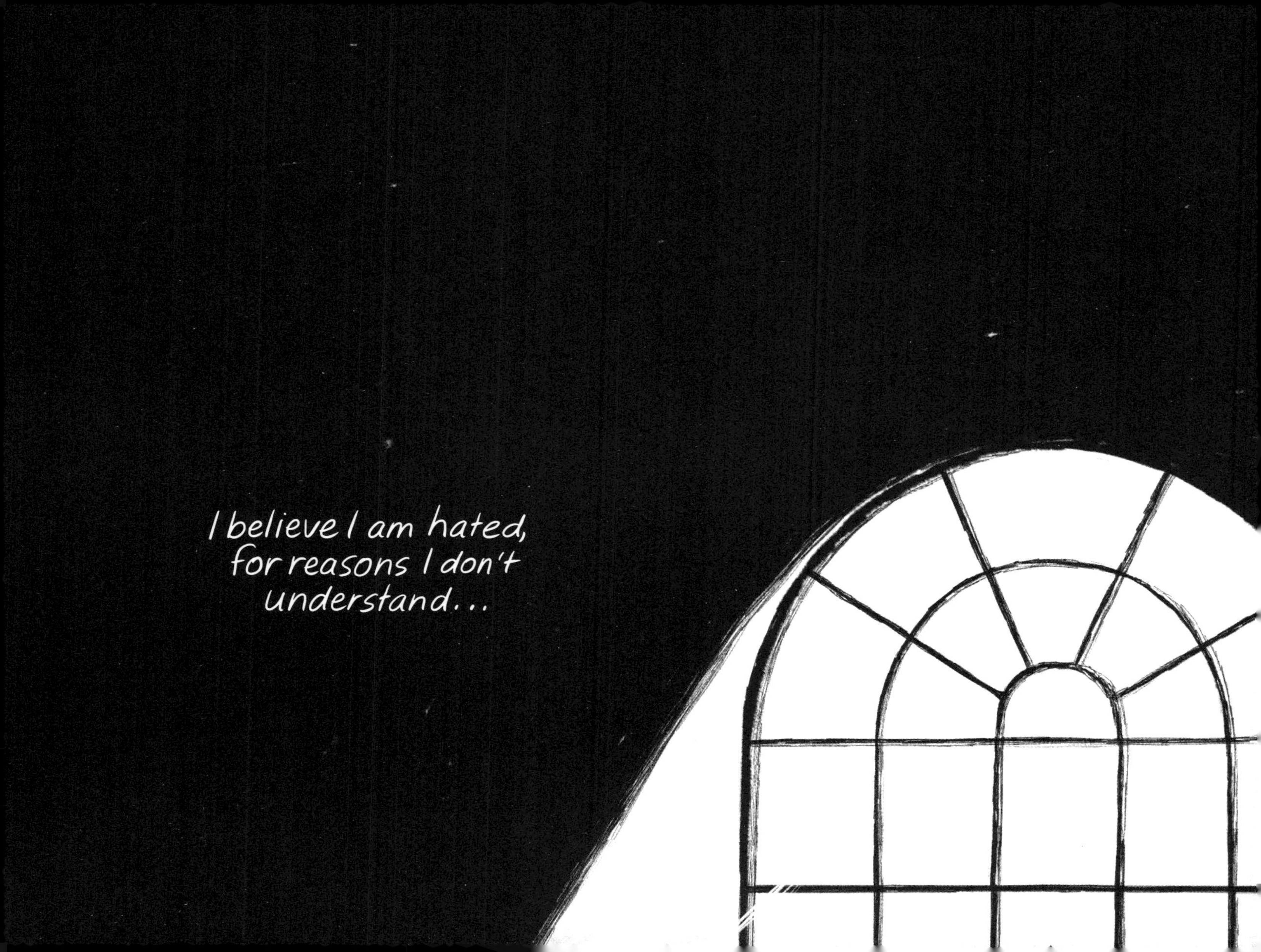
I believe I am hated, for reasons I don't understand...

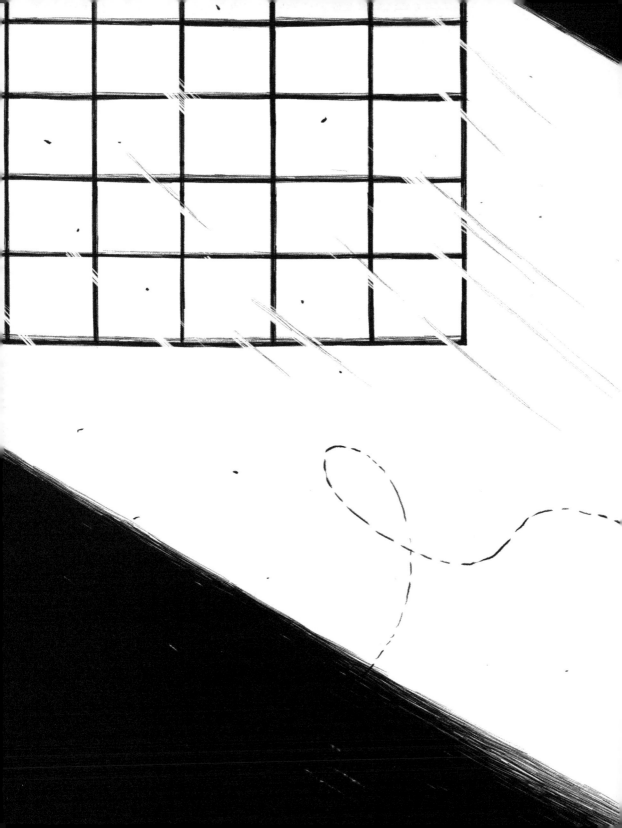

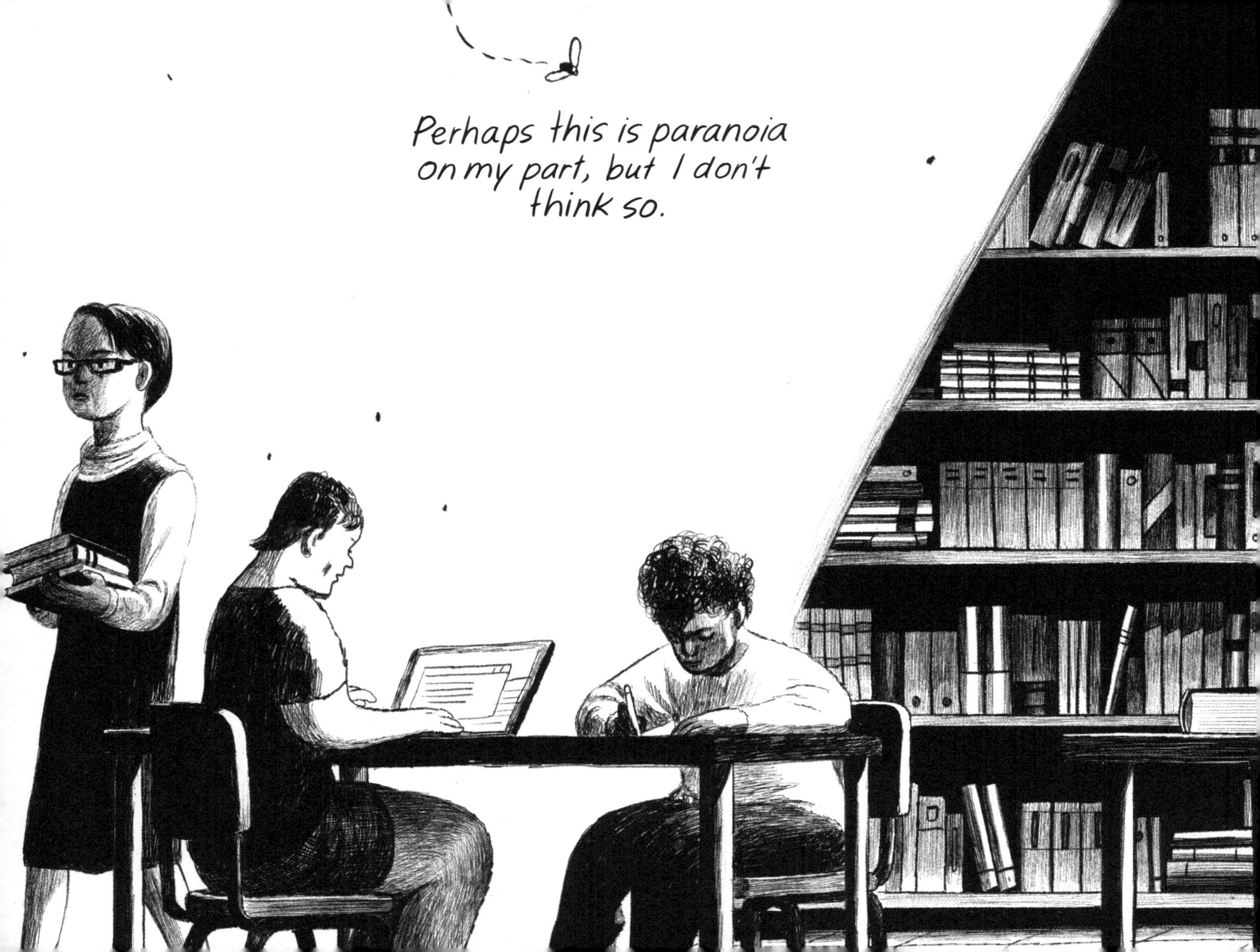
Perhaps this is paranoia on my part, but I don't think so.

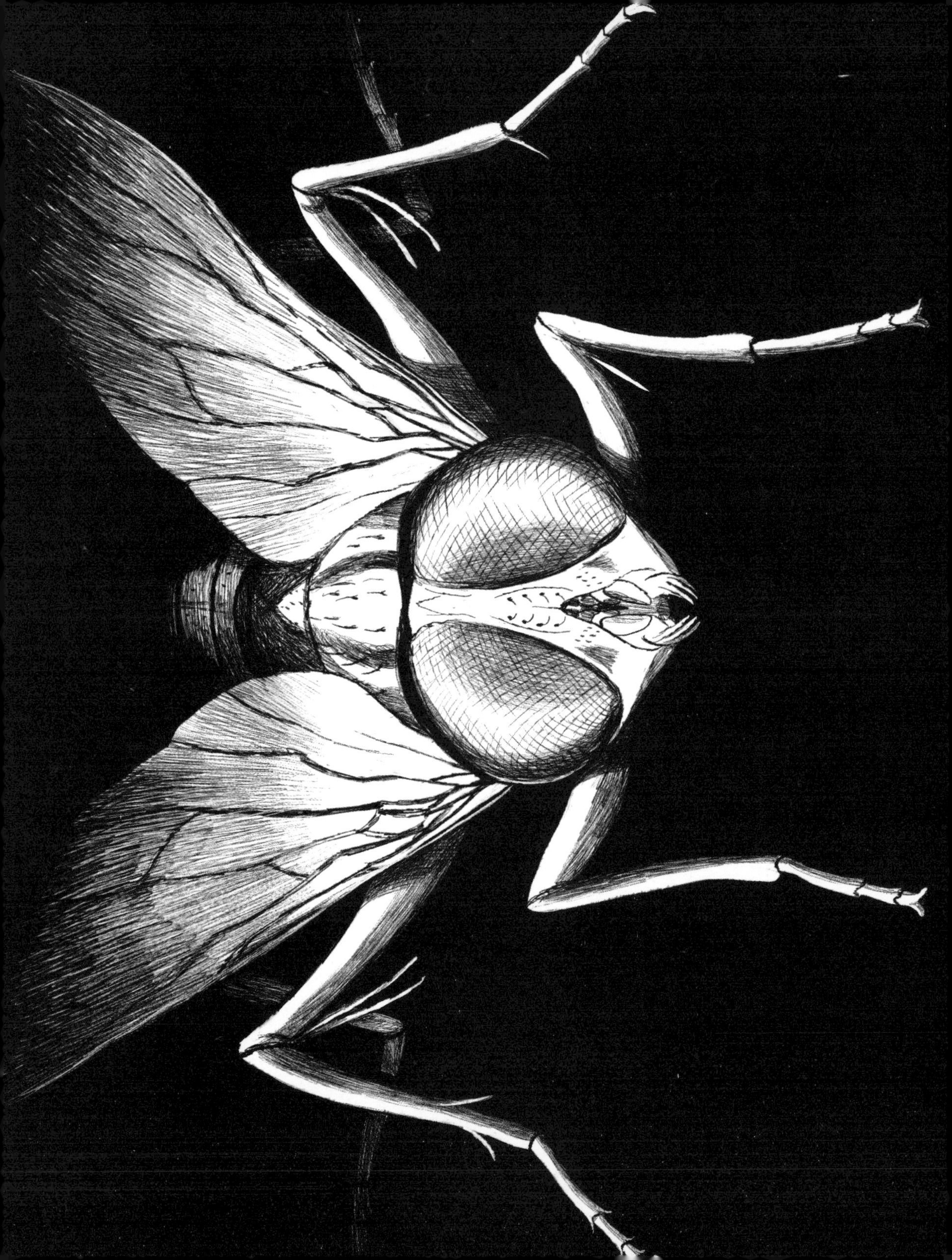

There are many dark corners to which I can retreat and live in peace. However, the simple act of moving creates a noticeable and irritating noise, which inevitably attracts attention in this quiet and serious world.

"Life is nasty, brutish, and short," said Hobbes. (I'm paraphrasing.)

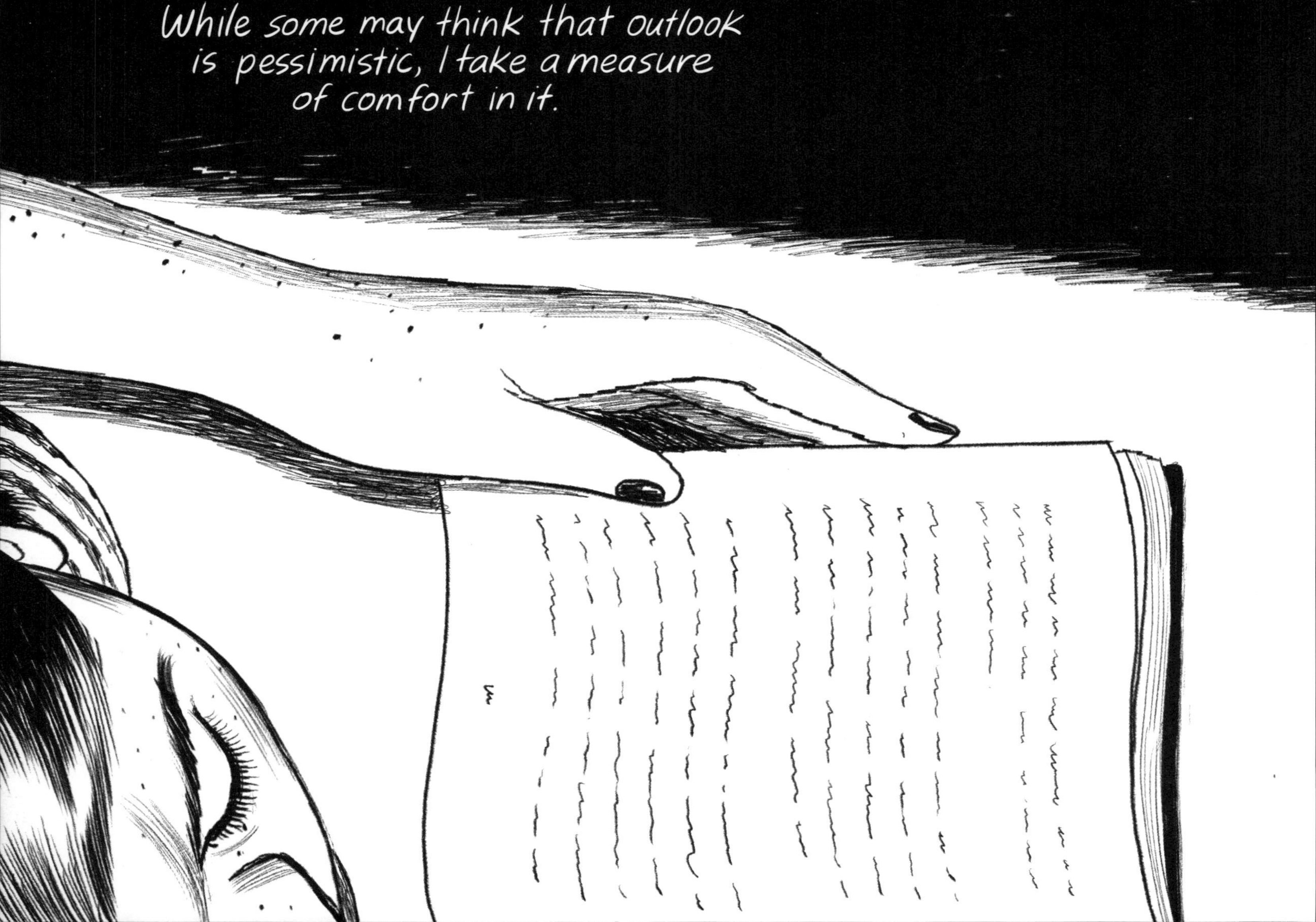
While some may think that outlook is pessimistic, I take a measure of comfort in it.

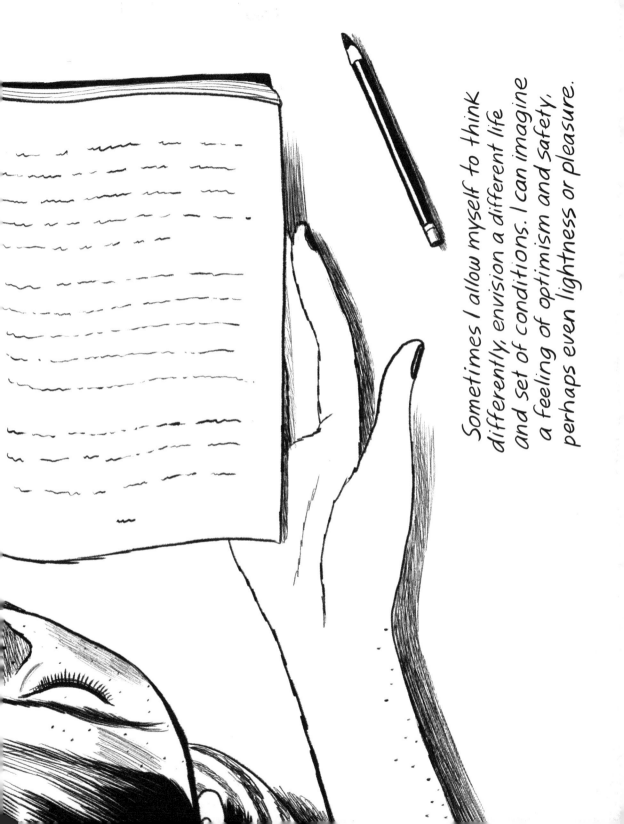

Sometimes I allow myself to think differently, envision a different life and set of conditions. I can imagine a feeling of optimism and safety, perhaps even lightness or pleasure.

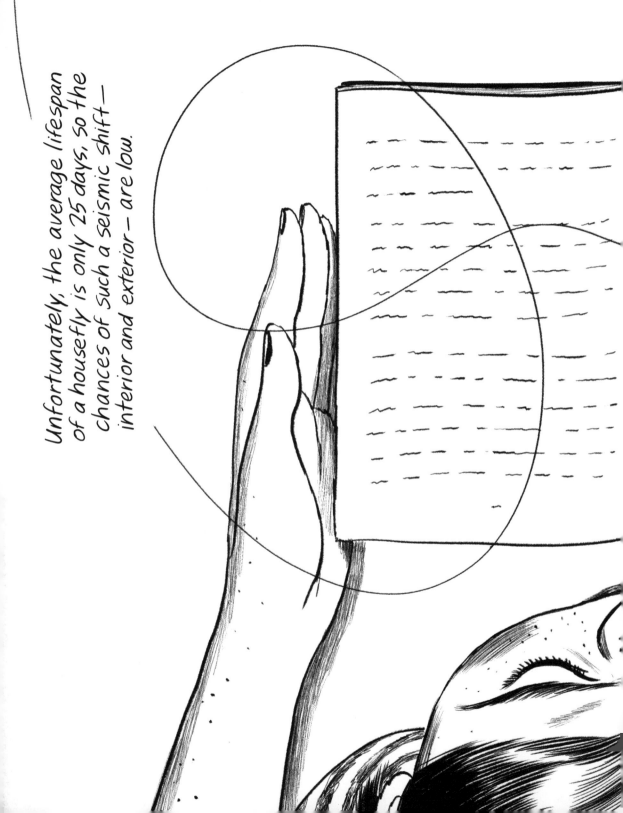

Unfortunately, the average lifespan of a housefly is only 25 days, so the chances of such a seismic shift — interior and exterior — are low.

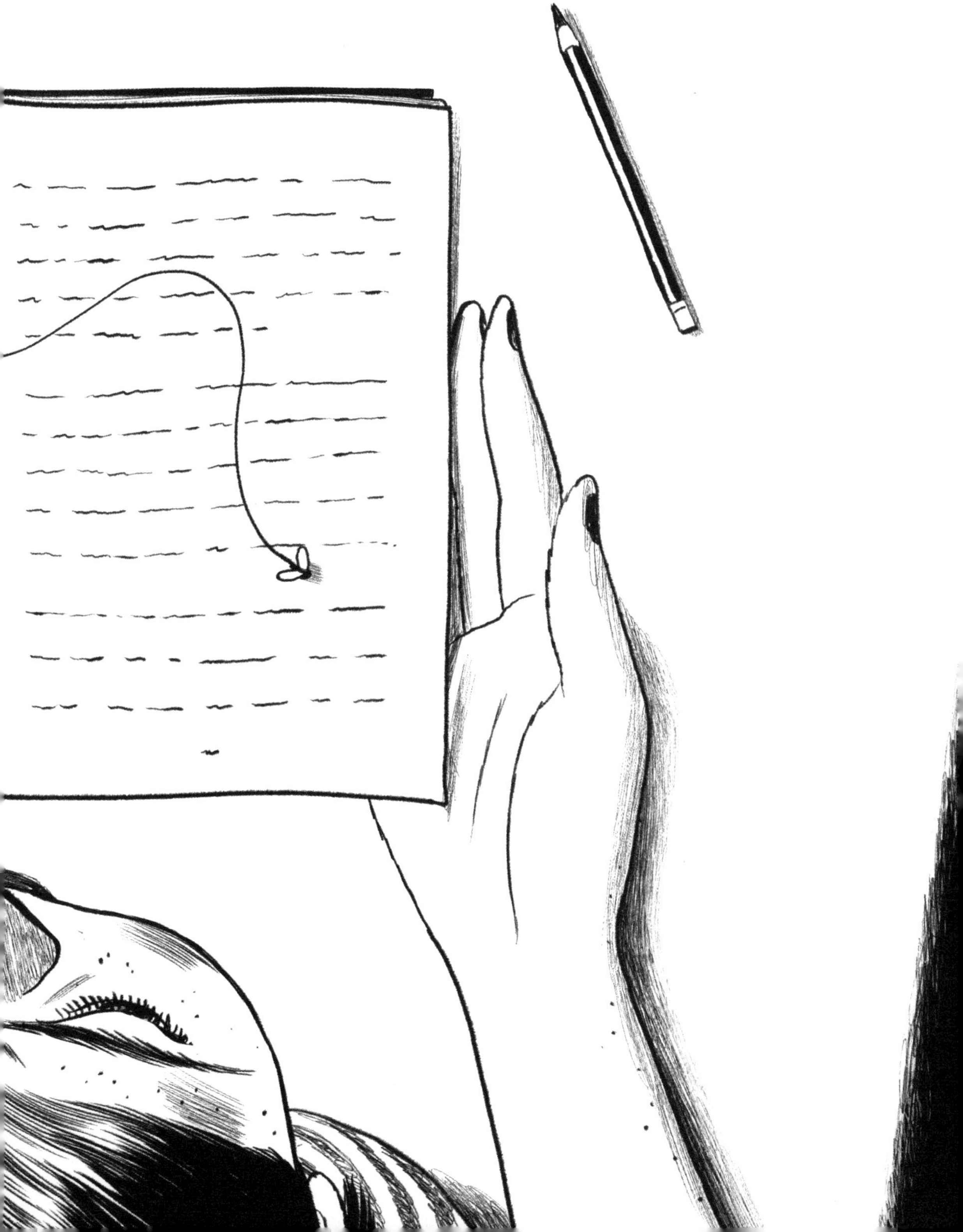

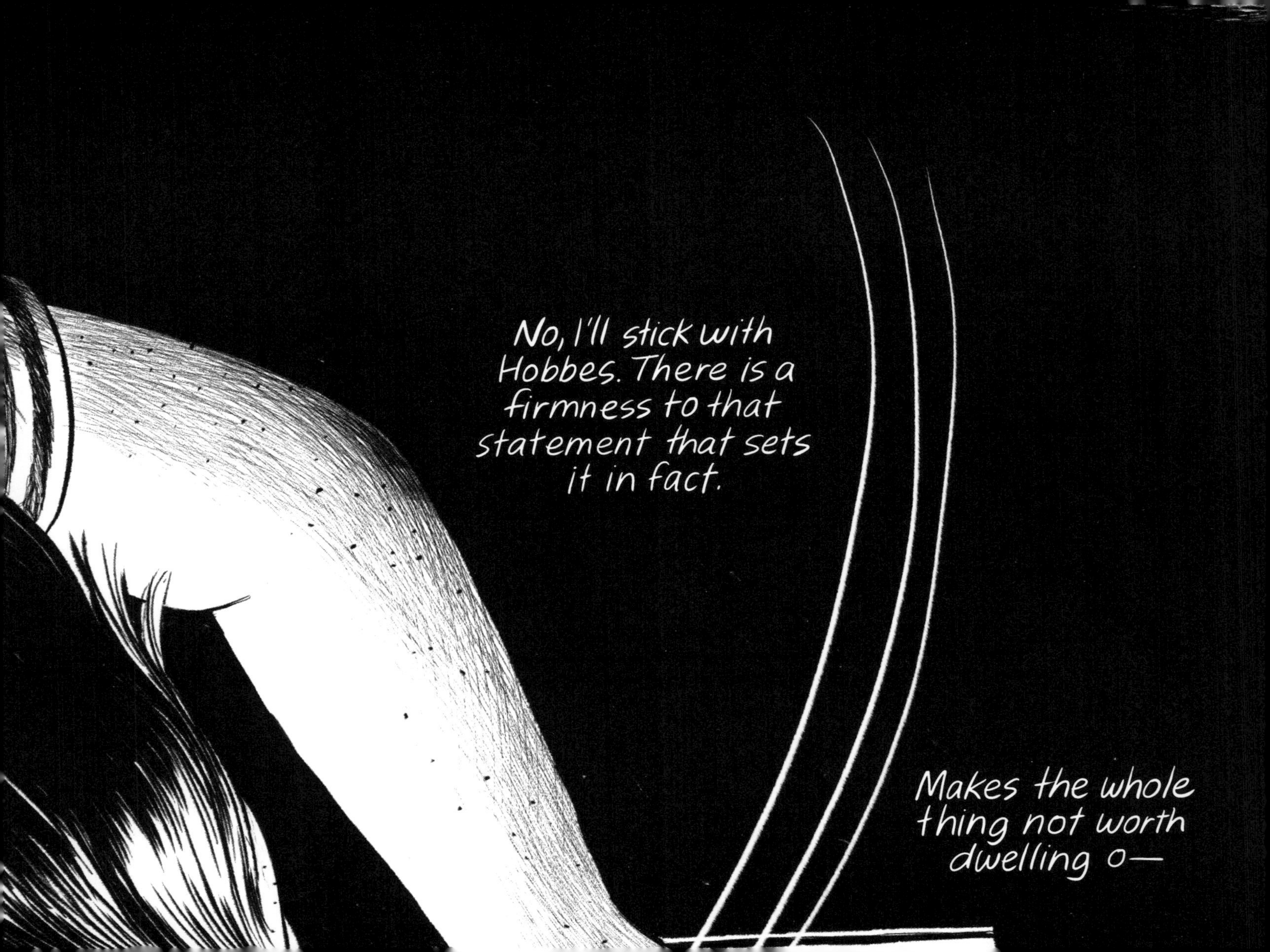
No, I'll stick with Hobbes. There is a firmness to that statement that sets it in fact.
Makes the whole thing not worth dwelling o—

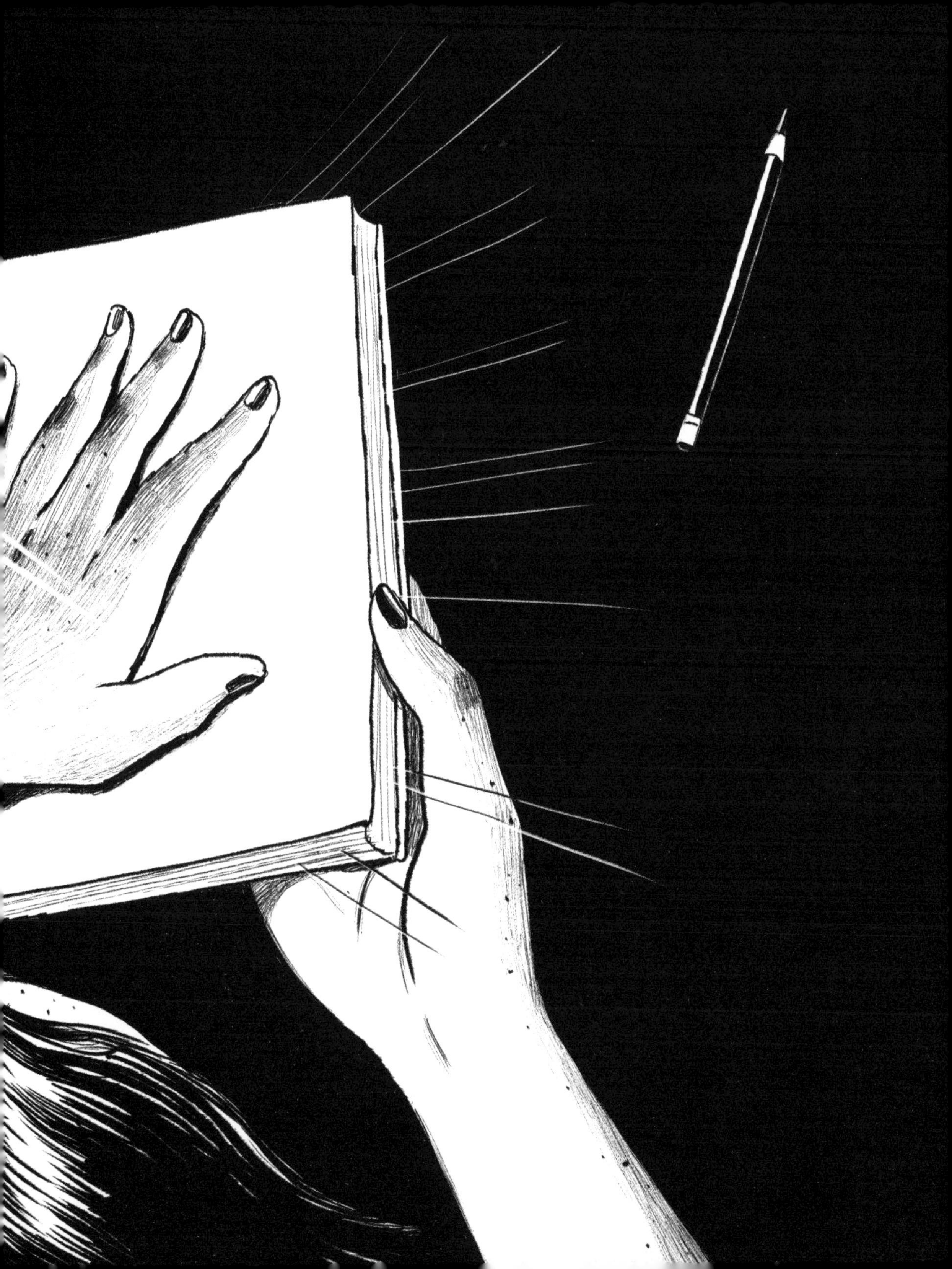

"Sex Coven" originally appeared in
Youth in Decline's *Frontier #7* in 2015.

"Half Life" originally appeared in
Nobrow 7 in 2012.

"Darla!", "Body Pods", "Boundless",
"Bedbug" and "The Clair Free System"
originally appeared on *Hazlitt.net*
in 2015 and 2016.

Thank-you: RYAN SANDS, ANSHUMAN IDDAMSETTY, MICHAEL DEFORGE, LAUREN TAMAKI, MARIKO TAMAKI, D+Q, S.T., AND THE MEMBERS OF SHEBOLA, ANNE ISHII AND CHELSEA CARDINAL

DRAWNANDQUARTERLY.COM
JILLIANTAMAKI.COM

First edition: June 2017
Printed in China
10 9 8 7 6 5 4 3 2 1

Library and Archives Canada Cataloguing in Publication
Tamaki, Jillian, 1980–, author, illustrator
    Boundless / Jillian Tamaki.
ISBN 978-1-77046-287-8 (paperback)
    I. Comics (Graphic works).
PN6733.T33B68 2017   741.5'971   C2016-906235-X

Published in the USA by Drawn & Quarterly, a client publisher of Farrar, Straus and Giroux. Orders: 888.330.8477

Published in Canada by Drawn & Quarterly, a client publisher of Raincoast Books. Orders: 800.663.5774

Published in the United Kingdom by Drawn & Quarterly, a client publisher of Publishers Group UK. Orders: info@pguk.co.uk

Canada

Drawn & Quarterly acknowledges the support of the Government of Canada and the Canada Council for the Arts for our publishing program.

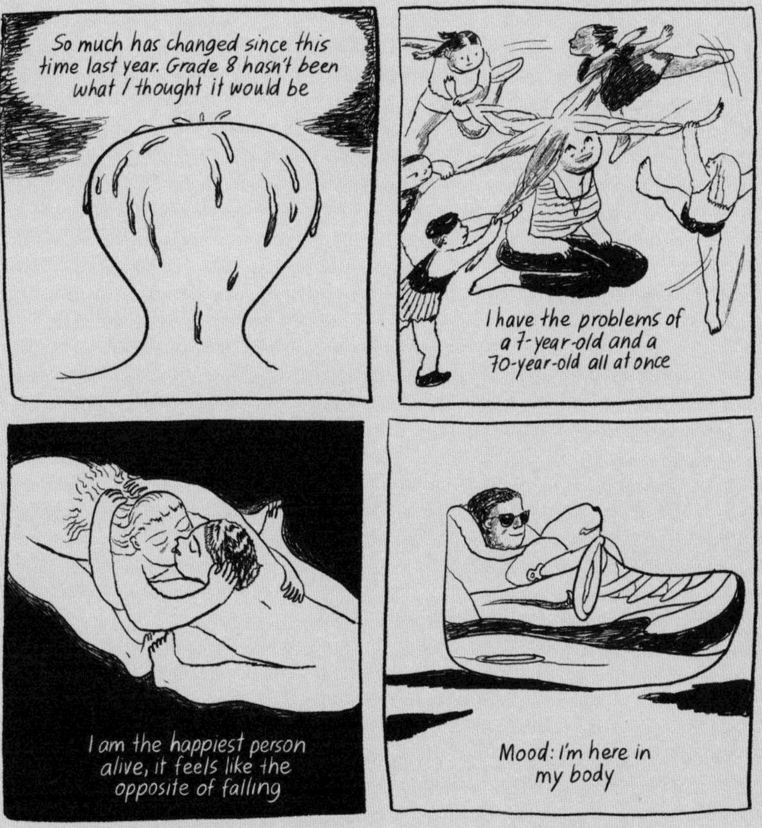
So much has changed since this time last year. Grade 8 hasn't been what I thought it would be
I have the problems of a 7-year-old and a 70-year-old all at once
I am the happiest person alive, it feels like the opposite of falling
Mood: I'm here in my body